Common Frontiers

of the

Social Sciences

MIRRA KOMAROVSKY
EDITOR

Common Frontiers
of the
Social Sciences

THE FREE PRESS
GLENCOE, ILLINOIS
&

THE FALCON'S WING PRESS

CONTENTS

INTRODUCTION, *by Mirra Komarovsky* 1

 A Guide to the Contents 2
 Some Recurrent Issues of Interdisciplinary Polemics 12
 Interdisciplinary Convergencies 22

PART I—HISTORY AND SOCIAL RESEARCH

THE DEBATE OVER ART AND POPULAR CULTURE IN EIGHTEENTH CENTURY ENGLAND, *by Leo Lowenthal and Marjorie Fiske* 33

 Introduction 33
 The Literary Media 34
 Audience Building 45
 Stages of Reaction 57
 Indictment 70
 The Defense 96

RESEARCH PROBLEMS IN AMERICAN POLITICAL HISTORIOGRAPHY, *by Lee Benson* 113

 Introduction 113
 Generalized Interpretation Analyzed in Terms of Time, Space, and Rate Dimensions 123
 Generalized Interpretation Analyzed in Terms of Historian's Space Dimension 146
 Generalized Interpretation Analyzed in Terms of the Historian's Time Dimension 155
 Analyzing a Hypothesis for a Specific Causal Factor 172
 Epilogue 182

v

PUBLIC OPINION IN FRANCE AFTER THE LIBERA-
TION, 1944–1949, *by Russell E. Planck*   184
    Introduction   184
    The French Political Experience, 1944–1949   187
    Political Alignments   193
    Religious Attitudes and Values   214
    Political Attitudes and Values   226
    Alterations of Attitudes and Values   231
    Conclusion   239

HISTORY AND PUBLIC OPINION RESEARCH,
    A DEBATE   242
    "The Historian and the Pollster," *by Paul F. Lazarsfeld*   242
    "The Historian's Concept of Public Opinion," *by Joseph*
      R. Strayer   263
    "Opinion Research in the Service of the Historian," *by*
      Henry David   269

PART II—ECONOMICS AND SOCIOLOGY

PLANT SOCIOLOGY: THE ELITE AND THE ABORIG-
INES, *by Clark Kerr and Lloyd H. Fisher*   281
    Industrial Sociology and Plant Sociology   284
    The Founders   288
    The Critics   290
    The Disciples   292
    Founders and Disciples—The Common Threat   300
    The Essential Choices   302
    Caveat Emptor   305
    Conclusion   308

PLANT SOCIOLOGY: REAL DISCOVERIES AND NEW
PROBLEMS, *by Conrad M. Arensberg and Geoffrey*
Tootell   310
    The Mayoite Middle Range Theories   312
    Beyond Teamwork to Processual Analysis   315
    The Problem of Fusion of Goals   319
    Permissive Leaders, Participation, Post Lewin 324
    Class Values and Motives for Work   328
    Processual Dynamics, Interaction, and Theory   333

THE NON-ECONOMIC ASSUMPTIONS OF JOHN MAY-
NARD KEYNES, *by Robert Lekachman*   338

THE FUNCTION OF SURVEY RESEARCH IN ECO-
NOMICS, *by George Katona*   358

Fact-Finding Through Surveys   359
Establishing Functional Relations   362
Values and Limitation of Survey Research in Economics 370
Research Tasks   372

KEYNESIAN THEORY AND EMPIRICAL INQUIRY

"A Note on Micro- and Macroeconomics," *by William
S. Vickrey*   376
"A Note on 'Middle-Range' Formulation," *by L. R. Klein* 383

REFERENCE GROUP THEORY AND TRADE UNION
WAGE POLICY, *by Seymour Martin Lipset and Martin

Trow*   391
Reference Group Theory and Economic Problems   394
The Social Structure as a Reference Group Determinant 396
Institutional Definitions of Reference Groups   397
"Legitimacy" of the Social Structure and the Choice of
Reference Groups   400
The Effect of Conflicts within and between Institutions
(The Manipulation of Reference Groups)   403
Non-Economic Institutional Variables Affecting Union
Behavior   406
Conclusion   408

Mirra Komarovsky

INTRODUCTION

The common frontiers of anthropology, social psychology, and sociology have been the subject of numerous books and articles. But the interrelations of the other disciplines dealing with social behavior and institutions, specifically those of economics, sociology, and history, have only recently begun to be explored.[1] The present symposium attempts to contribute to this relatively neglected task.

The interrelations of various disciplines may be studied in several ways. A common procedure is to essay a comprehensive portrayal of the province of each discipline in relation to some sister field. One of the earliest volumes on the social sciences published 30 years ago [2] as well as a recent one [3] followed this path. The contributors to the present volume, on the other hand, were invited to proceed differently. The examination of interrelations was to be conducted not through general essays but by means of a scrutiny, and frequently a reciprocal scrutiny, of some one specific topic or a group of studies in overlapping areas of research. In addition to the critical essays the volume contains three original monographs which exem-

The editor wishes to express her great indebtedness to Professor Paul F. Lazarsfeld for his encouragement and valuable suggestions throughout the preparation of this volume.

1. Karl Polanyi, Conrad M. Arensberg, and Harry Pearson, editors, *Trade and Market in the Early Empires*, Free Press-Falcon's Wing Press, 1957. Talcott Parsons and Neal Smelser, *Economy and Society*, Free Press, Glencoe, Ill., 1957.

2. W. F. Ogburn and A. Goldenweiser, *The Social Sciences and Their Inter-Relations*, Houghton Mifflin & Co., 1927.

3. John Gillin, editor, *For a Science of Social Man*, The Macmillan Co., New York, 1954.

1

plify an interdisciplinary approach in various ways, whether by applying a method developed in one field to the problems of another or by illuminating the data of one field with concepts and hypotheses of a neighboring discipline.

Admittedly such an approach could not yield a synoptic view of interdisciplinary relationships. But what is lost in comprehensiveness and unity may be gained in realism. There is no surer way to make explicit the differences and the similarities of the various disciplines than to examine them as they converge upon a common problem. Delusive harmony will be exposed when what hitherto appeared as a common concept is now seen to carry a different operational meaning to each specialist. Conversely, apparent differences may turn out to be merely differences in terminology. Emerging trends of interdisciplinary relations are more likely to be perceived through such case studies and less likely to be obscured by traditional cliches concerning the respective provinces of the various social sciences.

Such concrete examination of common interests has another and a more practical value. Interdisciplinary cooperation is generally felt to be desirable but difficult of attainment. Exhortations do little to further it. It is more likely to develop if a student is shown concretely that another discipline has something to offer in his own area of specialization.

This introduction is divided into three parts. The first section is intended to serve as a guide to the contents of the volume. The purpose of the second part is more analytical. In it we shall attempt to make explicit some differences which have emerged among the participating specialists with regard to the ideals of science, theories, and methods and finally in the last section we shall consider the implications of the volume for future interdisciplinary cooperation.

A Guide to the Contents

Part I of this volume contains monographs and essays which have grown out of a systematic effort to relate methods of empirical social research to historiography. Quantitative studies of contemporary society form an essential part of modern sociology. How are they related to the more comprehensive but also more speculative approach preferred by the humanist-historian? Three links are each represented in our three monographs.

It is in the nature of quantitative operations that they deal with discrete variables. A broader picture of a specific situation is obtained only by inter-relating these variables. Whatever the shortcomings of such atomistic procedures, they have certainly clarified the nature of causal interpretation. Lee Benson's contribution exemplifies this new awareness by applying it to selected problems in American political history. He treats election statistics in a way which makes them more suitable as evidence for historical analysis.[4]

In addition to progress in analytical *procedures*, social research has provided new types of *data*. Public opinion surveys report on the attitudes of people who in past periods left no such direct testimony. Will this material aid the future historian in his study of our times? The general issue is discussed in the three essays contributed by Henry David, Paul F. Lazarsfeld, and Joseph R. Strayer. A specific case study in point is Russell E. Planck's monograph. He had examined public opinion surveys carried out in France since the liberation. These were not collected for the purpose to which they are put now; while this imposes certain limitations, it permits the reader to consider the potential promise of an alliance between the polling expert and the historian under more favorable conditions.

Apart from new procedures and new types of data, empirical research can have another relation to history. Its findings may suggest *new problems* and *new hypotheses* for historical investigation. This link between the two disciplines is exemplified in the monograph by Leo Lowenthal and Marjorie Fiske. The problem which stimulated this study of 18th Century England arose directly out of recent investigations of mass media of communication.[5] The

4. Modern techniques of this kind are discussed in another publication of the present series, Herbert Hyman's *Survey Design and Analysis*, Free Press, Glencoe, Illinois, 1955, especially chapter 7. A first statement of the problem was by Robert Bower: "Opinion Research and Historical Interpretation of Elections," *Public Opinion Quarterly*, Vol. 12, No. 3, Fall 1948.

5. A review of the available data and the contemporary discussion can be found in the following papers by P. F. Lazarsfeld: "The Role of Criticism in the Management of Mass Media," *Journalism Quarterly*, Vol. XXV, No. 2, June 1948; "Remarks on Administrative and Critical Communication Research," *Studies in Philosophy and Social Science*, Zeitschrift für Sozialforschung, Vol. IX, No. 1, 1941, New York: Institute of Social Research; "Why Is So Little Known About the Effects of Television on Children and What Can Be Done?", *Public Opinion Quarterly*, Vol. XIX, No. 3, Fall 1955.

monograph also illustrates the mutual benefit derived from such a rapprochement between history and social research. The use of historical documents gives the sociologist access to new data with which to test generalizations derived from the contemporary study of communication.

The relation between sociology and history involves more facets than the three just listed. Sociological theory has developed concepts which have affected the writings of the historians. Sociologists in turn, and Max Weber is an outstanding example, have used historical materials. A comprehensive view of relations between the two fields would have to include other modes of collaboration not included in this volume which is limited to the relation of history and empirical social research.

We turn now to a more detailed description of the contributions.*

The first monograph, "The Debate over Art and Popular Culture in Eighteenth Century England" by Leo Lowenthal and Marjorie Fiske, traces the fundamental changes which took place in the relation of the writer to his public and in literary institutions in 18th Century England. "For the first time," write the authors: "the writer became dependent for his financial support on the public instead of aristocratic patronage. For the first time, the reading public ceased to be limited to scholars and members of the privileged classes and began instead to represent the population at large." The authors document the far reaching changes which have resulted in various types of literary institutions as well as in the nature of literary and ethical criticism. The most surprising feature of the study is the revelation of the extent to which the controversies over popular culture and problems of mass media of communication which we today consider so peculiarly our own were already present and being widely discussed two hundred years ago.

In the second monograph, "Research Problems in American Political Historiography," Lee Benson tries to make explicit some

---

* Administratively all three studies are part of a project on the relation between the humanities and social research carried out at Columbia University, under the direction of Paul F. Lazarsfeld. The funds for this program are provided by the Rockefeller and the Ford Foundations; Columbia University's Bureau of Applied Social Research has been closely allied with the development of each of the studies.

of the assumptions in the writing of political history. His theme
is the explanation of presidential elections. He shows that these
explanations are often not based on precise knowledge of how
the various subgroups of the population had voted. Furthermore,
election data cannot be interpreted unless seen as a point in a time
series. Because specific groups are usually studied in terms of specific
districts, Benson talks about the role of the time and space dimension
in such interpretations. Actually, to do his job fully, the historian
requires certain systematic data on elections not yet generally available and certain methodological techniques to handle such data.

The monograph examines a number of well-known historical
interpretations of elections and seeks to show that the lack of
requisite quantitative data "severely handicaps historians." These
examples are selected so as to illustrate various types of causal interpretations. Throughout these analyses the author attempts to distinguish the factual from the interpretative elements of a hypothesis
and to formulate the logical requirements for its test.

Russell E. Planck in the third monograph, "Public Opinion in
France After the Liberation, 1944-1949," notes that historical data
are particularly incomplete in the field of public opinion, the
opinions held by average people in everyday situations. He sees in
the development of attitude research a possibility of overcoming this
deficiency in the future. The study examines the materials of one
polling agency, the Institut Français d'Opinion Publique (IFOP),
for the light it throws upon French history from 1944 to 1949. It
thus illustrates the application of opinion research, a development
within the field of sociology and social psychology, to history.

Turning first to political alignments the author finds that several current ideas on the class composition of postwar political
parties are in need of revision in the light of the IFOP studies.
The study also brings a new understanding of the Communist Party:
the issues on which the rank and file Communists followed the
party line and those on which they showed considerable independence of attitude and action.

The major part of the monograph deals with religious and
political attitudes. We learn not only *what* these attitudes were at
various times but frequently *who* held them. Linking particular
attitudes to the social characteristics of the population is one of the

unique contributions opinion research can make to the historian.[6]
The final section of the monograph adduces some evidence on the
role of events in effecting changes in public attitudes.

Following the three monographs is a set of essays on "History
and Public Opinion Research, A Debate."

This debate begins with an article by Paul F. Lazarsfeld, "The
Historian and the Pollster." [7] The author illustrates, with selections
from well-known historical writings, that historians have frequently
been concerned with the attitudes and values of the periods they
investigate. By their own testimony, then, the study of public
opinion is part of the field of history. But the same historical selections show that the references to attitudes often lack adequate
documentation.

We find . . . statements which read like a Gallup poll, except, that
the tables are missing.

This might have been unavoidable before the development of
attitude research. Only to the extent that today's pollster can discern
and study issues of historical significance for the future, can the
situation be remedied. The body of Lazarsfeld's article explores the
problem of locating such significant issues.

Historical writings are recommended by the author as one
source of fruitful hypotheses. He illustrates several modes of historical analysis which, in the past, called for data relating to attitudes
and which therefore suggest problems for research.

The author recommends the establishment of a "commission for
the utilization of polls in the service of future historiography" to
consist of historians and social scientists who would help locate
significant problems and research technicians who could translate
these into research designs.

Joseph R. Strayer in "The Historian's Concept of Public Opinion" discusses Lazarsfeld's paper and expresses certain reservations
as to the potential value of attitude research for history. Not all
of the reservations are inherent in the methods of such research;

---

6. See Paul F. Lazarsfeld's essay, page 245.

7. This article is an extended version of the Presidential address delivered
by Dr. Lazarsfeld before the American Association for Public Opinion Research and published in *The Public Opinion Quarterly*, Winter 1950-1951.

some derive merely from the present emphases of the pollsters.

Historians, Strayer claims, consider verbal expressions of opinions with which the pollster deals much less important than actual behavior. Since the real test of opinion is action, the historian can learn what he needs to know from records of past actions and he is, in reality, not greatly handicapped by the lack of opinion research.

Secondly, even in recent and democratic periods, the shifting opinions of the masses of people have only limited influence upon the course of events. Opinion research would be more valuable if it could isolate the opinions of leaders and distinguish strongly held opinions from the lukewarm opinions of uninterested and uninfluential segments of the public. What matters more than superficial expressions of opinion about current issues are basic beliefs. Beliefs set limits within which policy leaders can operate. But can such basic beliefs and shifts in them, the author wonders, be studied by survey methods? May not traditional methods of the historian (the study of books read or movies patronized or the analysis of publications, such as the Saturday Evening Post) prove more reliable, after all?

Henry David in "Opinion Research in the Service of the Historian" specifies five distinct respects in which opinion research may be of service to the historian. These range from adding a new type of primary source materials to, in general, increasing our knowledge of man and society. But he does not expect the pollster to serve the historian of the future in the direct manner envisaged by Lazarsfeld. "The inquiries which future historians will conduct will in part be shaped by their own cultural setting and by what appear to be the compelling . . . issues of their day." The pollster will not be in a position to anticipate those issues and it is not for him to prescribe to the historian what the latter's concerns should be.

"Plant Sociology: The Elite and the Aborigines" by Clark Kerr and Lloyd H. Fisher and the following article by Conrad M. Arensberg and Geoffrey Tootell, "Plant Sociology: Real Discoveries and New Problems" are companion pieces opening Part II of the volume dealing with economics and sociology. They represent a double scrutiny of one particular branch of industrial sociology. The term "plant sociology" was coined by the economists Kerr and Fisher to describe the work of Elton Mayo and his followers. The authors of the first article set out to contrast the respective approaches

of the economists and the plant sociologists to problems of industrial relations. They find the differences sharp and pervasive and
deriving from fundamental ideological divergencies. The economists and the Mayoites are said to belong to two different traditions
with different views as to the nature of man and of society, different
values and prescriptions for social policy. The first article sets
itself the goal of discerning the ideological tenets of the Mayoites.
The authors seek to demonstrate that even the recent plant sociologists remained true to the Mayoite ideological heritage. They
seek to show that the ideological premises have determined the
focus, problems, methods, results and policy recommendations of
the school. Needless to add, Kerr and Fisher side with the economists
in this debate.

Arensberg and Tootell answer some of the criticism directly
but devote the major part of their article to a different kind of
rebuttal. They present what they deem to be the actual and potential scientific contributions of plant sociologists and maintain that
these can and must be judged independently of values and pro-
nouncements on matters of broad public policy.

The next unit of Part II consists of two articles by Robert
Lekachman and George Katona and accompanying discussions by
William S. Vickrey and L. R. Klein. The unit centers around two
related problems: the link between macro- and microeconomics
and the relation of economics to social psychology and sociology.
The particular material in the context of which these issues are
examined is the Keynesian theory of the business cycle.

Keynesian theory is an example of a macroeconomic theory.
It posits a set of determinate relations between a small number
of economic aggregates such as national income, level of investments, of savings, of consumption and so on. In "The Non-Economic
Assumptions of John Maynard Keynes" Robert Lekachman begins
with a resumé of the Keynesian theory of the business cycle. He
then proceeds to search out its socio-psychological premises. The
theory makes assumptions about human behavior at three points.
It imputes certain characteristics to consumers, investors, and
speculators. For example, the consumers as a class are said to be,
over the short run period, stable in their habits. They respond to
fluctuations in income but are powerless to initiate economic
changes.

The investors also constitute for the purposes of the theory a homogeneous class. Their decisions play a more dynamic role in the theory. The amount to be invested may be decided on the basis of a rational calculation of probable profits but uncertainty about the future forces the investors ultimately to rely upon "animal spirits," fluctuations of which Keynes doesn't claim to be able to explain.

Precisely because Keynes postulated relationships between a few measurable economic aggregates his theory stimulated the forecasting of levels of income and employment. Had the predictions based on the theory proved accurate the issues considered by Katona, Vickrey, and Klein may never have arisen. But it was unlikely that a theory erected as this one was "within a framework of short-run assumptions" (with, in other words, a host of variables held constant) could yield accurate predictions in the real changing world. Such a theory might, as Vickrey says, "provide insight into the functioning of the economic process and even provide prescriptions as to what to do in order to shift the course of . . . the economy in a desired direction" without, however, being capable of yielding accurate predictions.

This failure of Keynesian theory gives rise among others to the following questions: Are the patterns of motivations attributed by Keynes to consumers, investors, and speculators too simplified? What can we learn from a direct study of the economic behavior of consumers or investors? How can the inclusion of non-economic determinants of economic behavior improve our understanding and predictions of the latter? And finally, can the results of such studies be assimilated into the original macroeconomic theory?

"The Function of Survey Research in Economics" by George Katona attempts to answer these questions in general by considering the unique contributions of survey research vis-à-vis macroeconomics. Vickrey and Klein in subsequent articles bring these issues back to Keynesian theory.

Survey methods in economics involve direct questioning of individuals concerning their economic condition, behavior, or attitudes relevant to economic behavior. The questioning may be done by questionnaire or interview. Katona states that as a fact-finding technique the survey is accepted in economics. The usual aggregate statistics which can be compiled from records such as payroll data or retail sales often fail to give the microeconomic distribution of these total amounts. Budget studies, for example, have long supplemented aggregate statistics with sample surveys of consumers.

The most important function of the survey, however, goes beyond mere fact-finding; it is a tool, Katona claims, for establishing functional relationships between economic behavior and other variables. Even if the variables in question are traditional economic variables, survey methods may have an advantage over the macroeconomic approach. Using the relation of liquid assets to spending as an illustration, the author shows the difficulties of approaching this problem on the macroeconomic level, i.e., through "comparison of total assets with amounts spent in several periods or countries." Economies compared usually differ in many respects in addition to differences in asset holdings. On the other hand, survey research, "testing the hypothesis on the microeconomic level, enables us to hold many other factors constant and to test modifications of the hypothesis."

A more significant distinction of survey research is the possibility of including non-economic variables. Attitudes are measurable and must be introduced as consequences and causes of economic behavior. Attitudinal factors have a degree of freedom from their economic determinants and it is inadequate therefore to use only objective economic facts. Perceptions of economic events differ and these differences together with the factors which explain them are properly included in economic studies. Katona illustrates the superior value of the joint use of attitudinal and financial data in explaining the 1951 "spending lull."

Katona concludes with some general observations on the need to integrate economics, psychology and sociology into a theory of social action. This "economic psychology" in setting up its hypotheses would be as ready to draw upon Keynesian theory of the effects of income changes as it would upon theories of habit formation or of reference groups.

Returning to the consideration of macro- and microeconomics with special reference to Keynes, William S. Vickrey first defines the nature of the Keynesian contribution. Keynes provided a new way of thinking about the economy by singling out a new set of processes held critical in reaching an equilibrium. In relation to survey research the theory operated to direct attention to certain areas of study if not to specific variables within it. Survey research in turn has some bearing upon the original theory. Survey research on the consumer throws light upon four categories of variables which modify the simplified picture of consumer behavior contained in Keynes.

In the last article of this unit L. R. Klein attempts to show how these contributions of survey research on the consumer may be used to build a middle range theory of:

> . . . obviously greater applicability to real life situations than the purely pedagogical models (of Keynes) yet much less complex . . . than the Walrasian type network tying together all the fine details of microeconomic behavior. Something of the order of magnitude of five, ten or possibly twenty variables would be adequate and manageable.

Klein cites several illustrations of the refinements in the Keynesian consumption function effected by linkage of aggregate and sample survey data. For example, survey data on the marginal propensity to consume of wage earners, farmers, and businessmen may be used to estimate the macroeconomic consumption function with greater accuracy than would be possible on the basis of aggregative statistics alone.

Just as the choice with regard to the number of variables need not lie between the extremes of a handful and a hundred—so the alternatives in introducing non-economic variables need not be complete exclusion or infinite regress.

A step forward is taken if we can at least make numerical measures of psychological variables and quantify their effect on economic behavior.

The statistical distributions of these attitudes may then be included in the attempt to forecast economic events.

The last article of Part II is by Seymour M. Lipset and Martin Trow: "Reference Group Theory and Trades Union Policy." Among the various schools of labor economists our authors singled out a group of contemporary writers who, in contrast to the earlier macroscopic histories and theories of the labor movement, turned to concrete cases of industrial relations. Seeking to account for actual trade union behavior these writers have come upon facts which could not be adequately explained in terms of classical economics. To account for these facts the economists have begun to use such concepts as "equitable" or "invidious" comparisons. But the interpretations being developed by the economists remain ad hoc. On the other hand, turning to sociology and social psychology, Lipset and Trow find that the growing reference group analysis provides a fruitful theoretical framework for the study of the facts noted by labor economists; the phenomena are clearly a special case of the more general reference group theory.

The article thus confronts the empirical findings of one discipline with theoretical formulations of another and demonstrates various ways in which each would profit from such a confrontation. The article shows how reference group theory can direct further investigations and in turn assimilate their findings in a coherent and cumulative way.

Some Recurrent Issues of Interdisciplinary Polemics

The common frontiers of our three disciplines will be seen to be astir with intellectual skirmishes. Controversy both within and between disciplines is an inevitable feature of scientific development. It would be futile to attempt to "resolve" the various issues raised in the polemical sections of this volume. But not all intellectual controversy is equally beneficial. Pseudo-issues produced by verbal or logical ambiguities are much too frequent and waste our resources. They are usually occasioned by the failure to discern the tacit assumptions of the contending positions. Such is the case when contestants who disagree about the best method of dealing with a problem turn out upon analysis to have two different problems in mind. Consider the debate over the relative merits of processual as contrasted with factorial analysis. This debate may reflect some real differences in intellectual styles but frequently it continues only because the contestants fail to recognize that hidden in each position is a different quest.

Processual analysis is in fact often directed to the following problem: assuming phenomena A and B to be associated, can we discern the sequence of stages, the network of links which connects the two? By contrast, the factorial approach poses the problem:

why B rather than not-B? Under what conditions, that is, will B appear or fail to appear? For example, Waller criticized the usual factorial treatment of divorce and offered instead a processual analysis. He traced alienation in marriage as a process moving "in a cyclic fashion to its denouement in divorce." [8] In so doing Waller does throw a new light on the way in which some marriages come to divorce but he does not face the problem of why others remain stable. On the other hand the earlier correlation studies demonstrated the differential associations between regions, size of family, or economic conditions and divorce, but they failed to specify the links involved in these associations.[9]

To give another illustration of a pseudo-issue, some students look at society and find in it a predominance of processes which may be termed self-limiting or self-corrective because they generate counterforces which bring the system back to the earlier level. Other students emphasize cumulative processes. There is little doubt, for instance, that an inventory of social processes listed in each of the two sociology texts, that by Kingsley Davis, on the one hand, and by Ogburn and Nimkoff, on the other, would show such a contrast.[10] But what presents itself as a disagreement on facts may be a difference in purpose. As John Maurice Clark suggested in his essay on "Statics and Dynamics," [11] back of the preoccupation with self-corrective processes is a particular problem: how to account for the stability of a system and a tendency towards an equilibrium. On the other hand, the key to the emphasis on cumulative and irreversible processes is a primary interest in explaining change rather than stability.

---

8. Williard W. Waller, *The Family: A Dynamic Interpretation*, Cordon, New York, 1938.

9. For references on the processual vs. the factorial (or the "variable") approaches, see p. 326; Paul F. Lazarsfeld and Robert K. Merton, "Friendship as Social Process: A Substantive and Methodological Analysis" in *Freedom and Control in Modern Society*, Morroe Berger et al ed., D. Van Nostrand, New York, 1955; Solomon E. Asch, *Social Psychology*, Prentice-Hall, 1952, pp. 531-33; Bernard R. Berelson, Paul F. Lazarsfeld and William N. McPhee, *Voting*, University of Chicago Press, 1954, Chapter 13. H. Blumer, "Sociological Analysis and the Variable," *American Sociological Review*, 21, 6.

10. Kingsley Davis, *Human Society*, The Macmillan Co., New York, 1949; W. F. Ogburn and M. F. Nimkoff, *Sociology*, Houghton Mifflin Co., New York, 1950.

11. John Maurice Clark, *Preface to Social Economics*, Farrar and Rinehart, New York, 1936.

The clarification of verbal and logical confusion may on occasion result in complete agreement or it may transform what appeared originally as contradictory into complementary positions.

But not all inter- and intradisciplinary issues are pseudo-issues. Real differences exist. One theme frequently reflected in current literature and in the pages of this volume is the conflict between what is often termed the macro- and microscopic approaches. Several contrasts are enmeshed in this controversy and must be disentangled in the interest of clarity. From one point of view this is a version of the familiar problem of reductionism in science. In this sense macroscopic is usually identified with the institutional level of analysis while the focus of microscopic studies is the individual or aggregates of individuals. Such is the conflict between students of "political behavior" and the institutionalists [12] or between psychologically and sociologically oriented social psychologists.[13] The most extreme opposition to the macroscopic approach views it as merely a vague and misleading metaphor for the microscopic.[14] According to this view the macroscopic approach reifies concepts. "Social systems" or "institutions" are only certain features abstracted from the behavior of individuals and do not have an independent material existence. In order to be tested, any proposition about these abstractions must be expressed in terms of behavior or attitudes of human beings. Consequently, to the extent that this is done the macroscopic is reduced to the microscopic, ultimately without any remainder.

Without entering into an extended philosophical discussion of reductionism some observations may be offered on the uses of the macroscopic approach. An apparent paradox causes confusion. If "social facts" are merely abstractions from behavior of individuals, does it not follow that any proposition about institutions can be translated into or reduced to propositions about actions of individuals?

Some writers have questioned whether indeed such a translation

---

12. David B. Truman, "The Impact on Political Science of the Revolution in the Behavioral Sciences," *Research Frontiers in Politics in Government,* The Brookings Institution, 1955.

13. Theodore M. Newcomb, "Sociology and Psychology," *For a Science of Social Man,* John Gillin, ed., The Macmillan Co., 1954.

14. Floyd Allport, "The Nature of Institutions," *Social Forces,* December 1927, pp. 167-179.

can ever be made without some remainder of macroscopic terms.[15] If, as Allport once expressed it, the "church" cannot be said to control anything, if it is only the Pope or the minister who can exercise control, the latter terms do not avoid institutional connotations; they define statuses which can be understood only as part of a larger institutional complex.

But even if a particular generalization concerning "social facts" could, once it has been formulated, be reduced to terms of a lower level—the question remains whether such a generalization could have been made in the first place without macroscopic concepts. Without a concept of a social system a student is not likely to study "the organization of action about the exigencies of social systems as systems." [16] The psychologist, employing the model of the individual as a stimulating and stimulated organism, studied speech acquisition but it is no accident that he left it to others to explore speech as a communicative device in socialization. It was not the traditional psychologist who studied the role of speech and communication in the maintenance of the multi-person system.[17]

Another illustration may be drawn from a recent book on delinquency.[18] The author sets out to explain the culture of male, lower class gangs. The very formulation of the problem in terms of class and sex differences bears, of course, the imprint of a sociological orientation. His explanation draws upon such concepts as class, subculture, social roles, etc. He also draws upon perceptions of relations between social facts as, for example, Merton's observation that in our society "common success goals for the population at large" coexist with unequal "access to approved modes of reaching these goals." [19] A study of delinquent boys lacking this conceptual orientation and focusing upon the behavior of individuals would hardly arrive at the same conclusions. As the author explains, once the delinquent subculture emerges, it attracts individuals for a great

15. Maurice Mandlebaum, "Societal Facts," *The British Journal of Sociology,* December 1955, pp. 305-317; Talcott Parsons, *The Social System,* Free Press, 1951, pp. 541-555.
16. Parsons, *The Social System, op. cit.,* p. 539.
17. Theodore M. Newcomb, "Sociology and Psychology," *For a Science of Social Man, op. cit.,* p. 234.
18. Albert K. Cohen, *Delinquent Boys: the Culture of the Gang,* Free Press, Glencoe, Ill., 1955.
19. Robert K. Merton, *Social Theory and Social Structure,* Free Press, Glencoe, Ill., p. 125 ff.

variety of reasons. Suppose that the student approached the problem with concepts of individual psychology. That common core of motivations and circumstances which accounted for the emergence of the delinquent subculture would, unless organized by appropriate concepts, be hopelessly enmeshed with the motivations of all others who have joined the gang for a variety of reasons.

Most critics of the macroscopic approach, however, are not so extreme as to deny it any validity. They merely criticize its abuses on two grounds. The institutionalists have been held guilty of many unexamined assumptions about individual behavior and of holding too passive a view of the individual.[20] Secondly, they have been charged, and justly, with lack of methodological rigor in verification and, at the worst, with the reification of abstractions. Broad in scope, using concepts as explanatory principles when they were merely verbal metaphors, many a macroscopic generalization would have to undergo a radical translation to be susceptible of empirical proof. But the abstract level does not constitute in itself an intrinsic barrier to empirical verification. Several recent writers have pointed out that the concept of a "person" is as much of a construct as the concept of a group. A person can be "observed only through a series of actions," he is a conceptual rather than a perceptual unity.[21] The problem here as elsewhere in science is one of finding objective indicators of phenomena under study.

The "institutionalists" in their turn charge that the exclusion of the broader framework hurts the student of the microcosm even in his own bailiwick. He fails to give adequate consideration to the effect upon individual behavior of various patterns of organization.[22]

Apart from the issue of reductionism there are other contrasts embedded in the macro-microscopic debate. Macroscopic is sometimes equated with the study of formal and explicit institutional patterns as contrasted with informal social interaction. Such is the difference, among others, separating the economists and the plant

---

20. Newcomb, *op. cit.*, p. 232. See also Ernest Nagel, "On the Statement 'The Whole Is More than the Sum of Its Parts,'" *The Language of Social Research*, Paul F. Lazarsfeld and Morris Rosenberg, Free Press, Glencoe, Illinois, 1955.

21. Charles K. Warriner, "Groups Are Real," *American Sociological Review*, October 1956, p. 552.

22. Newcomb, *op. cit.*, 240 ff.

sociologists of our volume.[23] The focus on formal structures is termed macroscopic because it leads to greater concern with relations between broad institutional complexes. On the other hand the focus upon informal organization leads the investigator to minutiae of social processes within the organization. That, in turn, requires direct observation and interview of individual actors. The student of formal and larger structures typically accuses the other of neglecting the influence of the environment upon the internal processes; he is in turn charged with taking for granted the internal processes.

Finally, macro- and microanalysis is used also in the general sense of a focus upon large and complex as against limited problems. The historian Richard Hofstadter writes:

The historian who hopes to achieve important work is unable to rest content with the completion of a small but sound unit of craftsmanship because the tradition of his profession is not so much to reach for the perfection of microscopic units of research as it is to try to cope with certain insistent macroscopic questions. The historian deals with such categories as the Reformation, the Renaissance . . . with wars and social upheavals.[24]

Enmeshed in this issue is the debate over methods. The more precise quantitative research techniques and those which involve a direct study of individuals are felt by the macroanalysts to be suitable only for the limited and simple problems. V. O. Key, the political scientist, warns against "the hazards in transplanting conventional social science techniques to the study of politics." [25]

These techniques are unsuitable to the study of "large and complex political aggregates," i.e. "the analysis of the nature of bossism, of the process of legislative decision, of the impact of law and rule . . ."

The adherents of the more precise methods often maintain that the techniques held to be peculiarly suitable to complex and significant problems belong to the early stages of scientific exploration eventually to be replaced by improved methods. "Qualitative" methods in this view are preliminary approximations not yet satisfying scientific canons of proof.

23. See p. 281 ff.
24. Richard Hofstadter, "History and the Social Sciences," *The Varieties of History*, Fritz Stern, ed., Meridian Books, 1956, p. 369.
25. "Items," Social Science Research Council, Sept. 1956, p. 31.

The opponents, on the other hand, consider the link between scope of problem and method to be an intrinsic one. They are apprehensive about the extension of social research technology because they believe that it must produce a shift to less significant problems of study.

The premature closure of this issue would be a disservice to scientific development. Too ready an assumption of an intrinsic link between the large scope generalization and the "qualitative" mode of verification would freeze methods at the present level and discourage improvement. It is conceivable, for example, that a present day Max Weber would couple his significant and large scope generalization with "microscopic" methods. He might use more refined statistics and even interview samples of various religious groups to test his hypothesis as to the relation of religious and economic institutions. The contrary assumption that *all* problems of scholarly concern are susceptible of natural science methods is also undesirable in the present stage of our knowledge. It tends to deflect research effort from topics which, today in any event, (and maybe, ever) cannot be so studied. Fortunately, mutual criticism is beginning to exert some pressures upon both sides. There are indications that the "macroanalysts" are becoming somewhat more self-conscious about modes of verification whereas their opponents are under greater pressure to place research in a broader context.

Another promising development is the attempt to scrutinize qualitative methods and codify them. This would make more explicit the assumptions and the intrinsic limitations and values of various methods. We should in time know more about the types of problems or stages in research which can be best approached through this or that method.[26]

In addition to the problem of reductionism we shall cite another theme of intellectual polemics. The issue concerns the ideal of science. "The efforts of human intellect," wrote Morris Cohen, "may be viewed as a tension between two poles—one to do justice to the fullness of the concrete case before us, the other to grasp an underlying abstract universal principle that controls more than the one

---

26. Allen H. Barton and Paul F. Lazarsfeld, "Some Functions of Qualitative Analysis in Social Research, "*Sociologica,* Frankfurter, Beiträge Zur Sociologie, Band 1, 1955.

case before us." [27] Schools of thought differ in their orientation to one or the other of these poles; what kind of "science" to strive for?

In its most highly developed form science is a body of abstract, logically interrelated, and verified propositions. It abstracts from empirical reality selected aspects and attempts to make universal statements about them. Its method is to search for relatively few concepts out of which to build its own distinctive theoretical scheme. Scientific categories may bear no resemblance to common sense classifications of empirical events.

The second school of thought operates with a different model of scholarship. This is not the familiar contrast between pure theorizing and empirical verification. It is rather the difference between a generalizing and a more empirical discipline. Perhaps because they lack the faith in the underlying "lawfulness" of social behavior the second school is unwilling to strive for so high a level of abstraction and to stray so far from the common sense concepts.

"No amount of intellectual agility, for example," writes one adherent of this school, "can overcome the difference among the numerous revolutions that have taken place in human history and reduce them to a common pattern. Similarities there may be, but they are of such broad and general nature as to be unenlightening, and they become less enlightening the more cases one tries to cover with a theory." [28] The distinction between the "modern" and the "old-fashioned" approach drawn in this article is similar though not completely identical with the contrast under discussion here.

Instead, then, of vainly searching for a "law of revolutions" study them with familiar concepts common to educated men. Compare revolutions, by all means, because each may offer clues to a more complete understanding of the other.[29] Some factor neglected in the interpretation of one revolution may become visible in the case of another and require a re-examination of the earlier study.

Reflections of this controversy are to be found in several places. Recent developments in political science are a case in point. Truman reviews a number of books which are all characterized by a "more

27. Morris R. Cohen, *Reason and Nature*, Harcourt, Brace & Company, New York, 1931, p. 368.

28. Barrington Moore, Jr., "Sociological Theory and Contemporary Politics," *The American Journal of Sociology*, September 1955, p. 108.

29. *Ibid*, p. 110.

explicit pursuit of regularities" than is true of more conventional political science [30] and therefore by a search for categories which cut across the conventional formal categories like "executive," "legislature," "political party. . . ." The older categories may have been adequate for crude descriptions of formal political structures but they will not do for the construction of a "general theory of politics," an approach which rejects "the concentration on the study of uniqueness." [31] The terms "executive," "legislature," etc. are "not in fact comparable because they have no consistent meaning." With regard to the term "party" as used in comparative government one writer states:

> France has a multi-party system, the U. S. a two-party system. But is the French party similar to the American. . . . Perhaps a more significant correspondence to the French party is the American 'faction' of which there are at least four, and to the American party, the French groupement.[32]

Another writer concurs:

> Democracy, liberalism refer to such broadly aesthetic configurations that in many cases they are practically unique historically and not strictly comparable with anything else and at most allow the comparison of a handful of similar cases.[33]

The experimentation with new concepts takes many forms, such as the attempt to deal with nationalism in terms of a theory of communication, the study of international politics as types of decision-making or the application of game theory to political behavior.

Another illustration of the dilemma of comparability vs. uniqueness may be found in the literature of historiography and in more recent discussions of the relation of history to the social sciences.[34]

The adherents of the two approaches typically marshall certain

---

30. David B. Truman, *op. cit.*, pp. 217-222.

31. Paul T. David, "Comparative State Politics and the Problem of Party Realignment," *Research Frontiers in Politics and Government, op. cit.*, p. 170.

32. Herbert A. Simon, *American Political Science Review*, September 1953, p. 665.

33. G. Lowell Field, *American Political Science Review*, September 1953, p. 672.

34. "The Social Sciences in Historical Study," *Social Science Research Bulletin* 64.

arguments against each other. Those whose hope it is to build a generalizing science do not demand that any experimentation with theoretical schemes bear immediate fruit in the illumination of practical problems. Their opponents are less patient with what appears to them a doubtful, long-range investment and accuse the "generalists" of "scholasticism," "sterile formalism" and indifference to significant social problems of the age. Preoccupation with methodology which may be justified as another long-range investment appears equally trivial to those who do not share a similar faith in possibilities of social science.

The main counter argument of the "generalists" is that the resignation to the lower level of abstraction is nothing less than abdication of scientific aspirations. As to the contributions to social welfare, the pure rather than the applied science is the goose that lays the golden eggs. And pure science must transcend the use of "aesthetic concepts of large configurations" in favor of "narrowly defined variables rigidly abstracted from the aesthetic contexts in which they appear." [35]

The two approaches just outlined may derive from differences in the subject matter of various disciplines. History, for example, is likely to remain a more "empirical" discipline than economics precisely because it purports to deal with the totality of social life. But the two approaches may exist also as we have seen within a particular discipline, and a comment is in order concerning their respective functions. To have described the issue as that of "comparability vs. uniqueness" was to exaggerate the contrast. Our "empiricists" no less than the "generalists" employ concepts and abstractions. An intellectual apprehension of even a unique event involves the use of more general categories. The difference is in the level of abstraction and degree to which the concepts are systematized. The lower level concepts may serve a useful function in ordering empirical phenomena. An interpretation lacking the characteristics of a scientific law may still point up a trend, guide the mind to crucial factors in a situation, suggest policy in order to shift some social system in a desired direction. But to give up the ideal of a theoretical science is to give up the hope for a kind of knowledge which is both more intellectually satisfying and practically useful.

---

35. G. Lowell Field, *op. cit.*, p. 670.

The function of systematic theory is manifold; as Merton has pointed out, "It extends the scope and the cumulation of empirical findings and of theory." [36] Isolated or seemingly disparate phenomena are now seen to be interrelated. The ground for prediction becomes more secure both because of greater precision which the more rigorous ideal of science demands and because systematic theory provides a rationale lacking in mere empirical generalizations.[37] But systematic theory of this kind requires abstractions of a higher order because such interrelations can be expected only between selected aspects of empirical events, not their totalities.

To sum up, many issues of interdisciplinary polemics appear to center around the most fruitful allocation of scarce scientific resources. "Your approach has some merit" says one side to another, "but let us cut it down to size. Your theory will be found to apply only under restricted conditions; your method will be found to possess intrinsic limitations." Each position holds a different set of assumptions as to potentialities of different approaches and the implied predictions must await future developments for their ultimate test.

But if such issues of emphasis cannot be wholly resolved, they can and should be clarified. In the course of such clarification, each side to the debate is forced to make its quest and hidden assumptions more explicit and to delineate more sharply the special uses and limitations of its position. This may lead to greater recognition of mutual dependence.

Interdisciplinary Convergences

The analysis of the materials contained in this book suggests certain modes of potentially fruitful interdisciplinary cooperation. The first is a case in which the *empirical data being accumulated in one field could be illuminated by concepts existing in another.*

An illustration of this mode of convergence will be found in the article by Lipset and Trow.[38] As we have already stated earlier

---

36. Robert K. Merton, *op. cit.*, p. 93.
37. *Ibid.*, p. 94.
38. See p. 391 ff.

in this introduction, Lipset and Trow note that some contemporary labor economists in studying trade union behavior have been accumulating empirical data which traditional economic theory cannot explain. Were these economists satisfied to limit themselves to abstract economic models and define non-economic variables as exogeneous to the system, they need not have been embarrassed by such facts as the power struggles between unions or "uneconomic" wage settlements. But as soon as they set themselves the task of interpreting actual cases of industrial relations they had to take cognizance of non-economic determinants.

But labor economists who are thus entering the province of "non-economic" factors lack any previously developed concepts to deal with them and tend to formulate only ad hoc hypotheses. On the other hand, turning to social psychology and sociology, Lipset and Trow find that the growing reference group theory provides a fruitful theoretical framework for the facts described by the economists: these facts are clearly a special case of this theory. The term "reference group" pertains to the fact that individuals use for self-appraisal and evaluation standards of other individuals and groups. Reference group analysis is concerned with determinants and consequences of such comparative evaluations. For example, whom will a given group compare itself with and under what conditions? What are the factors which will determine the selection of reference groups? Do some individuals have conflicting reference groups? If so, how are these conflicts resolved? Lipset and Trow consider the relevance of these and similar problems for the labor economists.

Confrontation of the data being collected by the labor economists with reference group analysis would be profitable all around. For the economist the theory would provide an abundant source of new and related hypotheses. Because it contains a store of theoretically posed questions, it would direct investigations and in turn assimilate their results in a more coherent way. For the sociologist such collaboration will mean an access to a new body of materials with which to test and develop reference group theory.

A second and a closely related convergence exists when *concepts and hypotheses developed in one field open new problems and stimulate research in another*. History and sociology provide illustrations.

Prompted by the social sciences (states Richard Hofstadter) the historian begins to realize that matters of central concern to other disciplines force him to enlarge his conception of his own task. Problems associated with social status, social mobility, differences and conflicts between generations, child-rearing in its relation to culture, the sociology of knowledge and of the professions, are problems which he might properly take upon himself and which are interwoven with his traditional concerns. It seems inevitable, too, that some of the discoveries made by modern social research about current mass political behavior will have some effect upon the historian's conception of political behavior in the past.[39]

The monograph by Lowenthal and Fiske provides an illustration of this particular type of convergence. The two authors approached the historical materials of 18th Century England with categories, questions and hypotheses derived from the contemporary study of mass media of communication. This cross-fertilization proves fruitful for both the sociologist and the historian. The historical materials serve to test generalizations based exclusively upon the contemporary period. Many a sociological generalization is time and place bound and assumptions locked in it can be brought to light through confrontation with historical data. For example, the discovery that the controversy of art versus popular culture was already rife in the 18th Century belied the facile attribution of this whole problem to the introduction of electronics. Conversely, the very attempt to scrutinize the 18th Century scene in terms of sociological problems opened up a host of new perspectives for the historian. To cite one illustration, the authors have discerned changes in literary criticism and have attempted to account for them in social-structural terms, that is, by the relation between the class backgrounds of the writers on the one hand and their audiences on the other. The writers of the 18th Century faced a new and larger audience. They were no longer protected by the patronage of aristocracy but dependent instead upon the middle and working classes for support and acclaim. While in the earlier period the cultural backgrounds of writer and his audience were more often than not similar this was no longer the case with the new and broader market for literary products.

It is the authors' thesis that this change in the relation of the writer to his audience accounted for the changes which were

---

39. Hofstadter, *op. cit.*, p. 364.

taking place in aesthetic discussions. The change was in part the shift from a rational analysis of literary works to concern with the experience of the audience. In the earlier centuries the problems of the literati did not center on who was to be judge of literature but on such matters as the importance of classical rules, the limits of the genre, the role of literature in relation to other intellectual pursuits and so forth. This hypothesis as to reasons for the shift in literary criticism is cited as an illustration of the value that an historian may derive from a sociological approach to a problem of 18th Century English history.

The third kind of convergence may be regarded as a later stage in the development of the first two. It is a case in which *two disciplines bring their respective theoretical frameworks to the investigation of the same empirical problem.* Labor-management relations, worker productivity and morale have been the concern of the economists long before Elton Mayo and his followers entered the field. Collaboration is hardly the word to describe the process through which the convergence took place. But despite the lively debate between the economists and some industrial sociologists (many of them originally trained in anthropology), the scrutiny of their respective publications shows these two approaches to be not conflicting but complementary over wide segments of the analysis. Let us locate a few of the distinctive contributions which "plant sociology" has made and can be expected to make to the strictly economic analysis of labor-management relations.

In order to fill out lacunae in their interpretations economists occasionally resorted to "common sense" terms such as "mutual trust," "constructive leadership," and so on. One contribution of plant sociology lies in the further analysis of these "common sense" explanations. To have said, for example, that the impact of a given economic policy depended upon "mutual trust" or "constructive leadership" was to explain little. The definition of constructive leadership remained tautological, as the kind of leadership which brought about the desired results. The economists, lacking the conceptual tools for the examination of these phenomena, assumed that the common sense explanation of them was adequate. Arensberg and Tootell demonstrate, however, how much remains to be learned about leadership before its use as a modifying factor is theoretically satisfying and practically useful.

There is another way in which plant sociology sought to replace the "common sense" formulations of the economists: in scrutinizing the psycho-social nexus between phenomena asserted to be causally related. There are situations in which some economic variable makes such an immediate and understandable impact upon plant relations that no further scrutiny is called for. But this is not always the case. The effect of size of a company upon decision-making, or of the political climate of the country upon attitudes of management is a complex relation mediated by intervening steps. Even when such relations appear to be established and plausible much remains to be learned. It may be discovered that only some features of the "cause" are the decisive ones in bringing about the result and this discovery may suggest possibilities for control. Similarly, it may be discovered that certain intervening steps in the causal link are subject to modification. What starts, then, as merely a more complete description of a causal link may bring to light premises which were hidden in the original formulation, reveal the conditions under which the link obtains, and lead to the search for modifying factors.

Plant sociology, then, subjected to further scrutiny the unanalyzed "common sense" segment of the older interpretation. But its contribution went further. It revealed new variables, which on occasion have illuminated a situation for which the older framework offered no clues whatsoever. Such was the case when the discontent of design engineers which puzzled the management of one firm was attributed to the discrepancy between the actual lines of authority and the traditional norms of the company.[40] More frequently, the new variables served to round out the explanation of some plant phenomenon already partially understood in terms of economic variables by further specifying the conditions under which the latter operate. Plant sociologists, for instance, have explained why an incentive scheme has on occasion failed to produce the expected results by discovering a new variable: the amount of responsibility granted to the workers for setting production goals. The inadequacy of the earlier explanations was usually brought to light by some finding inconsistent with the existing economic theory as, for example, the continued high productivity of the Relay

---

40. Conrad M. Arensberg and D. McGregor, "Determination of Morale in an Industrial Company," *Applied Anthropology,* January-March 1942.

Assembly Room girls despite variations in working conditions. Plant sociologists suspect that many of the earlier generalizations would prove in need of qualifications if subjected to more systematic check.

The contribution of the plant sociologists just detailed would be minimized if it turned out to be true, as some critics charge, that the variables introduced can play only a descriptive and not an explanatory role. This would be the case if it could be shown that what appeared as explanatory factors were inevitable expressions of antecedent economic variables already included in the older conceptual framework of the economists. Let us suppose that in two plants A and B, identical incentive schemes were introduced with, however, different results; in plant A—high morale and increased efficiency while in plant B—unrest and impaired productivity. The plant sociologists discover that in plant A, but not in B, the incentive scheme was introduced with prior discussions and with responsibility for setting production goals given to the workers. Let us suppose further that the economists locate an institutional difference between the two plants. Plant A turns out to be a small and marginal concern struggling to preserve its competitive position which, the economists assume, predisposed the employer and the workers to cooperation. Plant B, on the other hand, is a rich company in which the interdependence of management and workers was not so obvious, and therefore mutual attitudes not so favorable.[41]

Is it valid, then, to assume that these differences in the economic status of the two plants explain adequately the different outcomes of the incentive schemes? This would be the case if the correlation were perfect; if, that is, in every small plant the introduction of the incentive plan would also vest responsibility in the hands of the workers themselves and, conversely, in every large plant a different procedure would be followed with the expected results. In other words, we could deny any explanatory role to the "human relations" factor if we found it not to have any degree of freedom. It is unlikely that the latter assumption is true. Economists formulated inquiries in such a fashion as to highlight the economic determinants. To ask whether firms with different competitive positions tend to exhibit differences in labor relations is obviously to couch

---

41. F. H. Harbison and R. Dubin, "Patterns of Union Management Relations," Science Research Associates, Chicago 1947.

the results in terms of these factors. But do all firms with similar competitive positions (or other economic characteristics) exhibit identical patterns of labor relations? Such an inquiry would bring into focus sociological variables. The question, then, is the limits which one class of variables sets for the operation of the other. It cannot be solved on *a priori* grounds because *a priori* arguments which minimize the role of "human relations" can be matched by others which accord it an important role. One writer holds that with the growing organization of labor and management the direct interaction of people in a local plant ceases to be an important determinant of industrial relations. The crucial decisions are made elsewhere.[42] But the same phenomenon of organization of labor led another writer to a different emphasis. He pointed out that with wage rates becoming more uniform as a result of unions other factors than wages account for variations in unit labor costs, among them labor productivity. Together with other non-wage factors, "human relations" in the plant assume thus an increasingly important role in at least this particular problem.[43]

As compared with the possible contribution of plant sociology, the function of the more traditional economic approach to labor management relations is so familiar as to require only a brief comment. It may be true that in so far as the "environment" affects in-plant life it must be revealed in the behavior and sentiments of plant personnel. It does not follow from this that minute observations of plant behavior constitute the only or the best way to grasp the influence of the "environment." Institutional factors must be related to other institutional factors in terms of economic theory. It would have hardly been possible to derive from the analysis of plant behavior the kind of knowledge we now possess as a result of the more impersonal macroeconomic study.[44]

While the *relative* usefulness of the two theoretical approaches can be assessed only by means of future research, they are complementary and used together can throw more light upon industrial relations than would be the case if one or the other were excluded.

---

42. H. Blumer, "Sociological Theory in Industrial Relations," *American Sociological Review*, June 1947.

43. F. H. Harbison, "Some Reflections on a Theory of Labor-Management Relations," *The Journal of Political Economy*, February 1946.

44. See pages 14-16 on the issue of reductionism.

The *fourth mode* of useful interdisciplinary cooperation arises out of what Paul F. Lazarsfeld has termed "*adjacent dilettantism.*" He notes:

> . . . certain procedures are used by a variety of social sciences. But in one discipline they are used competently and in another in a dilettante way. . . . Sociologists and social psychologists, for instance, have developed detailed skills in the writing of questionnaires. Economists, when they use questionnaires, often do so with . . . naivete. Historians use haphazard quotations from newspapers without any awareness of modern content analysis techniques. . . . Economists have discussed for 50 years, with great care, the logic of index formation. Sociometrists often slap together any index which happens to come to their minds.[45]

Since similar procedures are already employed in a given discipline no great resistance need be anticipated to the eventual diffusion of the improved version. While ignorance is thus the major problem in this case, greater obstacles stand in the way of the *fifth mode* of cooperation. This is a situation in which *a discipline adopts an entirely new method originally developed in another field.*

The borrowed method may serve the discipline in several ways. It may provide improved techniques of verification.

An illustration is provided by the use of public opinion research in the service of history in Planck's analysis. Using the data gathered by the French Institute of Public Opinion for the years 1944 to 1949 the author shows how a method borrowed from another discipline can serve history by providing, first of all, *improved techniques of verification.* French opinion research required a revision of several ideas on political alignments current in contemporary history. For example, survey research suggests that the intellectual component of the Communist Party may have been smaller and that of De Gaulle's forces considerably larger than was generally believed. Again, while the prevalent belief as to the strong Communist Party discipline was confirmed, the surveys show that on several specific issues anywhere from 20% to 50% of the Communist Party supporters displayed independent thought and action.

In addition to yielding more precise descriptions the survey method may be put to a more analytical use. Changes in social

---

45. Unpublished paper.

attitudes and values have always concerned the historian, but their explanation remains a peculiarly elusive problem. It is Lazarsfeld's thesis that the causal analysis of alterations in public opinion can be greatly advanced in the future by opinion research explicitly designed to meet this end. Planck's monograph takes a step in that direction by tracing the influence upon opinion produced by what A. V. Dicey called the "fait accompli" in history. Planck compares the attitudes towards De Gaulle as candidate of the Provisional Government just before he was designated and just after assembly's action in 1945. It appeared that the "fait accompli" converted nearly half of those who had previously hesitated and had reduced opposition by a small percentage. The author traces in a similar fashion changes in attitude towards Petain as a result of his imprisonment.

But the value of a new method may extend beyond the function of testing or refining the familiar generalizations already current in the discipline which has "borrowed" it. *A new method means new data and that in turn leads to the inclusion of new variables and to the formulation of new problems.* The essays by Lazarsfeld and David and the monograph by Planck contain many references to this mode of convergence with regard to history and sociology while Katona and Klein illustrate the same in the application of survey research to economics.

PART I

History

and

Social Research

Leo Lowenthal
and
Marjorie Fiske

THE DEBATE OVER ART
AND POPULAR CULTURE
IN EIGHTEENTH CENTURY ENGLAND

Introduction

The purpose of this study, which is one of a series eventually to include the nineteenth century in England, France and Germany, is to explore some of the antecedents of the popular culture issues, particularly those generated by the mass media, which we face today. Since its source materials are the works of writers and philosophers, and the background is one of social and economic change in eighteenth century England, this is a chapter of literary as well as of social history. As social scientists, we have ventured somewhat afield to explore what writers in eighteenth century England had to say about problems engendered when literary works began to be produced as marketable commodities.

The eighteenth century in England was selected for this first part of the series not because a "mass" audience in the modern sense developed in this period—that was to come only in the next century— but because, from that time on, a writer could support himself from the sale of his works to the public. In effect what took place was a shift from private endowment (usually in the form of patronage by the aristocracy) and a limited audience to public endowment and a potentially unlimited audience. At the same time, the production, promotion, and distribution of literary works became profitable enterprises. These changes affected the content as well as the form of literature, and therefore gave rise to many aesthetic and ethical problems. Not all of these problems were new; some had their origins deep in the seventeenth or even in the sixteenth century when there existed a popular audience for the theater. But in the eighteenth century, questions of the potentialities and predispositions of the audience assumed new urgency for the writer because his audience was now the exclusive source of his livelihood.

Section I is devoted to a brief summary, for background purposes, of the new literary forms which emerged during this period. Section II discusses the reactions of the literati to the various audience-building devices, largely commercial, which quickly came to dominate the literary marketplace. Section III shows how and why the optimism with which intellectuals initially greeted the increase of writers, readers, and reading materials gradually withered away. Section IV analyzes the specific criticisms which intellectuals brought to bear on the new literary products and their audiences. Finally, section V shows how they sought new standards which would be applicable in a literary democracy.

The focus is on how writers experienced and tried to work through these problems—in other words, the eighteenth century literary scene is presented as they saw it. Because the source materials comprise only small segments of the work of the writers with whom we deal, no writer emerges to his full stature. It is our hope, however, that despite such limitations this excursion into an area generally outside the purview of the social sciences, while not yet in itself a theoretical contribution, will provide some of the materials required for the development of a theory of popular culture in our own time.*

I. The Literary Media

During the first few decades of the eighteenth century, the growing industrialization and urbanization of England, together

* We are indebted to several scholars in English literature and the social sciences for valuable suggestions. The senior author's interest in sociological aspects of art stems from his lifelong association with Max Horkheimer and Theodor W. Adorno at the Institute of Social Research. This study was completed while the senior author was a Fellow at the Center for Advanced Study in the Behavioral Sciences. We wish to thank Edgar Rosenberg for his tireless work and incisive criticism, and the administrative and clerical staff of the Center—Mrs. Maria Paasche in particular.

with the cheaper production of paper and improved methods for producing and distributing literary goods, made reading matter less costly and more easily accessible than it had ever been before. Those who were literate read considerably more than their counterparts in the previous century; women were proving themselves to be particularly avid readers; and literacy was becoming a professional prerequisite for the merchant and shopkeeper classes. By the last quarter of the century even remote villages hired their own schoolmasters, or at least maintained Sunday schools in which the rudiments of reading were taught. Literacy estimates are scarce and unreliable, but it seems reasonable to conclude that from 1700 to 1800 the reading public expanded from one which had included mainly the aristocracy, clerics, and scholars to one which also included clerks, artisans, laborers, and farmers.

Despite the fact that new literary products were developing and that commercial competition became intense, each new form, or variation on an old form, found a ready market. In the 1790's, for example, the articulate though not always reliable bookseller Lackington estimated that the sale of books had increased fourfold in twenty years. In a glowing and much-quoted description (which, it should be added, has not gone without challenge from historians), he attributes this increase to the spread of literacy among the lowest socio-economic groups.

> The poorer sort of farmers, and even the poor country people in general, who before that period spent their winter evenings in relating stories of witches, ghosts, hobgoblins, etc., now shorten the winter nights by hearing their sons and daughters read tales, romances, etc., and on entering their houses, you may see *Tom Jones, Roderick Random*, and other entertaining books, stuck up in their bacon-racks, etc. . . . In short, all ranks and degrees now READ.[1]

Lackington may have been unduly optimistic about the heterogeneity of the audience, but the fact remains that literary production had become more highly differentiated. Many books were designed principally for the female audience; handbooks for young girls were greatly in demand, and toward the last quarter of the century, books were written especially for children. General periodicals almost invariably had sections for the ladies and for youngsters, and in addition there were professional and trade journals for lawyers, farmers, and musicians, as well as for a variety of hobbyists.

Toward mid-century, England experienced an unprecedented spate of encyclopedias, histories, almanacs, and other compendia, some of which were compiled with more attention to sales potential than to accuracy. Eminent writers (as well as many lesser) undertook compilations of one sort or another, usually when in financial straits. Tobias Smollett, for example, wrote a popularized history which met with great success, and did so quite frankly in order to supplement his income. This was certainly not the work of a scholarly historian, and Horace Walpole chided the hungry public to which "seven thousand copies of that trash were instantly sold while at the same time the University of Oxford ventured to print but two thousand of that inimitable work, *Lord Clarendon's Life.*" [2] But Walpole had no qualms about capitalizing on the fad himself; in 1760 he discovered that "natural history is in fashion," and shortly thereafter was at work simultaneously on six different scientific volumes covering such diverse areas as botany and husbandry.[3] Since not all popular science was as sound as his, so many absurd misconceptions of half-truths were spread about that several of the more conscientious magazines ran special columns devoted to correcting them.

This section comprises a brief summary of the growth of printed products and is intended merely to sketch in a background for the ensuing discussion. Three new or practically new forms will be touched upon: the popular novel, the magazine, and the newspaper—the latter two in their modern guise seeing light for the first time at the beginning of the century. A brief review of pertinent features of the stage is also included.

Magazines. It is sometimes difficult to distinguish between the newspapers and the magazines of this period. Both were likely to be folded, two-column, single-sheet folios. At first even their contents were similar: the periodical essayists (who usually edited their own periodicals) contributed features to the newspapers; conversely, many magazines included a great deal of news, often in the form of weekly summaries.

Two major changes took place in the periodical literature: a marked decline in publications supported by political parties or religious groups—the principal types to be found in the seventeenth century—and a notable increase in magazines supported by a paying readership and by advertising. Indeed, prototypes of nearly all periodicals familiar to us today were to be found in eighteenth-century England. The first magazine of miscellany, *The Gentleman's Magazine*, including news, fiction, poetry, social items, puzzles, and advice to the lovelorn, appeared in the third decade. In mid-century, the first fiction magazine designed especially for women readers, *Records of Love for the Fair Sex*, came off the press, and at the same time theatrical journals, weekly news digests, book condensations, and book reviews began to flourish.

At the close of the seventeenth century, the question and answer column had evolved as a successful device for covering a wide variety of topics. The first magazine to adopt this format exclusively was bookseller John Dunton's *Athenian Gazette*, which catered to the public demand for "information" and at the same time promoted the bookseller's wares. Some idea of the scope of these question-and-answers—which were to compose a major feature of most of the variety magazines to follow—may be gleaned from a sampling of the *Athenian Gazette*: What is the best poem which was ever made? Why are rats, toads, ravens, etc., ominous? Was it a sin for Noah to curse his son Ham for seeing his nakedness? Which is greater, the hurt or profit that comes from love? Where is the best place to find a husband? Very often, the questions and answers took the form of letters to and from the editor. On the subject of love, the problems were not very different from those confronted by Dorothy Dix.

Ques. I have by promise of marriage engaged myself to a young lady, and not long after my circumstances obliged me to travel, before which I conjured my mistress to be mindful of her contract with me; she at that time gave as great testimonies of her fidelity as I could desire but it was not long 'ere she entertained another gentleman, and so successful was my Rival, that doubtless he had married her, but being discovered the very night before it was to be put into execution, all their measures were irrecoverably broke, her Relations being bitterly averse thereto. At first knowledge thereof, I did not resolve what to do, but since (after mature consideration) I so resent her Behavior, as I believe I should be as willingly hanged as married to her, therefore I have secured a Discharge in writing, wherein we mutually and voluntarily acquit each other from all the Obligations of matrimony. *Whether my unhappy contract is not void, or how far it obliges me?*

Ans. Void, yes; we should be very unhappy creatures, if our vows must be of force, whether the women proved constant or not, for they have their share of Fickleness as well as we; and since your Reason has had the conquest, all you have to do is to pay it such a deference as to follow its advice in a second engagement.[4]

Daniel Defoe's *Weekly Review,* an eight-column, single-sheet periodical first published in February 1704, resembled the late seventeenth century political periodical in many respects. Defoe introduced several come-on devices into his paper, however, and thus paved the way for the variety magazines of later vintage. One of his innovations was a department called "Advice from the Scandalous Club, being a weekly history of nonsense, impertinence, vice and debauchery," [5] and while Defoe eventually developed a strong distaste for such deliberate bids for popularity, his successors in the periodical field did not share his scruples. There is considerable evidence that the *Review* profited from government subsidies, but Defoe claimed that advertisements constituted its principal means of support. As in the case of most other magazine advertising of the period, promotion of books accounted for about half of all commercially sold space.

At the peak of the success of Defoe's *Review,* Richard Steele hit upon an idea which resulted in a type of periodical unique to the eighteenth century, *The Tatler,* to be succeeded two years later by the *Spectator* * with Joseph Addison as principal editor and contributor. The *Spectator,* as *The Tatler* before it, was published daily in the form of single essays on social and cultural matters. Its tone was serious, its style elegant, and the fact that it quickly became the most popular journal of its day did much to contribute to a spirit of optimism about the potentialities of periodical literature.

The first journal of variety, the *Gentleman's Magazine,* was founded in 1731 by Edward Cave, a journeyman printer, post-office official, and one-time author of hand-written news letters. His professed objective was:

. . . to give Monthly a View of all the Pieces of the Wit, Humour,

---

* One of the characters in Richardson's novel *Sir Charles Grandison* distinguishes between the literature of the late seventeenth and that of the eighteenth century thus: "The reading in fashion when I was young was Romances. You, my children, have in that respect fallen into happier days. The present age is greatly obliged to the authors of the *Spectator.*"

or Intelligence, daily offer'd to the Publick in the News-Papers, (which of late are so multiply'd, as to render it impossible, unless a Man makes it a Business, to consult them all). . .[6]

As Cave's announcement suggests, his was at first a journal made up largely of extracts or summaries of news and entertainment items featured in the newspapers or in other magazines. By 1741 it had attained a circulation of 15,000 and was solvent enough to commission original material from an impressive array of contributors. Except for a short-lived excursion into more serious features in the mid-nineteenth century, it continued to flourish as a magazine of miscellany until 1907.

Imitations of the *Spectator* as of the *Gentleman's Magazine* were numerous—altogether, in the fifty-year period beginning in 1730, eighty-one magazines were published in London, Edinburgh, and Dublin.[7] Among the single-essay magazines notable for their literary quality if not for their popular appeal were the *Rambler*, published by Samuel Johnson for two years beginning in 1750, and the *Bee*, published by Oliver Goldsmith for a few months in 1759. Among the imitators of the *Gentleman's Magazine* were several which proved to be less worthy enterprises than their model, lifting all their material from other newspapers and magazines throughout their usually brief lives. One or two compounded the parasitism by abstracting and summarizing periodicals which were in themselves digests of second-hand material.

Popular Novels. Whereas the single-essay and the miscellany periodicals represented new literary forms, the novel, though not a new genre, found a new popularity, particularly after the middle of the century.

During the first two or three decades, the best selling works were more likely to have been reprints of seventeenth century romances than new fiction. Translations, notably from the Spanish, supplemented the meager supply of home-grown materials, and the *Arabian Nights* was published in six editions between 1708 and 1725.[8] The few new romances written during this period were dull and feeble, often nothing but poor imitations of the seventeenth century style.

The publication of Defoe's novels in the 1720's, but more particularly of Richardson's *Pamela* in 1740, marked a major change. With these first novels of the middle class the form was given the impetus which has made it a major literary medium ever since. For thirty years after *Pamela*, novels were characterized by a mixture of middle-class realism and sentimentality which the four major authors, Richardson, Fielding, Smollett, and Sterne, expressed in varying proportions. With them the eighteenth century novel reached its peak; after them came a period of imitation, repetition, and poor craftsmanship, so bleak the writers feared that this form was dying out altogether. Not so the audience, however, for whom this entertainment continued to be popular even when it consisted mainly of patch-works of several old volumes issued under catchy new titles.

Toward the latter part of the century, a revival if not of great novels, at least of more craftsmanlike work set in than had been seen in the 1720's. Harbinger of the new era had been Horace Walpole's *Castle of Otranto*, which added a fillip to the worn-out novel of sentiment by placing it in mysterious gothic settings and generously interlarding it with episodes of supernatural terror. The English public, sickened by the endless sentimentalities which had been paraded before it, eventually welcomed these innovations with enthusiasm. The fad spread, and by 1794 the Buckingham Palace librarian Thomas Mathias, author of a vigorous satire on contemporary fiction entitled *Pursuits of Literature*, was lamenting the consequences:

> [Walpole's] Otranto ghosts have propagated their species with unequaled fecundity; the spawn is in every book shop.[9]

Though the most widely read—or at least most widely approved—volume for children continued to be *Pilgrim's Progress*, by the late 1780's works more amusing if not less instructive began to become available to young readers. One such volume was *Sandford and Merton*. This novel was not written only for the juvenile market, although the two heroes are youngsters: Sandford, a boy endowed with natural wisdom and common sense, and Tommy Merton, a fitful product of luxury. The story was certainly didactic, though less pointedly so than its predecessors, and suggests a philosophy of education derived from *Emile*.[10] Toward the end of the century the Penny Chap-books, small paper-bound volumes illustrated with wood-blocks, long favorites with adults, began to be issued in titles suitable for children, including nursery rhymes, fairy tales, and extracts of longer works such as *Robinson Crusoe*.

As more people joined the ranks of the literate, novel writing became an increasingly lucrative affair. During the 1790's, even a relatively unknown writer could draw a comfortable income by writing serialized novels for enthusiastic publics. The three-volume novel format was especially popular with the ladies, it was said, because one section could be conveniently perused in a single sitting at the hairdresser's.[11] Small-sized books of all kinds were much in evidence throughout the latter half-century, both consequence and reinforcement of the interest in abstracts, abridgements, and anthologies. A popular example of the latter was Isaac D'Israeli's excerpts from famous writers, *Curiosities of Literature* (1792), designed as ". . . an experiment whether a taste for literature could not be infused into the multitudes." This small book quickly went through five editions, was revised several times over, and often imitated. The growing taste for what Dr. Johnson called "general and easy reading" seems to have been satisfied by these small and light books. He himself highly approved of the development: books, after all, should be held readily in the hand and should be easy to carry about; heavy books give a discouraging appearance of erudition and may succeed in frightening away the public altogether.[12]

Newspapers. The prototype of the modern newspaper came into its own soon after the lapse of the Licensing Act in 1695. Within a year or two, the Whigs and the Tories sponsored political newspapers, and by 1700 several papers circulated about London and were delivered to the provinces three times a week when the posts went out. Many English gentlemen living abroad or in the country subscribed to "newsletters issued by confidential sources" which in tone and substance resembled today's confidential and not so confidential newsletters and "dope sheets" on politics and finance. Newsletters, more often handwritten than not, had been a commonplace in the metropolis itself since the 1660's; in the eighteenth century they were more likely to deal with foreign than with domestic affairs.

At the beginning of the century the major source of news in the city continued to be the coffee house. Each class had its favorite rendezvous which, whether simple or elaborate, was invariably stocked with all periodicals available. Anyone willing to read aloud could attract a sizable audience at a moment's notice, and the news of whatever he read, whether of parliamentary debates or town gossip, spread rapidly. Perhaps rightly not trusting the loyalty of their papers, the leading politicians of the day employed "runners" who went from coffee house to coffee house, dropping tidbits and guiding the conversations along whatever lines their bosses happened to be espousing at the moment. Newspapers of the first half-century were singularly short-lived. However, two tri-weekly evening papers, *The London Evening Post* (1727) and *The General Evening Post* (1733) lasted into the nineteenth century; and *The Daily Advertiser*, established in 1730 and continuing for sixty-eight years, had by far the longest life of any daily.[13]

In the course of the century, the daily newspaper became self-supporting and self-respecting: self-supporting because of the spread of literacy, self-respecting because of a successful struggle against religious and political control.[14] In 1709 eighteen newspapers were published once a week or more in London, amounting altogether to some fifty issues. By 1730 the coffee house owners complained that it was impossible to subscribe to them all. Papers grew steadily in size as well, and in the middle of the century six-page editions were the rule. Furthermore, as Dr. Johnson observed, almost every important provincial town had its local organ.[15]

The stamp tax, imposed by the Tories in 1712 in an unsuccessful effort to crush the Whig papers, provides a cue for measuring the growth of the newspaper circulation. In 1776 approximately twelve million copies were sold in the entire year. Though this amounted to only one copy per day for every 300 persons,[16] at least one member of Parliament became alarmed and complained that newspapers were treated with more respect than the spokesmen of the nation.

> The people of Great Britain are governed by a power that never was heard of as a supreme authority in any age or country before . . . It is the government of the press. The stuff which our weekly newspapers are filled with, is received with greater reverence than Acts of Parliament, and the sentiments of one of these scribblers have more weight with the multitude than the opinion of the best politician in the kingdom.[17]

But the average reader viewed newspapers with mixed feelings. One correspondent to the *St. James Journal* for August 2, 1722, slandered *Mist's Newspaper*, a weekly, as being written only for "Porters and Cobblers and such dirty Customers as are his greatest patrons." If we are to believe a writer in another magazine of the same period, however, Mist's paper found an audience in more exalted social spheres.

> The Two famous Universities of this Land are the grand Centers of it: Men and Horses are employed to convey it in large Quantities to *Oxford* and *Cambridge;* where, senseless as it is, it is constantly read and applauded.[18]

On the whole those who paid attention to the growing literary market were more concerned with its potentialities for the intellectual and aesthetic development of the country than with the dangers of its possible influences on public opinion. Only in the early decades of the nineteenth century, when there were some four hundred newspapers in England and Ireland, did the problem of the newspaper as a manipulative device become a major concern to the intellectual.

Changes in the Theater. At the beginning of the eighteenth century the stage had long since been an English institution, rising and falling in popularity and prestige with changes in politics and religion, but always a major arena in which a writer could present his works.

Restoration drama, with its mirroring of the manners and mores of the aristocracy, had been sufficiently uninhibited to provide reforming pastors and laymen with ample reason for attack. In fact, in the first decade of the century neo-Puritans such as Jeremy Collier and Daniel Defoe waged campaigns to have the theaters, "those Houses of Sin and Nurseries of Vice" (Defoe),[19] abolished altogether. Assaults against the English stage were nothing new, and the moralistic and theological arguments brought to bear on them changed very little between the sixth and the eighteenth centuries.[20] The charges handed down by the grand jury of Middlesex in 1703 are typical.*

> We, the Grand Jury of the County of Middlesex do present, that the Plays which are frequently acted in the play-houses in Drury-Lane and Lincoln's-Inn-Fields in this County are full of prophane, irreverent,

---

* And they were by no means limited to the theater. All popular amusements were assumed to be conducive to excessive drinking, immorality, and breaches of the peace. (Vide, M. D. George, *London Life in the Eighteenth Century,* Knopf, New York, 1925, 287.)

lewd, indecent, and immoral expressions and tend to the great displeasure of Almighty God, and to the corruption of the auditory, both in their principles and their practices.[21]

As the Restoration play gave way to middle-class themes, play-going became more respectable and, with the licensing of the two patented theaters at Drury Lane and Covent Garden in 1737, the stage once more became a legitimate means of entertainment for the pious as well as the worldly—which is not to say that the zealots ceased to attack it.

Toward the middle of the century, when Garrick took over the management of the Drury Lane, the theater reached a new peak in popularity and in quality of production. In addition to the sentimental comedies of the day, Garrick brought Shakespeare back to the English public after a long period of neo-Puritan—and later neo-classical—obscurity. But despite the general excellence of their performances, both patented theaters, in order to keep their attendance high, resorted to elaborate pantomimes, "spectacular" operas, ballet operas, and a variety of sensational devices—different more in degree than in kind from those common in Shakespeare's day.

While even the clergy were now found in attendance at the theater, the actors themselves remained more or less outcast until the last quarter of the century. More than one debate in Parliament included attacks on the high salaries of actors, particularly those of Italian performers imported for the opera. In the course of one debate in 1735, a member of the House of Commons observed that

. . . it was astonishing to all Europe that Italian eunuchs and signoras should have set salaries equal to those of the Lords of the Treasury and Judges of England.[22]

Such complaints, however, only served to whet public curiosity about the private lives and morals of the theatrical world, a curiosity fed with increasing detail in the gossip-mongering parts of the press.

It was customary in Garrick's time to stage two performances every evening, one more or less serious, and one light. While many members of the audience who attended the first performance sat through the second, it is apparent from the financial records of the major theaters that an even larger group customarily came only for the latter half of the evening. Since the curtain rose at six, it was inconvenient for working people to attend the first performance. One "Citizen" in the 1730's wrote a letter of complaint to the Lord Mayor of London in which he pointed out that only the "mechanick of pleasure" could attend the theater at such an early hour.

> Gentlemen who have no employment may sleep whole days and riot whole nights . . . Compare the life of a careful honest man . . . with your mechanick of pleasure who is to frequent the theater . . . He must be a fine gentleman, leave his work at five at the farthest . . . that he may be drest and at the playhouse by six . . .[23]

Still more important was the prevailing custom of cutting the admission price in half after the first or "major" piece of the evening was over. On the one or two occasions when the theaters attempted to abolish this custom, public demonstrations and even riots quickly forced a reinstatement. The behavior of the English audience continued to be anything but passive. The noisiness of sailors and their girls and the preening of fops and dandies were ridiculed in many a prologue and epilogue and amazed more than one foreign observer.

The audience increased considerably in the course of the century. Not only did many smaller playhouses begin to flourish in the City and in the provinces, but theaters themselves were enlarged. The two patent theaters together could accommodate 14,000 persons per week in 1732, over 15,000 in 1747, and 22,000 in 1762.[24] Actual attendance, however, may have averaged considerably less than capacity.[25]

II. Audience-Building

Despite the lack of reliable literacy figures, there seems little doubt that two upsurges in reading took place among the English public during the eighteenth century. The first was in the thirties and forties, as the popular magazines and presently the novels began to flood the market. This spurt was due more to the fact that the literate were reading more material than to an increase in the numbers of people who could read. In the last two decades of the century, on the other hand, when the Bible societies, the political pamphleteers and the reformers produced reams of inexpensive literature in a concerted attempt to counteract the influence of revolutionary writers such as Tom Paine, the increased consumption was due to a growth in the reading public itself. In between, the village schoolteachers and the Sunday schools, the former in order to make a living, the latter in order to spread the Good Word, had gone about the business of teaching children of the clerical, working, and farming classes their ABC's.* Printing presses in London, according to contemporary estimates, increased from 75 in 1724 to 150-200 in 1757; the annual publication of new books quadrupled in the course of the century; [26] and the profession of letters became established as a respectable (and often very profitable) livelihood, indeed so well established that as early as 1752 Samuel Johnson labelled his the "Age of Authors." [27]

Part cause and part consequence of the increase in reading and the professionalization of the author, a number of channels for expanding the market for literary products sprang into being or took a new lease on life after the first quarter of the century, notably the circulating libraries, the bookselling and publishing trade, and the book-review periodicals. These institutions were closely related to each other as well as to the authors whose works they promoted or exploited and, as today, friction between authors and those responsible for the channels of distribution was not a rarity. Several non-commercial devices also served to promote the consumption of literary goods. Literary societies and reading groups spread throughout London and were eventually imitated in the provinces. The coffee houses in the City and in the towns continued to be centers where people gathered to read or to hear newspapers and magazines read aloud, and lingered to discuss what they had read or heard.

Some coffee houses were primarily literary resorts. Pope, for example, spent a great deal of time talking with fellow-writers in his favorite coffee house, until he found that the consumption of wine was beginning to get the better of his health. Among the more notable literary coffee clubs in the earlier part of the century was the Kit-Cat Club, which counted numerous leading writers of the

---

* Richard D. Altick suggests, in *The English Common Reader*, the manuscript of which he generously made available to us, that while the consumption of reading matter certainly increased steadily throughout the eighteenth century, it was only after the 1790's that the structure of the reading audience became democratic. On the whole, he feels, the seventeenth century may have had a more representative, and not necessarily a smaller, reading audience than the eighteenth.

period among its members and had Tonson, the outstanding book-seller of his time, as secretary. This club consisted mainly of Whigs, but it went out of its way to encourage young writers, presumably regardless of political persuasion, with financial prizes, particularly for comedies. Swift helped to found the Brothers' Club, whose members were mainly Tories, but whose interests were largely literary—and they, too, contributed to the support of promising younger writers.[28]

The bluestocking clubs, organized in mid-century by a group of literary-minded upper-class women, determined to substitute talk of letters for card games, were eventually imitated by middle-class women both in London and in the provinces. If nothing else, these groups did much to make reading (and writing) among women socially acceptable, even desirable. By the latter part of the century, informal book-discussion and book-buying clubs throve in every part of the country. How these clubs promoted the sale of books is described by Lackington in his *Memoirs:*

> A number of book-clubs are also formed in every part of England where each member subscribes a certain sum quarterly to purchase books: in some of the clubs the books, after they have been read by all the subscribers, are sold among them to the highest bidders, and the money produced by such sale is expended in fresh purchases, by which prudent and judicious mode each member has it in his power to become possessed of the work of any particular author he may judge deserving a superior degree of attention . . .[29]

Although would-be purchasers in the provinces sometimes complained that the metropolitan dealers ignored their mail orders, enterprising booksellers visited the clubs in outlying districts, sent them catalogues and in other ways offered moral if not material encouragement.

The principal audience-building efforts of the book dealers (who were publishers as well) were, however, directed to commercial channels.

Circulating Libraries. The first circulating library in England was founded in 1740, the same year in which Richardson's *Pamela* was published. The establishment of one of the major institutions for accelerating the spread of reading in the middle class thus coincided with the first important novel of that class.

It was customary for the libraries to charge an annual membership fee which entitled a subscriber to access to all books and magazines carried by the particular establishment to which he belonged. By the turn of the century, approximately one thousand of these profit-making institutions were scattered throughout the country, and their customers included members of the working as well as of the middle classes. Free public libraries, however, were noticeably lacking. The library of the Royal Society accumulated only a fair collection, and the British Museum, already distinguished for its collection of original manuscripts, made a poor showing in printed books. Edward Gibbon had reason to complain that "the greatest city of the world was still destitute of a Public Library." [30]

The booksellers at first viewed the development of circulating libraries with suspicion; but they soon recognized that, far from cutting off the sale of books, these outlets promised to constitute both an important market and a major advertising medium.[31] Not only did the circulating libraries provide books for families which could not afford to buy them, but they gave readers a chance to preview a book before investing in it.[32]

The ladies took to the new institution with delight. Toward the end of the century, there is scarcely a popular novel whose heroine does not in the course of her transports or travails select a novel from her circulating library or send her maid to fetch one. By that time, the booksellers were enthusiastic. Lackington was convinced that, along with his own bookshop of course,

> . . . circulating libraries have also greatly contributed towards the amusement and cultivation of the sex; by far the greatest part of ladies now have a taste for books. . . . Ladies now in general read, not only novels, although many of that class are excellent productions, and tend to polish both the heart and the head; but they also read the best books in the English language, and may read the best authors in various languages; and there are some thousands of ladies who frequent my shop, and that know as well what books to choose, and are as well acquainted with works of taste and genius as any gentleman in the kingdom, notwithstanding they sneer against novel readers, etc.[33]

While some of the literati toward the later part of the century blamed the circulating libraries for whetting the apparently insatiable appetite for novels which the booksellers were eager to feed by all manner of means, and while many writers poked light fun at the institution in their own fictional works, few serious attacks on this audience-building device were forthcoming in the course of the century.*

Bookselling. The conscientious man of letters was rather less tolerant of the booksellers. Possibly his newly acquired financial dependence on the publisher and dealer occasioned some degree of nostalgia for the days of aristocratic patronage; certainly the practices of a good many booksellers provided him with good reason for intolerance.

The Messrs. Tonson and Curll represent the two extremes of prestige and notoriety the bookseller could achieve in the days of Alexander Pope. Tonson, the afore-mentioned secretary of the Kit-Cat Club, left his mark on the history of the book trade as the esteemed publisher of *Paradise Lost* and numerous works by Dryden and Addison. He commanded the admiration of most of his authors, to whom he was generous in his commercial dealings and stimulating in his intellectual contacts.

Edmund Curll, one of the infamous names in the history of commerce, neither got nor deserved a modicum of respect from the literati. Unscrupulous and clever, he displayed a kind of stupid adroitness which repeatedly landed him in jail and encouraged him, on his discharge, to resume with redoubled vigor the very activities for which he had been imprisoned. He had a special knack for exploiting the scandalous, a thriving business in his as in more recent days, and while he did publish some useful works, given the length of his publication lists, he could hardly have avoided it. He dedicated most of his energy to a search for attractive titles and intimately personal (often scurrilous) advertisements for biographies and pornographic pamphlets which were thrown together willy-nilly by hacks to whom he paid starvation wages.[34] He came in for a lot of scathing criticism in Pope's *Dunciad*, and the reasons are not far to seek. Fielding tells the following story in the *Champion* about a fraud which Curll perpetrated by misusing the name of Pope:

But the most remarkable piece of ingenuity, if it had been done by

---

* Coleridge was later to speak scathingly of "devotees of circulating libraries" whose reading he considered to be on a par with reading word for word "all the advertisements of a daily newspaper in a public house on a rainy day."

design, was exhibited this winter, in which a poem was published with the following title-page, printed in the same manner as it is here inserted.

SEVENTEEN HUNDRED THIRTY NINE

being the sequel of

SEVENTEEN HUNDRED THIRTY EIGHT

WRITTEN BY MR. POPE

If this had been published by any other bookseller than Mr. C——l, we should have believed that it was intended to impose the year nine on the world as a work of Mr. Pope's, who is I think avowedly the author of the year eight, but the said Mr. C——l is too well known to have any such attempt suspected, both from the nicety of his conscience and his judgment, which should not suffer him to hope that he should be able to exhibit the pop of a pistol for the fire of a cannon.[35]

By 1800 the bookselling and publishing trade was one of the major industries in the country. Needless to say, both Tonson and Curll had their share of descendants. Lackington was the most successful as well as the most articulate book dealer of the latter part of the century: he went into business in 1774; in 1779 he published his first catalogue of 12,000 titles and estimated that some 30,000 people a year made use of it. It was Lackington who first hit upon the idea of remainder sales, and by the turn of the century he was selling over 100,000 volumes a year.[36] While he conceded that he made a substantial amount of money, he also took credit for making books available to groups who might not otherwise have been able to afford them:

. . . when I reflect what prodigious numbers in inferior or *reduced* situations of life, have been essentially benefited, in consequence of being thus enabled to indulge their natural propensity for the acquisition of knowledge, on easy terms: nay, I could almost be vain enough to assert, that I have thereby been highly instrumental in diffusing that general desire for READING now so prevalent among the inferior orders of society.[37]

After 1780 the cost of books, already high, rose further.* Well-

---

* Some indications of the comparative cost of books and other leisure activities may be found in the following figures given by H. W. Pedicord, and applicable for the mid-century decades: a seat in the first gallery at the Drury Lane 24 pence, a pot of beer 3 pence, cheapest dinner 3½ pence, a small book 36 pence.

established publishers were making their formats ever more elaborate and costly, in part because the etiquette of the more elegant members of the feminine audience demanded ostentatious bindings. But new booksellers soon entered the lists and issued reprints, including small modestly priced pocket editions of the classics. Another successful sales device adopted by the booksellers was the publishing of the classics, poetry, and fiction in newspaper-like serials, printed in weekly instalments at sixpence each.[38] After allowing a suitable period for the reader to forget the first version, the less scrupulous booksellers did not hesitate to reissue the trashier of these works, particularly the novels, under new titles, but otherwise unchanged.

Advertising methods ranged from the spectacularly absurd to the eminently reasonable and included, in fact, most of the devices which have remained the stock-in-trade of the publisher's business to this day. There was first the matter of the title. If it was catchy, slick, and sensational, it could not go very far wrong. There were *Beauty Put to Its Shift, Adultery Atomized, Female Falsehood*, and a thousand other titles like them. Old books in new titles were not limited to the folios; the salvation of many a hard-cover work came about by the simple expedient of removing the title page, replacing it with a more vivid or salacious one, and offering the renovated product as "Second Edition, corrected and improved." [39] A particularly successful device was to endow the author (or authoress) with qualities of fame, mystery, or notoriety, and writers said to have been "banished from the realm" were promoted with special avidity. Endorsements by "men of distinction," too, were a commonplace. On the whole the booksellers maintained close and friendly relations at least with their leading writers, and only one writer seems to have found his dependence on the bookseller sufficiently restraining to endeavor to free himself. In 1765, one John Trusler founded a Literary Society intended to eliminate the middleman and to secure all profits for the author by enabling him to bring out his own works independently. This society probably helped nobody but Trusler himself who managed, at most, to sell only one of his books.[40] Until the middle of the century, a great many books continued to be financed by advance subscriptions, but these were solicited by the bookseller himself, except for an occasional penurious and unknown author who went knocking from door to door.

Despite the thriving enterprises of the leading booksellers in

London in the second half of the century, their influence was not particularly strong in the provinces, except indirectly through the circulating library and the itinerant pedlar. Lackington describes a journey to Edinburgh in 1787, during which he made it his business to stop at every town with the twofold objective of keeping his finger on the pulse of his trade and picking up scarce or valuable books. His trip, on the latter count, was a notable failure: not only did he find depressingly few valuable books, but the shelves of the provincial bookshops were littered mainly with trash.[41] When he repeated his trip a few years later, he reported the situation very little changed.

Although an unscrupulous bookseller like Curll might arouse almost unanimous expressions of antagonism, the writers were rather less in agreement on the institution of book publishing itself. Both Samuel Johnson and Oliver Goldsmith, for example, were highly dependent on their publishers; but while Johnson was the nearest thing to grateful, Goldsmith—at best—viewed the situation with one auspicious and one drooping eye. Perhaps, as Krutch suggests,[42] Johnson's favorable disposition was the result of a very happy early experience he had with a bookseller who lent him enough money to keep him from starving. In any case, Johnson was not sparing of his commendations. In one of his *Idler* papers, for instance, he credits the booksellers rather than the schools with "popularising knowledge" among the common orders of England.[43]

In his early career as a writer, Johnson suffered from much keener poverty than did Goldsmith, whose main problem was that his money slipped through his fingers. Johnson's poverty was of a more spartan kind. We know how he wrote *Rasselas:* the book was dashed off in a few days to pay for his mother's funeral expenses. And Boswell reports that even when Johnson was finally paid for his *Dictionary* (first published in 1755) there was scarcely any money left after his expenses in compiling it had been met. Yet he countered Boswell's commiserations with a stout defense of the bookseller, justifying the lack of profit to the author by citing the risks to which the publisher exposed himself.[44]

Goldsmith was no party to this kind of defense. In his *Enquiry into the Present State of Learning* and in two of the letters in the *Citizen of the World,* one of which is devoted entirely to the dubious practices of the bookseller, he examines the bookseller's role in a forthrightly critical spirit. In his *Enquiry* he notes at the outset that the interests of the writer and those of the publisher are diametrically opposed:

> The author, when unpatronized by the great, has naturally recourse to the bookseller. There cannot perhaps be imagined a combination more prejudicial to taste than this. It is the interest of the one to allow as little for writing, and of the other to write as much as possible.[45]

And he directly attacks some of the more underhanded promotional techniques, particularly the device of attaching impressive status, real or invented, to the authors of books in the process of being promoted. Booksellers

> . . . seem convinced, that a book written by vulgar hands, can neither instruct nor improve; none but Kings, Chams and Mandarines can write with a probability of success.[46]

But it is in Letter LI of *The Citizen of the World* that we find the most biting sarcasm. Here Goldsmith describes a bookseller's visit to the ironically ingenuous Citizen. The bookseller begins by noting the seasonal appetites of his readers: "I would no more bring out a new work in summer than I would sell pork in the dog days." He next boasts that his works are always new, and that at the end of every season the old ones are shipped off to the trunkmakers. If he should have a scarcity of new books, there is no dearth of new title pages: "I have ten new title-pages now around me which only want books to be added to make them the finest things in nature." He is quite willing to make a virtue of his lack of cultural pretensions, modestly confessing that he has no desire to lead the public; on the contrary, the public—and the lowest stratum of the public at that—leads him.[47]

The writer's plight vis-à-vis the bookseller trade is well epitomized by a tragi-comic episode reported by Thomas De Quincey in his essay on Goldsmith:

> The pauperized (or Grub Street) section of the literary body, at the date of Goldsmith's taking service amongst it, was . . . at its very lowest point of depression . . . Smart, the prose translator of Horace and a well-built scholar, actually *let* himself out to a monthly journal on a regular lease of ninety-nine years. What could move the rapacious publisher to draw the lease for this monstrous term of years, we cannot conjecture.

"But think, Reader," De Quincey continues,

But think . . . of poor Smart two years after, upon another publisher's applying vainly to him for contributions, and angrily demanding
what possible objections could be made to offers so liberal, being reduced
to answer—"No objection, sir, whatever, except an unexpired term of
ninety-seven years to run." The bookseller saw that he must not apply
again in *that* century; and in fact Smart could no longer let himself
but must be sub-let, if let at all, by the original lessee.[48]

Book Reviews. Book reviewing came into being at the end of
the seventeenth century largely as a professional service. The review
journals of that time were limited to scientific and philosophical
works, and at first their principal purpose was to provide scholars
with convenient summaries, in English, of the works of their colleagues abroad. One of the earliest of the eighteenth century reviews,
the *Memoirs of Literature* (1710-1714), published by the Huguenot
refugee LaRoche, served as prototype for the scholarly review. This
periodical contained abstracts of English and foreign works in about
equal proportions. Critical comments were rare. In 1725, reputedly
with the help of a book publisher, LaRoche produced a second
journal, *New Memoirs of Literature,* in which he proved to be more
enterprising: this review—usually running to some seventy-five pages
an issue—not only abstracted but added comment to the works
selected for review. *The Literary Magazine,* first published in 1735
under the editorship of Ephraim Chambers, covered a wider range
of works, though it still limited itself to the "serious." It went
further in comment and biographical background than had its
predecessors, but was reluctant to set itself up as judge. In the words
of its editor, the responsibility of the reviewer is

. . . to give a faithful account of books which come into his hands. . . .
When he affects the air and language of a censor or judge, he invades
the undoubted right of the public, which is the only sovereign judge of
the reputation of an author, and the merit of his compositions . . .[49]

The first book review journal to move into the field of popular
literature and thus to qualify as an audience-building institution was
The Compendious Library, a one-hundred page bi-monthly publication printed in Dublin (1751-52). Its steps in this direction, however,
were both rare and gingerly. In introducing Fielding's *Amelia,* for

example, the reviewer first notes that romances and novels have no place in literary journals, but in this instance he justifies the exception on the grounds that fiction which serves "the reformation of manners and the advancement of virtue" may be allowed, and goes on to remark that "This seems to be one, if not the chief, point from which Mr. Fielding's performance ought to be considered. . . ." [50]

With the founding of the *Monthly Review* by Ralph Griffith in 1749, the book review purporting to cover all releases from the presses got its start. The *Monthly*, which at first had the reputation of being hostile to state and church, soon provoked the founding of a rival journal, the *Critical Review*, published by Archibald Hamilton, edited by Tobias Smollett from 1756-1763, and laying claim to Tory and Church support. Both reviews boasted eminent contributors: Goldsmith contributed twenty pieces to the *Monthly*, and Johnson as well as Smollett wrote for the *Critical*. Each journal dealt with the more important books of the month in considerable detail; in a "catalogue" appended to each issue, all other publications of the month were covered in three- or four-page reviews. The objective proclaimed by the *Critical* could be applied to the *Monthly* as well:

To exhibit a succinct plan of every performance; to point out the most striking beauties and glaring defects; to illustrate remarks with proper quotations, and to convey those remarks in such a manner as might best conduce to the entertainment of the public.[51]

The *Critical* successfully competed with the *Monthly* until 1790, but the *Monthly* managed to survive it well into the middle of the nineteenth century. Although criticized by authors for high-handedness on some occasions, these reviews and their competitors were inclined rather more to praise than to criticize. Witness, for instance, the prospectus of the *New London Review*, a short-lived publication of the years 1799 to 1800:

The Plan is suggested, and will be executed in the conviction, that few performances are wholly destitute of merit; that it is more useful to disclose latent excellence, than to exaggerate common faults; that the public taste suffers less from inaccurate writing than from illiberal criticism.

Criticism was to be reserved for the works of writers who went off any one of a number of beaten tracks:

Though no arrogance will be indulged in this Publication, whatever disturbs the public harmony, insults legal authority, . . . attacks the vital springs and established functions of piety, or in any respect clashes with the sacred forms of decency, however witty, elegant, and well written, can be noticed only in terms of severe and unequivocal reprehension.[52]

The task of covering all new books as they were released became more and more unmanageable. One of the *Monthly* reviewers in 1788 complained:

The Reviewer of the modern novel is in the situation of Hercules encountering the Hydra—One head lopped off, two or three immediately spring up in its place.[53]

The less conscientious journals solved the problem by a process of selection calculated to please the chief suppliers of their advertising revenue, the booksellers, who distributed review copies only to the journals in which they advertised. These books were reviewed first; time and space permitting, a reviewer might then send his "collector" around to other houses for books possibly deserving of his notice. Thus books often were reviewed months after they were released; in the case of particularly popular publications which were sold out by the time a collector arrived, no reviews appeared at all.[54]

As to the reviewers themselves, the *Monthly* and *Critical* and a number of similar journals had, in addition to eminent or well known contributors, other conscientious ones as well. More often, however, they were poorly paid devisers of makeshift who filled up page after page with direct quotations, selected, as one report has it, after first reading the preface, closing the book, sticking a pin between the leaves at random, opening and transcribing the page so chosen, or even a few pages, and then repeating the operation. One novelist of the 1770's accused the reviewers of passing on the merits and demerits of an author on the basis of the title-page alone. A correspondent to the *Gentleman's Magazine* in 1782 accused the reviewers of praising the works of those booksellers who owned shares in their journals and running down all others. Yet another novelist accused them of taking bribes from authors, sometimes even going so far as to let them write their own reviews.[55]

Samuel Johnson, as we might expect from his more favorable attitude toward booksellers, was considerably more indulgent toward the reviewers than was Oliver Goldsmith, who devoted a substantial portion of another of his *Citizen of the World* letters to a castigation of their practices. Goldsmith links the undiscriminating nature of the book reviewer's work to the fact that he is being paid by the bookseller or, worse still, to the fact that the bookseller himself sometimes writes reviews:

There are a set of men called answerers of books who take upon them to watch the republic of letters, and distribute reputation by the sheet . . . and to revile the moral character of the man whose writings they cannot injure. Such wretches are kept in pay by some mercenary bookseller, or more frequently, the bookseller himself takes this dirty work off their hands, as all that is required is to be very abusive and very dull.

The Chinese visitor goes on to ask his host whether this is the fate of every writer, to which the Englishman replies,

Yes . . . except he happened to be born a Mandarin. If he has much money, he may buy a reputation from your book answerers.[56]

Such was the ambiguous state of book-reviewing in the second half of the century. Only with the founding of the *Edinburgh Review* and the *Quarterly* in the early nineteenth century did the book reviewers begin to be free of publisher influence. If they kowtowed at all, it was likely to be in response to political party rather than to publishing house pressures.

III. Stages of Reaction

The acid comments of writers about the devices used to promote book sales did not herald an immediate negative reaction to the development of a literary market. Alexander Pope, to be sure, made dire prophesies about the low level to which literature was sinking; but though he was later to be looked back upon by Henry Fielding as "King Alexandre," the despotic ruler of the literary kingdom, Pope's "subjects" did not join in his protest against changes in the literary scene until much later. On the contrary, many literary figures in the first half of the century founded periodicals especially designed for the growing middle-class readership, and all of them contributed to magazines or newspapers at one point in their careers.

Their predecessors had been writing for a more homogeneous group: the nobility, the landed gentry, and scholars had composed the bulk of their readers. These readers debated about the "rules" and about good and bad writing along with the writers, just as they debated about good and bad music, architecture, and painting; but they did not distinguish between "high" and "low" art, nor did they discuss differences in aesthetic appreciation among different social segments of the audience. The growth of a broader market did not at first change the nature of these discussions. Each form was presumed to have its own special means of providing pleasure, but the accepted function of all writing remained similar to that summarized by the critic John Dennis in his discussion of "greater" and "less" poetry:

> 1. The greater Poetry is an Art by which a Poet justly and reasonably excites great Passion, that he may please and instruct; . . .
> 2. The less Poetry is an Art by which a Poet excites less Passion for the foremention'd Ends . . .[57]

Not all of John Dennis' contemporaries in the world of letters would have agreed with him that the excitation of great passion is the *sine qua non* of great poetry, but his view that the objective of all writing is to instruct would have evoked little controversy. The writer has a social task; he must use his gift as a means of contributing to the elevation of his readers. And just as the writers' creative gifts were assumed to go hand-in-hand with high moral responsibility, so was it assumed that a public which is responsive to moral teachings must also be capable of aesthetic appreciation.

This section will describe how, as writers, readers, and literary products multiplied, such initial optimism gave way to a mood very close to pessimism.

Optimism. Very early in the century, the English public had begun to display a powerful bent for reform of manners and morals, not the least manifestation of which was its wide-spread support of organizations such as the Society for the Propagation of Christian Knowledge and the Society for the Reformation of Manners—groups with far-flung networks through which numerous pamphlets and books of a moralizing, neo-Puritan nature were distributed.[58] The ideal of the "gentleman" to which tradespeople and aristocrats alike aspired was not the exaggeratedly ornamental and rakish figure which had become the stereotype of Restoration comedy, but the virtuous Christian citizen. In such an atmosphere it was taken for granted that the new literary forms would edify and elevate; an aristocrat, such as the Earl of Shaftesbury, and Defoe, a writer who saw himself as the very conscience of the middle and lower-middle classes, could agree with the crusading Sir Richard Blackmore that the responsibility of the writer is to "cultivate the mind with instruction of virtue." [59] To be sure, early magazines and newspapers were often attacked for their political bias—the fittest punishment Pope could conjure up for one of the "low" writers he attacked in the early *Dunciad*, for example, was to have him "[end] at last in the common sink of all such writers, a Political News-paper." [60] And Addison puffed his own journal at the expense of the newspapers, which he gently chided for emphasizing "what passes in Muscovy or Poland," rather than the "knowledge of one's self." [61]

The belief that the inclination for moral uplift so apparent in the audience presupposed a capacity for aesthetic advancement was at first reinforced by the success of the single essay type of magazine, which combined elegant writing with social and cultural purpose, and which first came into its own with the launching of Steele's *Tatler* in 1709. The *Tatler*'s immediate successor, the *Spectator* (1711), founded as a joint enterprise of Steele and Addison, became the most popular journal of its day. In one of the early issues, Addison announced that his publisher had just reported a daily circulation of three thousand copies for the journal, and goes on to estimate with some assurance that each copy had twenty readers (or "hearers," as the case may be).* Addison used these figures as a point of departure for a statement of objectives which is not only a succinct summary of the principle of "art as a means of instruction," but a statement of faith in the capacities of his readers:

Since I have raised to myself so great an Audience, I shall spare no

---

* Since there was no eighteenth century equivalent to a "continuing index of magazine circulation," these figures are debatable. Samuel Johnson (in *Lives of the Poets*) reckoned, on the basis of stamp tax figures, that the *Spectator* had an average sale of 1,700 daily copies. Addison's editor, Richard Hurd, and others offer average daily estimates closer to those ventured by Addison himself.

Pains to make their Instruction agreeable, and their Diversion useful. For which Reasons I shall endeavour to enliven Morality with Wit and to temper Wit with Morality . . . It was said of *Socrates*, that he brought Philosophy down from Heaven, to inhabit among Men; and I shall be ambitious to have it said of me, that I have brought Philosophy out of Closets and Libraries, Schools and Colleges, to dwell in Clubs and Assemblies, at Tea-Tables and in Coffee-Houses.

These worlds of tea-table and coffee house were not, in Addison's view, limited to the gentry and the scholars; in his "fraternity of spectators" he sees tradesmen as well as physicians, "statesmen that are out of business" as well as Fellows of the Royal Society, and all those "blanks of society" who until now have been "altogether unfurnished with ideas till the business and conversation of the day has supplied them." Finally he envisages the whole "female world" among his readers, but particularly the "ordinary" woman whose most serious occupation is sewing and whose drudgery is cooking. While there are some women who live in a more "exalted Sphere of Knowledge and Virtue," they are all too few, and he hopes to increase their ranks

. . . by Publishing this daily Paper, which I shall always endeavour to make an innocent if not an improving Entertainment, and by that Means at least divert the Minds of my Female Readers from greater Trifles.[62]

That most of what Addison called entertainment was indeed both morally and aesthetically "improving" is apparent to the modern reader who selects any issue of the *Spectator* at random. Between them, Addison and Steele covered the spectrum of their age from "Puritan Piety" (Addison) to "Miseries of Prostitution" (Steele). Addison informed his readers that he belonged to a club which served as a kind of "advisory committee" for the *Spectator;* in fact, his readers "have the satisfaction to find that there is no rank or degree among them who have not their representative in this club, and that there is always somebody present who will take care of their respective interests." He describes a recent meeting of the club during which he was congratulated by some members and taken to task by others. On occasion, members of this panel try to lobby for their special interests, but Addison hastens to assure the reader that he will remain unmoved by such pressures:

Having thus taken my Resolutions to march on boldly in the Cause of Virtue and good Sense, and to annoy their Adversaries in whatever Degree or Rank of Men they may be found: I shall be deaf for the future to all the Remonstrances that shall be made to me on this Account.[63]

Running throughout the series (the *Spectator* was published daily until December 6, 1712) is a strong admixture of literary criticism, mostly Addison's, clearly designed to establish a link between the "wit" of the elite classical tradition and the moral truths so in keeping with the ethos of the rising middle class.[64]

But that a moral reformation was inseparable from an aesthetic one became an assumption increasingly difficult to support. If it is true that the *Spectator* eventually attained a readership of twenty or thirty thousand, perhaps there came a point in eighteenth century England when the literary development of many persons hung in the balance, attracted to the refinements of an Addison who did not write down to his readers, and not yet seduced by the sensational or sentimental devices to be utilized by his successors. If so, it was for a relatively short period, and subsequent events have blurred the evidence. Historians of literature credit the essayists with high literary achievement, but suggest that they were victims of self-delusion if they believed that the moral concerns of their readers were in any way associated with a capacity for—or interest in—aesthetic growth. What Addison and the other essayists hoped for was a rapprochement between English classicism and middle class morality; what they paved the way for was compromise.[65]

Before the middle of the century the public was beginning to make its preferences abundantly clear. Defoe's *Robinson Crusoe*, which was mainly read as an adventure story, became an instantaneous bestseller seven years after the last copy of the *Spectator* was printed, and it went through numerous editions and translations during the next thirty years. In 1750, *The Oeconomy of Human Life* * was published, went through twenty-one editions in the 18th century (several more than that in the 19th) and was translated into six languages. This book, distinguished for its commonplaceness of thought, achieved unprecedented popularity and has been characterized as testimony to "the insatiable appetite of the eighteenth century for moral platitude." [66] In the same year in which the *Spectator* was founded, Shaftesbury had written, "Thus are the arts

---

* The authorship is disputed—some historians credit Dodsley, others Chesterfield, with the work.

and virtues mutually friends," [67] but that the mid-century audience thought differently is further attested by the fate of one of the *Spectator*'s more eminent imitators, *The Rambler*. This bi-weekly periodical was founded by Dr. Johnson in the same year in which *The Oeconomy* achieved its spectacular success. Like the *Spectator* four decades earlier, *The Rambler* aimed at intellectual and aesthetic as well as moral refinements. But except for one issue written by Samuel Richardson (Number 97) the peak circulation of *The Rambler* was 500, or one sixth of the circulation claimed for the *Spectator* after its tenth day of publication.[68]

Opportunity and Opportunism. While the hundred imitations of the *Spectator* published between 1712 and 1750 were remarkably short-lived, the *Gentleman's Magazine,* some fifty pages of news and entertainment features, went into five editions at its first issue in 1731. Twenty years or so later Johnson wrote of it as one of the most lucrative publications (it then had a circulation of 15,000), and its manager at the end of the century, John Nichols, reported it as still a highly successful enterprise.[69]

With the public expressing its interests by buying certain kinds of literary products and by not buying others, the publisher, book-seller, and writer with a knack for gauging public opinion could become, if not wealthy, certainly most comfortable. There were five thousand people subsisting by writing, printing, publishing, and marketing papers in the London of 1722,[70] and those who earned a living in the literary market by the middle of the century would probably have to be reckoned in the tens of thousands. It was no longer necessary to be a "man of letters" or a university graduate to be a professional writer. Housewives and bookkeepers who wanted to make a few extra pounds now wrote novels, as did country clergymen who had formerly dabbled in botany or archeology. Few of these writers felt any need to defend either their works or their profits, and few apparently were concerned about literary standards.

No longer were elegant and polished "wits" and intellectuals endeavoring to search out truth, beauty, and reason for themselves and a few readers much like themselves. Instead middle-class novelists such as Richardson and Fielding were writing for their social peers. They, and Smollett and Sterne after them, may have been concerned with truth and reason, at least insofar as these values were related to morality, but they were little concerned with beauty. Their world, as Leslie Stephen put it, had become that of "the middle-class John Bull . . . the generation which listens to Wesley must have also a secular literature, which, whether sentimental as with Richardson or representing common sense with Fielding, must at any rate correspond to solid substantial matter-of-fact motives, intelligible to the ordinary Briton of the time." [71] Fielding himself, satirist though he often was, offered a summation of this solemn atmosphere. Denouncing those writers who merely amuse or shock, he made it clear that he was even not "afraid to mention Rabelais, and Aristophanes himself," among those who have ridiculed the only means to moral health and wisdom: "sobriety, modesty, decency, virtue and religion. . . ." He then went on to state a precept which was adhered to—with varying degrees of sincerity— by most writers of his age:

> In the exercise of the mind, as well as in the exercise of the body, diversion is a secondary consideration, and designed only to make that agreeable, which is at the same time useful, to such noble purposes as health and wisdom.[72]

Indeed, so ingrained were these moral precepts that the majority of mid-century writers quite uncalculatingly fulfilled the reader's need to be convinced that he was being improved while being amused, diverted, or horrified. Adults told themselves that novel reading was instructive for young people, and the upper classes were persuaded that reading or play-going was uplifting for the lower. The actor, writer, and producer Garrick, in his *Bon Ton*, lightly ridiculed such rationalizations in a conversation between master and servant:

> *Sir John:* Why, what did I promise you?
> *Davy:* That I should take sixpen'oth at one of the theaters tonight, and a shilling place at the other to-morrow.
> *Sir John:* Well, well, so I did. Is it a moral piece, Davy?
> *Davy:* Oh! Yes, and written by a clergyman; it is called the "Rival Cannanites; or the Tragedy of Braggadocia."
> *Sir John:* Be a good lad, and I won't be worse than my word; there's money for you.[73]

A few writers, particularly lady novelists writing for the education of young girls, seem to have found it unnecessary to follow the caveat "to amuse," with apparently no great loss in sales. Parents of the innocents saw to it that they kept such books as Mrs. Chapone's *Letters on the Improvement of the Mind*—consisting of 200 pages of solid advice on religion, the Bible, the affections, the temper, and politeness—constantly by their sides. According to the moralizing novelist Hannah More, Mrs. Chapone's work "forms the rising age," and another contemporary, Samuel Hoole, has the heroine in his *Aurelia* envisage an ideal woman as one whose dressing table features Mrs. Chapone's volume:

> On the plain toilet, with no trophies gay
> *Chapone's* instructive volume open lay.[74]

At the other extreme were the sensational novelists who loaded their works with sex and sadism, inserting, as a kind of afterthought, a warning line or two, pointing out to the reader that his, or more frequently her, fate will be a ghastly one if he or she slips from the path of virtue. Under the guise of "satiric indignation," revelations of vice and licentiousness in high and low places were exploited in novels, on the stage, and in the magazines as well as in the press—some true, some offered under the pretext of being true.* Almost any device "enabled authors to pass in satiric review various classes and professions in corrupt society." [75] Charles Johnstone (1719-1800) suggested—with disarming candor in view of the fact that he himself was the author of *Chrysal*, one of the more notorious of these exposés—the extent to which the moralizing note was merely an excuse for feeding the appetite for prurient detail:

> There cannot be a stronger argument against the charge of degeneracy in moral virtue and religion brought against the present age, than the avidity with which all works exposing the breaches of them by the unerring proof of facts, are read by all people.[76]

---

* An idea of the topics covered is conveyed by the titles of a few of these novels:

Love-Letters between a Nobleman and his Sister.

The Unnatural Mother; or Innocent Love Persecuted; being the history of the fatal consequences that attended the . . . passion of a gentleman . . . and a young Lady.

The Cruel Mistress; being the genuine trial of E. B. and her daughter for the murder of Jane Buttersworth, their servantmaid, etc.

The Fatal Connexion, Colonel Digby and Miss Stanley.

In his preface to the first edition of the *Dunciad* (1728) Pope had made it clear through the words of a fictitious commentator on his work ("Martinus Scriblerus") that he was disturbed both by the pedants and fops of the literary world and by the sheer numbers of authors who cropped out all over the country once paper became cheap and plentiful in supply:

> He [our Poet] lived in those days, when (after providence had permitted the Invention of Printing as a scourge for the Sins of the learned) Paper also became so cheap, and printers so numerous, that a deluge of authors cover'd the land: . . . our author . . . did conceive it an endeavour well worthy an honest satyrist, to dissuade the dull and punish the malicious, *the only way that was left.* In that public-spirited view he laid the plan of this Poem. . . .[77]

Thus Pope, in the early third of the century of the Enlightenment, served as the conscience of conservatism. In challenging the idea of technical progress as a good in itself, he anticipated the coming debate about the defensive position of the creative individual in a mass society. His was not an article of faith but an article of doubt, and toward the end of the first edition he issues a strong warning not to underestimate these changes and the people who were capitalizing on them:

> Do not, gentle reader, rest too secure in thy contempt of the Instruments for such a revolution in learning, or despise such weak agents as have been described in our poem, but remember what the *Dutch* stories somewhere relate, that a great part of their Provinces was once overflow'd, by a small opening made in one of their dykes by a single *Water-Rat.*

He concludes the poem with a prophecy: "Art after Art goes out, and all is Night./ . . . Thy hand great Dulness! lets the curtain fall,/ And universal Darkness covers all." [78]

Fourteen years later, in the preface to *The New Dunciad* (1742), Pope writes that he is setting out "to declare the *Completion* of the *Prophecies* mention'd at the end of the former [Book]." [79] By that time his fellow authors had begun to wonder whether the first edition, outlet for injured professional pride though it may have been, did not also have some of the character of a true prediction.

Rising Dismay. After the middle of the century the writer faced

two problems which had not previously struck him as matters for
concern. Was the expanding audience for literary products (now
beginning to reach into the lower classes as well)* in fact capable
of, or interested in, being "improved" either aesthetically *or* morally
by means of the written and spoken word which it was consuming
in ever greater volume? And what was this new state of affairs—
in which he depended for his livelihood upon pleasing this broad
public instead of one or two aristocratic or political patrons—
doing to the integrity of the artist?

The writers who became most disturbed by these problems were
not members of the aristocracy who might have been expected
to look with some distaste on the cultural encroachments of the
nouveau-riche and the tradespeople. Nor were they embittered men
who had failed to achieve recognition. They were those writers,
mainly of middle-class origin, who had supported themselves by
producing serious works for the very public about which they
were now becoming skeptical. The *Spectator,* the *Tatler,* and most
of their imitators had tried to show these new readers what constituted good taste—in morals, manners, music, architecture, furniture, and landscape gardening as well as in literature. For thirty or
more years, the best had been made available to all who could read.
Those who had offered it, Garrick, Goldsmith, Johnson, and Fielding and others, began to echo Pope's early and not very exalted
opinion of public taste. He had worried about fashions in taste,
"snob appeal," and the fickleness of the public:

> Some ne'er advance a Judgment of their own
> But catch the spreading notion of the Town.
>
> Some judge of authors' names, not works, and then
> Nor praise nor blame the writings, but the men.
>
> Some praise at morning what they blame at night;
> But always think the last opinion right.[80]

---

* It is almost impossible to pinpoint the moment when the reading public
began to include a significant number of the working classes, but most literary
historians put it roughly around 1760-70. Tompkins, for example, in *The Popular Novel in England: 1770-1800,* reports that novel-reading had replaced
story-telling in the farmhouses, and that in town "the milliner's apprentice,
who turns up in contemporary satire with the regularity of Macaulay's school-
boy, spared twopence at the library for a volume of *The Fatal Compliance* or
Anecdotes of a Convent."

Now Fielding found the bulk of mankind "clearly void of any degree of taste" and suggested that the common denominator of the audience of his day was very low indeed:

> It is a quality in which they advance very little beyond a state of infancy. The first thing a child is fond of in a book is a picture; the second is a story; and the third is a jest. Here, then, is the true Pons Asinorum, which few readers ever get over.[81]

And from a less detached viewpoint a Mr. Jackson, who wrote essays but was primarily a designer and painter of wallpaper in Battersea, berated the level of public taste in a piece on engraving and printing:

> Persons who should prefer the gaudy and unmeaning Papers (so generally met with) . . . would prefer a Fan to a picture of *Raphael* . . . It seems also, as if there was a great Reason to suspect wherever one sees such preposterous Furniture, that the Taste in Literature of the Person who directed it was very deficient, and that it would prefer *Tom D'Urfy* [writer of scurrilous ballads and melodrama in the first quarter of the 18th century] to *Shakespeare*, Sir *Richard Blackmore* to *Milton* . . . an Anagrammatist to *Virgil* . . .[82]

He concludes, of course, with a commercial "snob appeal": the reader of his essay could demonstrate his sensitive taste in literature and on all other counts by buying Mr. Jackson's "classical" wallpaper.

Doubts about the capacities of their audience forced writers in turn to face the problem of the effects of a broadening market on the writer himself. Pope, himself an author living from the sale of his works, despite his general pessimism about the quality of much contemporary writing, was convinced that the literary genius would eventually win public support, and, conversely, that the writer who did not live well must also be dull. "To prove them *poor*," wrote an anonymous contributor to *Mist's Journal* in 1728, Pope "asserts that they are *dull; and to prove them *dull* he asserts they are *poor*." [83] His successors were not so sure; Johnson, Fielding, and Goldsmith were writing works that were certainly not "dull" in Pope's meaning of the word for an audience which made it increasingly clear that it was not capable of awarding the good writers with more popularity than the bad. How, they asked, does the author's conviction that his readers are both fickle and debased in their taste affect his integrity and creativity, and how does the book and periodical publishers' insistence on quantity affect the level of the writer's work?

For Oliver Goldsmith, who contributed to at least ten periodicals and was responsible for innumerable compilations and translations which he undertook in order to supplement the income derived from his other works, these were not academic questions. He debated them with all the fervor of a man who feels his professional reputation at stake. Consciously or otherwise, the writer is influenced by the preferences of his audience; it may mean, as Goldsmith said, in his early essay *Upon Taste*, that

> . . . genius, instead of growing like a vigorous tree, extending its branches on every side . . . resembles a stunted yew, tortured into some wretched form, projecting no shade, displaying no flower, diffusing no fragrance, yielding no fruit, and affording *nothing but a barren conceit for the amusement of the idle spectator.*[84] (Italics supplied.)

In the course of his prolific years to come, Goldsmith reflected often upon the ethical and artistic conflicts of the writer dependent on popular preferences and answered his own question whether genius must now produce only "barren conceit" alternately yes and no. His first original work, *Enquiry into the Present State of Polite Learning in Europe* (1759), explored the dilemma in which the writer for a growing market found himself. In this book, and in his *Citizen of the World* letters written during the next few years, he managed to place himself squarely on both horns of the dilemma.

For example, on the question of financial dependence on a paying audience, he wrote in Chapter VIII of the *Enquiry:*

> A long habit of writing for bread thus turns the ambition of every author at last into avarice. . . . he despairs of applause and turns to profit. . . . Thus the man who, under the protection of the great, might have done honor to humanity, when only patronized by the bookseller, becomes a thing little superior to the fellow who works at the press.[85]

A few years later (in the meantime he had published his short-lived periodical *The Bee*, written a life of Voltaire as hack-work for the booksellers, and received a much-needed advance of 60 pounds, presumably with the help of Samuel Johnson, on the *Vicar of Wake-*

field) he wrote a paean of thanks that the patronage of the public had replaced the "protection of the great." The writer comes into his own as the crucial shift from Patron to Public is completed:

> At present the few poets of England no longer depend on the Great for subsistence, they have now no other patrons but the public, and *the public*, collectively considered, *is a good and generous master* . . . A writer of real merit now may easily be rich if his heart be set only on fortune: and for those who have no merit, it is but fit that such should remain in merited obscurity. [Italics supplied]

Not only will he reap his due rewards; for the first time, he can now be self-respecting and independent:

> He may now refuse an invitation to dinner, without fearing to incur his patron's displeasure, or to starve by remaining at home. He may now venture to appear in company with just such clothes as other men generally wear, and talk even to princes, with all the conscious superiority of wisdom. Though he cannot boast of fortune here, yet he can bravely assert the dignity of independence.[86]

Or again, in the *Enquiry,* he had written that the author who turns to the bookseller because he can no longer find patronage gets paid for quantity and not for quality; that "in these circumstances the author bids adieu to fame, writes for bread . . ." with "phlegmatic apathy." [87] In the ninety-third *Citizen of the World* letter, on the other hand, he pointed out that "almost all of the excellent productions . . . that have appeared here [in England] were purely the offspring of necessity" and went on to recommend fasting for the sharpening of genius:

> Believe me, my friend, hunger has a most amazing faculty of sharpening the genius; and he who with a full belly, can think like a hero, after a course of fasting, shall rise to the sublimity of a demi-god.[88]

Johnson, usually less torn by conflicts between writer and market, raised similar questions. Who is to judge the merit of an author, he asked at about the same time that Goldsmith voiced concern about the fate of the literary genius, and how is he to find his way to recognition in all this "miscellany"? In discussing this problem, Johnson first described some of the needs and predispositions of a "mass" audience:

He that endeavours after fame by writing, solicits the regard of a multitude fluctuating in pleasures, or immersed in business, without time for intellectual amusements; he appeals to judges, prepossessed by passions, or corrupted by prejudices, which preclude their approbation of any new performance. Some are too indolent to read any thing, till its reputation is established; others too envious to promote that fame which gives them pain by its increase.

He then went on to develop a catalogue of audience reaction:

What is new is opposed, because most are unwilling to be taught; and what is known is rejected, because it is not sufficiently considered, that men more frequently require to be reminded than informed. The learned are afraid to declare their opinion early, lest they should put their reputation in hazard; the ignorant always imagine themselves giving some proof of delicacy, when they refuse to be pleased. . . .

If an author achieves recognition, he concludes, it will certainly not be attributable to the discernment of his readers:

. . . and he that finds his way to reputation through all these obstructions, must acknowledge that he is indebted to other causes beside his industry, his learning, or his wit.[89]

Such an audience cannot serve as judge; the writer therefore has to examine the literary scene himself. He must look at the works which are being purchased at so great a rate, and he must try to determine why the public had not soared upward on the two wings of morality and beauty as Addison had hoped they would, and as Pope, for all his self-assurance about the recognition of his own works, had feared they would not.

IV. Indictment

In asking themselves what effect the growing market for printed goods was having on the moral, intellectual, and aesthetic development of the individual and upon the country as a whole, English literati probably became the first group consciously to face the problem of popular culture in modern society. In examining the scene about him, the eighteenth-century critic was not so much concerned with the new format in which literature was being produced, such as popular magazines, newspapers, cheap editions or reprints of books; this concern was to develop later, when these new literary shapes had become firmly entrenched features of modern society. He tended, rather, to focus upon changes in content which resulted from the fact that many writers were deliberately catering to the lower levels of taste in the growing audience. The very term "popular writer," in the derogatory sense, came into usage for the first time in this period. Oliver Goldsmith, for example, used it in his *Enquiry* when he expressed fear that "affectation in some popular writer" would lead "others to vicious imitation." [90] While Pope did not actually use the word "popular" in his *Dunciad*, he believed that the drive for popularity accounted for the low level to which many writers of his time had sunk.[91]

Marked changes in the content of the drama and the novel took place in the first half of the century, changes which amounted to a whole-hearted espousal of character-types of the emerging middle class. The genre which replaced Restoration drama, sentimental or "weeping" comedy, centered around the professional and domestic problems of middle-class characters. The hero of these "realistic" dramas was likely to be an everyday sort of person who was a model of virtue, and the villain an everyday sort of person with familiar and commonplace vices. These changes may have contributed to the respectability of the theater but, according to at least one well-qualified observer, they also made it considerably less amusing. Fielding wrote: "In banishing humour from the stage, which was tantamount to banishing human nature, the dramatist made the stage as dull as the drawing-room." [92] This shift from socially elevated characters to city merchants and apprentices in private life—a shift epitomized by the domestic tragedies of George Lillo in the 1730's—brought about a notable change in the experience of the audience: it was now possible for the ordinary theater-goer to identify with the heroes and heroines on the stage. Restoration dramatists had created half-real people and completely unreal situations; in the new dramas of middle-class life, realism and believability were paramount goals.[93] This possibility for identification and imitation was the basis for many moral (as contrasted with aesthetic) anxieties which began to harass the intellectuals of the mid-century as they attempted to assess and to come to terms with the new literary phenomena.

It was the novel which stimulated most of the uneasiness about the consequences of identification with fictional characters. Many more novels were written in a year than there were plays produced, and for many it must have been easier to read novels than to attend the theater. A small book, to be sure, cost about three times as much as a seat in the upper gallery at one of the licensed theaters; but books could be borrowed from friends and from circulating libraries, and they could be read and re-read at the convenience of the reader. Not only was the novel a convenient form of recreation, but its length and considerably less rigorous construction made it more suitable to the limning of the details and nuances of middle-class life. In general, its contents differed from the romance of the seventeenth and early eighteenth centuries in much the same way as sentimental comedy differed from the Restoration drama. Realism of character and situation was, as Samuel Johnson pointed out in his *Rambler* essay, "The Modern Form of Romance," the distinguishing feature of the new fiction:

> The works of fiction, with which the present generation seems more particularly delighted, are such as exhibit life in its true state, diversified only by accidents that daily happen in the world, and influenced by passions and qualities which are really to be found in conversing with mankind.

Johnson goes on to demonstrate how this stress on realism creates a new problem for the writer. He can no longer rely on his book-learning alone, secure in the knowledge that he is better informed than most of his readers. He must become an astute observer of the world of people around him. Should he make a mistake, every "common reader" wil know it, because "our present writers" are "engaged in portraits, of which every one knows the original, and can detect any deviation from exactness of resemblance." [94]

Dangerous Realism. Restoration comedy had mirrored the foibles of the aristocracy with a light touch, with considerable humor, and with no small amount of caricature. The playgoer or the reader may well have been amused by the wit and elegance of these clever writings, but he would have been hard put to identify with its highly stylized characters. And the heroic romance of the same period, as Johnson remarked, had discouraged identification by resorting to machines and other convenient but far-fetched expedients such as "giants to snatch a lady away from the nuptial rites" and "knights to bring her back from captivity." [95]

While Samuel Johnson was not alone in his concern, his analysis of the problems raised by the new stress on realism is so pertinent that his essay on the modern novel warrants closer analysis. He asks the question whether, in his eagerness to portray reality, the contemporary novelist might not so closely interweave the reprehensible with the exemplary qualities of a character that the reader will become as favorably disposed to evil as to virtue:

> Many writers, for the sake of following nature, so mingle good and bad qualities in their principal personages, that they are both equally conspicuous; and as we accompany them through their adventures with delight, and are led by degrees to interest ourselves in their favor, we lose the abhorrence of their faults, because they do not hinder our pleasure, or, perhaps, regard them with some kindness for being united with so much merit.

In exploring this dilemma he points out that there have been, in the course of history, some "splendidly wicked" men whose crimes were never viewed as "perfectly detestable" because their often agreeable personalities cast a pleasing aura about them. He protests against true-to-life portrayal of such characters because they are "the great corrupters of the world, and their resemblance ought no more to be preserved than the art of murdering without pain."

For all his scorn of the *deus ex machina,* Johnson looked back with a tinge of regret upon the highly unrealistic romances which he had read in his youth:

> In the romances formerly written, every transaction and sentiment was so remote from all that passes among men, that the reader was in very little danger of making any applications to himself; the virtues and crimes were equally beyond his sphere of activity; and he amused himself with heroes and with traitors, deliverers and persecutors, as with beings of another species . . . who had neither faults nor excellences in common with himself.

He then formulates the processes of identification and imitation encouraged by the new realistic fiction.

> But when an adventurer is levelled with the rest of the world, and acts in such scenes of the universal drama as may be the lot of any

other man, young spectators fix their eyes upon him with closer attention, and hope, by observing his behaviour and success, to regulate their
own practices, when they shall be engaged in the like part.

While such processes could have unhappy consequences, Johnson
believed that identification with fictional characters might be put
to constructive use and realistic stories made a boon to the educa-
tor: "these familiar histories may perhaps be made of greater use
than the solemnities of professed morality, and convey the knowledge of vice and virtue with more efficacy than axioms and definitions." Perhaps, Johnson concluded (with notably greater emphasis
on effects than on artistic integrity), the author should manipulate
reality a bit. Virtue should be judiciously exalted, and vice, while
not to be eliminated altogether, should always be portrayed in a
way which leaves the reader with a feeling of repulsion:

> In narratives, where historical veracity has no place, I cannot discover
> why there should not be exhibited the most perfect idea of virtue . . .
> the highest and surest that humanity can reach . . . which . . . may,
> by conquering some calamities and enduring others, teach us what we
> may hope and what we can perform. Vice, for vice is necessary to be
> shown, should always disgust.

As though he were formulating a self-regulatory code for novel-
writers, he concludes with a plea for what amounts to "all-white
or all-black" character portrayals: *

> . . . nor should the graces of gayety, or the dignity of courage, be so
> united with it [vice] as to reconcile it to the mind: wherever it appears,
> it should raise hatred by the malignity of its practices, and contempt by
> the meanness of its stratagems; for while it is supported by either parts
> or spirits, it will be seldom heartily abhorred. . . . There are thousands
> of readers . . . willing to be thought wicked, if they may be allowed
> to be wits.[96]

Johnson was not alone in his complaints about the abuses of

---

* Johnson's criticism of Shakespeare was based largely on the grounds that
he did not do any judicious weighing of good against evil in his characterizations. In the preface to his edition of Shakespeare, he writes that on the contrary, Shakespeare "carries his persons indifferently through right and wrong,
and at the close dismisses them without further care, and leaves their examples
to operate by chance. This fault the barbarity of his age cannot extenuate;
for it is always a writer's duty to make the world better . . ."

realism. Lady Mary Wortley Montagu, a writer of charming letters though not a professional critic, touched upon the matter in a private correspondence. Referring to the realism of the character portrayals in Richardson's *Clarissa* and *Pamela,* she singled them out as the "two books that will do more general mischief than the works of Lord Rochester." [97] And Oliver Goldsmith went even further than Johnson in recommending that novels be especially adapted to youth. In an essay on education, he expressed concern about the effects of true-to-life characterizations and advocated that

. . . there be some men of wit employed to compose books that might equally interest the passions of our youth . . . to be explicit as possible, the old story of Whittington, were his cat left out, might be more serviceable to the tender mind than either Tom Jones, Joseph Andrews or an hundred others . . .

Instead of suggesting that professional writers adapt their works to the educational needs of youth, Goldsmith proposed that schoolmasters be put to work composing novels:

Were our schoolmasters, if any of them have sense enough to draw up such a work, thus employed, it would be much more serviceable to their pupils, than all the grammars and dictionaries they may publish these ten years.[98]

While both Johnson and Goldsmith drew fairly clear distinctions between mature and immature readers (that is, their worries about the effects of realism were largely confined to youth), they did not draw hard and fast lines between various levels of fiction. Moral problems, they felt, were posed by all realistic fiction, whether the work of a genius or of a hack.

Few writers maintained consistent viewpoints on questions of realism. Henry Mackenzie, for example, the author of what has become a proverbially sentimental novel, *The Man of Feeling,* followed this "all-white" product a few years later with *The Man of the World* in which the hero was from a quite different color of cloth. A contemporary reviewer of the second novel scolded Mackenzie for not sufficiently punishing his wayward hero, a reformed seducer, who "should either have been sent to the devil, or his reformation should have been in consequence of a long and

bitter repentance." [99] Mackenzie himself either changed his mind
or kept his various writing selves distinctly separate: ten years after
The Man of Feeling he wrote disparagingly, in his *Lounger*, of the

> . . . mingled virtue and vice which is to be found in some of the best
> of our novels. Instances will readily occur to every reader, where the
> hero of the performance has violated, in one page, the most sacred laws
> of society, to whom, by the mere turning of the leaf, we are to be
> reconciled, whom we are to be made to love and admire, for the beauty
> of some humane, or the brilliancy of some heroic action.[100]

Dr. Johnson, on the other hand, while he had on one occasion
recommended that characters be thoroughly good or thoroughly
evil, on another endorsed realism, though it necessarily involved
the picturing of wickedness. In his *Lives of the Poets*, published
nearly thirty years after the *Rambler* essay on fiction, he insists that
the writer, while occasionally justified in gratifying the audience by
making things pleasant, is bound also to show life as it really is.* [101]

True-to-life portrayals could easily become boring, and writers
resorted to many devices for sustaining interest in the ordinary
people and situations portrayed in their novels and plays. Two
methods for insuring audience appeal were full descriptions of tender
sentiments and, at the other extreme, detailed spellings-out of scenes
of aggression, violence, or horror. Very often, in the manner of
the Hollywood motion picture, these two sets of attractions were
combined in the same production, always making sure that the
sensitive hero was the victim and not the perpetrator of aggression.

These devices for offsetting boredom confronted the creative
writer with a number of additional problems.

First, does not the realistic portrayal of *crime and violence*, of
which the English audience was considered to be inordinately fond,
both reflect and encourage sadism in the audience?

Second, when everyday characters are made less boring by a
generous endowment of *sentimentality*, are not the heads of the
readers filled with romantic notions which will stand them in no
good stead as they go about the business of making a living (or

---

* This does not mean a victory of realism over moralism in Dr. Johnson's
approach to literature. As René Wellek points out, in his *History of Modern
Criticism*, the two strands—together with an element of abstractionism—were
closely interwoven in all of Johnson's criticism, but "more frequently the
moralist is dominant, to the exclusion and even detriment of the critic (V. I, p.
83)."

marrying a man) in the workaday world? Worse still, may they not use identification with the unreal world of emotion as a means of escape from the exigencies of everyday life?

Third, perhaps again because of the very familiarity of these realistic characters and situations, the audience began to attach increasing importance to *novelty and variety* as values in themselves. How, asked the writer, can we keep this desire for sensationalism from even further debasing the taste of the public?

Fourth, with an avalanche of mass-produced material which makes few demands on the reader and not many more on the writer, is there not a very real danger that the world of letters may be entering a period of *mediocrity?*

Crime and Violence. Though the modern media have more graphic, and more ubiquitous, representational devices at their disposal than did those of the 18th century, descriptions of sadism and brutality did not spring full-blown from the comic book or the television set. As a matter of fact, some of the "horror" novels which enjoyed popularity in the last three decades of the century make those "comic" books of sex and sadism which are sold from under the counter today look pallid by comparison.

The genre called "Gothic" romance, foreshadowed by Walpole's *Castle of Otranto* (1764), reached its peak a quarter of a century later in M. G. Lewis' *The Monk*, a romance built almost entirely around scenes of sadism, sensuality, and fright.* Lewis' work rapidly went through a number of editions and set a new standard for brutality which was to be imitated in most of the English Gothic novels to come. But while these horror tales stirred up small furors at the time of publication, the peak of popular as well as intellectual reaction was not reached until after 1800.

The debate over "crime and violence" in the drama, however, was waged with vigor throughout the eighteenth century. Concern about the murders and tortures which had long been commonplace on the stage had formed part of the objections to the theater raised by the neo-Puritans. But in general neither they nor their successors differentiated between profanity and lewdness on the one hand and

---

* Mrs. Radcliffe's *The Mysteries of Udolpho* was perhaps the outstanding novel of suspense of the period; in contrast to M. G. Lewis, Mrs. Radcliffe explained away the supernatural by rational means, and relied on curiosity rather than fear as the main appeal of her work.

criminal or brutal behavior on the other. Furthermore, when Defoe and others referred to the stage as a "nursery of crime," they were as much distressed about the behavior of the audience and about the "corrupting" environs of the theater as they were about what took place on the stage. Among less moralistic critics, aggression and violence on the stage were the main objects of concern. Even Addison, who was rather tolerant of the excesses of the opera and stage, raised the issue:

> But among all our Methods of moving Pity or Terror, there is none so absurd and barbarous, and what more exposes us to the Contempt and Ridicule of our Neighbours, than that dreadful butchering of one another which is so very frequent upon the *English* stage.

He sympathizes with French critics who had pointed to the sight of "Men stabbed, poisoned, racked or impaled" on the English stage as "the Sign of a cruel Temper" in the English national character. Addison goes on to decry the favorite climax of the stage tragedies of his day, wherein every prop for murder and torture is used in a grand free-for-all of mass slaughter:

> It is indeed very odd, to see our Stage strewed with Carcasses in the last Scene of a Tragedy; and to observe in the Ward-robe of the Play-house several Daggers, Poinciards, Wheels, Bowls for Poison and many other Instruments of Death.[102]

But in spite of such disdain, the English audience's love of blood and violence continued to be fed. In the mid-thirties, Henry Fielding published his skit, *Pasquin,* which ridiculed several of the dramatic excesses of the day, not least the addiction to slaughter and poison. Twenty years later, Oliver Goldsmith observed that

> . . . death and tenderness are leading passions of every modern buskined hero; this moment they embrace, and the next stab, mixing daggers and kisses in every period.[103]

And David Hume, in his treatise *Of Tragedy,* excoriated such realistic portrayals of horror because they interfere with the main objectives of tragedy:

> An action, represented in tragedy, may be too bloody and atro-

cious . . . Such is that action represented in the *ambitious Stepmother*, where a venerable old man, raised to the heights of fury and despair, rushes against a pillar, and striking his head upon it, besmears it all over with mingled brains and gore. The *English* theatre abounds too much with such images.[104]

Unlike present-day discussion of this topic, no eighteenth century critic seems to have condoned fictional or dramatic portrayals of "crime and violence," and reference to the Aristotelian concept of catharsis is in this connection (though not in connection with suffering from other causes) conspicuously absent.

Sentimentality. Goldsmith, in his *Essay on the Theatre*, reports the reaction of "a friend" to the unembroidered presentation of middle-class city-types and their practical problems. The friend left the theater in the middle of a play about a moneylender remarking, "it is indifferent to me whether he be turned out of his counting house on Fish Street Hill, since he will still have enough left to open shop in St. Giles's . . ."[105] While the drama tried to counteract such boredom with violence and other "special attractions," the novelists, for their part, had their own devices. Richardson had set the tone: portrayals of the plights and successes of the middle and lower middle classes could be invested with considerable appeal by the inclusion of detailed descriptions of their affairs of the heart. Goldsmith's *Vicar of Wakefield* is generally considered to be an outstanding work of this genre and Mackenzie's *The Man of Feeling* represents the extreme of the novel which combined the ordinary and the realistic in character and setting with detailed descriptions and exaltations of sentiment.*

In "the novel of sentiment" and the "novel of sensibility" (which differed from each other more in degree than in kind) the emotions were more important than behavior, and rationality in either thought or behavior was relegated to crude and insensitive souls. Forgiveness and repentance were the pinnacles of human feeling, and the reasons for actions which led to forgiveness or repentance

---

* The prevailingly sentimental tone of the novels of this period has been attributed in part to the fact that there was a great influx of women novelists who wrote for the largely female novel-reading public. Certainly contemporary satire on such lady novelists was not lacking: Tobias Smollett, among others, went out of his way, in *Humphrey Clinker*, to point out that the failure of one of his characters as a novelist was excusable because the ladies had the field of "spirit, delicacy, and knowledge of the human heart" all to themselves.

were as irrelevant as the murder which opens the modern mystery story. It was the detailed and lengthy portrayals of emotions that gave rise to the first discussions about the dangers of escapism.

Because of the improbable nature of the seventeenth and early eighteenth century romance, and perhaps also because it had been read by fewer people than was the novel of sentiment, few before the middle of the century had been concerned about the effect of fiction on the reader. Addison, to be sure, had poked mild fun at a gentlewoman who consumed many of these fanciful tales and eventually undertook to while away her time by re-doing her estate to resemble a romantic grotto,[106] but he was neither indignant nor alarmed about the social consequences of such indulgence.

The stress on sentimental bliss in the novels of the second half of the century gave rise to a more socially significant kind of concern. Over-indulgence in fiction has two serious consequences: it keeps the reader from useful endeavours and it fills his head with romantic dreams which it will be impossible to attain in real life. Oliver Goldsmith, despite *The Vicar of Wakefield*, often warned against the dangers of living in the transported world of sentiment. In a letter to his brother about his nephew's education, he even advised the father to prohibit novel reading altogether. Such romantic pictures of the world are snares and delusions to youth:

> They teach the young mind to sigh after beauty and happiness which never existed; to despise the little good which fortune has mixed in their cup, by expecting more than she gave . . .[107]

The reading of sentimental novels, in short, is not practical. But the pastime is perhaps more dangerous for the young girl than for the young man, because she who is fed on sentiment and sensibility will be hard pressed to love a man whose daily life is filled with the routine demands of earning a living for wife and family. Furthermore, as William Cowper noted with some indignation, the young lady is likely to become so over-stimulated by the reading of such "sentimental frippery and dream," of "sniv'ling and driv'ling folly," that no mere insertion of a warning will "quench the fire." [108]

The middle-class character had best be equipped with middle-aged sentiments, for too great a concern with tender feelings ill-equips a youth for bourgeois life. Richardson's Charlotte Grandison argues that "a mild, sedate convenience is better than a stark staring mad passion . . . Who ever hears of darts, flames, Cupids . . . and such like nonsense in matrimony? Passion is transitory . . ." [109]

But such warnings did not stem the tide of sentimental literature which provided readers with escape from the humdrum of everyday life. The middle class may have wanted to see itself in a mirror but it wanted to see its materialistic self dressed up and made more appealing with delicate sensibilities.

Novelty and Variety. Concern about man's search for distraction did not come into being with the dawn of the eighteenth century and the development of saleable literary goods. Montaigne, and later Pascal, had debated the issue in the sixteenth and seventeenth centuries.* But it was Voltaire's *Essay on Taste*, published in 1757, which alerted writers and scholars to the implications of the problem in a society rapidly becoming inundated with all kinds of written entertainment.

Voltaire, examining the general cultural scene of his times, found that

. . . the publick, fond of novelty, applauds their invention; but this applause is soon succeeded by satiety and disgust. A new set of artists start up, invent new methods to please a capricious taste, and depart still further from nature . . . Overwhelmed with new inventions, which succeed and efface each other with incredible rapidity, they scarcely know where they are . . .[110]

Looking at the growing market for literary products and at the manifest inclinations of the audience which was purchasing them, the English men of letters found ample proof that Voltaire's concern was justified.

David Garrick faced the public demand for novelty in his three-fold capacity as dramatist, actor, and theater manager. In the course of his thirty-year career he found it increasingly necessary to water down his artistic standards with "propping-up" devices and double feature billings which would supply "the many various objects that amuse these busy curious times." [111] Dr. Johnson devoted one of his *Idler* essays to "terrific" diction—a mannerism of obscurity adopted by some writers to add a note of novelty to the commonplace. In explaining the motivation behind this device

* See Leo Lowenthal, "Historical Perspectives of Popular Culture," *American Journal of Sociology*, January 1950.

(which he dubs the "bugbear" style), Johnson says that the demand to see "common things in an uncommon manner" is characteristic of the times. The kinds of devices which popular writers resort to are those on the order of telling time by algebra, drinking tea by stratagem, in short

> . . . to quit the beaten track only because it is known, and to take a new path, however crooked or rough, because the straight was found out before.

In another *Idler* essay he speaks of "the multiplication of books," particularly of compilations, and notes that they serve no real purpose but merely "distract choice." He concludes, however, that such writers do little harm in the long run because they are merely symptoms of a short-lived fad.[112]

It was the magazines which most conspicuously catered to the demand for variety, but oddly enough, these popular "miscellanies," whose number increased rapidly as the century wore on, were not attacked with any consistency by the serious writers.* Oliver Goldsmith, however, did devote one of his essays to some good-natured raillery of the magazines. He compares his lot as an essayist who can write upon only one subject at a time with those more "fortunate" magazine writers who can write upon several and thus avoid the risk of boring their readers. The magazine which he describes resembles the *Gentleman's Magazine* or some similar eighteenth-century original of *Reader's Digest:*

> If a magazine be dull upon the Spanish war, he soon has us up again with the Ghost in Cock Lane; if the reader begins to doze upon that, he is quickly roused by an Eastern tale: tales prepare us for poetry, and poetry for the meteorological history of the weather. It is the life and soul of a magazine never to be long dull upon one subject; and the reader, like the sailor's horse, has at least the comfortable refreshment of having the spur often changed.

Ironically complaining that he sees no reason why the magazine writers should "carry off all the rewards of genius," Goldsmith goes on to outline a plan for changing the format of his own

---

* It is possible that the intellectuals were inclined to consider the magazine beneath their notice, just as they seem to have left criticism of the popular novels of the latter part of the century to "middlebrow" writers.

essays, making them a magazine in miniature in which he proposes to "hop from subject to subject." He also gives notice that, if properly encouraged, he will decorate his magazine with pictures. The journal is to be called the *Infernal Magazine* and, unlike others of the same genre, it will live up to its advertised promise to astonish society. Obeisances are then made to the prospective audience in the usual style of eighteenth-century prospectuses, and Goldsmith assures his readers-to-be that the magazine is to be run by gentlemen of distinction (and means) who will perform this public service not for personal gain but purely for their own amusement.[113]

Nuances of feeling and sentiment offered one way to add appeal to the pedestrian characters and situations which dominated the popular writings of the time. Exotic settings provided another. The opening up of the Far East to British trade had resulted in what was perhaps one of the most sweeping fads England has ever experienced. Music, fabrics, dress styles, furniture, architecture, gardening, and painting—nothing escaped the great demand for the Oriental. The "nabob" who disappeared into China for a year or two and came home with his pockets full of gold became, for a time, a hero. Writers made short shrift of turning the situation to their own advantage. Nabobs were adulated on the stage where they often proved to be a great dramatic convenience, and essays, letters, and novels took the ordinary Englishman into extraordinary surroundings, replete with elaborate trappings and a heavy veil of mystery (it need hardly be added that the adventurer usually followed tradition and remained an Englishman for all that). In these tales of Oriental adventure, the "wisdom of the East" was often exalted, as in William Whitehead's prologue to Arthur Murphy's version of Voltaire's *L'Orphelin de la Chine* (1759)— "and boldly bears Confucius' morals to Britannia's ears. Accept th'imported boon." [114]

A few chauvinistic voices were heard saying, in effect, "What does the Orient offer that England cannot match or better?" But by and large the fashion for the Oriental, which was as popular among royalty as among shopgirls, was not considered as dangerous to the reader as was indulgence in the sentimental. Furthermore, it was good for trade and perhaps, with its tales of hard-won riches, even provided additional incentives, if any were needed, for concentrating on the practical (and remunerative) aspects of life.

For the most part, the world of letters confined itself to pointing to the Chinese fad as one more proof of the public's insatiable need for novelty and variety. The jaded European, as Goldsmith remarked with considerably more detachment than he had shown in his remarks about the novel of sentiment, "has, of late, had recourse even to China, in order to diversify the amusements of the day." [115] He himself, not without some apology, used the Oriental touch as a device for strengthening the appeal of his commentary on various aspects of contemporary life, as his *Citizen of the World*—"letters from a Chinese philosopher residing in London to his friends in the East"—testifies. In his introduction to these letters, he first complains about the fickleness of the audience and the indiscriminate way in which praise is lavished on the "mob" of popular writers, and then reports a dream in which

. . . the success of such numbers [of authors] at last began to operate on me. If these, cried I, meet with favour and safety, some luck may, perhaps, for once attend the unfortunate. I am resolved to make a new adventure.

He then comments that, while thus far the "frippery and fireworks of China" have merely served to "vitiate" the public taste, he will "try how far they can help to improve our understanding." [116]

Goldsmith and his fellow writers were less tolerant of the far reaches to which the public's desire for novelty had led in the opera and drama. The seventeenth-century theater had catered to a rather more heterogeneous audience than had the printed works of the time. To sustain the interest of people with diverse tastes it had made use of a variety of audience appeals. The "spectacular" or "sensational" devices to which eighteenth-century dramatists and theater managers resorted were, therefore, not essentially different in kind from those used in the days of Addison (or, for that matter, in the Elizabethan period). Addison had, in fact, devoted more than one issue of the *Spectator* to the abuses of the operatic stage, though his remonstrances were mild in comparison with those Pope was to write in twenty years and those of Goldsmith and Fielding forty years later. Addison found many of the popular attention-getting devices quite legitimate—his plea was merely for a more judicious application. Thunder and lightning, bells and ghosts, all have their "proper season" and, used with restraint, are to be applauded. The same is true of the much-maligned handkerchief, the "principal machine" for the "moving of pity": it should not be eliminated, but its flutterings should have some connection with the words of the actor.[117] About one minor attraction, however, he was not quite so tolerant. In another issue of the *Spectator* he writes that it is customary to impress the audience with the lofty character of the hero by the lofty height of the plumes on his head, as though "a great Man and a tall Man" were the same thing. Not only is this an affront to the audience, but most embarrassing for the actor because, "notwithstanding any Anxieties which he pretends for his Mistress, his Country or his Friends, one may see by his Actions that his greatest Care and Concern is to keep the Plume of Feathers from falling off his Head." [118]

Addison's sharpest sarcasm was reserved for the indiscriminate mixing of the representational with the real. In ridiculing the release of live birds from a cage on the stage of the opera house, he objected not that they were put there in the first place but that their songs emanated all too obviously from man-blown instruments hidden behind the scenery. Apparently intending to frighten stage-managers into their senses, he concludes with a description of where such absurdities might lead:

> I found . . . that there were great Designs on Foot for the Improvement of the Opera; that it had been proposed to break down a part of the Wall, and to surprize the Audience with a Party of an hundred Horse, and that there was actually a Project of bringing the *New-River* into the House, to be employed in Jetteaus and Waterworks.[119]

Had Addison lived on to the middle of the century, he would have found that instead of giving the stage-managers pause, he may have put new ideas into their heads, for audio-visual claptrap became more than ever the order of the day as the stage and opera had more strenuously to compete with magazines and novels for public attention.

Eloquent satirizers were not lacking as the abuses multiplied. Pope certainly did not overlook the stage as he lampooned the world of letters of his time:

> The play stands still; damn action and discourse,
> Back fly the scenes, and enter foot and horse;
> Pageants on pageants, in long order drawn,
> Peers, heralds, bishops, ermine, gold, and lawn . . .[120]

But again it remained for Goldsmith to conduct the most thorough-going analysis, this one in his *The Chinese Goes to See a Play*. First he points out that daggers and kisses are mixed in every scene. He then goes on to report an entr'acte episode which took place right after the curtain fell on just such a mixture of love and sadism:

> . . . my attention was engrossed by a new object; a man came in balancing a straw upon his nose, and the audience were clapping their hands in all the raptures of applause. To what purpose, cried I, does this unmeaning figure make his appearance; is he a part of the plot?

Analyzing the nature of the appeal of this vaudeville-like performance, Goldsmith postulates an ironic theory about its projective potentialities. Such a trick has something in it for everyone:

> Unmeaning, do you call him, replied my friend . . . this is one of the most important characters of the whole play; nothing pleases the people more than the seeing a straw balanced; there is a great deal of meaning in the straw; there is something suited to every apprehension in the sight; and a fellow possessed of talents like these is sure of making his fortune.

Between the third and fourth acts, the "Chinese" is surprised to see a child of six appear, "learning to dance" on the stage. At the end of the fourth act the heronie fell into a fit, whereupon the

> . . . fifth act began, and a busy piece it was. Scenes shifting, trumpets sounding, mobs hallooing, carpets spreading, guards bustling from one door to another; gods, daemons, daggers, racks and ratsbane. But whether the king was killed, or the queen was drowned, or the son was poisoned, I have absolutely forgotten.[121]

Another *Citizen of the World* letter is devoted to a description of the seasonal opening of the two licensed theaters, the Drury Lane and Covent Garden. Goldsmith first remarks on the competition between the two houses in which

> . . . the generals of either army have . . . several reinforcements to lend occasional assistance. If they produce a pair of diamond buckles at

one house, we have a pair of eyebrows that can match them at the other. . . . If we can bring more children on the stage, they can bring more guards in red clothes, who strut and shoulder their swords to the astonishment of every spectator.

He ridicules the idea that the audience—despite the virtuous platitudes of the times—can possibly derive any instruction from such performances, and reports that, "what with trumpets, hallooing behind the stage and bawling upon it," he himself always gets dizzy long before the performance is over. Calling the situation what it largely was—a money-making proposition—Goldsmith expresses surprise that the play-writing trade has not set up an apprentice system, since there would seem to be nothing easier than to write for the English stage:

> The author, when well acquainted with the value of thunder and lightning; when versed in all the mystery of scene-shifting and trap-doors; when skilled in the proper periods to introduce a wire-walker or a waterfall; . . . he knows all that can give a modern audience pleasure.

And—as in the case of the *Infernal Magazine*—he continues his essay with some ironic advice to the author who wishes to achieve popularity. First, he should never expect the actor to adjust to the requirements of a drama; it is the author's responsibility to appraise the particular abilities of each actor, and to write his play around their respective talents for expressing fear, pain or surprise. Such moans and groans and exclamations are the surest way to win the applause of the audience. There is, in fact, no other way to win an audience. The author will find his consolation in the knowledge that once having acquired such skills, he needs no other talents, and the playgoer can relax in the certainty that once in the theater he can "dismiss from the mind all the fatigue of thinking." [122]

To this facetious advice to the dramatist can be added a number of other examples. In his *Essay on the Theater* written two decades after the *Citizen of the World* Goldsmith formulates the problem of the "paying" audience in terms so modern that they might well be taken for a mid-twentieth century discussion of the motion picture. He begins with a criticism of sentimental comedy and suggests that such plays are largely popular because the dramatists go out of their way to cater to the public demand for novelty. He then acts as his own antagonist, saying that after all the theater is "formed to amuse mankind, and that it matters little, if this end be answered, by what means it is obtained." Whatever pleases the audience is good, "success . . . is a mark of [its] merit." Assuming his own role once more, he then raises the question—since become very familiar, but no more answered in our time than his—what would happen if the audience were provided with *good* drama? [123]

But the English audience continued to enjoy the various devices hit upon for its excitement and amusement. The grotesque effect of the "intermingling of daggers and kisses" is reported by a German visitor to a British play, in which the leading lady was so moved by her tragic situation that she was incapacitated for the rest of the performance

. . . and had to be carried off the stage unconscious. And the audience, too, unable to endure the strain, departed, so that the piece had to be finished without the leading lady, before a handful of unusually hard-boiled spectators.[124]

However powerful the appeal of the tragic emotions, it was for lavish displays that the eighteenth-century audience reserved its most unbounded enthusiasm. During Garrick's management of the Drury Lane, four lush pantomimes and Garrick's own "spectacular" *The Jubilee* all ran considerably longer than any serious drama produced in the same period. After a very brief initial run, most of the genuine works of art, as Garrick regretfully remarked even of his Shakespeare productions, had to be "propped up" by the addition of well-advertised and ever "new" baubles such as parades, masquerades, and dances.[125]

It was this demand for novelty from the reading and playgoing audiences which made it possible for almost any writer to have his day of popularity, provided only he could convince his public that he was giving them something they had never experienced before. Pope attempted to discourage the opportunists who catered to this propensity by deriding them with names and titles, but he had the advantage of perusing the scene fairly early in the century when one book could contain them all. His successors, unable to cope with the deluge case by case, were of necessity considerably less specific.

Mediocrity.   The idea of cyclical movements in the arts and sciences is to be found in almost any age. In eighteenth-century

England, this concept, together with the idea that his own period was one of decline, seems first to have been formulated by David Hume in the essay on *The Rise and Progress of the Arts and Sciences* (1742). He states that when the "arts and sciences come to perfection in any state . . . they naturally, or rather necessarily, decline . . . and seldom or never revive in that nation . . ." [126] A few years later, somewhat less dogmatically, Voltaire echoed Hume from across the Channel: "The taste of a nation may degenerate and become extremely depraved; and it almost always happens that the period of its perfection is the forerunner of its decline." [127]

Neither Hume nor Voltaire seem to have related their ideas about a decline directly to the growing audience and the popular literature with which it was being fed, though Hume did say that the public's desire for novelty "leads men wide of simplicity and nature, and fills their writings with affectation and conceit." [128] But other writers of the mid-century did connect their fears with the new tyranny of public demand and the new spate of popular works. Among the first protagonists of this concept, we find Pope and Swift complaining about the lack of literary qualifications of writers in general; we find less eminent authors complaining about hack novelists and their methods of production; and we find readers as well as writers complaining about the literary unworthiness of the new crop of fictional characters emerging in eighteenth century literature. Finally, we find a group of philosophers and writers seriously disturbed about the fact that, with the increase in literacy, anyone and everyone can become a literary critic, that incompetents are now passing judgment, and that literary standards may, as a result, be shattered altogether.*

---

* Thomas Carlyle, in reviewing English literature of the eighteenth century in his *Lectures on the History of Literature* (1838), regretted the quackery resulting from the selling of literary goods and reflected that it would bring about great confusion among "all men."

". . . an observer sees the quack established; he sees truth trodden down to the earth everywhere around him; in his own office he sees quackery at work, and that part of it which is done by quackery is done better than all the rest; till at last he, too, concludes in favor of this order of things and gets himself enrolled among this miserable set, eager after profit, and of no belief except the belief always held among such persons, that *Money will buy money's worth*, and that *Pleasure is pleasant*. But woe to that land and its people if, for what they do, they expect payment at all times! It is bitter to see . . . All men will suffer from it with confusion in the very heart of them."

Some time before the publication of the first edition of *The Dunciad* (1729), Pope wrote to Swift that it was the "little" writers of the world who made him angry, the "party writers, dull poets, and wild criticks."

> My spleen is at the little rogues of it; it would vex one more to be knocked on the head with a piss-pot than by a thunderbolt . . . But to be squirted to death, as poor Wycherly [the eminent Restoration comic playwright had died in 1716] said to me on his death-bed, by apothecaries' apprentices, by the understrappers of under-secretaries to secretaries who were no secretaries—this would provoke as dull a dog as Philips * himself.[129]

The objective of the book was, in his own words, to "dissuade the dull and punish the malicious" authors of his day. The poem consists of direct and often highly personal attacks not only on those writers whom Pope considered to be second-rate, but on the booksellers, book-puffers, and book-reviewers who by promoting such writers were assuaging the public hunger for information and novelty. The heroine, or better, the *bête noire* of the *Dunciad* is the Goddess of Dullness, a "laborious, heavy, busy, bold and blind" deity who seems to be coming into her own in the eighteenth-century world of letters. In addition to her coterie of writers and hacks, she is surrounded by a public whom Pope categorizes as Tasteless Admirers, Flatterers of Dunces, Indolent Persons and Minute Philosophers. Early in the poem the Goddess requests the Dunces to instruct a group of young students who enter the scene. The consequence of their teaching is that the youths taste the cup "which causes total oblivion of all Obligations, divine, civil, moral or rational" and are thus rendered unfit to play a constructive role in life.[130] In other words, the future of civilized society has become endangered because the students, who are the hope of that society, are being corrupted by dull, stupid, uncreative reading material produced by incompetents.[131]

The second edition of *The Dunciad* (1743) was considerably less personal and at the same time broader in scope than the first, going beyond the realm of literature proper to address itself to the theater, the opera, and even to education and politics. The two

---

* Presumably John Philips, 1631-1706, a nephew of Milton, employed largely as translator and hack-writer.

editions together compose the major broadside against particular writers; and the popular "little rogues" of literature whom Pope attacked have, as one of his recent editors has pointed out, all vindicated his judgment by sinking into oblivion.[132]

The fear of a decline centered on both the novel and the drama. In the case of the novel, the peaks attained by Richardson and Fielding, and later by Sterne and Smollett, were infinitely higher than anything achieved in the subsequent two or three decades of the century. Their works, in retrospect, were seen not as a starting point of a new era in the novel, but as its culmination. It was the serious-minded journalists rather than the few great literary figures of the latter half of the century who trained their sights on the cruder novelists.* To take one instance, *The Sylph*, a short-lived single-essay periodical published late in the century, devoted an issue to a lively parody of the way in which the popular novels were being slapped together: the trick is to spread the words mechanically across the page, shuffle them about to form sentences, and

. . . according to the arrangement and collection of them [they] become *narrations, speeches, sentiments, descriptions, etc.* and when *a very great quantity of them* . . . are wedged together after a particular form and manner, they are denominated a NOVEL . . .[133]

Another magazine writer recommended, in the manner of Swift, that engines be adopted to make the novel writing process easier, and contributors to several other respected journals of the latter half of the century made frequent quips about the plagiarisms, repetitions, and patchwork that often went into what was released as a novel. With such a multitude turning out novels, grumbled one, all themes have been used up; the novel has had its day:

The manufacture of novels has been so long established, that in general they have arrived at mediocrity. . . . We are indeed so sickened with this worn-out species of composition, that we have lost all relish for it.[134]

---

* In twentieth century terminology we might say that this is a typical example of the middlebrows criticizing the lowbrows. Highbrows, as we have seen, did not differentiate, at least not until the end of the century when Jane Austen's parodies of the novel of terror might be viewed as the highbrow singling out the middlebrow.

The deterioration in the English drama after 1740 has been attributed in part to the sheer accident that no great dramatist developed in this period; but the fact that audiences represented a broader social background and were at the same time artistically less interested than audiences of the first half of the century also deserves consideration.[135] Furthermore, as we have already remarked, middle-class realism tended to be more boring on the stage than in print. Another reason ventured for the decline in the drama was that the physical alterations made in order to accommodate larger audiences required adaptations by playwright and actor which militated against "good theater." The lighting was dim, the acoustics poor, and the exaggeration required to overcome these deficiencies lent a farcical note to the tragic and comic alike.

But for many artists it was the multiplication of "judges and critics" which seems to have been most portentous of a decline in the literary world. As the ability to read spread to all ranks of society, it seemed that anyone could become an arbiter of standards; "in short," as one periodical essayist remarked, "fiddlers, players, singers, dancers and mechanics themselves are all the sons and daughters of taste . . ."[136] Oliver Goldsmith, in his *Enquiry*, which he prefaced with the remark that he takes the decay of genius in his age for granted, placed much of the blame squarely on the multiplying number of critics or would-be critics.[137]

What rankled most seems not to have been the professionals but the amateurs in the audience. Writers had long had the field of literary standards to themselves, and the only threat to their self-imposed criteria was the necessity of now and then composing a paean of praise to a wealthy patron, when they were fortunate enough to have one. In the final analysis, this concern about the voices of the people amounted to a rallying behind Goldsmith in his pessimistic mood—"when only patronized by the bookseller the writer becomes a thing little superior to the fellow who works at the press"—rather than behind his optimistic formulation: "the public, collectively considered, is a good and generous master." Not only was "everyone" becoming articulate in the expression of literary judgments; worse still, there were so many levels of audience opinion that it seemed to the artists that their tastes were irreconcilable.

From all sides came the complaint. Fielding wrote: "How is it possible at once to please / Tastes so directly opposite as these?"[138]

and Garrick addressed the several levels of his audience as follows:

> What shall we do your different tastes to hit?
> You relish satire (to the pit) you ragouts of wit (to the boxes)
> Your taste is humour and high-season's joke. (First Gallery)
> You call for hornpipe and for hearts of oak. (Second Gallery) [139]

The critic Warburton sympathized with the fate of the dramatists who

> . . . are often used like ladies of pleasure: they are received with rapture and enthusiasm by the public on their first appearance, but on farther acquaintance are received very coolly, though they have indeed by this time greatly improved themselves in the *art of pleasing*.[140]

Cibber, speaking in his role of stage manager, was first to point out a new way of looking at the audience, one which was eventually to effect a compromise between the standards of the artist and the divers tastes of the new public. In one of his *Two Dissertations on the Theatres*, he speaks of the phrase "The Town" which was commonly used to designate the audience. Ask an author or an actor (individually) whom he has in mind when he uses this phrase, predicts Cibber, and he will tell you that he means the "judging few" —but if you ask him to specify these judging few you will see that each will point to his respective friends, to "those who approve, and cry up their several Performances." Ask a theatrical manager and he will also refer to those opinions of the Town which are most agreeable to him and which echo what he wants most to hear. Actually, Cibber continues, the matter is not so simple. It is necessary to distinguish several levels of influence within the audience. Regardless of walk of life, it is those people who are interested in and who, in their respective circles, give encouragement to the theater who constitute the true "opinion leaders."

> I think, the Town may be supposed to include all Degrees of Persons, from the highest Nobleman, to the lowly Artisan, etc., who, in their different Stations, are Encouragers of dramatic performances: Thus all persons, who pay for their places, whether Noble, Gentle, or Simple, who fill the Boxes, Pit and Galleries in a theatrical Sence, form the Town.[141]

In a way, Cibber's remarks might be construed as a plea for democracy in art. Many more gifted artists, in the face of the dilemma posed by the growing middle and lower class audience, were to attempt to find theoretical grounds for supporting this pluralistic viewpoint. But the task was difficult, and there were class as well as aesthetic barriers to be faced.

In the early half of the century, the middle class struggled successfully to assert its values and interests against those prevailing among the aristocracy. The increasing industrialization and the new importance attaching to the role of the worker in the latter half of the century, however, brought about a shift in focus: the middle class now began to suspect that its most dangerous enemies were below instead of above it. And while class lines in the world of letters were not sharply etched, neither were they altogether obscured.

During the latter half of the century the social status of fictional characters became an object of some concern. In the 1770's this form of snobbism was sufficiently recognized that the name *tapino-phoby* was coined for it. In 1773 the cleric-novelist Richard Graves used the term in his book *The Spiritual Quixote;* just after introducing a cobbler into his story, he interrupted the narrative with a warning to

. . . such readers, as are possessed with modern tapino-phoby, or dread of everything that is low either in writing or in conversation. If he is of the opinion that every representation of nature, that does not relate to the great world, is to be exploded as contemptible stuff; he will certainly repent of having read thus far; and I would exhort him, by all means, to return in peace to his card-assembly or to his chocolate house and pursue so low a subject no further.[142]

Tapino-phoby seems to have affected the literary elite as well. G. Sprague Allen, to whom we owe the above quotation, notes that the classicists—and here he names Goldsmith and Johnson among others—resented that such characters as Lillo's apprentice George Barnwell or Richardson's servant-girl Pamela should have serious attention paid to them in literature.[143] And the Buckingham Palace librarian, Thomas Mathias, in his vigorous (and very popular) satire on contemporary authors saw, among other evils accruing from the reading of novels, the possibility that young people might not only become morally corrupted thereby, but democratic as well:

Mrs. Charlotte Smith, Mrs. Inchbald, Mrs. Mary Robinson, Mrs. etc., though all of them are very ingenious ladies, yet they are too frequently *whining* or *whisking* in novels, till our girls' heads turn wild with impossible adventures, and are now and then tainted with democracy, and sometimes with infidelity and loose principles.[144]

As the charity schools and the Sunday schools went about fulfilling their missions of increasing the literacy rate among the workers and farmers, the problem of who should read soon became even more controversial than the problem of whom should be written about. In this case the anxiety seems not to have originated with the literati *—insofar as it can be located at all, it seems, rather, to have originated with the non-intellectuals of the middle class. The issues they raised were not aesthetic; they did not fear that literature might become debased in order to meet the tastes and capacities of a working-class audience. The problem was one of economic self-interest: if workers developed a strong predilection for reading, might they not acquire a distaste for manual work along with it?

The gist of the argument against workers reading was that the poor will remain tractable and useful only so long as they are kept in "some degree of ignorance." The Bible, perhaps, might be permitted, but any other type of reading is more than likely to make workers dissatisfied with the "manual labor" which is "destined to occupy their lives." [145] Correctives proposed ranged from putting a complete stop to the teaching of reading to children of the lower classes to censoring their reading so that only religious works would be accessible to them. A letter-to-the-editor in the *Gentleman's Magazine* proposed a rather modern-sounding method of censorship: a citizens' book-reviewing board should be established which would draw up approved reading lists for youth, workers, and other "lower orders." This committee, made up of "worthy persons," would peruse the novel output annually, print their lists in "a monthly publication" and point out "such as were of an improper tendency with candour, and recommending those of merit." [146]

It was in this atmosphere of aesthetic and class concerns that the debate about "taste" took place—what is it, who has it, how can it be acquired?

---

* Samuel Johnson, for one, asked by an affluent acquaintance whether his workers would become less industrious if they were to attend school and learn how to read, answered with an unequivocal "No, Sir."

V. The Defense

In the seventeenth and early eighteenth centuries the slowly expanding upper-middle class, composed of men of business and men of property, had tended to identify with the aesthetic tastes and aspirations of the aristocracy. There was no need for writers to adjust to the professed interests of this new audience because it was indistinguishable from the reading public which had existed before. The problems of the literati had not so much to do with who was to judge literature as with the role of literature in relation to other intellectual pursuits, the limits of the genres, and the place of the poet in the wide scheme of things. Questions might be raised whether the poet excelled the philosopher in his function as teacher (this in the sixteenth century); or about the comparative status of writer and scientist (this in the seventeenth century); or whether the classical rules were the only yardsticks to be legitimately applied in judging a work of literature (this in the early eighteenth).

By the middle of the century a middle class, not only consisting of wealthy businessmen and landowners, but of shopkeepers, clerks, apprentices, and farmers was becoming increasingly affluent, literate, and ambitious. Its literary interests were not necessarily identical with those of the upper classes, its educational background was certainly more primitive and, at the same time, its cultural pretensions were distinctly noticeable. It was, in short, an age when

> all men may procure
> The title of a connoisseur;
> When noble and ignoble herd
> Are govern'd by a single word;
> Though, like the royal German dames,
> It bears an hundred Christian names;
> As genius, fancy, judgment, gout,
> Whim, caprice, je-ne-sais-quoi, vertu;
> Which appellations all describe
> *Taste*, and the modern tasteful tribe.[147]

Or, in the even more pessimistic words of Oliver Goldsmith:

Without assigning causes for this universal presumption [of taste], we shall proceed to observe, that . . . this folly is productive of manifold evils to the community. . . . Hence, the youth of both sexes are debauched to diversion, and seduced from much more profitable occupations into idle endeavours after literary fame; and a superficial, false taste, founded on ignorance and conceit, takes possession of the public.[148]

As a result, a reorientation in aesthetic discussions began to take place. The change was dramatic and unprecedented in the history of letters; its essence was a shift from neo-classical objectivism with its stress on the rational analysis of literary works to concern with the experience of the public.

The new audience did not, by and large, have a classical education, and it placed more emphasis on feelings than on reason. Furthermore, middle-class realism did not allow for pleasure in purely intellectual pursuits. The problem was to get ahead, to improve oneself with practical information—a bent that was to reach a climax in the nineteenth-century craze for the statistical and instantly utilitarian, for the kind of guides and manuals on every activity under the sun which Matthew Arnold found so distressing and which he was to dismiss with the lofty phrase "culture works differently." In such a situation the lines between art and life, between literature and persuasion, between the aesthetic and the emotional experience became easily blurred and often indistinguishable.[149] After the middle of the century the position of the critic is therefore by no means unequivocal. He may speak about the qualities of a book, the intellectual and emotional processes involved in producing it, the critical process of evaluating it—but whatever approach he takes, concern with the experience of the reader or of different types of readers is rarely absent.[150] In short, once the profession of letters depended for support entirely upon the interest, good-will and purchasing habits of a broad public, it began to pay serious attention to the way in which this public experienced literary products and to raise questions about its role in the formulation of literary standards. The task was to distinguish, for the writer and for the public on which he was dependent, between the wheat of art and the chaff of trash.

Most mid-eighteenth century writers were themselves part of the bourgeoisie which came into its own in the course of the industrial revolution. Its empiricist spirit informed their approach to literary problems; and the ways in which they endeavored to cope with the demands of an increasingly diversified public were as pluralistic as the tastes of that public itself—ranging from Oliver Goldsmith's belief that the "universal presumption" to taste would have a "debauching" effect to Edmund Burke's faith in the idea of democracy in literary standards. By the middle of the century almost every writer of note could point to at least one essay—and often a volume —on the subject of taste.

This section will indicate briefly how the man of letters formulated the problem, how he searched for literary standards which would take the taste of "all men" into account; how this search led, at one extreme, to elite concepts and, at the other extreme, to the idea of diversity. Finally, we shall see how the concept of diversity in taste and judgment harbingered a change in the critic's role.

The Discussion about Taste.   In the debate about the validity of the classical rules, the issues had been rational and sharply defined: Should the writer adhere to the dramatic unities? Should he imitate the early Greek and Roman models or was he free to express his individuality in his own fashion? As the century progressed, individualizing, as it were, psychological aspects of a democratic society gradually came to take precedence over rationalist absolutes. Analyses of "wit" and "judgment," terms which were applied to the interplay of the sophisticated intellect with images and ideas, gave way to analyses of such concepts as "imagination," "enthusiasm," and finally "genius." "Genius," in turn, became synonymous with originality. Where the poet had in former times functioned as a high artificer, he emerged, toward the latter part of the century, as an inspired instrument of the poetic furor, working by seizure rather than by thought. The earlier set of critical categories had placed a premium on objectivity, reason, and knowledge; the new categories focussed on subjective qualities of emotion and spontaneous creativity.

Addison, though he wrote in the early part of the century when the discussion about the rules still flourished, had pioneered in the analysis of imaginative writing. He spoke of "imagination" not in abstract aesthetic terms but in terms of the appeal of imaginative works for the reader, using concepts related to everyday human experience. He addressed himself to all those "middle-station" people whom he conceived to be fit audience for the *Spectator*. His essays on imagination, indeed, predicated a great many categories which have appeared in most subsequent discussions of popular culture, including *variety, diversion,* the appeal of *facts,* and the emotional *gratifications* involved in hearing or reading about torture and other forms of horror.[151]

A later, less pedagogic and at the same time less optimistic approach than that of Addison was to differentiate among the various segments of the public in matters of literary judgment. Goldsmith, in examining the theater audience, observed that those who could afford seats in the pits at the Drury Lane and Covent Garden were ostentatiously eager to "show their taste," but "not one in a hundred," he felt, was qualified to do so.[152] And in less class-conscious but similarly statistical terms the critic Joseph Warton discriminated between two levels of the audience, one which could appreciate the works of genius, another sensitized only to commonplace products. Warton was rather more liberal in his estimate than Goldsmith:

> For one person who can adequately relish, and enjoy a work of imagination, twenty are to be found who can taste and judge of observations on familiar life and the manners of the age.[153]

In short, to the bewildering problem for the writer as to the kinds of standards which were to take the place of the now discredited classical rules, was added the cultural ambition of a public whose judgments often seemed "false" to him. The task for the writer, then, was to search out some means by which to reconcile these various tastes with his own artistic integrity.

Not the least conspicuous feature of mid-eighteenth century thought was a faith in the perfectibility of human nature which seemed to go hand in hand with faith in material progress. Is it not possible, several writers began to ask, that it is merely lack of proper education which keeps the audience from developing into true connoisseurs?

Turning once more to Oliver Goldsmith, we find him questioning whether "natural" good taste was not being corrupted by the numerous examples of "false" taste which prove singularly attractive to the "unwary mind and young imagination."[154] And this suggests, despite his disparaging remarks about the actual competence of the theater audience, that Goldsmith gave some credence to a concept of "innate" standards of judgment which, if they could be corrupted, could also be improved. Fielding, while he agreed that "natural taste" could so be corrupted, expressed even more aptly

than Goldsmith the characteristic faith in progress when he described
how the "small seeds of taste" which are present in practically all
men can be fructified by training and education. Fielding goes on to
say that he will "probably . . . in a future paper endeavour to lay
down some rules by which all men may acquire some degree of
taste." [155] That this paper was not written serves as one commentary
on the obstacles met in attempting to seek out and describe those
bases of judgment which all men were presumed to hold in
common.

The Search for Common Standards. Three paths were followed
in the search for common principles: (1) recourse to a feeling of
"inner conviction" that there must be such principles; (2) attempts
to prove their existence by deriving them from certain tests; and
(3) efforts to deduce them by determining how they work. At no
point, however, did any analyst of taste get so far as to describe or
define what those principles might in fact be.

(1) The first of the three approaches—the argument of inner
conviction—started early in the century and sought validation by
pointing to "simple" people who manifested clear judgment and true
taste. Anticipating the admiration later to be accorded the "natural"
man, the "noble savage," and the "unspoilt child," the *Tatler*, for
example, had presented a young woman "who had that natural sense
which makes her a better judge than a thousand critics," and the
Guardian pointed to a foot soldier as the "politest man in a British
audience, from the force of nature, untainted with the singularities
of an ill-applied education." [156] Later, in a philosophical vein, Hume
and Burke (the latter in his early aesthetic writings) based their
concepts of taste common to all men on their own inner conviction
that universal standards of judgment exist. Burke, in his *Essay on
Taste*, first defined his subject as "that faculty or those faculties of
the mind, which are effected with, or which form a judgment of, the
works of imagination and the elegant arts." The objective of his
inquiry is

to find whether there are any principles, on which the imagination is
affected, so common to all, so grounded and certain, as to supply the
means of reasoning satisfactorily about them. And such principles of
taste I fancy there are . . .[157]

As we shall presently see, however, though Burke continued his essay by discussing the human faculties involved in the acquisition of taste, he neither isolated any particular principles, nor did he demonstrate that "common" human faculties underlie them. Hume similarly postulated the universality of taste. All people whose "organs" are sound have a "considerable uniformity of sentiment" and from this uniformity "we may thence derive an idea of the perfect and universal beauty." [158] But Hume, too, failed to specify common aesthetic principles.

Even those who clung strongly to the idea of uniformity in taste in the abstract could not avoid the evidence of considerable disagreement when it came to judging a given work. Failing to define the common principles they sought, they could at least describe, and attempt to explain away, those tastes which were so deviant that they could not be considered manifestations of the assumed principles. Burke, who was echoed almost word for word by the Scottish literary critic Hugh Blair a few years later, resorted to the analogy of sensory taste in discussing these deviants. He pointed out that a man might be found who could not distinguish between milk and vinegar or who called both tobacco and vinegar sweet, milk bitter, and sugar sour. Such a man, said Burke, cannot be considered a person of taste, nor can he even be called a man of wrong taste. He is, quite simply, "absolutely mad":

> . . . when it is said, taste cannot be disputed, it can only mean that no one can strictly answer what pleasure or pain some particular man may find from the taste of some particular thing . . . but we may dispute, and with sufficient clearness too, concerning the things which are naturally pleasing or disagreeable to the sense.[159] *

It remained for Lord Kames to draw most unequivocally upon inner conviction as "proof" of the existence of a common set of artistic standards. When he attempted to demonstrate his belief, however, he moved far from the concept of universality.

Like most critics and philosophers who tried to reduce the multiplicity of tastes in the eighteenth-century audience to some common denominator, Kames began by asserting that there is a

---

* Blair, in his *Lectures on Rhetoric*, writes: "If any one should maintain that sugar was bitter and tobacco was sweet, no reasoning could avail to prove it. The taste of such a person would infallibly be held to be diseased, merely because it differed so widely from the taste of the species to which he belongs." [3 vols., Basle, 1801, V. 1, 35]

"universal conviction" in the sphere of morality and went on to state
that "This conviction of common nature or standard . . . accounts
not less clearly for the conception we have of a right and a wrong
taste in the fine arts." Kames disposed of the extreme exceptions in
the same way as Burke: "The individual who dislikes objects which
most people like or who conversely likes objects which most other
people dislike" is "a monster." His principal argument for the
existence of uniform taste is the fact that works of art are acknowledged as such:

> We are formed . . . with an uniformity of taste . . . if uniformity
> of taste did not prevail, the fine arts could never have made any figure.

A "conviction of a common standard," he concludes, is therefore
"part of our nature." [160]

(2) Further validation of the inner conviction theory was sometimes sought by the application of certain "tests." Cultural products
exist; those which have a universal appeal and which have stood the
test of time can be accepted as proof of the existence of common
standards. Addison had anticipated the universality test: the fact that
he, a cultivated English gentleman, could enjoy the folk songs of all
countries in which he traveled demonstrated that whatever is enjoyed by "a multitude" must have been judged by a universal
standard:

> Human Nature is the same in all reasonable Creatures; and whatever
> falls in with it, will meet with Admirers amongst Readers of all Qualities
> and Conditions. [161]

Joshua Reynolds in his *Discourses* picked up this argument—all questions of taste can be settled by an appeal to the "sense" which all
mankind has in common. He, too, avoided the question of what
standards, principles, or criteria compose this common sense. What
he does say is that the better acquainted a writer is with the works
of various periods and of various countries, the more likely is it that
he will be able to derive these unspecified—but uniform—standards.
To the test of universality, Reynolds then added the test of
permanence.

> What has pleased, and continues to please, is likely to please again:
> hence are derived the rules of art. [162]

If one accepts these two proofs of the existence of common artistic standards, as most mid-century writers evidently did accept them, it follows, as Hugh Blair put it in his *Lectures on Rhetoric,* that it is to the concurrence of the majority that one must look for standards of taste:

> That which men concur the most in admiring must be held to be beautiful. His taste must be esteemed just and true, which coincides with the general sentiments of men. In this standard we must rest . . . the common feelings of men carry the same authority, and have a title to regulate the taste of every individual.[163]

Thus did the writers of the mid-eighteenth century pay their respects to their new patrons, the great audience. But the discussion did not end on a note of faith in a common denominator.

(3) The works of Lord Kames, particularly his *Elements of Criticism,* illustrate the entanglement in which those who attempted to describe the workings of common principles found themselves.[164] He begins by equating the now familiar terms—common nature, common sense, common standards—with good taste. By and large, Kames observes, every man is aware that such common standards exist. Like Burke and Blair, he condemns the taste of the individual whose judgment deviates: "We justly condemn every taste that swerves from what is thus ascertained by the common standard." At the same time he postulates the mysterious "we" (which also appears in Burke's remarks on taste) endowed with the right to condemn.

The crucial question becomes, then, who constitutes this "we," and here, despite his use of the term "common" standards, Kames begins to differentiate. In the sphere of moral judgment he feels that one may rely on "everyone's" standards. When it comes to judgment in literature and the arts it will hardly do to "collect votes indifferently." In the aesthetic domain "a wary choice" must be made. His preliminary assumption of a "universal conviction" notwithstanding, Kames goes on specifically to exclude the greater part of mankind from the right to contribute to the "common" standard. "Particularly"—and here Kames establishes rigid class lines in what seems to have started as a democratic premise—"particularly all those who depend for food on bodily labor are totally devoid of taste." They can share in the formulation of moral principles and they must comply with them, but they can have no voice in the worlds of art and literature.* But Kames is not content to stop with the elimination of workers; there are others to be disenfranchised in cultural matters. At the other extreme are the rich and opulent who delight in conspicuous consumption, who are "voluptuous" both morally and aesthetically, and these, too, are disqualified. Since the manifest objective of this upper crust is simply to "amaze and humble all beholders," they can have no understanding of the "faint and delicate emotions of the fine arts." All that remains are those individuals who maintain a strict separation from the lower orders but who at the same time are free from envy or imitation of the members of the aristocratic remnants of the Restoration period and their obsolete style of life. Furthermore, within this group, which by now is defined as the middle class, only those can become judges who have "good natural taste . . . improved by education, reflection and experience." In other words, only the intellectual elite are qualified to evaluate cultural products—a clear instance of the intellectual defining his social role as the mentor and cultural leader of the new middle-class order.

Having narrowed those capable of aesthetic judgment to a chosen few, Kames then doubles on his tracks and once more assures his reader that the "good" and "bad" qualities in cultural products are clearly discernible and that "mankind" is able to distinguish between them. His elite theory becomes democratic once more by means of postponement: you have only to wait until the standards now formulated and applied by the select few will be recognized as universal by all mankind. And that time, Kames is confident, is bound to come.

For David Hume it remained to summarize most succinctly the contradictory position which was maintained by those who sought universal criteria for the judging of art. Hume stated that the principles of taste are universal "and nearly if not entirely the same in all men;" but he concluded this very sentence with the observation that "few are qualified to give judgment on any work of art, or establish their own sentiment as the standard of beauty." [165]

---

* This is a far cry from the unqualified remarks of Addison earlier in the century, before the middle classes were making their tastes clearly felt through purchases of literary products. Prior to his statement that "Human Nature is the same in all reasonable Creatures," Addison had said: ". . . it is impossible that any thing should be universally tasted or approved by a Multitude, tho' they are only the Rabble of a Nation, which hath not in it some peculiar Aptness to please and gratifie the Mind of Man." (*Spectator*, No. 70.)

Kames, Hume, and Blair are foremost among the critics who, beginning with the idea—or the hope—that standards for the judging of literary and other cultural products are held in common by all men, arrived at a conclusion almost the very opposite: the "all" spelled out to read a select few. Other writers and critics who looked for a common, egalitarian principle with as little success escaped from the dilemma by formulating concepts which may be subsumed under the rubric "the idea of diversity."

From Universality to Diversity. To recapitulate briefly, we have traced three phases in the discussion about the new public and the literary goods produced for it. First, a period of hope during which the men of letters waited for the aesthetic proclivities of this public to catch up with their moral inclinations. Second, a period of "opportunity and opportunism," when new writers and new products developed at a rapid rate, and the literati adopted a policy of watchful waiting. Third, a period of dismay among the intellectuals during which both audience and media were severely strictured. The controversy over "taste" might be said to constitute a fourth period. This discussion, as we have seen, was conducted as though the participants hoped that the manifold differences in taste, and the obviously low level of taste in some segments of the audience, were more apparent than real, and that they would eventually find underlying standards on which both artist and audience could agree. But the exploration came to nothing more than to a more or less general agreement: those literary and artistic accomplishments which hold up through space and time are "good," be they folk ballads or Greek sculpture, and the fact that some such achievements do so hold up indicates that common standards of judgment do exist. These assertions were of little practical avail in resolving the conflict between the integrity of the artist and the inclinations of the public which paid the piper. What did emerge from the exploration, however, was a widespread conviction that the experience of this public had to be taken into account in any discussions of literary standards.

As the search for common standards waned, such psychological and descriptive concepts as perception, individual differences, national differences, and "comparative" or "historical" views became increasingly conspicuous in the works of the critics, who paid increasing attention to the need for enjoyment, pleasure, amusement, and recreation. The emphasis, in short, was placed more and more on the analysis of the audience experience, as though in the hope that a study of reader gratifications would lead inductively to new knowledge about the nature of "common" standards.

To what extent this shift in emphasis resulted from the writer's dependence on his audience and to what extent it reflected the absence of powerful literary figures is a moot question. Fielding expounded a "great man" theory in an almost sociological vein. In a *Covent Garden Journal* article on the "Commonwealth of Literature," he traced the general state of literature through a variety of phases: first, an "ecclesiastical" democracy; then a period of absolutism coexistent with the political absolutism in the age of Henry VIII; next, an era of literary aristocracy, headed first by Shakespeare, Ben Jonson, and Beaumont and Fletcher, next by Dryden, and finally by Pope, whom Fielding always sees as literary autocrat. But in his own period, Fielding sees a decline in literary leadership; "after the demise of King Alexandre the literary state relapsed again into a democracy, or rather into downright anarchy . . ."[166]

While the stress on the effects of literary works on their readers became dominant, not all of the writers, philosophers, and literary critics involved in the discussion of standards were in agreement as to whether the experience of the audience should be looked upon as the only valid basis for literary criteria. Kames and Blair began their search for standards with the assumption that beauty lies in the eye of the beholder. Hume and Burke, on the other hand, began with the assumption that beauty is a quality residing in the object itself.[167] But it is characteristic of the descriptive approach which came into being at this time that even those who began with a premise of objective standards moved from the application of general principles such as reason, truth, and nature toward the development of long and detailed compendia of the attributes of literary works. Such itemizations may be found, for example, in Burke's *On the Sublime and Beautiful*, in which he isolates and describes literary qualities such as smoothness, sweetness, variety, smallness, color, aggregate words, abstract words, everyday words, and the like.[168] These compendia, in turn, served as a point of departure for an impressionistic analysis of reader experience.

In general, three early approaches to the problem of effects can be distinguished. The first we might call relative; the second psychological; the third descriptive. Needless to say, then as now these categories overlapped conspicuously.

Relative concepts had some history in the world of letters before the participants in the taste controversy got hold of them. The *Tatler*, as early as 1710, had suggested that the way of life and the peculiarities of a writer or a reader serve to some extent to condition their respective tastes.[169] This concept of "relativity" (which is in reality a qualified endorsement of diversity in taste) finds a good deal of application in the works of Addison and the later writers who explored such questions as the relationship between exposure and taste. The idea of relativity also became manifest in a new approach to the study of literature itself. Pope, for example, in the preface to his controversial edition of Shakespeare, had stressed the importance of historical, climatic, and national factors in the conditioning of ideas as to what constitutes good or bad literature.[170] But it was Johnson who, in his *Lives*, set the stage for the comparative historical study of literature as well as, incidentally, for exact textual study.[171] The comparative study of literature, in short, went hand in hand with the comparative approach to the study of the *impact* of literary works.

There was a strong relationship between such comparative or relative approaches and the psychological theories and hypotheses which were being aired at the same time. The expression "association of ideas" seems to have become a favorite one in the analysis of audience experience, and there was general agreement that a great variety of such associations could be expected when a widely assorted group of people were exposed to the same work. Pleasure in literary experience thus was more and more conceived as a matter of individual sentiment, not necessarily connected with objective standards of beauty or reason. Whatever a given individual with his own perceptive mechanisms found agreeable was also acceptable.[172] Even Johnson, despite his firmer adherence to rational principles, insisted that these were subordinate to individual response. If such principles are to be applied, he felt, they must be applied with caution, and he goes on to speak of "the cant of those who judge by principles rather than perception." [173]

At the other extreme of the descriptive approach we find those who brushed rules aside altogether, and justified their doing so on the grounds that the audience reacts impulsively in the process of reading and does not have time, even though it might have the capacity, to apply them. *The Monthly Review,* for one, supported Lord Kames' attack on the rules on these very grounds, and paraphrased him with approval:

> For when the mind is affected or disgusted, the affection or aversion takes place, as it were, by impulse and gives no time for the formal application of given principles to influence the judgment.[174]

The long-range effect of this new attention to audience experience was to legitimize emotional gratifications. While it is clear that an endorsement of emotion has persisted to the present time, it is by no means apparent to what extent the shift from the application of rational standards to the analysis of emotional response was the result of the need to take into account a new mass audience and a new group of literary products. What is clear, as a recent historian has put it, is that "examination of the mechanism of the mind by more philosophical thinkers like Hume resulted in the analysis of reason into imagination and belief, of common sense into intuition. The basis of classical art was shattered by these blows . . . and uncertainty paved the way for the emphasis on emotion as the most important factor in life and art." [175]

Recognition of this kind of gratification was comparatively unknown in the early decades of the century, when any literary or other cultural product had to subordinate (or pretend to subordinate) pleasure to moral uplift. For the first time in the century we find terms such as "relaxation" and "amusement" used without apology:

> Such is the nature of man, that his powers and faculties are soon blunted by exercise. . . . During his waking hours, amusement by intervals is requisite to unbend his mind from serious occupation. The imagination . . . contributes more than any other cause to recruit the mind and restore its vigor, by amusing us with gay and ludicrous images; and when relaxation is necessary, such amusement is much relished.[176]

This acknowledgment has no didactic overtones. It was as if a sense of defeatism in the search for a common aesthetic perception in the audience were accompanied by a sense of release from the obligation to assist in its moral reformation. Hume, for example, discusses how man seeks to escape from the pressures which weary him when he is alone with his thoughts:

> To get rid of this painful situation, it [the mind] seeks every amusement and pursuit; business, gaming, shows, executions; whatever will rouse the passions, and take its attention from itself.

He proceeds to list the kinds of passion that may be aroused by such means and remarks that whether they be agreeable or disagreeable, happy or sad, confused or orderly, they are still preferable to "the insipid languor" of a man thrown back upon his own inner resources. He points to the gambling room to validate his thesis; wherever the most exciting play is going on, most members of the company may be found, even though that table may not have the best players. To identify with people who are experiencing the passions of loss or gain is to relieve oppression:

> It makes the time pass the easier with them, and is some relief to that oppression, under which men commonly labour, when left entirely to their own thoughts and meditations.[177]

Archibald Alison, a critic writing later in the century, analyzed the various "qualities of mind" which can be evoked by reading. He even distinguished between passive and active gratifications:

> The qualities of mind which are capable of producing emotion, are either its active or its passive qualities; either its *powers* and capacities, as beneficence, wisdom, fortitude, invention, fancy, etc., or its *feelings and affections*, as love, joy, hope, gratitude, purity, fidelity, innocence, etc.[178]

As in many analyses of audience experience undertaken after the middle of the century, one is struck by Alison's pragmatism, which is in such strong contrast to the moralizing tone uppermost in the middle of the century. It was this almost scientific approach to the experience of the audience which paved the way for a new conception of the critic's role.

The Critic as Mediator. Dissatisfaction with the kinds of rigid and pedantic literary criticism which had prevailed in the early part of the century had been brewing for some time. Swift already had attacked such pedantry; his *Battle of the Books* overflows with denunciations of the "malignant deity, called Criticism." The mixture of bookishness and glibness in these critics was of no benefit other than to give "the coffee house wits some basis for literary pretensions." [179] Pope, who needed no inspiration from Swift on the subject (although he apparently got a great deal of it), similarly attacked the destructiveness, or at best the futility, of those who lived by petty and often meaningless attacks on the writing of others. Nothing is sacred to these critics; on any subject "they'll talk you dead/ For Fools rush in where Angels fear to tread." [180] Later Goldsmith, in discussing German writings, echoed the disdain of his eminent predecessors for this type of critical hairsplitting:

> Their assiduity is unparalleled; . . . they write through volumes while they do not think through a page. Never fatigued themselves, they think the reader can never be weary; so they drone on, saying all that can be said on the subject, not selecting what may be advanced to the purpose.[181]

Again it was Addison who presaged a new concept, this time of the critic's role. He was to be creative and constructive: in a word, a "revealer of beauties." Beginning with Addison's influential pieces on *Paradise Lost* in the *Spectator*, almost every important author had at least one book-length criticism written about his work entitled *The Beauties of* . . . .[182] This concept of a revelatory function for the critic implied that he was to assume a role of responsibility in relation to the general public as well as to his fellow writers and intellectuals, and most of the writers and critics of the mid-century followed suit. It was the critic's function, as Johnson put it, to help men "to enjoy life or to endure it." [183] At the same time, it was characteristic of the mid-century writers—in their optimistic mood —to view the critic's contribution as a means of raising the aesthetic level of the public. In this light, the critic has an educational role. Goldsmith sees him—and he is speaking of the "man of taste" as contrasted with the scholar or compiler—as "placed in a middle station, between the world and the cell, between learning and common sense."

But perhaps the most far-reaching change which took place in the concept of the critic was that a two-way function was premised for him. Not only was he to reveal the beauties of literary works to the general public by means of which, in Goldsmith's terms, "even the philosopher may acquire popular applause"; he must also interpret the public back to the writer. In brief, the critic not only "teaches the vulgar on what part of a character to lay the emphasis of praise," he must also show "the scholar where to point his application so as to deserve it." Goldsmith believed that the absence of such critical mediators explained why wealth rather than true literary fame was the goal of so many writers. The result, he feared, might be that nothing would be remembered of the literary works of his time.[184]

We have observed that Goldsmith, in his endeavor to come to grips with the dilemma of the writer, represented a variety of sometimes conflicting views. We have seen, however, that it was likely to be Goldsmith in his optimistic rather than in his pessimistic vein who set the tone for what was to come. So, too, his view of the "ideal" critic, of his function as one of mediation between the audience and the writer, was to prevail. Critics, writers, and philosophers, such as Johnson, Burke, Hume, Reynolds, Kames, and the Wartons, all adopted his premise as they began to analyze the experience of the reader.

A critic must try to understand what goes on in the minds of the readers. In Johnson's words he must

. . . improve opinion into knowledge, and . . . distinguish those means of pleasing which depend upon known causes.

Johnson then outlines what we might today look upon as a scientific, descriptive approach to the study of media experience, pointing out that

. . . literary criticism, which has . . . hitherto known only the anarchy of ignorance, the caprices of fancy and the tyranny of prescription . . . can now be placed under the dominion of science.[185]

Joseph Wood Krutch points to him as the formulator of the concept that the critic "derives his right from the rights of the general public of which he is a part—not from the fact that he *is* a critic. He will generally agree with the public's considered judgment because literature is to be judged, not in the light of learning . . . but in accordance with the same common sense which guides us as we go about the business of life." [186] It was this orientation to audience experience which opened up an entirely new dimension in the debate over art and popular culture. In spite of their conflicts and contradictions, the mid-eighteenth century English writers paved the way for the nineteenth century critics and philosophers who were to formulate the metaphysics of cultural democracy. They were the first to recognize the importance, in an increasingly industrialized and mobile society, of relaxation, amusement, and escape from the pressures of work, whether the individual be a tired businessman or a manual worker, and in so doing were far more detached than were their counterparts across the Channel. While Hume, for one, analyzed the psychological factors involved in "distraction" or amusement, Schiller and Goethe were to take a moral position: the public may need distraction, but unless they find a less passive way to achieve it, culture will surely degenerate.

Lee Benson

RESEARCH PROBLEMS
IN AMERICAN POLITICAL
HISTORIOGRAPHY

I. Introduction

An American historian's lot is not an easy one. His beat is a country of continental proportions, peopled by an incredible number of intermingled ethnic and religious groups physically and socially mobile to an unparalleled degree. Moreover, it is a country settled at different times and in different ways. The economy and its re- source patterns have been. and are. extraordinarily diverse and dynamic. Small wonder that of the making of "new" interpretations there is no end. Probably one major reason for the rapid fluctuations and relative lack of consensus characterizing our historiography is the difficulty inherent in explaining American political development. In the absence of a well-defined common methodology, and the presence of a near-universal dependence upon impressionistic tech- niques and data, one might reasonably expect to find that different frames of reference, training, interests, access to data, etc., result in a splendid profusion of varying interpretations. Such expectations are satisfied by a survey of the literature of American political history. If it does nothing more, a survey of this kind demonstrates that among historians—if nowhere else, "rugged individualism" still holds forth.[1]

Scholarly initiative and independent-mindedness can only be applauded, but it is suggested here that fluctuating views and lack of consensus among political historians are best attributed to other factors. For example, presidential elections have tended to be the major foci of American political history, and usually they also have been taken, in some degree at least, as measures of economic, social, cultural, religious, and other developments. Setting aside the basic theoretical question of whether such an orientation is really desirable, it seems correct to assert that historians *do not yet have available the systematic data necessary to begin to interpret voting behavior, nor the methodological techniques to handle such data were they available.* (The terms, "systematic data" and "systematic methods," will be defined below.) In effect, historians are called upon to answer the "why" of American presidential elections without knowing the "what" and the "who." That is, historians do not now have available to them, in meaningful and easily workable form, the basic election statistics over time and space, nor anything but the scantiest verified data on who (what groups) voted for whom, when.[2] *It is the central proposition of this study that historians, therefore, have found it extremely difficult to function as historians and view political developments in long-term perspective. Instead, each election is usually treated as a separate phenomenon, and interpretations of voting behavior at one time do not rest upon detailed comparison with voting behavior over time and space.* As will be emphasized below, this *ahistorical* tendency is not attributed to the failings of individuals; on the contrary, it is believed to reflect the difficulties confronting all students of political behavior in the United States.

Primarily, the study is designed to focus attention upon problems of interpretation which result from lack of detailed voting data over time and space, and from the present unsystematic techniques of handling available data. It also discusses a tentative method *to identify potentially verifiable hypotheses* originally derived from impressionistic research, and, conversely, one which can be carried further *to formulate potentially verifiable hypotheses.* The concept, "potentially verifiable," will be considered later.

Perhaps the best perspective for the reader to adopt is that the study is basically designed to raise questions, call attention to research problems in political history, and serve as a springboard for their discussion. It does not report the results of intensive research in political history based upon primary or secondary sources, nor does it do more than sketch in rough outline a methodological procedure to facilitate intensive research in political history. But in order to demonstrate the need for such a procedure, as well as the possibility of its attainment, the study analyzes conclusions reached by qualified scholars concerning a variety of significant political contests.

Understandably, because the data concerning spatial distribution of voting behavior over time are not available in manageable form, historians have tended to treat each election in isolated fashion. This observation applies even to presidential contests where national and state totals at least are not difficult to ascertain; when historians deal with Congressional results for the country at large, or state and local elections, their problem regarding statistics is much greater. Yet it is almost axiomatic that without the voting data for elections on *all levels*, interpretations of American elections on any *one level* cannot be regarded as comprehensive.

That the inadequacies of available quantitative data severely handicap historians in interpreting elections can be seen from the examples which follow. In one form or another they show the same basic pattern: voting determinants are deduced from impressionistic research and little attempt is made to specify the conditions under which they operate, or the type of data necessary to establish that they actually are the voting determinants in a given election. Prominent historians and highly regarded works have been deliberately chosen to point up the representative quality of these examples, as well as to demonstrate a variety of interpretative problems. But the choice of particular hypotheses for examination *was not* based upon an evaluation of their intrinsic significance, nor the importance attached to them by their authors. The hypotheses were selected because their formulations permit unambiguous evaluation, because they reflect the impressionistic approach long dominant in American political historiography, and because they fit in with the structural design of this study. I trust that the tone of the analysis is non-polemical and therefore consonant with its purpose. Employment of the case method, it is anticipated, will focus attention upon some basic historiographic problems rather than upon specific elections and interpretations of them.

Since the analysis focuses upon secondary works which treat a wide range of complex developments, data is marshalled in a manner designed to evaluate hypotheses or propositions already stated to be valid or proven. But the preliminary results of research now in progress indicate that the technique can also be applied to the *formulation* of hypotheses when the requisite systematic data is collected, analyzed, and organized into easily-worked categories.

Time, Space, and Rate Dimensions. In their explorations, historians are limited to three dimensions: time, space, and rate. Though no meaningful inquiry into human behavior can really dispense with the time dimension, until now the historian has been distinguished from workers in other disciplines by his unique emphasis upon the chronological order of events. But emphasis on the recording, analysis, and relationship of events over time hardly means that the more removed the investigation is from the present moment the more "historical" it is. Studies of ancient Egypt can be fundamentally "unhistorical," and studies of contemporary phenomena might be historical in the best sense of that much abused word.

For our purposes the problems of securing access to contemporary source materials and acquiring historical perspective are irrelevant. As employed here, the time dimension essentially connotes the *process* of charting, analyzing, and relating the chronological distribution of events. But, if the requisite data is available, it is also possible to handle similarly the spatial distribution of phenomena at any given moment in time. Combining the two dimensions, that is, studying both the chronological and spatial distribution of phenomena, permits one to obtain a far closer approximation to reality than if either dimension is employed alone. To make the study really dynamic, however, it is necessary to introduce the rate dimension, or the dimension which measures the *pace* of events as well as their chronological and spatial distribution.[3] Basically a function of the time dimension, the rate measure is important enough in its own right to warrant separate demarcation. One might know that certain phenomena almost uniformly succeed other phenomena, but the historical processes of development would differ significantly if the rate of succession varied from place to place.

Under ideal conditions, the historian, fully armed, can be expected to carry out his explorations in three dimensions. He is able to study the unfolding of events over time, their distribution over space, and their *relative rate over both time and space*. But conditions are rarely ideal and in practice more or less of his time and resources are given to one or the other dimensions according to the

here deal with American presidential elections, the primary test is to state the hypothesis' claims in terms of the systematic data most pertinent to it, i.e., the statistics of voting behavior. If the hypothesis fails to satisfy those stipulations when the pertinent voting statistics are made available and subjected to close analysis, it either must be reformulated or held to be demonstrably invalid. *That is, for our purposes, a potentially verifiable hypothesis is one consonant with the statistics of voting behavior, systematically collected, organized, and analyzed.* In the present monograph testing will not go beyond a systematic analysis of pertinent voting statistics. But that operation might be clarified by noting that the likelihood of verifying a hypothesis is increased if additional kinds of data are stipulated and their satisfaction demonstrated.

Possible Contributions of Systematic Research Methods to Political Historiography. Perhaps another useful preliminary to the concrete case studies presented below is to discuss briefly some of the contributions systematic research methods might make to political historiography. Stated in oversimplified terms, let us consider a hypothesis which claims that the nomination of a candidate possessed of a blemished political past led to sharp departures from normal voting patterns in a certain presidential election. Though his nomination by the party long entrenched in power is stated to be the *direct causal factor*, the *basic condition* shaping the election outcome is held to be a widespread, deeply-felt conviction that his party's growing corruption made a political change imperative.

Assuming the hypothesis to be valid, a difficult problem must be faced at the outset. How can we go about *establishing* its validity so that experts will attach a *substantial* degree of credence to it? (*Substantial* is deliberately not defined more precisely here. It only implies a greater degree of credibility for one hypothesis than for any other suggested as an explanation of the same phenomenon.) What is necessary is to marshal systematic data supporting the hypothesis' claims concerning both the basic condition governing the election and the causal factor directly determining voting behavior. In the first instance, in line with the discussion above, it is necessary to demonstrate that the hypothesis is consonant with the systematic data derived from voting statistics.

But before we can begin to marshal the requisite data it is necessary to reformulate the hypothesis. As it stands it is too general.

Among other things, we cannot tell as yet what stipulations the voting data must satisfy for the hypothesis to be potentially verifiable. The direct causal factor can be taken as a case in point, i.e., a particular candidate's nomination by the party in power. Obviously, we are not required to show that *every vote* cast in the election was determined by his candidacy. Equally obvious, we do not have to show his candidacy to have been the *sole* determinant of any *single* vote. But the hypothesis does require us to make some explicit statement subject to verification. Merely asserting that the candidate cost his party enough votes to lose the election puts the problem in so general a form as to prevent demonstration that he cost them any votes.

Depending upon the degree of precision and persuasion sought, it is necessary to state the *number* and *kind* of voters who decided to vote against the party in power, to a greater or lesser extent, because its candidate was suspect. Moreover, it is not enough to say that certain votes were determined by his nomination. To carry conviction the hypothesis must offer some explanation of why those votes were affected adversely from his party's viewpoint, and why *others were not.* Again, no implication is intended that the hypothesis must account for all voting decisions in the election or assign an exact weight to a causal factor as a determinant of any single vote. But it is worth repeating that the hypothesis' verification requires us to provide systematic data supporting our interpretation of two different kinds of voting behavior; voters who were sufficiently disturbed by the nomination of a suspect candidate to express their dissatisfaction at the polls, and voters who were not affected. Nonetheless, though the problem now is somewhat more clearly defined, we still have not indicated how to go about securing the requisite data.

It is a key proposition of this study that no interpretation of an election outcome can begin to be verified until the description of what happened is translated into who (voting groups) caused it to happen. The term, "who," refers to any characteristic distinguishing certain voters from other voters. The distinguishing characteristic can range from full socio-economic descriptions to the extremely specialized case of voters who listened to a particular campaign address. That is, even a systematic descriptive statement of party victory or defeat, gain or loss, etc., does not permit interpretation.

We must designate explicitly the group, or groups of voters, affected by an issue, or set of issues—in this case, past political corruption—before we can systematically marshal voting statistics and other data to support our interpretation of what happened. In other words, using the time dimension, this question must be answered before we can proceed: "Who voted for whom, when?" Broadly speaking, distinguishing features can be of two types: *group characteristics* of particular voters (religion, economic class, ethnic origins, urban-rural, socio-economic status, etc.); or *operative conditions* in a certain place at a certain time (economic depression, heightened sectional conflicts, intense religious or ethnic antagonisms, etc.), without direct reference to the group characteristics of voters living in that area. It is also possible to combine the two types of distinguishing features so as to specify the different responses of particular groups of voters (e.g., "Yankees" and Irish-Americans) living in areas affected by certain conditions (e.g., low socio-economic-status districts in an area experiencing economic depression). Subject to the number of variables introduced, combinations of the two broad types of distinguishing features can be devised to achieve greater precision.

The *group characteristics* and *operative conditions types* of distinction have at least one feature in common. They enable us to make some specification concerning *differentiated* patterns of voting behavior which are subject to systematic verification. For example, if in our hypothetical study the Republicans were the party in power, we might claim that as a result of the corruption issue Yankees *generally* were "less Republican than usual," Irish-Americans *generally* were "as Republican as usual." We could then go on to make more precise claims: Yankees in both high and low socio-economic-status areas experiencing depression were "*much less* Republican than usual," Irish-Americans were "less Republican than usual" only in depressed, low socio-economic-status areas, Yankees in both high and low socio-economic-status areas enjoying *prosperity* were "less Republican than usual," etc.

Implicit in these claims is the premise that Yankees as a group were historically more responsive than Irish-Americans to the issue of corruption; a premise which would require demonstration for the hypothesis to be verified. Moreover, although these claims specify certain *operative conditions* and non-ethnic *group characteristics* as

increasing or decreasing the impact of corruption upon voting behavior, they also hold that "Yankees" as a group were demonstrably
more responsive to the issue in the particular election studied.

Granted our ability to employ systematic methods to compile
the data and construct the indexes implicit in the factual claims made
above concerning voting performance, they can be demonstrated to
be valid or invalid. Obviously, such demonstrations would not
"prove" the causal inferences but their consonance with the systematic data of voting performance would give some credence to
them. Having identified "Yankees" as a group responsive to the corruption issue in a given election, and having demonstrated their
actual voting performance to be consonant with that interpretation,
we could then attempt to present other supporting data. *In sum, only
after we have stated and demonstrated who voted for whom, when,
can we tackle the far more complex problem of establishing why
they did so.*

Though anything but easy in reality, the process of specifying
differentiated types of voting behavior patterns is simple compared
to that involved in assigning *relative weight* to a given causal factor
as a determinant of voting behavior. Probably few historians mean
to contend that a *single* factor is the *sole* determinant in any election,
despite the fact that their terminology frequently lends itself to that
conclusion. Thus two separate but interrelated types of problems
exist: how to assign different weights to more than one causal factor,
and how to assign *different* weights to the *same* causal factor according to the distinguishing features of voters, i.e., *group characteristics*
and *operative conditions*. For example, to use the example above,
how much weight should be assigned to an anti-corruption campaign in determining its impact upon "Yankees" of high and low
socio-economic status, in areas experiencing depression, and in those
enjoying prosperity?

Hopefully, introduction of the additional problem of assigning
relative weights to causal factors has clarified the proposition that
the voting groups affected by given causal factors must be designated
explicitly before interpretation can begin. Because it raises extremely
complicated and difficult questions, it seems best to reserve discussion
of the problem of assigning relative weights to causal factors for
another methodological study now in progress.

II. Generalized Interpretation Analyzed in Terms of Time, Space, and Rate Dimensions

The election of 1884 put a Democrat in the White House for the first time since the Civil War and various historical explanations have been offered for Grover Cleveland's hairbreadth victory over James Blaine. Not surprisingly, the closeness of the election has been used to reinforce the doctrines of that "fortuitous" school of history which minimizes the possibility of discovering causal patterns in human behavior. Since various "accidental" factors of that campaign usually have been pointed to as determinants of the final result, the conclusion could be drawn that sheer chance was responsible for Blaine's defeat. But Allan Nevins, in his Pulitzer Prize biography of Cleveland, attempted to reformulate the problem in such a manner as to place "accidents" and petty factors in perspective, and thereby dispose of the fortuitous explanation. Discussing the situation in New York, the one "close state" whose electoral votes could have decided the outcome in favor of either candidate, Nevins dismissed the charge that Democratic fraud cost Blaine the election:

The whole cry of fraud like the charges of mismanagement shortly [thereafter] brought against Chairman Elkins and Jones [Republican campaign managers], was essentially an effort to obscure the real cause of Blaine's failure. The vote cast in Republican districts for St. John [Prohibitionist]; the rain that kept rural Republicans at home; the loss of more than 2,000 Republican votes in Conkling's [Republican rival of Blaine] home, Oneida County; the Burchard alliteration [Rum, Romanism, and Rebellion]—these all counted. But the great central explanation of the defeat was simply that Blaine was morally suspect.[4]

In effect, what Nevins did was to set down the *basic condition* under which accidental factors operated to cause Blaine's defeat. They "counted" only because Blaine was morally suspect, otherwise their effect would have been unimportant. Whether his interpretation is correct or not, it is not too much to say that Nevins persuasively disposed of the fortuitous explanation the moment he reformulated the problem. Clearly, rain in the rural districts, Republican desertions to minor parties, politically embarrassing oratorical

1896 campaign, for example, when more basic issues were sharply drawn between the two parties and the Republican plurality in New York State was over 250,000. In all likelihood, under those circumstances similar campaign "accidents" would have had little influence in determining any but a small number of votes. In any event, the number of votes "accidentally" determined in 1884 hardly would have dented the Republican plurality of 1896.

Stated in other terms, the significant question posed by the 1884 election is not whether chance factors affected the small number of ballots which were enough to give the Democrats the winning electoral votes. Narrowly conceived, this may be a "correct" explanation of the 1884 election. Seen in meaningful perspective it is a gross distortion because chance factors are made out to be of major importance in accounting for voting behavior, whereas, at best, they affected a minute percentage of the total vote either in New York or the nation at large. The significant question is the very reverse of whether or not accidental developments determined a small number of votes. *Why was the outcome so close, why were chance factors of any significance in the election of 1884?*

To begin with, let us assume that Nevins' hypothesis is verifiable and restate it as presented in his two chapters dealing with the 1884 campaign:

The great central explanation of Blaine's defeat is that he was morally suspect because of unethical conduct in public office. At that particular time in American history *men all throughout the nation were in revolt against the entire system of government by special favor of which Blaine was simply the emblem. Under those conditions, the national contest became so close that a Democrat was elected president because of accidental factors.* But accidents determined the outcome only in the sense that the nomination of Blaine created a situation in which the election could turn on the relatively insignificant number of votes they directly influenced.[5]

To support the hypothesis' claims that no issues were of major significance except the public integrity of the major party candidates, stress was given to the neat manner in which one of Cleveland's supporters summed up the "real issue" of the campaign:

We are told (he said) that Mr. Blaine has been delinquent in office but blameless in private life, while Mr. Cleveland has been a model of official integrity, but culpable in his personal relations [fathered an illegitimate child]. We should therefore elect Mr. Cleveland to the public office which he is so well qualified to fill, and remand Mr. Blaine to the private station which he is so admirably fitted to adorn.[6]

In assessing the relative weight assigned to Blaine's integrity as a determinant of voting behavior no attempt is made here to interpret strictly the description, "real issue." A reasonable interpretation would be that in general, among groups and in areas where the Republican party percentage declined, Blaine's candidacy operated as a significant determinant of that change. It would not be expected to have acted with equal effect everywhere, but, according to our hypothesis, it must be shown to have acted generally, and to a greater extent than any other factor. To demonstrate the impact of Blaine's candidacy, therefore, it must be demonstrated that some measurable pattern of changed Republican strength actually exists. We must also specify the *group characteristics* or the *operative conditions* which can be shown to have been associated with Republican percentage declines resulting from Blaine's candidacy.

Questions of this order need to be posed: Did Blaine's candidacy merely result in a slight percentage decline in a few normally closely balanced states, or was there a nation-wide Republican percentage decline of considerable proportions? Which, if any, distinguishable groups of voters were influenced by charges against his public integrity? Under what conditions, if any, did voters in specific areas become receptive to such charges? In other words, the hypothesis must make some explicit statement concerning who (i.e., voters by group or area, or both) cast less than normal Republican votes because of Blaine, *and why they did so and other voters did not.*

Both the generalized nature of the causal factor and the stress given it as the "real issue" in the campaign are sufficient to negate the possibility that it could have been operative only in one state, or a few states. If it were the real issue in the nation, why, for example, should Blaine's integrity have been a determinant of voting behavior only in New York State? To make such a claim, one would have to provide detailed, verifiable evidence that though it was the real issue everywhere, Blaine's questioned integrity was a significant voting determinant only in New York because of group characteristics or operative conditions, or some combination thereof, peculiar to that state. Moreover, it is not necessary to rely solely upon logical argument. Two full chapters are given to the 1884 campaign in the book from which the hypothesis is drawn and they make it abundantly clear that the "morally suspect" explanation is not confined to New York but is applicable to the nation at large. Those chapters maintain that the impact of Blaine's nomination was not only widespread but considerable. It is described as the single, most important factor causing marked Republican losses throughout the country. The extensive quotations strung together below are from different pages but are in context and provide an accurate summary:

> For several reasons the campaign of 1884 will long be counted among the most memorable in American history. It is the only campaign in which the head of a great party has gone down to defeat because of charges impugning his integrity . . . [Blaine's] nomination [on June 6] was the signal for a revolt which took the most experienced observers by surprise, for in volume and intensity it surpassed the hopes of the Democrats and the fears of the Republicans . . . [Before Cleveland's nomination on July 11] The campaign had already taken on the quality of a great moral crusade. The uprising of the independent voters to vindicate the principle that the presidency must forever be barred to any man of doubtful integrity had gained tremendous momentum, arousing a fervor such as tens of thousands had not felt since the Civil War. . . . The hour was ripe for precisely such a movement. The health of a nation requires, from time to time, a far-reaching moral movement to awaken men from old lethargies and fix their eyes upon some new city in the heavens. Ever since Appomattox the government had in great part been subject to the selfish materialism of the worst wing of the Republican party . . . [details of corruption] men were in revolt against the entire system of government by special favor of which Blaine was simply the emblem. They knew that he would not take bribes in the White House. But they also knew that by virtue of his record, his associates, and his coarseness of fibre, his election would give new encouragement to the crew of lobbyists, spoilsmen, and seekers after privilege. They wanted an honest man who stood in hostility to the whole discreditable and dangerous tradition.

> At the Republican Convention the rebels had mustered but a corporal's guard. Before the week was over, it was a brigade; before June ended, an army . . . It was impossible to conduct such a campaign except upon an emotional plane. Men who were intent upon a change in the very spirit of government could not be bound down to prosaic issues like the tariff and currency. Seldom has so little account been taken of platform or pledges, for as George W. Curtis truly said, "the

platforms of the two parties are practically the same." . . . It was evident that the real issue was the public integrity and capacity of the two candidates, and that old questions of private conduct [Cleveland's social indiscretions] were essentially irrelevant.[7]

What has been done here so far is to state in general terms the relative weight assigned to the causal factor, its widespread operation, and its considerable effect in changing voters' party support. It occasioned a revolt which "in volume and intensity . . . surpassed the hopes of the Democrats and the fears of the Republicans"; before June ended the rebels had mustered "an army," etc. But we have not identified *any particular groups* who were affected by Blaine's candidacy, nor *any particular conditions* which could distinguish voters in areas affected by the issue from voters in areas not affected by the issue. ("Independent voters" obviously does not provide such identification.) Though the relevant chapters give no clue in this regard, since the hypothesis is assumed to be verifiable, it becomes necessary to devise a procedure yielding some specific statement concerning voting behavior subject to systematic demonstration.

Precisely because statements of the following kind seem to be obvious and are therefore frequently overlooked, one of the things we must demonstrate is that considerable *changes* actually took place in voting behavior adverse to the Republicans. Men could not have been ripe for a political revolt precipitated by Blaine's nomination if, for example, the 1884 election returns showed little variation in the normal relative strength of the Republican and Democratic parties throughout the nation in general, and each state in particular. Thus, a logical way to begin to evaluate the hypothesis is to tackle the task of specifying *whom* the issue affected, and why, by employing systematic methods to learn what actually happened in the election of 1884, i.e., what spatial voting patterns can be distinguished in 1884, *in contrast to previous elections.*

The Importance of Constructing Time Series.   The two chapters discussing the 1884 campaign made little comparison between it and previous elections but did present statistics indicating that Cleveland won a very narrow victory over Blaine:

His [Cleveland's] margin in New York was of less than 1200 votes, but it was decisive. He had carried every Southern state, together with

Indiana, New Jersey, and Connecticut, and though his popular majority over Blaine was less than 25,000 in a total vote of more than ten million, he had 219 electoral votes to Blaine's 182.[8]

Since the 1884 election was extremely close, *for a marked change to have taken place, the Republican vote in previous elections must have provided that party with a comfortable margin of victory.* If we could identify in geographic terms, i.e., states, counties, townships, etc., the areas where its vote declined perceptibly, we would be in a better position to identify the groups among whom vote-switching took place, and then attempt to demonstrate that Blaine's candidacy explained the switching. *But, conversely, if in fact no general pattern existed of marked Republican decline, the hypothesis would rest on an erroneous factual assumption.* In other words, attention is directed here to the necessity of demonstrating the accuracy and inclusiveness of the factual elements in the hypothesis before attempting to demonstrate the validity of its interpretative elements. And that it is possible for erroneous assumptions to be accorded status as accepted facts relative to the 1884 campaign is readily indicated.

Has the common assumption really been established that even in New York accidental features of the campaign "all counted" against Blaine? Though one can cite numerous *assertions* to this effect, to my knowledge no one has demonstrated that the much discussed "accidents" actually swung any votes from him. In fact, given the prevalence of anti-Catholic sentiments, it becomes a difficult problem even to think of how one would go about attempting to show that the Burchard incident *hurt or helped* Blaine. But perhaps the possible usefulness of systematic research methods for political history can be illustrated by examining another assertion concerning the impact of accidental factors upon voting behavior in 1884.

In the book from which the hypothesis is drawn, stress was given the idea that the 1884 Prohibition Party vote was a consequence of actions taken at the Republican nominating convention; there "the Republicans painfully humiliated the temperance forces." This humiliation was said to have been a definite factor in the events which led to the decision to run an erstwhile Republican, John P. St. John, on the Prohibition ticket; "The Republicans were to rue their indifference to him." [9] Since in 1884 the Prohibition vote was about 150,000 for the nation and 25,000 in closely contested New

York, it might appear that Republican arrogance did swing enough votes from Blaine to have been of some significance, given the central hypothesis that Blaine was "morally suspect."

But when one constructs *a time series for voting behavior,* the candidacy of St. John and the vote given him are both seen in a considerably different perspective. The temperance forces had been running presidential candidates since 1872 and continued to do so after 1884. *Even more important, though the 1884 Prohibition vote in New York was much larger than in the previous presidential election, it was slightly smaller than the party had polled in 1882 for Governor. That is, the Prohibition candidate for Governor received 25,783 votes in 1882. Two years later the party's presidential candidate received only 25,006 votes, although the total was 200,000 more than in 1882.* Further, in 1882, the Democratic gubernatorial candidate, Grover Cleveland, was given a majority of unprecedented proportions. In 1884, Grover Cleveland, the Democratic presidential candidate, carried New York by a scant 1,149 votes out of 1,167,189 cast.

That the Prohibition vote in the state had been growing after 1880 is shown in the table below.[10] But in broad terms, the table also indicates that the Prohibition vote was relatively stable between 1882 and 1888, inclusive, whether it was cast in a state or national election.

Table I—New York State Vote for President or Highest State Officer, 1880-1888

	Rep.	Dem.	Prohibition	Proh. Percentage
1880	555,544	534,511	1,517	0.13
1881	416,915	403,893	4,445	0.53
1882	342,464	535,318	25,783	2.81
1883	446,108	427,525	18,816	2.08
1884	562,005	563,154	25,006	2.16
1885	490,331	501,465	30,867	2.98
1886	461,018	468,815	36,437	3.75
1887	452,811	469,888	41,850	4.00
1888	650,338	635,965	30,231	2.28

When the New York Prohibition vote is viewed in historical perspective, i.e., over time, it obviously cannot be taken as an accidental product of the 1884 campaign. In assigning weight to Republican defections to the Prohibitionists, it must be recognized that these defections, if they were *Republican* defections, on balance, occurred before Blaine's candidacy. In New York, and elsewhere, compared with 1882, sharp losses were suffered *not by the Republicans with Blaine but by the Democrats with Cleveland*. For in 1882 the Democrats had achieved a "political revolution" throughout the country which may be said to have marked the first major post-Civil War switch to them from the Republicans. And since the Prohibition vote in New York was practically constant in 1882 and 1884, an assessment of its impact upon Blaine's defeat focuses attention instead upon the sharp Democratic retrogression from 1882, and the extent to which the Republicans had recovered.[11] Thus, the conclusion appears warranted that the hypothesis concerning the 1884 election which assumes that the Republican party underwent a general, marked decline, runs counter to the fact that with Blaine as a candidate the Republicans *gained ground* compared to the major election contests immediately preceding. One index of their recovery is the close vote in New York (and elsewhere) compared to the 1882 Democratic sweep; another is the Republican gain in Congress. The party composition of the House of Representatives demonstrates the shift.[12]

Table II—Congressional Election Contests, 1876-1886

	1876	1878	1880	1882	1884	1886
Rep.	140	130	147	118	140	152
Dem.	153	149	135	197	183	169
Other	0	14	11	10	2	4

Republican Performance in 1884.   Republican gains in 1884 with Blaine as a candidate do not in themselves indicate that he failed to hurt the party. Conceivably, certain events after 1882 could have improved the Republicans' position to such an extent that another candidate might have won. If this were the case, however, the historian would have to identify those events and demonstrate their political impact. For example, the argument might be advanced that a situation had developed analogous to the Republican recovery in 1880, which, the claim could be made, resulted from the end of depression in 1879 and the great burst of prosperity preceding the election. Just a reverse situation obtained, however, in 1884. After four years of high prosperity a recession did set in shortly before the 1882 elections, but it was not until the Spring of 1884 that the depression of the mid-eighties really developed. Since a Republican administration was in office, if it had any political effect at all, economic depression worked against, not in favor of Blaine. Under these circumstances, a "great moral crusade" which by June had enlisted "an army" against Blaine should not have resulted in a Republican political resurgence. Other events would have to be subjected to similar analysis if it were argued that they explained Republican recovery.

Even if the significant political developments of the four years between elections are ignored, the 1884 voting record shows little evidence of a nation-wide revolt against Blaine's candidacy. Despite the fact that in 1880 the Republican percentage of the total vote was higher than in any election between 1876 and 1892, inclusive, *Blaine had only 00.09% less of the total vote than James Garfield, the victorious Republican candidate of 1880,* and the Democratic increased share was only 00.28%! [13]

Table III—Presidential Elections, 1876-1892, Percent of Popular Vote Cast for Republican and Democratic Candidates

	Rep.	Dem.
1876	47.87	50.86
1880	48.31	48.20
1884	48.22	48.48
1888	47.83	48.63
1892	42.96	45.90

Possibly the most remarkable feature of the election of 1884 was that in terms of net shift, compared to its predecessor, it showed *less* arithmetic percentage change than any other in American history.[14] Actually, Blaine received about 400,000 more votes than Garfield. An additional 9,000 votes would have enabled him to match the latter's percentage exactly because the total vote was larger in 1884. It cannot therefore be demonstrated, as our hypothesis requires that it must, that Blaine's candidacy cut into the popular vote attained by the Republican party at preceding elections. His vote actually represented *increased* Republican strength as compared to 1876, and greater strength than in 1888 and 1892. An unchanged popular vote means that if the Republicans suffered losses in certain states due to Blaine's candidacy, these losses *were counterbalanced* by Republican gains. At best, a hypothesis which can only be applicable to Republican losses must be considered partial. But this line of reasoning can be carried further. If Republican gains and losses were of equal magnitude, and if in certain states no change occurred, the hypothesis making Blaine's candidacy the "great central explanation of the [Republican] defeat" must be *capable of explaining all three sets of voting data if, without explicit restricting conditions, its general explanation of any one set is to be considered potentially verifiable.*

In view of the remarkably small net shift in 1884 party strength as compared to 1880, no more justification exists for regarding Republican gains and constancy as deviant cases from a hypothesis based upon Blaine's *weakness* as a candidate than for regarding Republican losses as deviations from a hypothesis postulating Blaine *as a strong candidate.* Though numerous types of causal factors might have differential effects upon voting behavior among different groups or in different areas, the hypothesis under consideration does not offer one of that nature. Particularly since it makes no attempt to identify groups or areas more susceptible to charges against Blaine's integrity, the hypothesis in fact offers no explanation for the different types of voting behavior revealed in 1884 when the voting data is arranged systematically. For example, if sectional conflict were designated as the "real issue" of the 1884 campaign, and if each party were identified with a particular section, then in comparison with 1880 one would expect to find differential effects upon party strength consistent with the parties' sectional identification.

But if Blaine's nomination precipitated a widespread and considerable revolt against the Republican party in 1884, why should voting performance in 1884 have shown no net change in the parties' relative strength, as well as a markedly irregular pattern throughout the country when analyzed over time on a state level? Yet systematic analysis yields voting patterns of such irregularity as to prevent one from specifying the groups of voters, i.e., "Yankee stock," "voters in rural-agricultural or urban-industrial states," etc., *who* voted against the Republicans because of Blaine, and then attempting to explain *why* they did so. Because the hypothesis postulates that Blaine's nomination led both to widespread and considerable decline in Republican percentage strength, it is regarded here as demonstrably unverifiable. As shown below, it cannot satisfy the systematic voting data obtained when the time, space, and rate dimensions are employed.

Time, Space, and Rate of Change. Though even a crude index such as net change over time is of considerable utility in testing a hypothesis concerning voting behavior, more intensive examination of the voting data suggests a standard procedure for handling the problem in terms of the three dimensions available to historians, i.e., time, space, and rate of change. The popular national vote showed less net change in 1884 than in any election before or since but it would be inaccurate to conclude that only an insignificant proportion of voters changed allegiances. Gains and losses might have been so closely balanced that a *gross turnover* of significant proportions could have occurred yet not be reflected in the *net turnover*. To study the extent to which voters switched allegiances, it is necessary to combine the time and space dimensions, i.e., break down the net turnover in the total *national vote* to the net turnover in the *individual state's vote*. If more precise data were desired concerning the gross turnover, the state totals would have to be broken down further and the units of analysis arranged in descending order, counties, towns, wards, election districts, or variations thereof. But for our purposes changes in the state totals are all that is necessary.

As indicated above, comparison of the Republican vote in 1880 and 1884 permits classification of state voting behavior in three distinct categories: states where the Republican party increased its percentage of the popular vote; states where its percentage decreased; states where its percentage remained constant. Constant is defined here as ±.99, an increase is +1.00 and over, a decrease is at least −1.00. Like all definitions of categories the criteria are arbitrary. But only under unusual circumstances would they significantly distort the patterns of voting behavior because they operate identically in both directions, and there is room for movement in both directions. A larger number of categories would cut down the possibility and extent of distortions due to cluster around the criterion points, ±1.00, but would be less convenient to handle. Actually, the 1884 results are such that the amount of distortion due to specific criterion points is insignificant and can be ignored.

(Slightly different results would be yielded if the criteria were ±.50 or ±2.00, but the basic picture would not be altered.) The table below is arranged in descending order of Republican improvement in 1884 compared to 1880; the second set of columns gives the improvement in 1888 compared to 1884.[15]

Table IV—Republican Improvement, 1880-1884, and 1884-1888; Arithmetic Percentage Change in Popular Vote by States

	1	2	3	4
State	Rank	% Change 1880-1884	Rank	% Change 1884-1888
Virginia	1	+9.4	15	+0.6
Nevada	2	+8.7	8	+1.5
Missouri	3	+8.3	22	—0.7
West Virginia	4	+6.7	6	+1.7
Mississippi	5	+6.5	37	—10.2
Louisiana	6	+5.4	38	—16.0
Texas	7	+4.7	30	—3.9
Maine	8	+3.9	5	+2.2
Tennessee	9	+3.5	25	—2.0
Colorado	10	+3.0	11	+1.2
Kentucky	11	+3.0	4	+2.2
Pennsylvania	12	+2.1	19	—0.2
California	13	+2.1	26	—2.4
Alabama	14	+1.5	34	—6.0
Florida	15	+1.2	36	—7.0
Oregon	16	+0.4	3	+3.7
Maryland	17	+0.4	9	+1.4
Arkansas	18	+0.4	27	—3.2
Georgia	19	—0.7	33	—5.5
Ohio	20	—0.7	24	—1.5
New Hampshire	21	—0.8	23	—0.8
Illinois	22	—0.9	21	—0.6
Indiana	23	—1.2	13	+0.9
New Jersey	24	—1.7	10	+1.2
North Carolina	25	—1.7	14	+0.8
New York	26	—2.1	12	+1.0
Kansas	27	—2.3	28	—3.4
Connecticut	28	—2.5	16	+0.4
Vermont	29	—3.4	2	+4.8
Wisconsin	30	—3.7	20	—0.6
Rhode Island	31	—4.2	31	—4.2
Michigan	32	—4.2	7	+1.6
Minnesota	33	—4.4	32	—4.7
Delaware	34	—4.5	17	+0.2
Iowa	35	—4.5	18	—0.1
Nebraska	36	—5.6	29	—3.8
Massachusetts	37	—10.1	1	+5.0
South Carolina	38	—10.6	35	—6.2

The table shows that if only two categories are used, i.e., gains or losses, then in 1884 the Republicans gained in 18 states compared to *all parties* and lost in 20 states. Gains ranged from +9.4 (Virginia) to +0.4 (Arkansas); losses from —0.7 (Georgia) to —10.6 (South Carolina). Rather than a uniform trend below 1880, an arithmetic range of 20.0 existed between Republican performance in Virginia and South Carolina. The fact that a relatively smooth curve results when the improvement (positive and negative) in each state is plotted in graph form confirms the impression gained from the table that the 20.0 range does not simply reflect changes in Virginia and South Carolina. But dividing the data into two categories tends to obscure the fact that at least three basic patterns of voting behavior can be observed in the 1884 election. (A more precise analysis would distinguish at least five categories; the ±1.00 criterion, and a ±5.00 criterion to subdivide further, gains and losses.)

Any hypothesis concerning the 1884 election must be consonant with the fact that 15 states recorded gains for the Republicans, 7 were constant, and in 16 states the GOP lost support either to Democrats, minor parties, or both. More than that, the hypothesis has to be consonant with the *group characteristics* and *operative conditions* of the individual states within each category, the magnitude of the shift in each case, and the *rate* of shift. The magnitude can be calculated from the state totals for 1880 and 1884 but the *rate* of shift requires at least one more datum point, the vote in 1888.

If statistics are available only for one election the historian's analysis is restricted to the space dimension; if two elections are known he can use both the time and space dimensions to indicate party gains and losses in different states; three elections enable him, in addition, to make some limited statement concerning the *rate* of change between 1880 and 1884 in different states. That is, one must have two sets of successive elections in order to have the basis of comparison necessary to establish a rate. An arithmetic increase of 10.0 from 1884 to 1888 might be steep if the increase from 1880 to 1884 were 1.0, it would be shallow if the increase had been 30.0 instead of 1.0. If we introduce the rate dimension, therefore, instead of three categories reflecting a direct comparison between 1880 and 1884, it is possible to classify voting behavior in at least eight distinct categories. Before describing these categories it might be well to discuss their utility for evaluations of a hypothesis such as the one under consideration.

The contention might reasonably be made that systematic demonstration of three different categories of irregular state voting behavior (gains, losses, constancy) definitely requires restatement of the hypothesis but does not invalidate it entirely, nor limit its potential verifiability to a certain number of states. Conceivably, Blaine's candidacy checked a sharply rising *long-term trend* of Republican strength in the 22 states which showed increases or were constant in 1884, and accelerated a trend away from the party in the 16 states where losses were recorded. If we could determine the trend in each state, and the rate of change in 1880-1884 compared to 1884-1888, a more precise and meaningful statement would be available concerning voting behavior. We could then judge Republican performance in 1884 in short-run historical perspective and better identify those states which could have been affected adversely by Blaine's candidacy.

For example, there would be little likelihood that a Republican *down-trend* state showing a steep Republican *increase* in 1884 reacted unfavorably to Blaine; a steep *decrease* in a Republican *up-trend* state might have been due to him. The most significant states, therefore, are those which display counter-trend movements in 1884, and the rate dimension enables us to identify them. Less significant are those states which display uniform trends (up or down) from 1880 to 1888. Nonetheless, even where the trend is uniform, the rate dimension enables us to distinguish further between Republican performance in 1884 and 1888.

Categories of Voting Behavior. The table above contains all the information necessary to form eight categories of voting behavior. A state such as Virginia, represented by a plus sign in both the second and fourth columns, is one in which the Republican trend was upwards from 1880 to 1888. Kansas has minus signs in both columns and exemplifies a continual Republican down-trend. Mississippi has first a plus sign and then a minus sign indicating that the Republican vote in 1884 was *higher* than in both 1880 and 1888. Not only did the Republican 1884 performance improve over 1880, it was clearly *above* the trend for the three elections. Contrariwise, Massachusetts has first a minus sign and then a plus sign. The Republican vote was *less* than in both 1880 and 1888 and clearly *below* the trend.

So far a method has been described to establish four categories of states to evaluate Republican performance. Category I comprises states such as Virginia in which the Republican trend was continually upward. Category II, states such as Kansas where the Republican trend was continually down. Category III, with Mississippi the prototype, states where Republican performance was better than trend. Category IV, Massachusetts, where Republican performance was worse than trend. Applying this method to the table above the 38 states participating in the three elections fall into these categories:

I (8 states)	II (11 states)	III (10 states)	IV (9 states)
Virginia	Kansas	Mississippi	Massachusetts
Colorado	Georgia	Alabama	Connecticut
Kentucky	Illinois	Arkansas	Delaware
Maine	Iowa	California	Indiana
Maryland	Minnesota	Florida	Michigan
Nevada	New Hampshire	Louisiana	New Jersey
Oregon	Nebraska	Missouri	New York
West Virginia	Ohio	Pennsylvania	North Carolina
	Rhode Island	Tennessee	Vermont
	South Carolina	Texas	
	Wisconsin		

Simply in terms of gain and loss, without the constancy criterion, these categories show that in 1884, Republican strength increased in 18 states (I and III), continued a down-trend in 11 more (II), and in 9 states declined counter to trend (IV). Thus, before the rate dimension is introduced, the trend data indicate *that only the 9 states in Category IV displayed adverse Republican voting patterns which might be attributed primarily to Blaine's candidacy.* For example, it would be illogical to offer this explanation in the case of a category II state such as Kansas where Republican strength declined *at every election after 1864 until 1896.*[16]

Table V—Republican Percentage of Popular Vote, Kansas, 1864-1900

Year	Percentage	Arithmetic Change
1860	—	—
1864	81.7	—
1868	68.8	—12.9
1872	67.0	—1.8
1876	63.2	—3.9
1880	60.4	—2.8
1884	58.1	—2.3
1888	54.8	—3.4
1892	46.7	—8.0
1896	47.5	+0.8
1900	52.6	+5.1

Not every state in category II shows a similar pattern of unbroken decline but with rare exceptions the Republican percentage in 1884 was *below* that recorded in all previous elections and *above* that recorded in all subsequent ones until 1896. And when the rate dimension is employed, as can be seen from the Kansas table, even more precise statements can be made. Though the Republican party continued to give ground in 1884 in Kansas, its rate of decline was *less* than in the two elections before and after.

The rate dimension now enables us to subdivide further the four categories and describe eight patterns of voting behavior in 1884. For example, the Republican gain in Virginia (Category I) from 1880 to 1884 was +9.4, much steeper than the +.6 recorded for 1884-1888. Had the Republicans continued to increase their strength at the same rate, the latter figure should also have been +9.4. Had their rate of increase in 1888 bettered that of 1884 it should have been at least +9.41. In Oregon, another Category I state, the Republican rate of increase did pick up in 1888, +.4 was followed by +3.7.

Similarly, it is possible to compare the rates of increase or decrease for the three other categories, and subdivide them accordingly. Diagrams A and B below represent a steep and shallow rate, respectively, in an uptrend state; C and D represent a steep and shallow rate in a favorable counter-trend state. Actually, D represents steeper than short-run trend gains in 1884 rather than what might be termed a true counter-trend movement. That is, the Republican percentage in 1888 is also higher than in 1880, although it is below that of 1884. In contrast, C represents an 1884 reversal of a short-run down-trend for 1888 is lower than 1880. Of these four patterns of voting behavior, only Diagram B could be offered as an example of a state in which the voting statistics show Republican improvement was possibly retarded by Blaine's candidacy. The other three represent more favorable than trend Republican voting in various degrees of *improvement*.

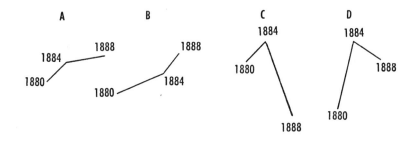

The four diagrams below represent the same patterns in down-trend states. Here G is the true counter-trend type, and F is a state such as Kansas where Blaine's candidacy might have slowed down the rate of Republican *decline*.

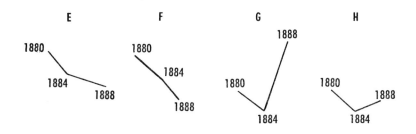

Evaluating Republican Performance in 1884. The information which can be obtained from analyzing the 1884 vote would increase with the number of datum points utilized to establish trends and rates. If the diagrams above were extended to include elections from 1860 to 1900 the short-run movements from 1880 to 1888 could be seen in terms of a long-run perspective, and interpretations of the 1884 election might be expected to fit not only the immediate events of the campaign but more fundamental patterns of American politics in the post-Civil War decades. According to the degree of precision desired, we could use more than three datum points, set up more than eight categories for all parties, and thereby obtain a clearer description of American voting patterns. Particularly if the analysis were carried down to the county level, where in the states the number of units occasionally runs in the hundreds and for the country at large, in the thousands, an increased number of categories would facilitate accurate thinking about the results of any one election. We would then know what we are attempting to explain, and, presumably, be in a better position to do so.

A uniform distribution of units in the various categories would indicate one pattern of national voting behavior; a sharply skewed distribution would have another meaning entirely. For our purposes such detailed diagrams are unnecessary and their results can be summed up in this fashion: With few exceptions the Republican party's state percentages declined perceptibly after 1872 in comparison with the average percentage of elections from 1860 to 1872 inclusive, and the process was not reversed until 1896. The exceptions are states in which recovery began one or two elections before 1896. In every state the party more or less declined after 1872.

Seen in long-run perspective and broken down into meaningful categories, Republican performance in 1884 obviously takes on a different aspect than the one usually given it. But even the information gained from analyzing the three elections, 1880-1888, is of considerable aid in evaluating the hypothesis under consideration. *It demonstrates that no factual basis exists for a possible assumption that Blaine's candidacy checked the rate of Republican increase and accelerated the rate of decline throughout the country.* Had this assumption been true the number of states in category G, unfavorable counter-trend, should have been large, and the number in C, favorable counter-trend, should have been small. The reverse pattern is found; there were six states in category C, and only one in G. Moreover, there were three times as many states in category A (steeper increase) than in category B (shallower increase), but categories E and F were equal in number. The 38 states break down as follows:

A	B	C	D
Virginia	Maryland	Mississippi	Missouri
Colorado	Oregon	Alabama	Pennsylvania
Kentucky		Arkansas	Tennessee
Maine		California	Texas
Nevada		Florida	
West Virginia		Louisiana	

E	F	G	H
Illinois	Kansas	Vermont	Connecticut
Iowa	Georgia		Delaware
Nebraska	Minnesota		Indiana
South Carolina	Ohio		Massachusetts
Wisconsin	Rhode Island		Michigan
			New Jersey
	New Hampshire (—.79 and —.79)		New York
			North Carolina

What emerges from a systematic analysis of the statistical data available on state voting behavior, therefore, does not support the hypothesis that Blaine's candidacy was "the great central explanation" of the Republican party's defeat in 1884. (Affirmative results which emerge from this analysis will be discussed in another section.) *Its arithmetic net loss in the national total vote was only 00.09%. The party had been declining since 1872. In a considerable number of states its performance was better than the short-time trend and in six states it clearly reversed an unfavorable trend.* At best, only in certain states (G and H) could the party be said to have done worse than might have been expected from the trend of presidential elections. *And this takes no account of the stunning defeats suffered by the Republicans in 1882 and other adverse political developments after 1880 for which Blaine cannot be held responsible,* nor the fact that both major parties were under increasing attack after 1872. Thus, in both New York and New Jersey where the Republican party declined slightly from 1880 and recovered slightly in 1888, Democratic strength also diminished in 1884. Moreover, if one examines in detail the political situation in the other seven states in categories G and H, additional possible explanations for Republican losses suggest themselves.

In Massachusetts, for example, where the party's percentage of the popular vote was 10.1 below its 1880 percentage, the decline might be explained by the vote polled for ex-Governor Ben Butler on a combined Anti-monopoly and Greenback ticket. Examination of the Massachusetts annual voting statistics from 1876 to 1884 indicates that when Butler ran for state office on a Greenback fusion ticket with the Democrats, as he did in 1878, 1879, 1882, and 1883, significant inroads were made into Republican strength. Thus, in 1880 he was not a candidate and the Republican presidential percentage was 58.5. Nor was he a gubernatorial candidate in 1881, and the GOP vote increased to 61.3%. But in 1882 Butler won the race for governor on a fusion ticket and Republican strength plummeted to 46.8%. He lost his bid for re-election in 1883 to a Republican but only by a small margin, and in 1884 his presidential campaign gave him 8.1% of the Massachusetts vote. Though Blaine's percentage was 10.1 lower than that attained by Garfield in 1880 and 9.1 lower than Hayes' in 1876, the Democratic party with Cleveland as its candidate only registered an increase of 0.7 over 1880 and was 1.7 less than the vote given Tilden in 1876. In other words, the marked decrease in Republican strength was not accompanied by anything like a corresponding increase in Democratic strength.[17]

Table VI—Massachusetts Popular Vote; Party Percentages
for President or Governor, 1876-1884

Year	Office	Rep.	Dem.	Greenback
1876	Pres.	58.0	42.0	—
1877	Gov.	49.5	39.7	1.9
1878	Gov.	52.6	4.0*	42.7*
1879	Gov.	50.4	4.1*	44.8*
1880	Pres.	58.5	39.6	1.6
1881	Gov.	61.3	34.6	3.1
1882	Gov.	46.8	52.2**	**
1883	Gov.	51.3	48.1**	**
1884	Pres.	48.4	40.3	8.1

* Democratic party offered candidates but bulk of party fused with Nationals (Greenbackers) to support Ben Butler.
** Fusion of Democrats and Greenbackers to support Butler.

The statistics above are not offered to "prove" that Butler's candidacy explains the Republican decline in Massachusetts. They are cited to indicate that even in a category H state such as Massachusetts little basis exists for the *automatic* assumption that Blaine was solely responsible for the decline. In similar fashion, having once identified the states in categories G and H, it is possible to show that other explanations than the one given by our hypothesis may account for Republican losses.

Surely the fact that in 1882 Cleveland had scored the greatest victory in New York Democratic annals is worth consideration in explaining the slight Republican decline in that state during a political era when native sons were expected to attract votes. (Actually, the Democrats also declined slightly in Cleveland's home state, New York; their arithmetic percentage decrease was 0.1. Contrariwise, in Maine, the home state of Blaine, the Republican arithmetic increase was 3.9, the Democratic decrease was 6.0, and minor party increases made up the difference. If the real issue had been the public integrity of the two candidates, among people who presumably knew them best, Blaine had been given a vote of increased confidence, Cleveland had not.)

Even if other possible explanations are ignored, however, the procedures carried out above of reformulating our hypothesis and analyzing the pertinent voting data systematically have demonstrated that it is at best applicable to a small number of states. Logically, therefore, the hypothesis also must be required to state, and shown to be consistent with, the conditions which produced the different voting patterns described in the eight categories, A to H; a requirement which it cannot satisfy. Of more importance, however, is the logical requirement that it also state the conditions which made the personal characteristics of the Republican and Democratic presidential candidates the "real issue" of the campaign!

Just as Nevins acutely observed that accidental factors such as "Rum, Romanism, and Rebellion" were only significant under specific circumstances (assuming now that they were), analysis of the 1884 campaign indicates that the candidates became *the "real issue" only because certain conditions then prevailed in the country*. Again the 1896 election can be used as a reference point. After several years of deep depression and growing social conflict it is almost inconceivable that hypothetical indiscretions by Bryan and dubious transactions by McKinley could have replaced "free silver" and sectional antagonism as the primary issues in 1896. A comprehensive hypothesis concerning the 1884 campaign, or any other, must not only identify the causal factors which explain the systematic data, it must also answer the more fundamental question of why those specific causal factors were operative. If this contention is accepted, then the need becomes obvious to develop at least a crude body of theory concerning American presidential elections—a task, however, to which this study will only call attention but prudently will not attempt to undertake.

The 1884 Election Reconsidered. Having been employed above to evaluate Nevins' hypothesis as unverifiable, the systematic data presented can also be employed to designate another impressionistic explanation of the 1884 election as *potentially verifiable*. This explanation also puts the fortuitous interpretation into proper perspective by answering the significant question posed by the campaign. The question: Is it possible to identify the basic conditions which explain why the candidates' personal characteristics dominated the 1884 campaign? Historians, it is contended here, would answer that question with impressive unanimity. There simply were no significant issues which distinguished the national Republican and Democratic parties in 1884, nor indeed, at a minimum, between 1877 and the early 1890's. Nevins clearly should subscribe at least to the first part of that proposition, for he quoted George W. Curtis approvingly, "the platforms of the two parties [in 1884] are practically the same," and himself affirmed that "Seldom has so little account been taken of platform or pledges . . ." [18] His explanation was that Blaine's candidacy precipitated such a state of affairs. But after all, with virtually identical platforms, with both parties animated by the same philosophy and controlled by essentially the same groups, what else could Democrats and Republicans stage an election "contest" around other than Cleveland's private, and Blaine's public, indiscretions?

To borrow Harry Carman's and Harold Syrett's neat phrase, the period between the end of Reconstruction and the emergence of Populism can be described as "the politics of dead center." [19] Under such circumstances the election of Cleveland or Blaine simply was fraught with insignificance, except, of course, to the politicians involved, their entourages, and the "special interests" which expected to benefit if "their" candidate won. It was hardly an accident that

Republican gains and losses were nearly equal, that no new patterns emerged and that a Republican net decline of 00.09 from 1880 in the percentage of the popular vote was barely overbalanced by a Democratic increase of 0.28. Reinforcing this point is the fact that the net turnover from 1884 to 1888 was the second smallest in American history. Republicans won the election although they recorded a —0.39 arithmetic percentage change, and Democrats lost though they improved their showing with a +0.15. (Gross turnover was even more restricted than in 1880-1884.)

Obviously, the voting data cited above do not prove the "politics of dead center" explanation. But they do indicate how systematic methods can be used to evaluate conflicting hypotheses derived from impressionistic research. Moreover, it seems reasonable to assert, by demonstrating the factual error in the "moral crusade" interpretation the systematic voting data have pointed up the methodological dangers of judging history from the documents, records, and publications of contemporary elite groups. (Here the term "elite group" embraces the political, economic, social, and cultural leaders of a given period in a broad sense; it does not refer to "social position" in the conventional usage.)

Impressionistic research is particularly vulnerable to the dangers of unintentional distortion and one-sidedness because, to a striking degree, source materials reflecting elite groups' views and experiences are the ones most frequently preserved and readily accessible to later scholars.[20] Perhaps the "Mugwumps" who led the "moral crusade" genuinely believed that Cleveland's election was imperative if American political institutions were to be preserved. (The genuineness of their moral crusade is debatable.) Perhaps they also were convinced that they embodied and reflected the nation's will and wisdom. (This point is more easily conceded—that is, their conviction as distinct from the fact.) But in the 1884 election, the voting returns appear to demonstrate that they can hardly be said to have represented anyone but themselves.

In New York County, for example, where the "crusade" attained its greatest publicity and commanded its most powerful press support, the Republican party percentage was almost identical in 1880, 1884, and 1888. The Democratic party percentage in 1884 was actually 1.4 *less* than in 1880, and 1.6 *less* than in 1888. (See the table on p. 168 below.)

Less intriguing than cryptic entries in carefully preserved private journals, less colorful than professional politicians' speeches or the public rhetoric of articulate leaders, *systematic voting statistics are more reliable indicators of popular attitudes and beliefs.* This is not to argue that impressionistic source materials such as the records and writings of elite groups in a given period are valueless. On the contrary, they are indispensable and can provide the historian with valuable insights into the whole range of contemporary politics. Nonetheless, the records of elite groups which happen to be preserved and accessible do not constitute an adequate basis for the description and interpretation of an election outcome. Their representative quality and accurate depiction of reality can best be evaluated when they are employed in conjunction with systematic data. Another key proposition of this study holds that such data give the historian a solid foundation upon which to stand in working through those documents fortunate enough to withstand the hazards of time, and the whims of mice and men.

III. Generalized Interpretation Analyzed in Terms of the Historian's Space Dimension

The space dimension becomes particularly valuable to a historian whenever a substantially new phenomenon occurs, or when the available data preceding or following the phenomenon under study is too fragmentary for adequate comparison. In those situations, though it can be put to limited uses, historians are largely deprived of their basic methodological tool, the recording and analysis of phenomena as they occurred over time. If the requisite data are available, it is possible to analyze phenomena in terms of subsequent developments or of other phenomena which preceded it, no matter how fragmentary the data. But the value of the time dimension is considerably diminished as a result. To paraphrase artillery gunners, when the "target" is not bracketed between "before" and "after," its significance is difficult to gauge. More than ever, it becomes necessary to utilize the space dimension fully in attempting to understand and explain the phenomenon at issue.

The space dimension is not only valuable in dealing with "new" developments; as the case study in Section II was designed to demonstrate, it is far more effective when combined with the other historical dimensions. But whether used alone or in conjunction with time and rate, spatial recording and analysis of data has two essential characteristics of particular interest to political historians; above all to American historians who must deal with a federal system placing a high premium on geography.

Plotted in spatial terms, a party's voting support, for example, can be recognized and described as widespread or restricted, random or regular in pattern, concentrated or spotty. Such determinations are extremely useful in describing *what happened,* and they are also good ways to begin the difficult task of learning *who voted for it to happen.* Once voting data are plotted spatially in units such as wards, townships, counties, states, etc., all other data which might help to answer the question, and capable of representation in the same form, can be similarly plotted. In effect, data pertaining to various kinds of designated voting groups are superimposed on voting performance data arranged in ecological unit order.

Consciously or otherwise, the two characteristics of the space dimension sketched above are almost invariably used by political historians, indeed, by political pundits of any kind or lack of qualification. For example, if the present farm price support issue becomes a topic of conversation, one "instinctively" thinks of particular geographic areas where it might be a significant voting determinant, and of particular voting groups in those areas who might be affected (corn-hog farmers, wheat farmers, dairy farmers, and the like).

Precisely because it is so conveniently and casually used, the space dimension lends itself to marked confusion and error in impressionistic research. A phenomenon which appears to be common and widespread may actually be rigidly restricted or erratically spotty. And voting performance apparently associated with a particular occupational group in a given area may actually cut across class lines and be far more accurately associated with religious affiliation. No claim is made here which even implies that systematic research methods and data eliminate all error and solve all problems connected with the space dimension's use. It is contended, however, that they can substantially increase its effectiveness and reliability when employed in political historiography. The case study in

Section III is designed to illustrate these claims in practice, as well as amplify the points made above.

The Election of 1824. The election of 1824 is of considerable interest to historians because it marked the break-up of the one-party rule developing after Jefferson's victory in 1800, because it was the first in which a country-wide popular vote was cast, and because Andrew Jackson, though unsuccessful in his bid for the presidency, was thereby established in national politics on a firm footing. Placing stress upon the latter point, Arthur Schlesinger, Jr. stated in his Pulitzer Prize work: "His immense popular vote in 1824 came from his military fame and from the widespread conviction of his integrity." [21] The sentence clearly offers an explicit explanation of voting behavior throughout the country in 1824 and will be analayzed in those terms.

At first sight Schlesinger's explanation might appear to be of the type which cannot be verified but only argued about. The causal factors, i.e., Jackson's military fame and widespread conviction of his integrity, are of such a highly generalized nature as to make it difficult to measure their impact and separate them out from other possible determinants of voting behavior. Stated in terms of the original formulation, the explanation would force historians to rely upon impressionistic data, and scholars of equal competence might reasonably be expected to offer contradictory albeit plausible estimates of its validity. How, for example, could one even begin to attempt to determine whether an *undifferentiated* number of men voted for Jackson because they were impressed with his heroism and integrity or because he was, as an alternative hypothesis has it, a representative of the frontier? Without fairly precise delineation of the *kind* of men who voted *both for and against Jackson*, explanations of why a certain number of men voted for him are not subject to systematic tests of their potential verifiability.

But it is possible to reformulate Schlesinger's original statement and thereby render the hypothesis more susceptible to verification. The factual elements in the hypothesis are that a widespread conviction existed of Jackson's integrity, that his military fame was at least equally widespread (by implication), and that his popular vote was "immense." Thus, the common denominator in the factual elements of the formulation is their "widespread" incidence. Neither the size of the vote for Jackson nor the influence of his fame and integrity upon voting behavior is described in local or sectional terms but in terms of the nation as a whole. The relationship between fact and interpretation is clear when the implications are made more explicit. Stated in other words, Schlesinger's hypothesis is that a large if unspecified proportion of the "masses" throughout the country were impressed by Jackson's military fame, were convinced of his integrity, and, primarily for those reasons, voted for him in the 1824 election. That such formulation does not distort his position is evident, it would seem, from this quotation:

> In the republic's early years, martial reputation had counted little for future political success. But the broadening of the suffrage, the thrill of surging nationalism and the declining glamour of the old ruling class created a favorable atmosphere for new idols, and the War of 1812 promptly produced the military hero. The old aristocracy resented such vulgar and *parvenu* prestige, and a man wtih Jackson's credentials was almost forced into the opposition. Moreover, while the newly enfranchised and chauvinistic masses regarded the military hero with wild enthusiasm, to the old aristocracy, raised on classical analogies, no figure could seem more dangerous to the republic.

Particularly when put in those terms, the assertion seems warranted that Schlesinger's thesis has to satisfy at least two stipulations: Jackson obtained *a large proportion of the "masses" vote; his support was not restricted to specific states and sections but was national in scope.* When the thesis is restated it is more subject to verification and calls for analytical emphasis to be placed upon the historian's space dimension. The presidential contest in 1824 was the first in which the American people directly participated to a measurable extent, or as H. J. Ford has put it, the first to mark "the beginning of a concentration of popular interest on the presidential election." [22] No comparable statistics of the popular vote are available before 1824 and in that election the national vote stood: [23]

Jackson	153,544
Adams	108,740
Clay	47,136
Crawford	46,618
	356,038

These statistics make it possible to translate the vague factual description, "immense vote," with its connotation of extremely widespread support, into an explicit statement that Jackson received approximately 43% of the popular vote, his nearest rival 31%, and his two other rivals, 13% each. (No statistics were presented by Schlesinger for either the popular or the electoral vote on a state or national basis.) Once the verbal description is translated into even such gross quantitative terms as the national totals and percentages, once the problem is not to explain why an "immense," or "overwhelming," or "very large" proportion of the American people wanted Jackson to be president, but why 43% of the "small" (defined below) number of people who actually cast ballots voted for him, the problem becomes easier to handle.

Who Voted for Jackson? Since Jackson received less than 50% of the vote, the statistics appear to rule out the likelihood that all throughout the country the majority of the "chauvinistic masses" who voted cast ballots for Jackson, unless it can actually be demonstrated that his support was more or less uniformly distributed along tight class lines. This follows since the "masses" must logically be expected to outnumber the other classes or the term "masses" is not revelant to the election of 1824. If Jackson's support was very heavy in some areas and very light in others, in some places both the masses and the other classes voted preponderantly for him, and in other places both groups voted preponderantly against him. This conclusion would have to follow unless two conditions obtained; a different proportion of voters are to be designated as belonging to the "masses" and "other classes" in different areas, and both groups displayed uniform voting behavior throughout the country.

To my knowledge no evidence has ever been offered that in 1824 significantly different proportions of the masses voted in the different states where popular suffrage obtained; moreover, breaking down the returns by states demonstrates anything but a uniform distribution. It suggests that if Jackson's widespread military fame and reputed integrity actually do explain his lead in the popular vote, then these generalized factors operated in a remarkably selective manner which demand both explicit statement and further specification. For he carried but eight of the eighteen states in which popular votes were cast, only in six did he get 50% or better, and as the table below shows, Jackson's margin over his nearest rival was 2 to 1 or better only in Alabama, Tennessee, and Pennsylvania.

The approximately 50,000 *plurality* given him in the last two states more than accounts for his lead over John Q. Adams in the nation-wide vote, a fact which should be central to any interpretation of the 1824 election results and of Jackson's popular lead. That is, roughly 42% of Jackson's entire vote came from three states which cast only 23% of the national vote. In these three states he got about 80% of the vote, whereas he had only 43% of the national total, and 32% in the other 15 states.[24]

Table VII—Popular Vote, 1824—States Carried by Jackson

State	Jackson	%	Adams	%	Craw-ford	%	Clay	%	Total
Tennessee	20,197	97.5	216	1.0	312	1.5	—		20,725
Pennsylvania	36,100	76.2	5,440	11.5	4,206	8.9	1,609	3.4	47,355
Alabama	9,443	69.4	2,416	17.8	1,680	12.3	67	0.5	13,606
Mississippi	3,234	64.1	1,694	33.6	119	2.4	—		5,047
North Carolina	20,415*	56.7	—		15,621	43.3	—		36,036
New Jersey	10,985	51.6	9,110	42.8	1,196	5.6	—		21,291
Indiana	7,343	46.6	3,095	19.6	—		5,315	33.7	15,753
Illinois	1,901	40.4	1,542	32.7	219	4.7	1,047	22.2	4,709

* "Peoples Ticket," or anti-"Caucus" vote

Several pertinent facts concerning the election in general, and the strong Jackson states in particular, further indicate the partial nature at best of an explanation which attributes his support primarily, if not exclusively, to "his military fame and . . . the widespread conviction of his integrity." That approximately 350,000 votes in all were cast, out of a population of nearly 11,000,000, indicates how small a percentage of the "chauvinistic masses" actually voted. (The comparable figures for 1828 were 1,150,000 votes, 12,250,000 people.)[25] And to quote Stanwood's standard work on American presidential elections, the figures given above credit to Jackson:

. . . a great many votes which, like the 20,000 in North Carolina, were cast for no candidate in particular, but in opposition to the caucus ticket generally [opposition to nomination by a Congressional party caucus of Crawford as the "regular," albeit unofficial, candidate], and of which it was estimated at the time that 5,000 were given by friends of Adams; and other votes which, in some Northern states, were cast against Adams generally, without being for any particular candidate.[26]

A major source of distortion relative to the popular vote is that the statistics do not include six states where the Legislatures made the choice. In three of the states Jackson received none of the electoral votes; in New York, the most populous state in the Union, he received one out of 36; he took 3 out of 5 in Louisiana, and all 11 in South Carolina. Hence as Jackson received but 15 of the 71 electoral votes of these states, pending a detailed study, the presumption seems reasonable that their popular vote would have substantially decreased his percentage of the national total. Such reasoning is speculative, yet to indicate how little is really known about the popular sentiment in 1824, Stanwood observed that: "there were real contests in very few of the States, so that the partisans of neither [sic] candidate were fully represented at the polls." [27] Thus, Massachusetts, home state of John Q. Adams, where Jackson did not get a single vote, cast more than 66,000 ballots for governor in 1823 and only 37,000 in the presidential election a year later.

Viewed in light of the above considerations, the conclusion seems warranted that Schlesinger's hypothesis regarding the extent and reasons for Jackson's vote in 1824 is not consonant with the election statistics. *The factors denoted by him as voting determinants throughout the country could have been operative only in certain localities, states, and sections; they could not have had the unrestricted nation-wide impact demanded by his hypothesis.*

Conditions Favorable to Jackson. When attention is turned to the three states in which Jackson was strongest, the historian's obligation to specify the conditions under which causal factors actually function becomes more obvious. In states where Jackson secured few votes, or only a minor percentage of the total vote, either his fame and integrity were unknown and unpublicized (subject to investigation if deemed important), or far more likely, they were ineffective as determinants of voting behavior. On the other hand, it is possible that these alleged causal factors were operative in Tennessee, Alabama, and Pennsylvania. Schlesinger's hypothesis then could be restated to set forth the conditions under which Jackson's military fame and integrity determined voting behavior and those which yielded opposite results. By way of illustration, among other conditions which it might be necessary to take into account: Tennessee was Jackson's home when such a factor was extremely important, particularly in a western state seeking national influence (he ran about 40 to 1 in Tennessee). Neighboring Alabama was a frontier area strongly responsive to the victor of the Creek War of 1813-1814 which opened it to settlement. Jackson was of Scotch-Irish descent when marked conflict existed between the New England "Yankee" element, strongly based on the seaboard, and the Scotch-Irish and German elements west of the Alleghenies. Probably associated with these ethnic loyalties and conflicts as a determinant of political behavior—here research using manuscript sources would be indispensable to verify the assumption—is the fact that as early as 1821 the leading politicians of Pennsylvania had decided to run Jackson as a candidate.[28] Local, sectional, and ethnic influences aided his rivals as well, but this only underscores the point that *the significance of the voting statistics is not apparent if only the national totals are considered in isolation and the basic conditions affecting voting patterns in various areas are left unspecified.*

The main point of the discussion has been that the greater the precision achieved in breaking down voting statistics over space, the greater the possibility of fixing the conditions under which a given explanation can be valid. Hypotheses take on more precision, and a greater possibility of verification, if the factual stipulations which they must logically be expected to satisfy are carefully thought out and then demonstrated rather than assumed.

In frontier Tennessee the vote for Jackson was "immense"; in neighboring Kentucky, the home of Henry Clay, Jackson was badly beaten (roughly 17,000 to 6,000). Obviously, in Kentucky military fame and reputed integrity were not key determinants of voting behavior. But it is possible, and, for purposes of illustration, it will be assumed here as fact, that in a number of Kentucky counties Jackson did run ahead of Clay. A comprehensive explanation of the 1824 election would have to explain such phenomena, or at least it should state explicitly that it does not satisfy certain systematic findings.

If the deviant cases not satisfied by the explanation were of the magnitude indicated above—a number of Jackson counties in a strong Clay state—then it would be logical to expect the historian to deal explicitly with questions of this nature: What conditions, if any, differentiated the Jackson counties from those voting for the native son, Henry Clay? Was Jackson's fame greater, and belief in his integrity more firm, in certain counties than in others? If opposite voting patterns occurred in counties where detailed investigation leads one to conclude that his fame and integrity were uniform, what other conditions were different? Given Schlesinger's primary causal factors, why should these different conditions have operated to bring about different patterns of voting behavior?

The last question, the "why" question, would be the interpretative element in formulating that part of the hypothesis covering the deviant cases; the previous "what" questions are in the category of factual description. Factual questions yield information analogous to the natural scientist's statement of the conditions under which water boils at a certain temperature, but they fail to explain why the phenomenon occurs under those conditions. To take a hypothetical case: We might factually demonstrate that in all counties where over 50% of the entire population was Scotch-Irish, over 50% of the popular vote went to Jackson. To explain why this result occurs in such counties is a job of another order and explicit recognition of the distinction between fact and interpretation favors progress towards its solution.

The following possibility is suggested to bring out the potential dangers of generalized explanations which do not attempt to specify the conditions necessary for them to be verifiable. A careful analysis of the areas of Jacksonian strength and weakness, in order to state the conditions under which his military fame and reputed integrity operated as determining factors, might lead to the unanticipated conclusion that they were of relatively minor importance everywhere. It might be observed that Jackson was strong only in areas having certain characteristics: frontier areas not settled by New England migrants and no "native son" candidate; areas dominated by Scotch-Irish and German voters; agrarian areas dependent upon certain staple crops; and so forth. It might also be observed that in a number of areas where detailed investigation demonstrated little or no perceptible differences in awareness of Jackson's heroism or stress upon his integrity, his proportion of the vote *varied widely* depending upon the extent to which the area possessed the characteristics denominated above.

If Schlesinger's explanation could be valid only in areas having specific characteristics in common, and does not hold true when these characteristics are absent, it would be more logical to try to explain the vote for Jackson in terms of these specific characteristics rather than general causes which did not in fact operate generally. No implication is intended that any of these developments took place in fact. The point is that the procedure of attempting to specify the conditions under which a given set of causal factors operate might yield systematic findings not consonant with the hypothesis. These findings might then lead to reformulation of the hypothesis, or to construction of a series of new hypotheses more consonent with the data. In turn these hypotheses would be subject to additional testing through the re-analysis of existing data and the collection of additional data necessary to their verification.

Because the amount of data bearing upon voting behavior in 1824 is circumscribed by the nature of that particular election, and because the time dimension cannot be adequately utilized, a more elaborate example follows of how the potential verifiability of a generalized explanation can be evaluated. The time period covered will be somewhat longer than in Section II, and the spatial units much more delimited than in either Sections II or III.

IV. Generalized Interpretation Analyzed in Terms of the Historian's Time Dimension

As suggested above the historian's time dimension is a complex construction; it is simultaneously a methodological tool and a subtle concept. Although this study confines itself to the methodological aspects of the time dimension, they are pointed up by discussing briefly the time dimension's conceptual role.

To convey more vividly the idea that "a historical phenomenon can never be understood apart from its moment in time," Marc Bloch quoted a nicely turned old Arab proverb: "Men resemble their times more than they do their fathers." [29] Though this idea of historical context is easily accepted and freely talked of, it is terribly difficult to apply in practice. Among other things, it calls for a creative, disciplined imagination, as well as an impressive store of substantive knowledge. The concept associated with the time dimension, therefore, is much less easily handled than the method of recording and analyzing phenomena chronologically.

Notwithstanding the consideration that a really thorough historical analysis must employ both the concept and method inherent in the time dimension—their separateness has been exaggerated here to clarify the point—the mere chronological recording of data is extremely useful in beginning an inquiry into voting behavior during a particular campaign. Just as one thinks in terms of the spatial distribution of voting performance, one "instinctively" thinks in terms of time. Members of some group voted as they "normally" did; others were "more Republican than usual"; still others "sharply broke with tradition," etc. To refer back to the example given in Section III: We would use the space dimension to locate the farm price support issue as a voting determinant for Iowa corn-hog farmers because they have been thought to be strongly Republican over time, and because essentially we want to know whether they cast a higher or lower than "normal" Republican vote.

But as in the case of the space dimension, it is dangerous to use the time dimension impressionistically. And perhaps because chronology is more subject to blurring than geography, the dangers are actually much greater. For unless we really know what normalcy (sic) is, we are easily liable to come a historical cropper. Down is up, up is down, climaxes beginnings, beginnings climaxes, unless we have some accurate objective historical standards to measure from and contrast with, and systematically do so.

The Election of 1896.   Apart from its intrinsic importance, the election of 1896 is of particular interest to students of methodology in political history. It is particularly interesting because the Populist campaign of the nineties coming to a climax (of sorts) in 1896 has long been taken as proof of the Turner frontier thesis covering all phases of American history. Without going into the complicated material involved, the alleged closing of the frontier in 1890 was said to have been directly responsible for the emergence of Populism as a major current in American politics. And Turner and his followers claimed that the emergence of Populism after 1890 proved the broad thesis that the presence or absence of "free land" was the key factor in American history. Again, without going into details, a vital sub-proposition of the frontier thesis held that the dominant conflict form in the United States was sectional, i.e., conflict between the inhabitants of different geographic areas rather than conflict between groups or classes. Though Turnerians recognize the existence of socio-economic group and class conflicts, they essentially regard them as subordinate. In fact, "Un-American," in the best sense of the phrase, describes the view taken by Turnerians of group and class conflicts in the United States (particularly the latter); "Un-American" because their relative insignificance was viewed as stemming from the uniqueness of American society. Class conflict was looked upon as a foreign importation, untrue to the American genius and spirit.[30]

Since the Populist demands of the 1890's were held to be new departures in that they advocated collective action by government to benefit individual entrepreneurs or citizens *directly*, since the voting patterns show distinct sectional differences, since in 1896 the Populists fused with the Democrats, the election of 1896 was taken by Turner to prove his frontier thesis and its sectional subproposition. Note the logical consistency: after 1890 demands were made for collective action, "proof" that the alleged traditional individualism allegedly caused by the presence of alleged free land no longer had a basis in material conditions; the political conflict over the question of collective action found effective *sectional*, not *group or class, expression.*

During the 1930's the Turner thesis came under increasing attack and alternative theses were proposed to explain American history. One alternative thesis, of which Arthur Schlesinger, Sr., was probably the chief proponent, attempted to substitute the rise of the city and the urban movement in America for the significance of the frontier and the westward movement. In place of sectional conflict as the dominant form, Schlesinger postulated the "clash between two cultures—one static, individualistic, agricultural, the other dynamic, collectivistic, urban." [31] The "urban thesis" attracted wide attention in the 1930's, and, in turn, was subjected to criticism. Probably the most elaborate and penetrating attack upon the thesis was made by William Diamond at the close of the decade. The quotation below suggests his main line of criticism:

though urban-rural conflict may be as important as sectionalism, the significance of either one as the basis of an American history is open to serious question. It is certainly legitimate to ask whether emphasis on the existence and importance of the antagonism of city and country does not frequently obscure the further facts (true of sections as well) that "city" is a collective term and that in it lives a heterogeneous population made up of many interest groups and classes leading more or less different ways of life. The question of the meaning of urbanization requires further examination, for if the determining forces in human behavior are to be found in economic and social distinctions rather than in geographical or political groupings, then such a judgment as the one suggested [i.e., increasing urban-rural conflict] becomes not only of little value as a clue to the study of American political history but invalid as well. Nevertheless the flow of people into cities has changed the face of the nation, as once the westward movement did. The conflict of urban and rural populations must, therefore, be given its place as a factor in American history—a factor which has been perhaps as important as the frontier and the westward movement.[32]

In place of sectional or urban-rural conflicts, Diamond was suggesting that the *basic* determinants of American history were conflicts between interest groups and classes. As he saw it, whether in the form of sectionalism or urban-ruralism, political conflicts in the United States really stemmed from socio-economic entities because, dependent upon their socio-economic composition and functions, fundamental differences existed *between* cities, e.g., industrial, commercial, financial cities, metropolises, seaports, inland centers, etc.[33] But though the cities differed from each other, Diamond accepted the view that they had at least one common feature, they all had significant conflicts with their surrounding rural areas. Whatever the *real basis* for the antagonism, therefore, urban-rural conflicts were characteristic of American life. In his words, as applied to the election of 1896:

> But whatever the basis of urban-rural antagonism, whatever the forces that accentuate or soften the clash of city and countryside, the fact remains that in the election of 1896 there was a high urban-rural tension.[34]

That sentence was stated as a proven proposition at the end of a factual demonstration rather than as a hypothesis to be tested. Quoted out of context here, the hypothesis is not clear. But before attempting to remedy the deficiency it is desirable to discuss briefly the challenging and important task Diamond set himself. Though his own approach differed from the urban thesis, it differed even more sharply from the frontier-section thesis. Since he was working at a time when the latter was dominant, and since the urban thesis was consonant with his own in form, if not content, his study concentrated upon establishing that:

> The urban-rural conflict has been of some importance in American history. Little, however, has been done to measure that importance. It is the purpose of this article to take a step in that direction by making a study of the conflict at one fixed point in American history, the first Bryan-McKinley campaign: to establish the existence of that conflict in the nation as a whole and to see whether or not it followed *a recognizable pattern* [italics added].[35]

The Real Significance of Urban-Rural Conflicts. Diamond conceived his first task to be the demonstration of significant urban-rural conflicts throughout the nation. But stated in such terms, the demonstration would support the urban thesis against which his study was directed perhaps as much as against the frontier-section thesis. However, if instead of a general pattern of urban-rural conflict, there was "a recognizable pattern" then, Diamond contended in effect, the urban thesis really would be specious. That is, if voting behavior in 1896 (and elections generally) could be shown to take different patterns according to the different socio-economic structures of given urban-rural areas (Eastern industrial-dairy agricultural, Western commercial-staple agricultural, seaport-perishable agricultural, etc.), Diamond believed his broad thesis of group and class conflicts as the determinants of American history would be supported. Urban-rural tensions affected voting behavior all throughout the country, he maintained, but some cities voted more heavily for McKinley than their hinterland while other cities voted more for Bryan. According to him, these differences were not random but could be shown to follow "a recognizable pattern," i.e., they were associated with a definite socio-economic pattern.

Diamond's article contains so many suggestive ideas that it is difficult to summarize his views without distorting them, but the quotations below provide us with a specific hypothesis subject to systematic analysis:

> It has become a commonplace that Bryan directed his entire campaign in 1896 to both farmer and laborer, to the inarticulate but potentially powerful workers and the vast lower middle classes that make

up the bulk of the population of cities as well as to the farmers of the West and South. Yet because "a solid East and Middle West," the most highly urbanized sections of the nation, overwhelmed and defeated Bryan, it has gone almost unnoticed that he occasionally scored heavily in Eastern cities, the foci of the "toiling masses" to whom he addressed himself. John Giffin Thompson has pointed out—though without statistical evidence—that the "fact that Bryan carried a number of the agricultural states of the West, in 1896, while the East voted against him has obscured the further fact that he received strong support in many of the eastern urban centers while heavy majorities against him were in many cases rolled up in the rural sections of the East." This, if accurate, would be a highly significant comment on the factors which determined the election of 1896, and it would at the same time bear witness to the political cleavage between urban and rural populations.[36]

The hypothesis still has not been made clear but another quotation facilitates doing so. (It is clear in context, the difficulty lies in making it clear in abbreviated form.)

The cities of the East, with the highest *urban-rural tension* [italics added], were the oldest cities in the nation. In the northeast many of the cities were the products of the factory, sometimes the centers of finance. There the large laboring and immigrant populations were set off against a rural background of conservative landowners. There the cities were more radical than the countryside. Most of the cities between the Alleghenies and the Rockies were the offspring of the railroad; they were trading posts and transportation centers. In them frequently were centered the influences against which the farmer of the West rose in protest. They were often the centers on which they [sic] depended for the marketing of their products. Those cities, it has been shown, were more conservative than their surrounding rural populations.[37]

The 1896 Campaign as Catalyst.   Put in other words, Diamond's hypothesis really was that the Bryan campaign of 1896 *increased the intensity of urban-rural political conflicts throughout the entire country*. In given urban-rural political entities (cities within a state) possessing different socio-economic structures the intensified conflicts expressed themselves in different political forms. Northeastern cities were "more radical" than usual; the surrounding rural areas were "more conservative" than usual. The reverse was true in the West; there the rural areas were "more radical," the cities "more conservative." Whether in particular areas the city or its hinterland was "more radical," the same pattern held throughout the country;

the Bryan campaign acted as a catalyst to intensify urban-rural political conflicts having their roots in persistent socio-economic antagonisms.

Before discussing the meaning of "radical" or "conservative," it is necessary to indicate what Diamond meant by "urban-rural tension." He constructed an ingenious index to measure the differences in voting behavior between a city and its hinterland. The relationship was expressed in a "percentage ratio":

> The percentage ratio of a city is the ratio of Bryan's percentage of the votes in that city to the percentage of votes he received in the nonurban sections of the state. The percentage ratio of a state is the ratio of Bryan's total urban percentage to his rural percentage. The result in either case is a number which may be either greater or less than one. If greater, it means that the percentage of urban votes given to Bryan was greater than his percentage of the rural vote of the state. If less, then Bryan did better among the rural population. . . . Ratios from .9 to 1.1, while they show a clear-cut difference in urban and rural votes, will be called the range of low urban-rural tension. Ratios below .9 and above 1.1 will be regarded as representing a high degree of tension between city and country.[38]

Though his definition of urban-rural tension is exceedingly useful, his definition of "radical" is much less so. That the problem is more than semantic is evident to scholars familiar with the difficulties "radical" and "conservative" have caused for political historians. What "radical" means at a given time in American history has never been agreed upon, and Diamond's arbitrary definition, unfortunately, led him into serious trouble. Since Bryan was the nominee of more than one party—though the other parties were really insignificant in 1896—the statistical comparison was made between the returns for Bryan and McKinley, not for the Democratic and Republican parties:

> The Bryan vote, from no matter what source, was basically a radical vote. Given that definition of radicalism, the urban-rural percentage ratio of Bryan votes represents the degree to which cities were more or less radical than rural sections of the states in which those particular cities were located.[39]

Such a definition of radicalism is open to at least two kinds of objection, "substantive" and "methodological." Without attempting to do so here, a good case can be made out for the proposition that the majority of Bryan votes cannot in any meaningful sense be regarded as radical; indeed, in my opinion, it is better characterized as "reactionary." That proposition is certainly debatable but the "methodological" objection is not. The campaign of 1896 was not *tabula rasa*. Deeply felt, persistent traditions and party loyalties are basic to American political history and, in the short run at least, changes in voting behavior are confined to relatively narrow limits. *Within reasonable limits, no matter who ran on the Democratic ticket in 1896, or what kind of campaign the party waged, its nominee would have received a substantial percentage of the total vote.* As in the case of the 1884 election, the table below emphasizes the remarkably broad continuities in American voting behavior during the late nineteenth century despite basic socio-economic changes.[40]

Table VIII—Presidential Elections, 1808-1900
Percent of Popular Vote Cast for Republican and Democratic Candidates

	Rep.	Dem.
1868	52.7	47.3
1872	55.6	43.9
1876	47.9	50.9
1880	48.3	48.2
1884	48.2	48.5
1888	47.8	48.6
1892	43.0	45.9
1896	50.9	46.8
1900	51.7	45.5

The "net turnover" in Democratic strength from 1892 to 1896 was only an insignificant +0.9, a figure which certainly indicates that a substantial number of people who voted for "conservative" Grover Cleveland in 1892 on the Democratic ticket voted for Bryan in 1896 on the Democratic ticket. The inference is undeniable that any political John Doe would also have attracted a considerable number of votes if he had been the Democratic standard bearer.

A definition of "radicalism," therefore, which holds that it can be applied to *every vote for Bryan* "from no matter what source" is meaningless at best, and in this instance, positively harmful to Diamond's own intelligently conceived broad study. For had he attempted to find out *which votes* could reasonably be termed "radical," he would have been forced to examine both *the net turn-over and the gross turnover in voting behavior.* And had he done so, unlike the 1884 election, he would have found that the *gross turn-over* was not only considerable, but that it followed a definite *sectional pattern which invalidated his generalized hypothesis concerning the 1896 election.* Rather than follow the same procedure employed in the 1884 and 1824 analyses, attention here will be focused upon only one state. Such restricted scope enables us to demonstrate that the procedure applied broadly throughout the nation for those years can yield much more precise and definite results when the requisite data is available.

It must be emphasized that the concern here is not with the in-appropriateness of "radical" as a description of all Bryan votes in 1896. In reality, the terms "radical" and "conservative" were irrelevant to the hypothesis under examination, and only served to confuse its conception and attempted verification. When reformu-lated, the hypothesis actually claimed that the dominant determining factors in the 1896 election were certain socio-economic antagonisms taking the shape of urban-rural political conflicts, and that these antagonisms and political conflicts were *intensified* in 1896. Whether the result was increased or diminished "radicalism" really did not matter. The point at issue was that "the determining forces in human behavior are to be found in economic and social distinctions rather than in geographical or political groupings."

The claim that political conflicts were *intensified* in 1896 was not made explicit in Diamond's article but his hypothesis is meaning-less if it does not include that claim. Clearly, if "urban-rural tension" in all Northeastern states, for example, was identical from 1880 to 1900 it would make no sense to maintain that Bryan "occasionally scored heavily in Eastern cities, the foci of the 'toiling masses' to whom he addressed himself." Similarly, the designation of certain cities as "more radical" than their hinterland in 1896 requires not only comparison between given urban and rural entities in 1896, but comparison of their "percentage-ratio" *over time.* Possibly the confused definition of "radicalism," a definition which ignored the time dimension, contributed to the more serious confusion in the hypothesis. For the evidence supporting the claim that voting behavior in 1896 was primarily determined by certain socio-economic antagonisms not covered by the frontier-section and urban theses consisted of a statistical index interpreted as proof that "in the election of 1896 there was a high urban-rural tension."

But *high* in relation to what? Clearly, higher than the urban-rural tension in the previous election, or more meaningfully, higher than the *normal* urban-rural tension. But what was *normalcy* in this case? To find out, one must compile the data over space, as Diamond painstakingly and systematically compiled it for 1896, *for a number of elections and then demonstrate that the tension was higher than normal.* If the tension for a given urban-rural entity were the same in 1896 as in 1892 and 1900 one would hardly conclude that Bryan "scored heavily" in the city as contrasted to the countryside, or *vice versa.* If both the *urban-rural tension and the urban Democratic party percentage were considerably lower,* then there would be solid support for a hypothesis that either certain socio-economic antagonisms, and the political conflicts stemming from them, between the city and its countryside were *diminished* in 1896, or that they became *less* weighty determinants of voting behavior.

An Alternative Hypothesis and Its Implications. Had Diamond been able to carry out his systematic statistical analysis of urban-rural tension *over time* as well as over space, and introduced the rate dimension, in my opinion, he would have rejected the hypothesis holding that Bryan occasionally "scored heavily" in Northeastern cities because of vaguely defined, increased socio-economic antagonisms between "laboring and immigrant populations" and rural "conservative landowners." On the contrary, the hypothesis might then have been postulated that the traditional antagonisms of these groups or classes were diminished, or were overshadowed, in 1896 *by shared antagonisms directed against other groups or classes.* That is, some other form of "tension" such as "sectionalism" might have assumed more importance as a voting determinant than the persistent socio-economic antagonisms reflected in "urban-rural tensions," as Diamond defined them. And once this conclusion had been arrived at, one might well have gone on to make a higher level generalization for all American history—political and non-political—which subsumes several essential features of all three theses, i.e., the "frontier-section," "urban," and "interest groups and classes" theses. For, again in my opinion, all three are partially correct, although, as they are usually stated, even their verifiable elements need considerable modification and reformulation.

If the reader anticipates an attempt to demonstrate the validity of that sweeping judgment, what follows will come as anti-climax. The analysis is confined to demonstrating that in New York State, the systematic statistics of voting behavior indicate that intersectional antagonisms modified the determining impact of intrastate, or intra-section urban-rural antagonisms, and that the Bryan campaign raised issues which tended to narrow rather than widen the area of political conflict between the urban and rural populations. *That is, the issues raised by the Bryan campaign were such as to cut across group or class lines, and, in relative terms, united voters normally antagonistic to each other against voters in another section, also normally mutually antagonistic.*

Thus, whatever the political weight assigned to factors associated with the "frontier-section," "urban," "interest groups and classes" theses for longer periods of American history, *in 1896 more weight* should be given to the "frontier-section" factors and *less weight* to those associated with the other two. Actually, this formulation implies that *some* weight should be given to all three types of factors, and that estimates of the relative amount of weight could only be made after an exceedingly thorough, systematic, and complicated analysis. Moreover, the formulation implies that similar results would be found if the same procedure were followed in states other than New York. It does not imply, however, that the pattern would be the same everywhere.

The Bryan Vote Compared with the "Normal" Democratic Vote. Perhaps the discussion has wandered far enough afield to justify repetition in the interests of greater clarity. In the study under analysis, apart from other methodological objections, the failure to compare the 1896 election with those preceding and following it makes the real significance of the results impossible to comprehend. Though the space dimension was systematically employed to analyze voting behavior, the analysis was fundamentally ahistorical. Compilation of data over time, the basic tool of the historian, was ignored.

It is a major proposition of this monograph that quantitative data are meaningless when isolated from either their spatial or chronological contexts. Presented in ahistorical fashion such data might seem to have one meaning; in historical context they may have entirely opposite meanings. Were urban-rural conflicts a constant factor in American politics, were they in 1896 the start or culmination of a long-time trend, was the 1896 election a deviant?

Similar questions need to be asked in regard to sectional, as well as group and class, conflicts. Comparison with other elections was even more necessary than usual since the hypothesis claimed that intensified socio-economic antagonisms resulted in Bryan occasionally "scoring heavily" among the "toiling masses" of Northeastern cities. Yet, in chronological isolation, the 1896 election returns cannot be taken to prove any proposition other than the relative strength in that year of the Republican and Democratic parties in given localities. Certainly they provide little factual basis for a hypothesis which assumes that workers in a number of Northeastern cities responded favorably to the Bryan campaign. (Actually the claim was made that this situation obtained in all five New England states having at least one city of 45,000 population, and in New York.) Reformulated, the hypothesis must demonstrate factually that *the Democratic vote among the working classes in those cities was heavier than usual, and that the increase can be definitely attributed to Bryan's campaign.* Only a factual demonstration of this kind would provide a systematic basis for the hypothesis under examination, i.e., that intensified socio-economic antagonisms between the urban and rural populations in the Northeast were the major determinants of voting behavior in 1896.

In point of fact, when comparison is made with preceding elections, support appears to be lent to a hypothesis—advanced here solely for illustrative purposes—that the Bryan vote in New York and other Northeastern states, far from reflecting intensified "urban-rural tension" in 1896, *was a sharply diminished remnant of the normal Democratic vote.* Just the reverse appears to be true of the assumptions that Bryan occasionally scored heavily in the Eastern cities, and that acute urban-rural tension, intensified by his campaign, was responsible for the Democratic vote in that section. So far as can be determined readily from the *Tribune Almanac, every* major urban area in the Northeast gave Bryan a considerably lower vote than it had usually cast for Democratic candidates in previous elections. The decreased Democratic urban strength in 1896, and to a lesser extent in succeeding campaigns, is consonant with our hypothetical thesis; it is in flat contradiction to the hypothesis which claims that intensified socio-economic antagonisms taking the form of "urban-rural tensions" were the major determinants of voting behavior in the Northeast. One is even tempted to go so far as to speculate that the Bryan campaign *in 1896 perceptibly weakened the Democratic party for a number of elections thereafter in the Northeastern cities.*

Though the real concern here is not with the question of what "radical" and "conservative" means, or whether it is correct to characterize the Bryan vote as "radical," a reference to the latter question throws light on the hypothesis' basic weakness. The inappropriateness of denoting all votes in 1896 for Bryan as "radical" without examination of previous voting patterns perhaps is best seen in this paradoxical situation: If all votes for Bryan be taken as "radical," then New York and Kings counties, for example, were more "radical" than most rural counties but they were much more "conservative" in depression-ridden 1896 when Bryan vigorously denounced Wall Street than in relatively prosperous 1892 and 1888! (Brooklyn is Kings County.) Table IX below [41] appears to demonstrate convincingly that the urban-rural conflict in presidential elections needs to be considered in historical perspective.

Possibly it is belaboring the point but preparing such a table on a national scale would have presented enormous difficulties and it is easy to appreciate why the author of the 1896 study confined his statistical compilation to a single election. However, it seems obvious that the value of his study would have been greatly enhanced had he not only suggested an interesting approach to the Bryan campaign but been able to carry his work to its necessary conclusion. Of course, it is easy enough to write that the work should have been carried through to its "necessary conclusion." The fact that that numerous historical studies have made statistical analyses based solely on a single set of election returns indicates that the procedure cannot be attributed to personal failings but has its roots in the nature of the material. At the same time it is necessary to recognize that there has been a basic conceptual weakness in American political historiography. Studies in political history which make anything like a systematic analysis of voting behavior over time and space are the exception rather than the rule.

Table IX—Presidential Vote—1900, in Urban Counties, the Strongest Democratic Rural Counties, and New York State, in Percentages

	New York County (Urban)		Kings County (Urban)		Schoharie County (Rural)		Seneca County (Rural)		New York State	
	Dem.	Rep.	Dem.	Rep.	Dem.	Rep.	Dem.	Rep.	Dem.	Rep.
1860	65.2	34.8	56.4	43.6	56.2	43.8	49.7	50.3	46.3	53.7
1864	66.8	33.2	55.3	44.8	62.6	37.4	54.9	45.1	49.5	50.5
1868	69.4	30.6	59.0	41.0	59.1	40.9	53.9	46.1	50.6	49.4
1872	58.7	41.3	53.3	46.7	56.1	43.9	49.7	50.3	46.8	53.2
1876	65.7	34.2	59.5	40.4	59.9	39.9	46.8	47.8	51.4	48.2
1880	59.9	39.8	53.9	45.7	58.7	40.7	52.5	46.9	48.4	50.3
1884	58.5	39.5	54.8	42.4	59.2	38.5	51.6	46.5	48.2	48.2
1888	60.1	39.9	53.7	45.6	56.1	41.4	49.8	48.1	48.0	49.1
1892	61.5	34.7	56.8	40.0	55.3	39.5	47.7	46.4	47.9	44.6
1896	44.0	50.8	39.7	56.3	51.0	46.6	44.6	53.5	38.7	57.6
1900	52.2	43.9	48.3	49.6	51.6	46.2	46.8	51.2	43.8	53.1

Studying the table one can observe that the decline in normal Democratic strength was *much sharper in the cities of New York and Brooklyn than in the rural Democratic counties, and considerably more than in the state as a whole.* Thus, in 1896 compared to 1892, the Democratic percentage of the total vote was 17.5 less in New York County, 17.1 less in Kings (Brooklyn), only 4.3 and 3.1 less in Schoharie and Seneca respectively, and 9.2 in the entire state. In fact, Schoharie became the banner Democratic county in the state, and even Seneca, for the first time since at least 1860, cast a heavier Democratic vote than either New York or Kings counties. The Bryan campaign for monetary inflation, it might therefore be speculated, in relative terms was more favorably received in rural farming areas suffering from commodity price declines than in urban areas consuming farm commodities. And the inappropriateness of applying the term "radical' to groups waging such a campaign perhaps is underscored by the recognition that "tinkering with the currency" required no structural changes in American institutions or principles. Here again the time dimension is indispensable to historical analysis, for such "tinkering" had long been a part of the American political tradition.

Did Urban or Rural Voters Respond More Favorably to the Bryan Campaign? If urban-rural tension in New York is calculated from the ratio of the urban vote percentage to the rural vote percentage for the Democratic party—the index used by Diamond—then Bryan's campaign had the effect of reducing urban-rural tension in the state to a lower point than in any election from 1860 to 1900! This can be seen most readily by comparing the Democratic percentage in the most urbanized counties, New York and Kings, with the party's percentage in the state from 1860 to 1900. The extent to which the Democratic campaign in 1896 alienated the party's urban followers can also be gauged by comparing its sharp decline in New York and Kings with the relatively small decline in Schoharie and Seneca.

Contrasting urban and rural Democratic response in New York to Bryan's campaign illustrates the inaccuracy of what Diamond accepted as a valid "commonplace," i.e., "that Bryan directed his entire campaign in 1896 to both farmer and laborer, to the inarticulate but potentially powerful workers and the vast lower middle classes that make up the bulk of the population of cities as well as the farmers of the West and South." More precisely, if the group which controlled the Democratic party in 1896 actually believed that a program to raise commodity prices and the cost of living for urban dwellers, couched in terms of sectional conflict, was destined to win votes in that depression year, then the urban election returns in the Northeast must have come as a rude shock. (Whatever Bryan may have said in specifically addressing himself to Eastern audiences, a dominant theme in the free silver "crusade" was the conflict between the allied South and West against the Northeast—and the "goldbugs" made certain that this fact was brought home to Eastern voters.)

The objection might be raised that the statistics cited above showing sharp decreases in Democratic strength in New York and Kings counties do not necessarily indicate that Democratic "workers" or members of the "lower middle classes" deserted the party in 1896. Conceivably, non-working and non-lower middle class Democratic support in New York County, for example, could have fallen off to such an extent as to account for the party's decreased percentage. *Probably this was the case to some extent, but it also appears clear that this was far from the whole story.* Unfortunately, the

Assembly Districts were reapportioned between the 1892 and 1896 elections so direct comparison is difficult. But that Democratic support fell off in working class as well as in non-working class areas is seen in the much smaller Democratic pluralities *in every Assembly District.* (Not even the most intricate pattern of gerrymandering could have eliminated a substantial number of "lower-class" districts in New York in the 1890's, and the larger number of Assembly Districts probably resulted in more homogeneous units.) Whereas in 1892 the Democrats carried every one of the thirty Assembly Districts, for the most part by extremely wide margins, in 1896 they only took eighteen of the thirty-six Districts by more than 100 votes, the Republicans carried fourteen, and of the remaining four, the Democratic plurality was less than 100 in two, and the Republicans also took two districts by a few votes.[42]

In an attempt to achieve greater precision a convenient device was employed to identify the working class districts without exhaustive research. The assumption was made that they were likely to be those in which the Socialist Labor Party was strongest. Party percentages were calculated for the two "most Socialist" districts in 1896 and are shown in the table below.[43]

Table X—Party Percentages, 1896, in the Most Socialist Assembly Districts

	12th A.D.	16th A.D.
Republican	39.6	43.3
Democratic	45.1	43.0
Socialist Labor	14.0	12.6

In 1892 the Socialist Labor party did not achieve anything like these percentages in any district; almost certainly, this indicates that its strength was augmented in 1896 by defections from the Democrats. *But the extent to which the Republicans also must have made inroads into the working class vote is suggested by the fact that even in the two "most Socialist" districts the combined Democratic (including the Populists) and Socialist Labor vote was less than the Democratic vote alone for the entire county in 1892.* The county Democratic vote in 1892 was 61.5%; in 1896 the 12th A.D. combined vote was 59.1%, the 16th A.D., 55.6%. If the 1892 county vote is combined for the Democratic, Populist, and Socialist Labor parties, the contrast is even greater, for it came to 64.6%. And in

1892 there were a number of Assembly Districts in which the Democratic vote alone was well above 70%, whereas in 1896 no district approached that figure.

That conclusions concerning voting behavior require painstaking analysis is illustrated by the paradox seemingly involved in the following statement. Both these propositions might well have been true in 1896: workers made up a *higher proportion* of New York County Democratic voters in 1896 than in any previous election; a *smaller proportion* of workers voted Democratic in 1896 than in any previous election. Given a much sharper decline in Democratic support among non-workers than among workers, both propositions would be accurate and consistent with each other. But if considered alone, the first proposition lends itself to the erroneous conclusion that Bryan scored heavily among the New York masses to whom he allegedly addressed himself.

Table XI—Comparison of Democratic Percentages, 1892 and 1896, in New York County and in "Most Socialist" Assembly Districts

Year	Dem.	New York County Combined (D., Pop., S.L.)	12th A.D. Combined	16th A.D. Combined	12th A.D. Dem.	16th A.D. Dem.
1892	61.5	64.6	—	—	—	—
1896	44.0	47.2	59.1	55.6	45.1	43.0

The statistics cited above appear to invalidate the hypothesis which rests on the assumption that the Bryan campaign attracted greater than usual Democratic support in New York lower class districts; instead, they indicate a marked shift to the Republican party. Inspection of election returns in numerous cities, as printed in the *Tribune Almanac for 1897*, reveals that the pattern was uniform in the Northeast. The conclusion seems warranted, therefore, that both the space and time dimensions need to be utilized systematically by historians if accurate *descriptions* of voting behavior are to be achieved, let alone if verifiable *interpretations* are to be advanced for voting behavior.

V. Analyzing a Hypothesis for a Specific Causal Factor

Until this point hypotheses have been examined which did not differentiate between voting groups, or offered only generalized causal factors, or both. Section V deals with a hypothesis which is explicit in its identification of the group it claims to have been affected by a specific set of causal factors. Unlike the 1884 election, for example, the problem is not to find a way to learn which group's voting behavior could have been determined by a generalized causal factor. The problem tackled here is to establish that a specific causal factor, or set of factors, actually operated in accordance with a hypothesis' claims.

Necessarily, all explanations of voting behavior couched in group terms depend upon characteristics common to most, if not all, members of that group. Those characteristics may not be actually shared by every member of the group, nor are they rigidly confined to its members. But the logic underlying any claim that a certain group is responsive to a specific causal factor is that its members are more likely than non-members to possess the characteristics making voters responsive to that causal factor. Since few individuals other than hermits belong only to one group, explanations of group voting behavior have another logical premise which is best stated in connection with a concrete example.

Suppose a hypothesis to be offered claiming that Irish-Americans voted "strongly Democratic" because that party favored easier immigration and naturalization laws. In effect, this type of explanation connotes that one set of characteristics, i.e., those associated with Irish descent, is assigned greater weight in determining the voting behavior of individuals possessing them in common than unspecified characteristics of those same individuals which place them in other group classifications (class, education, etc.).

Our hypothesis gives primary emphasis to a specific causal factor but it does not rule out the possibility that other factors and characteristics associated with membership in other groups affected the voting decisions of Irish-Americans. It means only that their common ethnic characteristics or loyalties resulted in a common voting pattern cutting across the lines of class, education, etc. However, although other possible determinants of Irish-American voting behavior are not ruled out, at best our hypothesis assigns them a subordinate role. The main point might be stated in this form: For a hypothesis based upon group characteristics to be considered potentially verifiable, it must increase our predictive ability. Other things being equal, according to our hypothetical explanation, Irish-American workers should vote more Democratic than non-Irish workers; and so on for all economic classes, or other non-ethnic group categories. *But it would be entirely consistent with the hypothesis if Irish workers were more Democratic than Irish employers.*

Taking leave of the balmy realm of logical abstraction, an attempt now will be made to test the line of reasoning sketched above on the rockier terrain of reality.

The Election of 1860. A considerable number of explanations have been offered for the outcome of the 1860 election and two foremost American historians, Samuel E. Morison and Henry S. Commager, synthesized the material in this fashion:

> Apart from the Democratic split, northern labor was the decisive force in the election. The German-Americans for the most part had joined the Democratic party as soon as they became naturalized; but they had suffered too much from tyranny in the fatherland to support it in any new shape. The personality of Lincoln swept them into a new party allegiance, and in conjunction with the New England element they carried the northwestern states . . . And in some obscure way northern labor had come to look upon slavery as an ally of the northern capitalism that exploited him [sic].[44]

Of the various hypotheses which this paragraph holds to be valid, analysis is given here to the one explaining why German-Americans switched to the Republicans in 1860. For purposes of illustration the assumption will be accepted that such a switch took place.

It is important to note that the hypothesis holds that voters of German descent *all over the country* were more or less influenced by the combined impact of the same two causal factors; experience with tyranny in Germany led them to support the party (Republican) opposed to tyranny (slavery) in the United States, and the personality of Lincoln swept them from erstwhile political moorings. Precisely because the causal factors were ascribed to *group characteristics* of German-Americans, the hypothesis may reasonably be interpreted to mean that throughout the country members of that group "for the most part" cast Republican ballots essentially for the same reasons. The phrase was used to describe their former allegiance and, while not precise, "for the most part" conveys the idea that considerably more than 50% of the German-Americans voted Republican in 1860. Their voting behavior was described as a decisive factor in the Northwestern states not as a result of sectionalism, or of any particular conditions obtaining there, but because they constituted a sizeable voting group only in that section. (In other areas their numerical strength was so limited as to be of only local significance in the popular or electoral vote.)

Though the hypothesis does not necessarily imply a rigid, uniform voting pattern among German-Americans the country over, it must mean that their votes were cast in somewhat the same proportion in most areas. Of course, variations are to be expected; other factors may have influenced German-Americans of different classes, sections, religious persuasion, etc. The hypothesis, therefore, is consonant with some variation in the group's voting percentage for the Republican party. For example, if good grounds existed for the belief that Northern capitalism was allied to slavery, other things being equal, German-American workers in the North might have cast a heavier Republican percentage than their compatriots who were capitalists.

Perhaps it is useful to translate the verbal formulation into statistical terms in order to develop the logical implications of the hypothesis more clearly, as well as to indicate the kind of systematic voting data which would make it potentially verifiable. As noted above, one cannot be expected to support a hypothesis based upon ethnic characteristics by demonstrating that members of all possible subdivisions within the group (class, section, religion, etc.) voted in the same proportion for a political party. What must be demonstrated, however, is that in *comparison* with voters in similar categories outside the group, German-Americans consistently voted higher. That is, the hypothesis in effect predicts that if the Republican percentage in 1860 among all workers were 60%, among all Northern employers 40%, among all voters in the Northwestern states 65%, among all Catholics 30%, etc., the Republican percentage among *German-American* workers, employers, Northwesterners, Catholics, etc., would be *higher* than 60%, 40%, 65%, 30% respectively. (To achieve greater clarity the important problems will be ignored of whether the German-American vote has to be consistently higher in *every* significant category, and how much above the average it has to be.)

Obtaining the Systematic Data. Having indicated the kind of systematic voting data required, the task now is to find real-life data to support our hypothesis. That is, we must demonstrate that in 1860 voters of German descent "for the most part" switched over to the Republicans because of the combined impact of two causal factors: Experience with tyranny in Germany led them to oppose the party of tyranny in the United States, i.e., the Democratic party now dominated by slaveholders; Lincoln's personality appealed to voters of German descent. In reality, the hypothesis makes a considerable number of factual assumptions apart from its causal inferences, but attention here is only focused upon its assumptions concerning actual voting behavior.

For the hypothesis to be potentially verifiable it is necessary to demonstrate that a common pattern exists for German-American voting behavior in 1860. In other words, within "reasonable" limits of variation, German-Americans grouped in subdivisions of one broad category such as economic class, geographic location, religious persuasion, etc., must be found to have made similar voting decisions. If, when classified in terms of a meaningful criterion which divides them systematically into subdivisions also containing non-Germans, the voting patterns of German-Americans do not vary greatly from subdivision to subdivision, and consistently tend to be more Republican than the average for their subdivision, then the systematic data would support the hypothesis. But the heavy weight given by the hypothesis to its claimed causal factors as determinants of German-American voting behavior does not permit a great deal of variation because of other factors.

Fortunately, long historical interest in the question of whether the "German vote" in the Northwest decisively affected the 1860 election outcome provides us with some systematic, albeit imprecise, group data in terms of geographic location. That is, we cannot classify German-Americans throughout the country according to economic class, social status, religion, etc., but we can roughly ascertain their voting patterns in terms of geographic entities such as wards, townships, counties, states, sections.

For reasons perhaps reiterated too frequently, while no rigidly uniform pattern is necessary, given the nature of the hypothesis, German-American voting percentages in the separate geographic entities must be expected to show some degree of consistency. To take an extreme case, suppose it were found that the patterns were completely random within states and between states. If that were true, German-Americans clearly were not generally affected by the causal factors the hypothesis holds to be the most weighty determinants affecting them *as a group*.

A random pattern means that German-American voters were no more likely to cast Republican ballots than the average voter in the different geographic entities. Yet if we cannot show that our causal factors had sufficient impact upon *enough* members of the group to make them *more likely* to have cast Republican ballots than the average of all voters in the different geographic entities, what warrant would there be for assuming that those causal factors influenced *any* member *because of his ancestry?* That is, some voters who happened to be of German descent may have decided to vote for the party of Lincoln because they believed it opposed tyranny, and because his personality appealed to them. But the same proportion of members of all other ethnic groups also might have voted Republican for the *same reasons*. If this were so, the hypothesis based upon German characteristics would be specious. Under those circumstances the problem would be why certain German-Americans voted Republican, not why members of that group in general voted Republican. Perhaps those individuals could be placed in another group but its criteria would not be characteristics associated with German descent.

Since the hypothesis is couched in terms applicable to German-Americans throughout the country, and our data is classified in geographic units, it is not enough to show that *German*-Americans in several localities or states voted preponderantly Republican. Even a factually correct statement that in the Northwest members of the group preponderantly voted Republican would not in itself lend support to our hypothesis. Such a statement in no way provides the requisite systematic data to demonstrate that German-Americans in the Northwest, let alone throughout the country, were *more likely* to vote Republican than non-German-Americans. If it could be shown historically that *as a group the German-Americans had never displayed any homogeneous voting pattern in the nation but tended to conform to the dominant pattern of the area in which they resided, if it could be shown that this pattern obtained in the 1860 election,* then clearly a different explanation would be called for than the one given in our hypothesis.

The Spatial Incidence of German Voting Patterns Over Time. Various historians have commented upon German voting behavior in 1860 but probably the most comprehensive study, based largely on quantitative data, offers a hypothesis which is consonant with the systematic voting data pertinent to it. Moreover, it differs markedly from the one based on opposition to tyranny and the personality of Lincoln as distinctive factors affecting the decisions of German-American voters. According to Andreas Dorpalen:

> From the earliest colonial times the German element in this country had shown itself particularly susceptible to environmental pressure. It accepted, and adopted, conditions as it found them.[45]

Though his study hardly provides sufficient evidence to support this arresting thesis adequately, it is at least suggestive. Of more importance for our purposes, he analyzed in some detail the 1860 voting behavior of German-Americans throughout the country in terms of response to sectional environmental pressures. Rather than the German-American vote exhibiting the uniform national pattern demanded by our hypothesis, in percentage terms, it varied according to sectional, state, and even local patterns. Though the dominant patterns differed widely throughout the nation, to the extent that the German-American vote could be identified it *generally* tended to *conform* to the vote pattern of the section, state, and locality. It must be emphasized that the identification of the German vote necessarily was crude because of the study's national scope, but Dorpalen's work suggests that more intensive research and more precise methods might support the following formulation:

In different geographic subdivisions (sections, states, etc.), German-American voting percentages *tended to conform to the average of all voters* within each subdivision. But compared to members of their own ethnic group, German-American voters' behavior in one subdivision *varied widely* from German-American voters' behavior in other subdivisions. Stated in other words, German-American *group variations* in the different subdivisions tended to parallel the *average variations* in the different sub-divisions. Thus, the systematic data Dorpalen marshalled supported his hypothesis of German-American conformity to environmental pressures.

Probably because the German influence in the Northwest had long been cited as *the* cause, or *a* cause, of the Republican victory in 1860, Dorpalen's most intensive analysis was given to that section. He employed a variety of quantitative techniques to determine the degree of Republican strength among Germans in the Northwestern states. The size of the area covered, and the difficulties in identifying the German vote apparently caused him to use fairly crude quantitative tests. But in the absence of more refined analyses yielding contrary results, Dorpalen's statistical findings appear to be convincing, and are reinforced by impressionistic evidence. Perhaps a seeming digression here really is pertinent.

Although this study is designed to suggest the contributions systematic research methods might make to historical studies, it hardly means to imply that impressionistic methods and data are valueless. On the contrary, as historians are painfully aware, there are valuable kinds of evidence which it is difficult, if not impossible, to convert to quantitative form. No doubt it is far harder to devise and *consistently apply* methods or rules which evaluate impressionistic evidence and enable scholars to arrive at some consensus (factual or interpretive) than it is to do the same thing for quantitative data. Yet efforts toward that end are more likely to be rewarded if the historian adds another set of tools to his intellectual equipment. That is, if historians explore the possibilities of simultaneously employing traditional impressionistic methodology and systematic quantitative techniques in attacking the complex problems involved in understanding man's past, they are likely to come closer to their goals and improve both types of methodology to boot.

To resume the discussion of Dorpalen's use of both quantitative and impressionistic evidence to support his hypothesis: Once he reformulated the long-debated problem to take into account the time and space dimensions of German voting patterns, Dorpalen, in effect, neatly delineated the systematic voting data which must be considered by any hypothesis treating any segment of those patterns in 1860. Whether his hypothesis is verifiable or not, the quantitative and impressionistic evidence cited by him demonstrates the factual inaccuracy of the interpretation which assumed that the "German vote" in the Northwest (or other sections or areas) was determined by causal factors which did not similarly influence non-German voters.

For example, Dorpalen showed that in the ten Indiana counties where Germans had mainly settled, Lincoln only carried three. Of more importance is the fact that though the Republicans scored considerable gains over 1856 in all ten counties, *the increases were not disproportionate to its gains* in other Indiana counties where few German-Americans lived! And in the nine Wisconsin counties with the strongest German-American concentration, Lincoln only carried five to Douglas' four. Again, as in Indiana, Republican gains in counties of German concentration were not disproportionate to those in non-German counties.[46] If in areas where the dominant voting pattern was not Republican the German-American vote also was not Republican, if in areas where German-Americans apparently gave strong support to Lincoln other groups also gave him strong support, if in certain states or sections Lincoln ran strongly both in non-German and German areas, then the thesis of German-American conformity to environmental pressures is given considerable credence.

The heart of Dorpalen's analysis was a comparison of statistics for German settlement and the vote in 1860 throughout the Northwest;[47] it affords little justification for a hypothesis requiring disproportionate German-American support for the party opposed to tyranny and offering a candidate with the personality of Lincoln. *That the interpretation of a fact depends on whether the fact is treated in haphazard isolation or seen as part of a body of systematic data* is nicely illustrated in Dorpalen's summary of his findings:

. . . while it is correct to say that Lincoln's victory in the northwest would have been impossible without German support, it is wrong to conclude that his German vote was out of proportion to the size of the German element in the northwestern states. In reality the Germans did no more to assure Lincoln's victory than did their American-born neighbors. Nor did they do so in any other section or in the nation as a whole.[48]

If more intensive and comprehensive research than has been undertaken to-date confirms Dorpalen's description of the German-

American voting pattern in 1860 and previous elections—that is, it closely conformed to dominant sectional or other spatial patterns—an excellent example would exist of the utility of stating a hypothesis in terms of the systematic voting data necessary to satisfy it. The hypothesis offered at the outset of Section V rested upon the assumption that German-American voters possessed characteristics which made them more likely to vote Republican than the average of all voters in the Northwest. *Although the hypothesis might appear to be consonant with the "facts" if attention were confined to the German-American vote in the Northwest, it does not hold true when the German and non-German vote in the Northwest, and throughout the country, is examined.*

Which Hypothesis to Test? Since our concern with this material is essentially illustrative rather than substantive, let us assume that Dorpalen's description of German and non-German voting patterns is accurate, and his thesis of German voting conformity to environmental pressures is verifiable. Now if we are interested in finding out why the Germans in the Northwest preponderantly switched to the Republicans, we must *first* determine what caused a significant proportion of the Northwestern population as a whole to switch over to the Republicans. (It is easily demonstrated that such a switch did take place when the Northwestern population is considered as a whole.) *Precise, comprehensive, and systematic statements of the facts of voting behavior are necessary to evaluate a hypothesis, but they are also necessary to arrive at a logical priority for which hypothesis to test out of a multitude of possibilities.* It seems logical to claim that even if data for German-American and non-German-American voting patterns were available only for the Northwest, any historian blessed with a normal amount of insight would give higher priority to the hypothesis of German-American conformity than the hypothesis resting upon German-American characteristics making them peculiarly responsive to the Republican party. Such a priority would be especially logical because recent studies emphasize the conformist tendencies of immigrants in general.

When the problem of German voting behavior in the Northwest is stated in terms of why the section went over to the Republicans, a persuasive answer is given by Paul W. Gates' recent study.[49] Gates' work in the field of land history entitles his views to attention and his hypothesis can be stated in this oversimplified fashion: The position taken by the Democratic administration of President Buchanan on the public land question after the Panic of 1857 was favorable to Southern pro-slavery interests, certain land-speculator-politicians, and other interested parties identified with the South, and unfavorable to actual squatter-settlers, settler-speculators and "antislavery" land monopolists from the East and Middle West. The Buchanan administration's policy was so unfavorably received in the Northwest that large numbers of voters in the public land states swung over to the Republican party which promised to enact a genuine homestead measure. Hence, Republican victory in the Northwest resulted from its campaign promises on the land question, and from the actual performance of Buchanan's administration which ran counter to the desires and needs of a majority of the section's residents.

Clearly, if Dorpalen's description of the German-American voting pattern in the nation is accurate, then Gates' hypothesis is consistent with it and is a logical one to explore in examining the Republican victory in the Northwest. Whether the hypothesis is more than potentially verifiable is immaterial here. The crux of the discussion has been to underscore the importance of recognizing the logical implications of a hypothesis based upon group voting behavior. Once such recognition is attained, it is possible to marshal the requisite systematic voting data and determine whether the hypothesis is potentially verifiable. If this procedure is not followed, however, the danger exists that specious causal factors may appear to be so plausible as to gain wide acceptance and thereby divert attention from the real determinants of voting behavior.

VI. Epilogue

Until this point the study has essentially dealt with the problems of learning what happened, where and when it happened, and who did it. In a sense, although filled with technical difficulties and demanding arduous research, these phases of inquiry are relatively the easiest in terms of satisfactory resolution. They call for a high order of intellectual clarity and articulation but the major difficulties they present might really be viewed as mechanical and administrative, requiring efficient organization and adequate forces rather than highly skilled, intelligent, imaginative historical research.

When attempts are made to answer questions involving the why and how of American political behavior, a considerably more complex field is entered. Granted that we were able to describe what happened accurately, and who voted for it to happen, we still would not know why they voted as they did, and how their beliefs came to be formed. In other words, what are the opinion-making and opinion-manipulating devices and institutions utilized at various times to persuade various groups that they should vote for a particular party or individual, for particular reasons? How effective are these several instrumentalities in achieving such persuasion, and under what conditions? To what extent does tradition condition voter beliefs; to what extent are voter beliefs the specific result of purposive action by specific individuals, groups or institutions; to what extent are these beliefs by-products of ostensibly non-political groups, activities, social processes, and institutional patterns; to what extent are these beliefs consciously or unconsciously acquired or inculcated?

Obviously, questions involving the why and how of political behavior are extremely difficult to answer for so heterogeneous and dynamic a country as the United States. It cannot be overstressed that establishing the objective correlations indicated above does not automatically solve these questions. On the contrary, *they merely allow these questions to be put forth in meaningful form.* That is, questions can then be derived from known facts, not erroneous or metaphysical impressions, and the answers to the questions can be tested to conform with all known facts. Moreover, attempts to answer these questions may reveal that insufficient correlations have been established and lead to efforts to establish additional correlations.

But if one essays beyond simple description, correlations can only point the way for historical research, they cannot take its place. One may be able to establish beyond reasonable doubt, for example, that for given time periods German-Americans tend to conform to the dominant patterns of their community without knowing why they do so, how they came to be persuaded, and under what persuasion they ceased to do so. Correlations thus can be thought of on two levels, descriptive and interpretative; they are adequate for the first but merely suggestive for the second.

This study is not designed to deal with the complicated problems involved in the attainment of genuinely objective historical interpretations of systematic, well-described, known data; that is, interpretations which can be described accurately as consistent with scientific procedures. Yet it seems reasonable to maintain that before we can have such interpretations, or even argue logically whether they are possible under any circumstances, *we must have known data in manageable form.* Lacking sufficient data of this character, statements on the subject, both *pro* and *con*, really are incapable of resolution. No implication of mechanical separation is intended here. Self-evidently, the processes do not take place independently of each other, nor would it be desirable that they do so. Nonetheless, at the present stage of controversy and development, known data of the type called for above and techniques to handle them would seem to be a prerequisite if historiographic advances are to be made, and if arguments relative to "scientific history" are not to remain at the mercy of the rapid changes of intellectual climate so characteristic of the twentieth century.

Russell E. Planck

PUBLIC OPINION IN FRANCE
AFTER THE LIBERATION, 1944-1949

I. Introduction

History presents many unsolved problems because the past has not preserved all that the historian needs to know. Historical data are particularly incomplete in the field of public opinion. The inarticulateness of the majority of people adds to the difficulty of finding "historical data on average people and everyday situations." [1] As a result, the historian who deals with group attitudes is forced to rely on the testimony of the few who speak rightly or wrongly for the many. These problems would not exist, at least in their present form, had people's attitudes on important issues been investigated in earlier times in much the same way as they are in today's public opinion polls.

Public opinion matters are not the express business of all historians, though at some time most encounter problems which would at least be simplified if information about the structure and the molding of opinion were at their disposal. The absence of such information is serious for those historians who are concerned with the climate of opinion of a given period and with the influence of public opinion upon institutions—and especially for political historians since the end of the 18th Century when in the western world steadily growing numbers of the populace were more directly drawn into public activities.

It is hardly fruitful to linger on the obvious deficiences in historical sources and, therefore, in historical knowledge. A more

The author wishes to express his gratitude to Professors Shepard B. Clough and Paul F. Lazarsfeld for their encouragement and help.

constructive approach would be to attempt to remedy the situation by coordinating the efforts of the historian and the polling specialist in the spirit expressed by the Committee on Historiography in *The Social Sciences in Historical Study*.[2] The historian would do well to examine the progress of public opinion research for its potential usefulness to historiography. The present study is designed to aid the historian in this task by examining the material of one polling agency, the *Institut Français d'Opinion Publique* (IFOP) from the end of 1944 to the beginning of 1949.

Whatever the success of the present investigation, it can at best only suggest the possible uses of opinion research in the writing of history. The potential value of this research can be fully realized only through interdisciplinary efforts by the historian and the public opinion student. In another article of this volume, Paul F. Lazarsfeld sets forth some specific recommendations for such co-operation. The historian and the pollster share several areas of concern. We shall presently see that the polling method can supply the historian with factual data, data relative to attitudes, and data concerning prevailing values. Furthermore, in connection with both attitudes and values, polls can reveal changes over time and open the possibility of studying the influences causing such alterations.

Two types of factual data are obtainable through surveys: those relative to conditions and those relative to past actions. The first result from asking respondents questions about matters like employment status, educational level, health, etc., answers to which are not practically realizable for the entire populace. Data such as these are an extension of social bookkeeping and are regularly solicited by both private and government agencies, particularly census bureaus. The second type of factual data comes from requests that respondents indicate the course they have already pursued in regard to a given situation. The social historian may learn from queries of this sort how people employed themselves in their leisure time and the political historian may discover more about the way in which people cast their ballots in an election.

The historian and poll-taker frequently share an interest in the attitudes and opinions expressed by a public. More selective in his interests than the opinion specialist, the historian understandably concentrates on what are to him significant attitudes relative to events of historical moment. Attitudes may vary by reason of their end-product: some are indicators of future action and others present views not expected to result in action. The former may be called action-centered relating to intended activity such as the kind of school parents will select for their children, or the degree of support a group may offer a political candidate under present or altered conditions. These action-centered attitudes may refer to a single event like an election or to a succession of similar events or trends. The study of long-term patterns of opinion with which this succession of events may be interwoven is an attempt to use opinion data for purposes of comparison; i.e., to study spatial distribution within a country, international differences, etc. The second type of opinions here under discussion—the non-action-centered—involves neither the necessity nor the probability of a follow-up act. These may be opinions about specific events, proposed government actions, personalities, etc. Just as the action-centered opinions, these can be linked with unique events or with a succession of events to study long-term opinion patterns.

A third link between the historical and polling disciplines lies in the study of fundamental values, so-called because they reflect a more permanent and basic outlook on life's central problems than the more superficial opinions just considered. "Thus," as Hyman and Sheatsley explain, "the citizen opposes brutality, shuns the unnecessary use of force, avoids attitudes of cynicism and complacency, values loyalty, trust and helpfulness." [3] Reliable information on these prevailing values is far more significant to the historian than evidence on specific opinions, although it is somewhat harder to obtain, the benefit of modern psychological techniques notwithstanding. Yet basic values are reflected in opinions about everything of consequence, since the processes by which attitudes are formulated are often guided by fundamental philosophical convictions.[4] Opinions about one or another issue may not be connected with particular values through conscious recognition of what is happening but the association of issue and value remains close and real. For example, the Frenchman who is asked his attitude toward his country's participation in Western European Union would be expected to speak within the framework of his religious, ethical, cultural, social, economic, and political values. His judgment would certainly be affected by his predispositions toward communism, the USSR, Germany, nationalism, war and peace, etc.

The attention of polling experts and historians is often fastened on changes of opinion, the way in which attitudes and values may affect or be affected by propaganda or particular events. The examination of "who [has said] what to whom with what effect" [5] is a legitimate enterprise for social scientists in view of the importance of opinion formation and guidance in contemporary society.

In the discussions to follow these ways in which public opinion data may aid the historian will be illustrated by French survey material. But before the central features of this study are turned to, a brief review of the major political events which occurred in France between 1944 and 1949 is in order. Those who wish more detailed information on these events are recommended to one or more of the several excellent works in English on the period. [6]

II. The French Political Experience, 1944-1949

In June of 1940 France went down to defeat at the hands of the Nazi war machine. The government of Marshal Henri Philippe Pétain, hero of World War I, succeeded that of Premier Paul Reynaud and immediately requested a separate armistice. German occupation of two-thirds of France followed and the remainder was left under French authority with its capital at Vichy.

After being voted full powers by the Parliament, Pétain, in collaboration with Pierre Laval and others, proceeded to establish the authoritarian "French State." Meanwhile, in London, General Charles de Gaulle, long the leading French advocate of a modern mechanized army, renewed the call to arms and founded the Free French movement which was later to become a Provisional Government in exile. De Gaulle and his followers labored long and hard to organize all French patriots outside the mother country against both Germany and Vichy. Inside France concerted resistance sprang up, gathering momentum after the Communists had committed their resources to the underground in response to the invasion of Russia by the *Wehrmacht* in June 1941. Two years later a National Council of the Resistance (CNR), made up of representatives of diverse political and labor groups, was formed in alliance with De Gaulle to direct the activities of the numerous underground contingents within France. Reflecting a spirit of dedication to high aims, the CNR was guided and supported by men of apostolic faith and zeal, many of whom optimistically—but unrealistically—believed that out of the suffering to which they had been subjected a new spirit of brotherly love and cooperation would emerge to fashion a better France. The lessons of the past and the challenges of the future would abolish fundamental differences and unite all patriots in a humanitarian crusade to bring about a glorious French political, economic and social renaissance. The nature of this renaissance and the method of its realization were contained in a series of vaguely phrased resolutions comprising the CNR program.

Late in August of 1944 Paris was freed and the Provisional Government, now containing men of the internal resistance, grasped the reins of power. The rejoicing which accompanied liberation was tempered by a recognition of the arduous task of reconstruction and rehabilitation which lay ahead. On all sides the leaders of the new regime could espy Herculean labors, for the effects of the war and occupation were staggering. The economic and political structure of the country had been shattered. Communications and transportation had to be restored; factory, farm and mine production had to be revived; other material destruction had to be repaired; the war had to be continued and its requirements, including those of the British and American "occupiers," had to be met; problems of inflation had to be contended with; the Vichy regime and its legislation had to be eliminated; collaborators had to be apprehended, tried and punished and republican legality had to be assured.

In these first few weeks of the post-liberation experience the earlier aspirations of the CNR seemed practicable but as months wore on the genuine and traditional divisions of public sentiment were again reflected in the multiplicity of political patterns. As it busied itself with everyday jobs the cabinet operated in an atmosphere of growing political strain and economic crisis. The Communists seemed to arrogate the resistance leadership unto themselves and to keep the military and political elements of the resistance powerful within the framework of the Provisional Government. The threat of a state within a state was slowly dissipated, however, so that it became clear, after the municipal elections of the spring of 1945, that resistance thought and pressures would in future be effectively presented not by resistance organizations as such but by political parties. Old political tenets were soon dusted off, and eulogized and the expression of national, unanimous aims was modified by partisan political outlooks. Still sharing vague golden dreams, the former resistance chieftains found that fraternal good will alone could not close the chasms which separated their respective philosophical systems. The eventual aim of peace and brotherhood could be esteemed by all, but on the explicit character of the goals to be pursued and the methods to be employed there was wide division.

The future seemed to belong to the Left, for the old Right was closely and unpopularly identified with the collapse of the Third Republic and with wartime collaboration and "Vichyism." At the extreme Left the *Parti Communiste* (PC), which had supplied many military and active civilian resistants, hundreds of whom presumably had given their lives in the struggle, reorganized under Maurice Thorez.[7] One of the chief projects of the PC was to unite all former resistants in a great political movement and, more particularly, to establish one large working-class party through a Communist-Socialist fusion. The reconstituted *Parti Socialiste* (SFIO-*Section française de l'Internationale Ouvrière*), the largest of the prewar political groups, entered negotiations with the Communists to this end. Progress was limited to several joint policy declarations and within the next two years disagreements between these two Marxist parties accentuated their individuality over their common bonds.

One new party, the *Mouvement Républicain Populaire* (MRP), took its place beside the older political formations. The MRP, with some ties to the prewar popular Democrats but largely the product of the resistance, was established by Catholic leftists in sympathy with the CNR Program but naturally antipathetic to traditional leftist anticlericalism which deprecated the existence of private schools and assailed state financial assistance to them. Among the older parties to reform their ranks were the *Parti Radical et Radical*

Socialiste, commonly referred to as bourgeois and centrist in inspiration and aspiration, and some small elements of the traditional Right.

During the winter and spring sharp differences of opinion over economic matters appeared. The CNR Program called for nationalization "of the sources of energy, underground riches, insurance companies and big banks," and in December the first nationalization bills were hurriedly adopted under strong pressure from the Left. To some observers this marked the inauguration of a postwar condition in which doctrinaire politics frequently seemed to outbalance sound economic thinking in the attempt to resolve the grave financial and economic problems which challenged the country. They hold that too much was attempted in too little time and believe that political intransigence tended to breed resentments which contributed much to the revival of economic conservatism as a political force. These disagreements dissipated energies and divided parliamentary majorities, thereby preventing the root problems of wages and prices and fiduciary circulation from being successfully attacked, a situation which became chronic in the postwar era.

Essentially De Gaulle headed a trustee or caretaker administration. He considered himself responsible only to the sovereign people, who could not be consulted until the prisoners of war and deportees had returned and life had been somewhat normalized. This consultation came in the national referendum and election of October 1945 in which women exercised their recently granted franchise. The referendum expressed an incontestable wish for a new constitution, for which the Communists, Socialists and Popular Republicans had campaigned. The assembly chosen thus became constituent. In the election the Communists commanded the largest single segment of the electors, about 26%. The MRP and SFIO, with about 24% of the vote each, became the other members of the Big Three. Not unexpectedly the Radicals and the Right sustained an unqualified defeat. After a struggle with the PC over the formation of the Cabinet, De Gaulle was elected President and the job of governing and constitution framing proceeded. De Gaulle's military background did not equip him for the game of political give and take and his actions were increasingly regarded as dictatorial by politicians, especially those of the Left who viewed with alarm the general's attractiveness to rightist elements. On January 20, 1946, as a result of a dispute with the Left over military appropriations, General De Gaulle abruptly submitted his resignation. A tripartite government consisting of PC, SFIO and MRP members under Socialist Félix Gouin was put together within a few days and De Gaulle retired to the country.

Under the domination of a Marxist coalition the constitutional committee submitted a draft which provided for an all-powerful unicameral legislature and a President of the Republic with substantially reduced powers. The MRP joined the Radicals and the Right in campaigning against this constitution before the May 1946 referendum. The Communists argued vigorously for adoption of the draft while the Socialists, less positively enthusiastic, stressed the necessity of ending the provisional regime and establishing permanent institutions. In the voting 53% opposed the document and 47% favored it. This was a major setback for the PC and in the June elections for a new Constituent Assembly the MRP gained the ascendancy by capturing 28% of the vote. The Communist total remained about as it had been in October but the Socialist strength fell to approximately 21%. MRP leader George Bidault organized a new tripartite cabinet at about the same time that General de Gaulle first broke his self-imposed silence by speaking up loudly for a strengthened presidential office and a bicameral parliament. To many Frenchmen—as opinion surveys confirm—De Gaulle was now apparently grooming himself for the role of a new Bonaparte.[8]

The Second Constituent revised the rejected constitution chiefly by approving two legislative chambers, the National Assembly, before which the cabinet was to be responsible, and the Council of the Republic, which was to be essentially advisory, and by broadening the presidential powers. When this document was submitted to the electorate in October, De Gaulle's relentless opposition was well-known, but all three major parties called for its adoption. And, although the constitution was accepted by a vote of 52% against 47%, a large number of eligible voters—nearly one-third—abstained in obvious protest.

In the November elections for the National Assembly the Communists regained their earlier lead with 28% of the vote and the Popular Republicans came next with 26%. The Socialists trailed with 18%, having lost over a million supporters since October 1945. With the two biggest parties unwilling to cooperate in a coalition, an all-Socialist government led by Léon Blum was installed pending the organization of the Council of the Republic and the election of a President by the two legislative houses. Directly after his election to that office in mid-January 1947, Vincent Auriol appointed fellow Socialist Paul Ramadier as the first Premier of the Fourth Republic. Under Ramadier disagreements over economic policy and the prosecution of hostilities against the Communist-dominated Viet Minh in Indochina provoked a split in the cabinet between Communists and non-Communists. When the Communists refused further support of the government's deflationary salary policy, Ramadier decided, early in May, to drop them and to seek a vote of confidence from the Assembly. Ramadier's tactics were approved and from that time the PC has remained out of the government.

About a month earlier Charles de Gaulle presided at the birth rites of his *Rassemblement du Peuple Français* (RPF). Although the RPF was not to be a political party but a national movement working chiefly for constitutional revision, within a few months the Gaullists organized a parliamentary intergroup and prepared to enter lists in the fall municipal elections and to ally themselves with various political groupings. In these contests the new Rally won a distinct victory especially in the larger cities. Nearly 40% of the vote went to the RPF candidates or those affiliated with the RPF and about 30% went to the Communists at the other extreme. The middle-of-the-road parties, soon to be known as the Third Force, seemed to be threatened, for both extremes talked and acted as if they would soon take matters into their own hands. By this time there was general dissatisfaction with Ramadier, who resigned at a moment when social unrest was on the upswing. Labor troubles, originating in Marseilles, spread into other areas and various industries in the course of November and early December. The new ministry of MRP Robert Schuman rode through the storm, in the progress of which the General Confederation of Labor (CGT) was split between a Red-dominated majority and a non-Communist minority, the *Force Ouvrière* (FO). Both groups had been united on the necessity for wage increases but the non-Communists opposed the use of the strike for specifically political purposes.

Within the Third Force itself there were fundamental differences over the existence and subsidization of Catholic and other private schools, the length of military service, the conflict in Indochina, social and economic policy. Finally, over a question of military appropriations, Schuman threw in the sponge, to be followed by the short-lived ministry of André Marie, which, in turn, was succeeded by that of Henri Queuille, another Radical. The Premier was confronted immediately by a new strike situation, spawned by demands for wage adjustments and by Communist challenges to the government and to the new European Recovery Program. By the beginning of November the backbone of the strikes had been snapped and the violence gradually abated.

Despite a noticeable improvement in material conditions in 1948, inflation continued its destructive course. The standard of living remained low and the appallingly inadequate housing conditions were not bettered. As a result a majority of the public demonstrated in several opinion polls that it could marshall no real confidence in the government or in the immediate future.[9] The fundamental problems had yet to be solved. If any sort of order and stability was to be achieved, if the great promise of the liberation was to be realized, France would have to grapple with and resolve many deep-seated political, economic and moral problems. It is to a few of these problems and their ramifications that attention is now directed as the contribution of French public opinion data to questions of historical interest is examined.

III. Political Alignments

In the following discussions of French material pertinent to the expression of attitudes and opinions only certain action-centered opinions will be included and the historically important information gathered from them will be spotlighted. These data suggest that (1) several ideas regarding postwar party stratification in France may need revision; (2) new hypotheses regarding party composition should be investigated; (3) the Communist Party, although the most homogeneous in France, possessed a non-conformist minority of challenging proportions.

REVISION OF THE IDEAS ON PARTY STRATIFICATION

The revival of old-time political habits and divergencies in the post-liberation period quite understandably intrigues the historian, who seeks to know, among other things, what types of people supported each of these parties, what religion they embraced, what social position they occupied, where they lived, etc. Speculation and research on the recruitment of parties has of course produced a considerable literature in many countries. One is reminded, for example, of Trevelyan's generalization concerning the Glorious Revolution of 1688-1689: "The Whigs represented mainly the wealthier landowners, the Dissenters and the mercantile community; the Tories mainly the Squirearchy and Church.[10]

To the postwar French writings dealing with political parties the survey method can contribute information which helps to present a more precise picture of voting patterns. The breakdowns of the French Institute of Public Opinion question on voting intention [11] contain important material on the sex, age, occupational and social status of the sample. Many of these facts sustain the conclusions of expert observers who have employed other methods. These will not be repeated in this study. Some which do not coincide with expressed ideas have been selected to illustrate the value of survey data as a check on evidence obtained from electoral statistics, studies of party structure and other sources. Though this group of conclusions is not disproved by survey figures, the apparent discrepancies in the information cast doubt on the accuracy of earlier testimony, making further studies incumbent on the researcher.

Four instances of this type of data have been drawn from a survey of July 1948. Since the political balance was not then markedly disturbed by acute social and economic unrest, this period may be termed, within understandable limitations, "normal" for the early postwar years. The propositions dictated by public opinion findings are: The strength of the MRP among the workers, both in the pre-RPF and post-RPF era, may be overestimated; Socialist losses among the lower middle classes may also be overstressed; the decline of Gaullist enthusiasm among the rich and business groups may not have been so great as some authors claim; the intellectual component of the PC may have been smaller than originally estimated and that of the Gaullist forces may have been considerably larger.

The MRP and the Workers. Some commentaries on the working class following of the MRP would appear to be misleading. Largely because leaders of the *Confédération Française des Travailleurs Chrétiens* (CFTC) have tended to support the MRP some writers have called the influence of that party among the workers significant.[12] Survey results indicate, however, that not even in its heyday in 1946—prior to the creation of the RPF to which it lost the larger proportion of its voters—did the MRP attract many more than 15% of the workers and that by mid-1948—a year after the organization of the RPF—the MRP attracted only about 8% of the proletarian voters, who made up roughly 10% of the total voting strength of the party.[13] Constantly, over 60% of the workers cast their ballots for one of the Marxist parties, the larger group going to the PC. Therefore, although the MRP might have possessed "an authentically proletarian wing"[14] within its membership, that representation was not great in comparison with the party's total voting strength.[15] Small before the foundation of the RPF, the number of worker-voters in the MRP was even smaller thereafter. In the summer of 1948, for example, Popular Republican worker support was only slightly greater than that offered the pro-capitalist *Rassemblement des Gauches* (RGR)[16] and the rightist *Parti Républicain de la Liberté* (PRL).[17]

Also, the assumption that the CFTC "was at least as strong a workers' movements as the *Force Ouvrière*"[18] or that in itself the CFTC was importantly a proletarian group would seem gratuitous unless the term "worker" is mistakenly stretched to include salaried employees, many of whom belonged to the CFTC.[19] An IFOP inquiry of February 1948 indicated, for example, that less than half the CFTC membership—variously estimated as between 400,000 and 800,000—consisted of manual workers and somewhat over half was in the category of salaried employees and civil servants. The same survey points to the fact that more workers subscribed to the FO than to the Christian unions.

The SFIO and the Lower Middle Classes. In the early postwar elections the Socialist party consistently lost popular support. Between October 1945 and November 1946 over 1 million voters deserted the SFIO for other formations. Many were the reasons advanced for this collapse. Among these were the failure of the SFIO to bring its doctrines and policies into line with current needs and its inability to compete with the excessive program of the non-governmental PC in the fight to enlist and retain influence among the working class elements.[20] During these years the Socialist Party suffered, too, from lack of funds and dynamic leadership.[21]

In analyzing the electoral losses of the Socialists some authors, like Henry W. Ehrmann, have maintained that the continuing economic crisis siphoned off many of the petit bourgeois voters, particularly those who lived on fixed incomes.[22] Most observers also noted that the SFIO became in postwar times a real middle class party. Survey figures indicate that the falling off of lower middle class and rentier support was probably not of primary significance, for in the summer of 1948, 82% of the Socialist voters were in the two middle class categories, 48% being in the lower. At the same time one-third of the SFIO electors were rentiers, retired people or women without profession. More importantly, a comparison of responses gathered in several surveys conducted between the fall of 1945 and the fall of 1946 clearly implies that about 30% of the rentiers and retired people backed the SFIO in the first general election and that this total fell only to about 27% in November 1946. Worker strength, appearing to decline to 20% from an original level of 25%, was more adversely affected. Support from the manufacturers and merchants as a whole fell from just over 20% of their entire voting number in 1945 to about 15% in 1946 and the backing offered by the farmers was also lower in 1946 than in 1945—perhaps dropping from over 20% of the total to about 17%. The losses sustained by the SFIO in small business man and rentier strength are here seen but defections were even more notable among other occupational groups, perhaps most importantly, from the point of view of numbers, among the workers. The alterations in socio-economic following of the SFIO are unknown, for in this period IFOP had not yet classified people's responses according to class position.

The Gaullists and the Rich. On heralding the birth of the RPF in the spring of 1947 General de Gaulle emphasized that the movement was not a political party but a rally to unite Frenchmen of various political inclinations in a campaign to liberate the state from its dependence on political parties and to establish a stronger executive force in government. Soon Communism was defined as the primary enemy and in August there was established a new Gaullist parliamentary intergroup to which deputies were asked to affiliate themselves while retaining membership in their original party groups. Both the Radical Socialists and the Right tolerated this arrangement but the MRP, originally the party most loyal to De Gaulle and still strongly Gaullist in its rank and file, fearing a rift with its Socialist allies in the government and sharing the leftist suspicion of De Gaulle's protestations of democratic intentions, rejected the double membership scheme. Meanwhile, survey data registered a mass movement toward the new Rally which, along with the PC, stressed in the municipal election campaign of October the national political significance of the balloting. The candidates of these two parties and their affiliates polled nearly 70% of the total vote, a result generally interpreted as a protest against the government and its policies. From this high point the strength of the RPF tapered off in the following year to a level of between 25% and 30%.

François Goguel, Charles Micaud and others have hinted that this decline of support was especially notable among the business and wealthier classes who apparently were either frightened by De Gaulle's efforts to woo labor or reconciled to the centrist government as material conditions improved.[23] Because of the late adoption of the class position breakdown by IFOP, there are no 1947 figures on the RPF following among the richer voters. However, in the spring, summer, and fall of 1948 General de Gaulle and the RPF commanded the support of between 45 and 50% of the Class A or wealthy electors. In April, 46% wanted De Gaulle to return to power; in the summer approximately 45% opted for the RPF in preference to other parties; and in October, 50% stated that General de Gaulle was right in his program and should be followed. In the winter there was an indication of a slight fall in De Gaulle's popularity among the rich, for in January 1949, 42% expressed the desire to see General De Gaulle stage a comeback.

Thus a small loss among the Class A voters, only about 200,000 in all, could in no wise play an important quantitative role in a period when RPF defections apparently rose to a million or more. On the other hand, the loss of a few very rich and influential backers might have immense qualitative significance and might contribute to the defeat of candidates in one or more districts. Of course neither of these possibilities can be traced in survey results in their present form.

Between the 1947 municipal elections and the end of 1948 there was no positive demonstration that the merchants and manufacturers turned in large numbers from De Gaulle. At the end of April 1947 37% of this group wanted De Gaulle to come back to power. In the next month 40% wanted De Gaulle and 52% said they would prefer a Gaullist bloc to an anti-Gaullist bloc.[24] In the summer 38% favored De Gaulle's return and in September this number increased to 42%. In December positive approbation of a comeback by De Gaulle fell to 36% and fluctuated by only a few points in the coming year.[25] About 35% of the merchants and industrialists said they would vote for the RPF in July if elections were held at that time and three months later a similar number claimed that De Gaulle was correct in his political views and should be supported. This view had not altered since May 1947. Only in the fall of 1947 did the support given De Gaulle by the commercial and industrial classes rise above the standard 35-40% which was noted in the months before the municipal elections of 1947 and in the year after. In this way public opinion data testify that there was no numerically significant walkout by these voters after the elections and, additionally, that there was no evidence to substantiate a belief that De Gaulle's labor policy, first announced at St. Etienne in January 1948, had an adverse effect on his popularity with the merchants and manufacturers, over 70% of whom belonged in the upper two socio-economic brackets.[26]

The PC and RPF and Intellectuals. Many reasons have been proposed for the electoral triumphs of the French Communist Party in the postwar period. The resistance record of the PC, its identification with the prestige-laden Russian war machine, its freedom from responsibility for prewar governmental blunders, its superior organization and discipline, its vigorous, corruption-free leadership, its dogmatic certainty regarding the solution of the problems of society, its appeal to the traditional leftism of the revolutionary inheritance, its function as a magnet for the discontented are among the factors cited by authorities.[27]

Most discussions of the party's composition include references to the many intellectuals who have embraced Communism in the postwar era "in which Communism, peace, liberty, country, social justice were closely associated and evoke[d] one another re-ciprocally." [28] On the other hand, the intellectual component of the RPF has been termed weak.[29] Although the words "intellectual," "intelligentsia," etc., are meaningful in only a relative sense, it is not unreasonable to assume that the members of the liberal pro-fessions and/or the superior school alumni constituted the bulk of the intellectual voters in the sample. If these two variables are taken as indices of intellectualism, one finds that survey data raise the possibility that the strong intellectual composition of the PC and the weakness of the RPF in this respect have been overstressed. For example, no party had fewer ex-superior school students in its ranks than the PC in April 1947. Of all those who had once gone to a superior school fewer than one-tenth voted Communist. Among the members of the liberal professions, well over 60% of whom were alumni of superior schools, only a small percentage—under one-tenth —supported the PC. In July 1948 this was less than one-third as many liberal profession electors as the RPF had, and about half as many and three-fifths as many as the PRL and MRP respectively possessed. Each of the latter parties could claim approximately one-half the total following of the PC, and the RPF had about the same strength as the PC.

The survey of April 1947 was conducted prior to the organiza-tion of the Rally of the French People but 25% of those with superior school educations were at that time in favor of De Gaulle's return to power in government. In May 1948 such a tie-up was not made, but of the 74% of the superior school alumni who selected a morning Paris paper for regular reading almost one-half—35%— preferred *Figaro* and about one-ninth—8%—selected *Aurore*, both of which could boast of a Gaullist majority among their readers. Besides this, the consistent following of De Gaulle by the members of the liberal professions has been noteworthy. With minor changes, in the vicinity of 40% wished De Gaulle back, believed he should be supported because his program was correct and selected the RPF.

All the figures given above, then, seem to indicate that in 1947 and 1948 the RPF was backed by a relatively large minority of the voters who might be classified as intellectual, far more in fact than the PC, the intellectual composition of which was more frequently observed by students.

It is also interesting to note that in the spring of 1947 about three-fifths of the former students in superior schools chose one of two parties: 40% the MRP and 18% the PRL. Since it was from the ranks of these two parties that subsequent RPF support came, it may not be too far afield to assume that a substantial group of these more highly educated voters migrated to the Gaullist Rally.

NEW HYPOTHESES ON PARTY STRATIFICATION

The survey data cited in the preceding pages call for some revision in the existing hypotheses concerning the composition of political parties. But the I.F.O.P. data also give rise to some new hypotheses not previously listed in the studies of this period.

First, it has generally not been noted that Socialist support, while relatively greater than that of the Communists among voters between 50 and 64, was smaller among the oldest group of electors, those 65 and over. The SFIO has been widely dubbed an old people's party in postwar times, but of all political formations the SFIO had the lowest relative as well as absolute strength among the older citizens.[30]

Secondly, it was generally appreciated that the poorest segment of the population (Class D) would vote in great strength for the extremist Communist and Gaullist movements (32% and 24% respectively), but it was not customarily acknowledged that the Republican Party of Liberty captured the third largest portion of these citizens in the summer of 1948 (13%). The PRL probably served as a rallying point for those conservative petit bourgeois and impoverished rentier voters who eschewed the RPF and De Gaulle.

Thirdly, the fact that the MRP had within its ranks in 1947 nearly one-half of the voters who had attended secondary schools, almost one-third of those who had gone to technical schools and just under one-half of those who had pursued superior school courses is certainly worthy of mention and further investigation.

COMMUNIST PARTY HOMOGENEITY

Under the Third Republic, with the principal exception of the PC and SFIO, there were no great political parties organized in hierarchical fashion on a national level. Seldom were so-called parties more than parliamentary groups with a central bureau which functioned as a clearing house for information and propaganda and as a general staff for planning and establishing periodically required electoral coalitions and strategy. When the regime collapsed, its parliamentary system was denounced in many quarters for having bred an irresponsible individualism among the deputies, a condition which could in the future be rectified by highly disciplined, monolithic parties. The early postwar years witnessed the development of such party organizations on an extreme scale and the Fourth Republic helped to nurture that transformation by its electoral laws which favored large national organizations.[31] Strict party discipline on the parliamentary plane was required and frequently major policy decisions were reached by non-parliamentary executive committees and imposed on deputies in the interest of party tactics and sectarian concerns. It has been charged that in many instances deputies, especially those of the PC, SFIO, MRP and RPF, served their party first and the people second, and in the long periods between elections sovereignty of party executives was substituted for the sovereignty of parliament.[32] Too much discipline within the leftist parties and the RPF—until a break came in the Gaullist ranks after the period of this survey—posed a real conflict of loyalties among a large number of their deputies, whereas the representatives of rightist and centrist groups often split among themselves in the traditional spirit of individualism. In short, party dictatorship seemed to be the working alternative to individual anarchy.

Although party directors, militants and other members may have demonstrated a more disciplined approach to political life in these postwar years, it is debatable whether the mass of voters followed suit. Survey results provide some important information regarding the effect of stronger party organizations on the voters. Inquiries into party loyalty which investigate past electoral behavior and future intentions confirm the general belief that the PC was the most homogeneous party, with the RPF running second, the SFIO third and the MRP fourth. The voters of the rightist PRL and the conservative Left Rally followed in that order. Since other sources and other studies satisfactorily attribute to the Communist voters the most highly developed spirit of orthodoxy among the French electors, the IFOP survey material relevant to this central fact may be regarded as primarily confirmatory information which does not require further elaboration.

But the survey data have enabled us to go beyond this generally recognized fact. The results of over a dozen separate IFOP inquiries show that the hold of the Communist Party over its followers varied from issue to issue and that on some controversial questions anywhere from 20 to 50% of the PC supporters voted independently.

The questions which have been selected to illustrate the varying degrees of opinion among the Communist voters will be studied under three major headings: Loyalty to Party Voting Instructions; Loyalty on Economic Issues; Loyalty on Questions of Foreign Policy and Cold War Issues.

LOYALTY TO PARTY VOTING INSTRUCTIONS. Five indices of party loyalty have been constructed from IFOP inquiries into voting habits after the May 1946 referendum, the June 1946 election and before and after the October 1946 referendum. These indices which are listed in Table I have been derived from responses to the following questions:

1. "Does the party for which you voted (June) correspond perfectly with your ideas?" The alternatives offered were "perfectly, fairly, well, not very well and not at all."

2. "Did you vote 'Yes' or 'No' in the referendum of May?"

3. "Would you vote for the constitution if the party for which you intend to vote recommends voting for the constitution?" "Would you vote against the constitution if the party for which you intend to vote recommends voting against the constitution?" (Before the October referendum.)

4. "How far in advance did you reach the decision to vote as you did?" The alternatives presented were "the day of the vote, two or three days before, within the last week, more than a week before."

5. "Did you change your decision once or more often?" (Before the June election) "Did you change your decision?" (Before the October referendum) The June alternatives were "changed or did not change decision"; the October alternatives were "changed decision once, twice, more often, did not change decision."

Table I—Indices of Party Loyalty in 1946
(as percentages of total voters of each party)

INDEX	TOTAL	PC	SFIO	RGR	MRP	PRL
1. Stated Satisfaction with Party Platform. % of voters stating their party corresponded perfectly with their own political ideas.—June	28	58	29	16	31	24
2. Issue Loyalty. % of voters who voted in the May referendum according to their party's instructions.	94	74	78	93	93	
3. Loyalty to Hypothetical Instructions.						
a. % who would vote Yes in Oct. referendum if party wanted Yes.	50	85	65	45	42	35
b. % who would vote No in Oct. referendum if party wanted No.	43	62	40	39	48	39
4. Reluctance. % of voters who made their June voting decision in the final week.	26	14	32	40	33	37
5. Oscillation. % of voters who changed their voting decision once or more often.						
a. In the June election	16	8	16	22	24	29
b. In the October referendum	16	5	14	22	27	16
RANK OF PARTY		A	B-2	C-2	B-1	C-1

Observers have remarked that before World War II party platforms generally incorporated neither the serious hopes of the voters nor the genuine intentions of the party leaders or candidates. Rather, the programs provided "a comparatively small idea of the position of the author on the immediate questions of the day" [33] and were far "less important than relative positions." [34] In postwar France authorities like Domenach have held that the four-fifths of the Communist voters who were not party members voted for Communist candidates "for reasons which often have little to do with the special nature and aims of the French communist party and which can even be the very opposite of those aims." [35] The testimony of this survey apparently mitigates the extremism of Domenach's belief. Three-fifths of the PC respondents asserted that their political ideas—admittedly, a vague entity—were in perfect correspondence with those of their party. Another third—bringing the total to over nine-tenths of the Communist electors—stated that their party's platform corresponded fairly well with their convictions. On the other hand, only about three-tenths of the Socialists and Popular Republicans saw such perfect correspondence and roughly one half of each group maintained that they had reservations about their party's platform. It is illuminating to observe here that in their study of the Willkie-Roosevelt election campaign in the United States in 1944, Paul Lazarsfeld and his associates found by late October in Erie County, Ohio, that only 25% of the respondents signified whole-hearted agreement with their own parties. This might suggest that the non-Communist French fitted into a pattern not unlike that discoverable in other countries.[36]

The second question on fidelity has reference to the observance of party instructions for the May 1946 referendum. Although Communist efforts to win the adoption of a document tailor-made to the specifications of a highly disciplined, centralized party organization failed, the inquiry uncovered no appreciable defections from the PC ranks. Ninety-five per cent claimed to have voted Yes at the polls and a mere one per cent revealed a vote contrary to that desired by the party executive.

Also effective in disclosing the solidarity of the Communist Party's electoral body are the answers to the third set of questions concerning the voters' willingness to accept or reject the October constitution in accordance with official instructions regardless of individual predilections. Thus, of all the PC electors, 85% said they would support the constitution if their chieftains wanted them to. By this time the Communist directors were resigned to the fact that this redrafted document was all they could legitimately hope for in the line of government by assembly in the teeth of De Gaulle's powerful "authoritarian" demands for a stronger executive. But in case of a highly unlikely reversal of this policy about three-fifths of the PC supporters were prepared to go along and vote for the rejection of the draft. Less than one-fifth were prepared to go against their party's wishes.[37] In a certain way these three million odd voters of the PC represented a tough core of internal discipline, one which becomes even more significant with the realization that, at the extreme, only one-third of these electors were party members and, therefore, more "professionally" Communist.

The incidence of tardiness in reaching voting decisions and of alteration of voting decisions may also provide good indices of the strength of a party's hold on its followers. Late decisions are often due to a voter's lack of interest in a particular campaign or in politics in general, to his disgust with the operations of the political machine, to his subjection to strong cross pressures, etc. In the campaigns which preceded the June 1946 election and the October 1946 referendum, deficiency of interest cannot be dismissed, but perhaps both periods were more remarkable for the counterpulls that had been activated. A determination to capitalize on the May victory gripped the non-Communists in June and a spirit of tactical moderation appeared among the Communists. Of all the voters the Communists were the least reluctant to make an early decision. Defeat in the referendum had apparently not caused many of the PC voters to reassess their political aims and to speculate about changing their vote. Only eight per cent were involved in decision changes and some 14% waited until the last week to reach their decision to vote as they did. The relative number of late decisions within each of the other major parties, however, was over twice as great as this Communist figure. In October the major conflict was between loyalty to De Gaulle and his views and loyalty to one's preferred party and its wishes if the two were at variance. This problem did not harass the PC voters so that only 5% changed an original voting decision once or more often. This should be contrasted with oscillations among other party supporters which ran from over two to over five times larger.[38]

LOYALTY ON ECONOMIC ISSUES.   Surely one of the most interesting indications of Communist disaffection on domestic policy dates from July 1947 when the respondents were asked whether, in a general way, price fixing was necessary, and from September 1948 when they were questioned regarding their acceptance or rejection of complete liberty of prices and salaries. These were questions of vital import, for the principal economic problem which had tortured French governments was that of inflation.

Between the spring of 1944 and the end of 1948 the retail price index in Paris increased by 650%.[39] Other prices rose in similar fashion. As prices skyrocketed, new wage increases were granted but, as is almost always the case, the discrepancy between the two remained great.

Very naturally these postwar experiences with rising prices were responsible for the growth of pessimism regarding the efforts of the various cabinets to stabilize the cost of living. In the summer of 1947, when the first inquiry on price fixing was made, an average of about 85% could only see further price increases, and by September 1948, the date of the second survey, pessimism was even more widespread, 91% believing that prices would continue to go higher.

Through all this time state controls remained in effect but the successive ministries failed to check the debilitating upward spiral of wages and prices. The black market flourished and the rich grew richer, serving to accentuate both the failure of government efforts and the unequal distribution of wealth. Thus, the 1947 and the 1948 inquiries concerning the durability of economic controls affected the participants closely and personally and consequently a highly crystallized opinion was to be anticipated. In 1947 only seven per cent refused to answer the question. Fifty-nine per cent believed that prices should be free and 34% held that they should be controlled. There was more hesitation in 1948 when both wages and prices came under specific consideration, but at that time the larger number, 47%, backed liberty and the 33% championed state regulation. The greater percentage of PC voters also leaned toward economic freedom, just over half in 1947 and somewhat under half in 1948. In the light of the collectivist principles of the Communist Party it is surprising that only about ⅖ of the PC voters in each survey espoused economic controls. It would have taken a more refined IFOP inquiry to ascertain the reasons for this discrepancy between collectivist principles in the abstract and views on economic controls in practice. Perhaps some voters would have favored controls had the PC had a share in government. Possibly some dyed-in-the-wool Communists wanted the removal of controls precisely because the ensuing chaos might benefit the Party. Whatever the reasons the fact remained that a large proportion of Communists opposed the existing price and salary regulations.

LOYALTY ON FOREIGN POLICY AND COLD WAR ISSUES. The attitudes of the Communist voters on foreign policy will be treated in chronological sequence and will point up the varying levels of dissidence within the Communist electorate.

In April 1946 the IFOP sample was asked what country would aid France most in her recovery. Nearly two-thirds of the Communists named the Soviet Union but somewhat over one-fifth thought, along with a majority of all the respondents, that the United States was a better bet. Fourteen months later, after the USSR had declined to associate herself and her satellites with the "imperialistic blandishments" of the Marshall Plan, the French were asked if they considered France right or wrong for participating in the Marshall Plan discussions. About 45% of the Communist voters maintained that their country should have followed the Russian lead to eschew the American project but a large 30% assumed a more nationalistic and independent point of view, holding that, despite Russian objections to the Plan, France should continue to negotiate with the West toward constructing a workable mutual assistance program.

In October and November 1947 General De Gaulle's Rally of the French people reached its zenith. During the latter month IFOP asked its respondents to state which of nine principal points in the RPF program they endorsed, which of them they disliked, which particular one they approved the most and which they disapproved the most. The following were the points listed:

1. Maintenance of the French occupation in Germany; division of Germany and collaboration with her in the economic field.
2. Regulation of trade unions by the state and the institution of a collaboration between employees and workers.
3. Recognition of a community of interest between France and the United States.
4. Distrust of the USSR.
5. Liquidation of communism.
6. Dissolution of the present parliament.
7. Replacement of proportional representation by the majority-list with one ballot.
8. Fight against political parties.
9. Creation of a strong state with extensive powers for General de Gaulle.

Data gathered in this type of inquiry are of special significance in public opinion research, for they illuminate attitudes toward the central issues of a campaign and thus help to clarify the reasons which lie behind a vote for a given political party or candidate. Our present interest lies in this direction only insofar as we wish to examine the viewpoints of the PC voters in order to bring further material to bear on the question of Communist homogeneity. A large proportion of the Communists understandably expressed disagreement with the RPF platform. Only three planks gained the support of over 10% of the PC electors. These were the propositions referring to points (1) Germany, (3) the community of interest with the USA, and (6) the dissolution of parliament. The discovery of this minority in the first two instances invites investigation.[40]

THE PC VOTERS AND THE GERMAN PROBLEM. In the four years which followed liberation French foreign policy was molded largely by fear of Germany which had inflicted three invasions on France in less than a century. Pierre Bertaux, sometime postwar chief of the Sureté Nationale, the non-political internal security force of France, was not atypical in remarking: "it's always the Germans—for my grandfather, 'Les Prussiens,' for my father, 'Les Boches,' for us 'Les Fritz.' " [41] As the European war ended, Frenchmen of every political conviction seemed to be as one in their determination to prevent Germany from again reaching the point where she would be economically and militarily able to threaten the security of France. Allied leaders pondered French demands for the internationalization of the Ruhr, the creation of a separate state in the Rhineland, and for French exploitation of the mineral resources and industrial power of the Saar.[42] Consistently maintaining that the postwar German state should be decentralized to prevent a recurrence of Prussian predominance, French officials early encountered divergences between their way of thinking and that of the British and Americans, who after reappraising what appeared to be an earlier advocacy of federalization, came to favor the speedy creation of a central German administration which would represent a democratic, peaceful and economically progressive nation.

The British were especially desirous of rebuilding the German industrial machine so that their zone of occupation would cease to be a drain on the weakened British treasury and become self-sustaining. Consequently, the British opposed the separation of the Rhineland and the Ruhr from Germany. With this American Secretary of State James Byrnes placed himself in agreement when he spoke to German leaders at Stuttgart in September 1946. Only in regard to the Saar did the French pleas fall on sympathetic British and American ears. Meanwhile, before the Russians took a public stand at the Paris foreign ministers' conference in July 1946 by repudiating the political detachment or internationalization of the Ruhr and advocating four-power control, the French Communist Party enjoined a policy consistent with French security ideas and the German Communist Party reflected German nationalistic thought. Finally, at the Moscow conference of March 1947, the Russians favored a unified Germany which would include the Rhineland, the Ruhr, as well as the Saar, and the French Communists promptly adopted a new party line. Throughout 1947 a veritable diplomatic impasse existed. The French policy makers tried at one and the same time to hold their ground with regard to Germany and to avoid positive commitment to either of the great colossi which were rapidly dividing the world into pro-American and pro-Russian spheres. Increasingly, pressure was placed on the French by the Anglo-Americans to cooperate in the integration of the economy of the Western occupation zones as a first step to uniting the three. It was at this point that the survey on the RPF platform was conducted.

The cards were now on the table in the grim game which had the future of Germany as its stake. The entire sample was generally sympathetic with the French nationalistic approach of General de Gaulle to the German settlement (60%) and not strikingly opposed (17%). The Communists were the only electors who failed to offer majority approval of the German plank of the RPF. The fact that three-fifths of this group did not favor this proposal was to be expected in the light of the contrary stand espoused by the USSR and the native Communist leadership. Within this body of voters, however, nearly one-third went against the PC line, thus appearing to subordinate to their Communist loyalties to their national patriotism. Despite the indoctrination attempts by the party on behalf of Russia's aims to unify Germany—a reversal of earlier propaganda which, as Domenach has observed, was formerly significant in exploiting French fears of Germany—this substantial bloc of voters clung to traditional viewpoints which now strayed from those publicly preached by the directors of their party.[43]

Before considering the second RPF plank for which some Communist support was discernible, we should conclude this discussion of the German problem with a consideration of an important survey which was conducted in February 1948 on the very lively issue of German zonal unity.

In the face of stubborn Russian disapproval the Quai d'Orsay had already begun to entertain seriously the idea of cooperation with the United States and Great Britain on zonal unification. A conference in London of the Big Four on the Austrian and German peace treaties had been stalemated in December of 1947 and had widened the breach between the East and the West which the French government had hoped to close. French leaders were more than ever aware that Russian intransigence was pushing France into the Western camp. The possibility of mutual action by the three powers of the West on Germany was bound, therefore, to provoke vehement opposition from the Communists as well as to stimulate reappraisal of the situation by non-Communists. Actually 73% of the PC voters disparaged the idea of fusion and only 8% praised it. The rest, amounting to 19%, were evidently not sufficiently swayed by Communist propaganda to avow their support of its objectives. It is perhaps unjust to overemphasize the significance of this fifth of the PC followers, for there were proportionately more Don't Knows among other voters, for example, the Socialists and Popular Republicans, although a majority of each expressed sympathy for the policy being forwarded by the Anglo-Americans. Uncertainty now flourished among all political groups because the German problem had developed into a real dilemma for France: it could stand alone in the gathering gloom of Europe's diplomatic climate or it could elect to stand with the West. The former course might perhaps prove suicidal from the economic if not the military viewpoint as well. The second might be equally suicidal, for it required apparently major concessions in the struggle of France for fundamental security against Germany. This was a dilemma not to be resolved easily in the coming years.

THE PC AND ANTI-AMERICANISM. A majority of the sample (55%), including the largest numbers of all non-Communist voters, approved the recognition of a community of interest between the United States and France as it was stated in the RPF platform. Approximately seven-tenths of the Communists, in keeping with their party's verbal assaults on American imperialism and war-mongering, were not in sympathy with this plank, but a minority of 15% were. This latter group had positively resisted or ignored the Communist hate-America campaign and were to be regarded as neither anti-Russian nor anti-American. Another 14%—a sizeable number among PC supporters on questions of vital public concern and wide knowledge—had not made a decision on the question. Of this group perhaps five per cent or more were genuinely hesitant and confused and, therefore, not converted to the policy of aspersing the USA. This estimate is based on the average indifference rate of 10% or less among the Communist voters.[44]

An interesting brace of questions was presented in December 1947: "Do you think the USSR would launch a war of conquest or that it would fight only to defend itself?"; and, "Do you think that the USA would launch a war of conquest or that it would fight only to defend itself?" Only a handful of PC supporters asserted that Russia would take aggressive action and over four-fifths declared that she would fight only to defend herself. Nearly seven-tenths of this group of voters accepted the possibility of an American of-fensive and only ten per cent were of the opinion that the United States would limit a war to self-defense.[45] But on the second question there was a noticeably greater hesitation than on the first—20% versus 10%. Again it was manifest that an attitude toward the United States which was not definitely hostile characterized between one-fifth and one-fourth of the PC voters.

THE PC AND NATIONAL COMMUNISM. Reference to lack of complete homogeneity among Communist supporters raises the question: Do survey data shed light on the extent to which French Communism has been infected by nationalism or Titoism? Since there is reason to believe that Thorez and other PC leaders have on occasions exhibited nationalistic tendencies, may one conclude that these ideas were representative of important numbers among the rank and file? Writing two years after the terminal point of this study, Mario Einaudi believes that "National Communism in the West is only a generic and distant threat," although in an atmosphere of democratic freedom which does not permit the mass elimination of strong dissenting views "even communist dissent might flourish." He concludes that the effect of Titoism will remain small among the French Communists so long as they remain in opposition, for thus "relieved of the responsibilities of government, they will not be required to carry out policies dictated solely by the interests of the Soviet Union" and "as long as they cannot set up a slave state under Russian control, they will parade as the champions of freedom and national independence," a circumstance which deprives any growing Titoism of its chief stimulus.[46] Vernon Van Dyke, who maintains essentially the same view, adds that "if Titoists gain any significant influence, they are more likely to split the party than to capture it —more likely to weaken the party than to strengthen it." [47]

The results of only two additional inquiries seem to be of assistance here and, since the data are limited, they must be accepted with caution. In the summer of 1948 IFOP called attention to the then recent rupture between the Cominform and Marshal Tito and asked its respondents if they believed Tito would remain in power, and if they wished him to so remain. Much uncertainty was obvious, for 50% of all the sample refused to essay a prediction. Twenty-eight per cent thought the Yugoslav dictator would continue to rule and 20% were of the opposite view. One-fifth of the Communists both thought and wished that Tito would retain his position despite the execrations and threats of the USSR and international agencies of Communism. Although the PC voters possessed the most crystallized opinions, about two-fifths of their number—a very large percentage—were silent on the issue.

At the same time the respondents were asked whether they thought France, Britain and the United States would remain in Berlin and whether they wished the Western powers to stay. Only 43% believed in the possibility of their overcoming the obstacles of the Russian blockade of the ex-German capital but 66% desired that France, Britain and the United States remain in Berlin against 12% who wanted the three powers to evacuate. Only the Communists in large numbers—50%—wanted the Western allies to leave Berlin to the sole occupation of the Russians. Yet a sizeable minority of nearly one-fourth of these voters expressed a preference for the contrary development. At 27%, hesitation was stronger among the Communists than among any other electors.

CONCLUSION. The foregoing discussion of Communist orthodoxy can be summarized and clarified by dividing the key questions which have been examined into three categories according to the amount of dissent and lack of positive response they elicited.

Any standard based solely on disagreement might tend to mislead by failing to indicate the occasional high rate of Don't Knows among the Communist partisans, a condition which exhibits an absence of certainty among many respondents and, therefore, a lack of positive enthusiasm for their party's viewpoint, an ignorance of it or an indifference to it.

The first category would contain those questions toward which the Communists demonstrated rugged orthodoxy in that less than one-fifth were at odds with the party line and at least four-fifths pronounced positive judgment. Actually, on most of these issues four-fifths or more of the voters identified their attitudes with those of the PC leadership. The questions which fell under this first heading were those related to voting instructions, real and hypothetical; the organization of the legislature; the appointment of the Premier by the President of the Republic; a foreign policy founded on Franco-American community of interest; and the military intentions of the USSR.

Questions in the second category provoked greater heterogeneity of outlook among the PC electors. Here the level of nonconformity ranged between 20 and 30% and the level of hesitation, as in the first classification, did not exceed 20%. Ordinarily, three-fifths of the Communists revealed their loyalty on these issues. Such a record of faithfulness excelled that of other voting groups and was generally not even approached except by the followers of the RPF in 1947 and 1948. Inquiries in this class pertained to the President's general role in political life and his specific right to dissolve Parliament; expectation of financial help from Russia and the United States; and advocacy of a politically divided Germany. In short, most foreign policy problems concerning Germany and the cold war were in the second category.

Finally, the few questions in the last category were those which engendered marked disharmony, evident either in an opposition of over 30% to the official PC viewpoint or in a combination of dissent and lack of expressed opinion of at least 50%. Included in this division which obviously spotlighted serious differences of opinion or uncertainties among Communist voters were questions on the necessity for wage and price controls; French participation in the Marshall Plan; Marshal Tito's position in Yugoslavia; and the continued occupation of Berlin by the three powers of the West.[48]

An analysis of the issues which stimulate an above-average heterodoxy suggests well-developed resistance to party propaganda when the voters were confronted with official party views which ostensibly threatened their economic well-being or to do violence to their deep-rooted nationalistic convictions. No dogmatic statements are yet justified, for they should await the accumulation of more data over a period of years. Yet it now seems reasonably clear that the postwar accomplishments of the French Communist Party, once characterized by Léon Blum as a "foreign nationalist party," [49] must be qualified by the fact that a significant minority of its supporters between 1945 and 1949 manifested important attitudes identifiable less with Marxist theory and Soviet Russian objectives than with patriotic French and selfish individual interests.[50]

IV. Religious Attitudes and Values

Frequent references have already been made in this study to underlying values as differentiated from surface opinions. These values are considered by historians under such varied headings as climate of opinion,[51] spirit of the age, the intellectual environment, underlying preconceptions, *Zeitgeist*, *Weltanschauung*, or world pattern. No matter what the terminology, values are given some attention by all historians who attempt to present a well-balanced portrait of an age.

The great obstacle to ascertaining the values of a period lies in the paucity of information concerning the great masses of people as contrasted with the articulate few. What starts out as an attempt to portray the climate of opinion of an age turns out frequently to be a description of its intellectual leadership or of some other limited group. It has been suggested, for example, that the characterization of the Middle Ages as predominantly spiritual in its values may have come about because the major primary sources for the period are the products of the clerical pen and mind, and that if a larger number of extant sources about medieval attitudes had been written or compiled by non-ecclesiastics our modern conceptions might well be open to modification. Surely this hypothesis is not beyond the range of possibility, for, as Louis Gottschalk argues, the historian of the future might be easily misled into overemphasizing the influence of our present-day intellectuals on human affairs if the writings of these leaders of thought were to become the principal or exclusive sources of historical knowledge of our contemporary world.[52]

In his first Storrs Foundation Lecture at the Yale University School of Law, Carl Becker dealt with the climate of opinion of the eighteenth century, holding that the values of the *philosophes* "were still, allowance made for certain alterations in the bias, essentially the same as those of the thirteenth century." [53] Astutely analyzing the contrast between medieval and modern points of view, Becker confines himself exclusively to the appraisal of a climate of opinion of the intellectual segment of the population, ignoring entirely his own indirect caution that the term "climate of opinion" should be applicable not only to "the best thought of the time" but to popular thought as well.[54] By so restricting himself the author does not really present the ideals of the age in a fully balanced manner. The fact, for example, that "the faith was still intact in Dante's time," although "it was just ceasing to be instinctively held" may be true of what Becker describes "its ablest adherents," [55] but was it equally true of those preponderant numbers who were divorced from the intellectual vanguard? How well in fact was "the wide world . . . so neatly boxed and compassed, so completely and confidently understood" [56] by men in general rather than by certain men in particular? This is not to call into question Becker's conclusions as far as they go, but to raise the point of their completeness in describing the nature of a "medieval world pattern." [57]

Preserved Smith in his book on the Reformation also fails to give a balanced interpretation of climate of opinion despite his endeavor, in an introductory discussion of individualism, to differentiate, albeit obliquely, between the masses and the intellectual elite. He does this by raising the point that "to a large extent the undisciplined mind in all periods of life and history is conscious only of object" but that "the trained and leisured intellect discovers, literally by 'reflecting' the subjective." [58] In his chapter entitled "The Temper of the Times" Smith considers matters like tolerance, witchcraft, education, art and books, stressing the acts and words of leaders and implying, without attempting any distinctions, that they reflected and molded the popular temper. He offers some attractive but perhaps unwarranted generalizations. For example, the claim is made that "the love of the beautiful was universal," [59] that "poetry was in the hearts of the people; song was on their lips," that "wit and humor were appreciated above all things," [60] and that "the people were no longer content to leave the glory of life to their superiors." [61] To some these citations may seem carpingly critical of a treatment which in places honestly attempts to assay the true temper of the times. Nevertheless, much of the time Smith neglects to make necessary distinctions and to emphasize the impressionistic character of his evidence.

When considering the spirit of official tolerance of the period Smith notes a few exceptions, although he maintains, and probably with reason, that "the consensus of opinion was overwhelmingly against liberty of conscience." [62] And to him the "witchcraft craze" was one "of those manias to which mankind is periodically subject." [63] Again, because of the dearth of evidence Smith fails to qualify his conclusions.

Some historians have, of course, attempted to distinguish more carefully values held by various segments of the population. G. M. Trevelyan, writing about England, states that "a sincere belief in the reality of witchcraft [was] held by all classes," a belief which was weakened only among the educated classes in the late seventeenth and eighteenth centuries while the mass of the population remained credulous.[64] Shortly after he has distinguished between acceptance of witchcraft according to level of education, Trevelyan tries to establish a factual foundation for his statements by extracting evidence from Sir John Reresby's report on a witch trial held in 1687 at the York Assizes in which it is clear that educated people like the author and the judge were far more skeptical than the members of the Jury, a soldier and a turnkey, all of whom were on a lower educational plane.[65] Checks of this nature from sources revealing the convictions of the people as well as their leaders are not always available.

The foregoing brief illustrations will suffice to demonstrate that historians are indeed concerned with values and are often troubled by paucity of information especially about values held by the masses.

We shall now turn to the survey results on French religious and political attitudes. The IFOP inquiries were not designed for a systematic study of values and did not employ the more refined techniques already available in opinion research. Proper survey techniques can pry beneath the level of ephemeral opinion. Even if the IFOP surveys fall short of revealing the full potentialities of opinion research, the data on some of the religious and political attitudes of the French are of considerable interest and occasionally point to the preconceptions or values which underlie opinions.

THE EXTENT OF RELIGIOUS CONVICTIONS

Since the eighteenth century, when the deistic and agnostic conceptions of the *philosophes* challenged the philosophy and faith of the Catholic Church, France has been a nation religiously divided within herself.[66] Rationalism seemingly triumphed in the great revolutionary years so that in the Napoleonic Era Cardinal Consalvi, sent by Rome to negotiate the Concordat, could conclude that "the people . . . were indifferent in the great majority." [67] The post-Napoleonic religious revival and the return to faith which followed the revolutionary year of 1848-1849 among the bourgeoisie were obviously followed by new setbacks for the church as secular dogmas were more insistently propagated in the second half of the century and a new irreligious proletariat arose.

The far-reaching effects of the rationalist movement on the masses of the French population can only be roughly calculated. The anticlerical Aulard taught, for example, that the peasantry in the revolutionary epoch was not truly Christian.[68] The skeptic Rivarol in his memoirs notes "that at the approach of the Revolution the enlightenment of the clergy equalled that of the philosophers." [69] Perhaps, on the other hand, Horace Walpole's observations of the 1760's that "impiety is less a conviction than a fashion" [70] and those of the Catholic de la Gorce, who holds that the masses continued to lean towards traditional religious beliefs and execute the motions of formal observance are correct.[71] Other interpreters have disagreed as to the influence of traditional religious values in the population at other times, and no attempt is made to evaluate or criticize these contradictory and often impressionistic conclusions. Faith, as Dansette has remarked, can be discovered only through its manifestations and even then, who can tell from diocesan, parochial or other figures, say of Easter communions, how many are faithful, for who has looked into their consciences and who can describe their motives? [72] May there not be real differences between those who are psychologically religious and those who are institutionally religious? [73]

Nevertheless, even the most conservative estimates acknowledge a notable reduction in the ranks of practicing Catholics which probably both accompanied and strengthened post-revolutionary skepticism, indifferentism and anti-clericalism.[74]

The historian who is concerned with religious values in France —as elsewhere—probably has a three-faceted investigative task. First and foremost, he seeks to know the extent to which religious sentiments were reflected in the views and actions of the people. In short, he inquires how frequently and how profoundly fundamental religious convictions impinged on everyday life. Secondly, the historian searches for valid data concerning the affiliation of the masses with organized religion. This is an institutionalized interest distinct and apart from, but yet related to, the spread and depth of religious values in the community. Surely, for example, the historian of the revolutionary epoch in Franch would like to know more about:

> Jean François, laborer of Quercy, [who] wrote no thing and . . . [whose] thoughts no one cared to collect. Did he practice? Did he have the faith? Did he think? Did he live as a good Catholic? The question is immense; it is the life of the French people under one of its essential aspects.[75]

And, lastly, the historian wants to ascertain how the various population groups conceived the role of the church in the political, social and economic activity of the time. How, then, should the institutional needs of religion be interpreted?

If the historian of today is desirous of obtaining satisfactory answers to these questions of the past, the historian of the future will certainly look for answers to the same questions as they relate to contemporary conditions.

The first area of inquiry is perhaps the most significant and, by the same token, the most difficult. As far as IFOP is concerned we have only one study conducted at the end of 1947 by Gallup affiliates in twelve countries which states in some short and un-refined terms that about two-thirds of the French sample believed in God and three-quarters in a personal life after death.

The international character of the inquiry permits a comparison between the religious convictions of the French and those of nationalities with divergent religious backgrounds. And by virtue of these comparative data a clearer view of French religious faith emerges. Of all national groups tested the French were the most inclined towards atheism and were the least willing to respond to the question about belief in God.[76] Sixty-six per cent of these respondents affirmed and 20% denied God's existence. Apparently the most important single variable was sex: 75% of the women but only about 55% of the men acknowledged a God, a relationship amply confirmed by other data. The kind of God the French believed in is not evident from these data, for those interviewed were, regrettably, not asked to explain their understanding of the term.[77]

The French results compared with a 96% level of belief in Brazil, 95% in Australia and Canada, 94% in the United States, 84% in Norway and Great Britain, 83% in Finland, 80% in the Netherlands, Sweden and Denmark and 77% in Czechoslovakia.[78]

The next question, pertaining to the immortality of the soul, is perhaps slightly more useful in our attempt to ascertain the broad lines of French religious faith. Among the various national groups French belief in a personal life after death was relatively stronger than French acceptance of a Divine Being, for the French figure of 58% was considerably greater than the British and Swedish 49% and somewhat greater than the Szechoslovakian 52% and the Danish 55%. Of the remaining two-fifths of the French sample 22% rejected the doctrine of individual immortality and 20% refused to answer the question.[79] Again sex differences appeared to be significant, as 68% of the female respondents against 47% of the males espoused the belief in immortality.

It may be contended that correlation of the data obtained from both questions indicates a traditional interpretation of God by the French. The results of the two questions reveal a difference of only 8% between French acknowledgment of the existence of God and the soul. This disparity—except in the case of Britain—may very well represent among the various nationalities the approximate number of those who, while claiming to be theists, viewed God as an impersonal power or Prime Mover. The British data add weight to this tentative inference, for the marginal difference between those British respondents who bespoke faith in a personal God (45%) and those who avowed belief in the immortality of the soul (49%) was the smallest to be found.[80] There were, therefore, strong implications that, since 85% of the French theists also confessed a belief in an immortal soul and since 97% of those with faith in eternal life affirmed the existence of God, the IFOP respondents envisaged the deity in terms of Judaeo-Christian teachings rather than in terms of Enlightened thought.

This study has but brushed the surface of the problem of religious sentiments and beliefs. The relationship between belief and action also remains to be explored. Ethical problems—hypothetical or real—could be presented to the respondents and their recommendations correlated with beliefs ascertained independently. Again, the role of religion could be explored by ascertaining the situations in which an individual seeks a religious experience.

AFFILIATION WITH ORGANIZED RELIGION

One standard criterion for determining the seriousness with which people embrace their religious principles is their formal affiliation with an ecclesiastical organization. Such affiliation is seldom sufficient in itself to demonstrate the influence of religion in the life of the church member. His participation in the activities of the church, his attendance at services, his reception of the sacraments are, of course, better indices, although not necessarily valid, of his attachment to the dogmatic and ethical values of a specific religious institution. Accurate statistical information on the formal observance of religion in France is hard to come by. Church agencies do not normally release these data and independent surveys, though conducted scientifically, have not been sufficiently broad or numerous to reveal precise information on the religious habits of the people as a whole.[81] Some investigators have concluded that no more than 45% of the adults in most of the religious sections of France are fairly regular in their attendance at Sunday mass and make their obligatory communion during the Easter season. Le Bras estimates that of the 38 million baptized Catholics a majority are *conformistes saisonniers:* they satisfy church obligations on four major occasions in life-baptism, first communion, marriage, and burial.[82] Boulard has categorized areas according to their degree of religious observance. He and others have directed attention to the vast chasm between the religious practice of residents of departments like the Finistère in the West, which is thoroughly Christian; the Bouches-du-Rhône in the South, which is indifferent; and large sections of the Yonne to the southeast of Paris, which are "mission territory." [83] Furthermore, studies of voting statistics in these areas have uncovered a close relationship between religious fidelity and party selection.[84] Survey results supply some figures on attendance, although many authorities, including the directors of IFOP, have expressed the belief that the percentages are perhaps too high, therefore lacking the validity of other poll findings. This may be true, but in the absence of other completely reputable data, the results of these inquiries probably yield the best available information on French religious fidelity between 1946 and 1948. They suggest that on a national basis only one fourth of the French adults at the extreme were faithful to their religious duties. From one-third to two-fifths of the population might perhaps be classified as less regular participants in religious services and perhaps nearly one-half of the sample went to church, other than for other people's weddings, funerals, christenings, etc., at least once during the year.

When the respondents were asked in March 1946 if they went to mass regularly, thirty-three per cent claimed to be habitual mass-goers and 55% stated that they were not.[85] The sex variable was of course important, for 42% of the women and barely 25% of the men were "pratiquants." [86]

Over a year and a half later, at the same time as the sample was quizzed on belief in God and the immortality of the soul, another question on religious practice was presented: "Did you go to Divine Worship last Sunday or the preceding Sunday?" Thirty-seven per cent affirmed such participation on one or both occasions and 58% stated that they had not gone to church on either Sunday.[87] Again the female population was far more faithful than the male: 47% to 27%. Ninety-eight per cent of those who said they had gone to church believed in God and 95% believed in the immortality of man's soul. Nearly one-half of those who had not been at mass believed in God and over one-third acknowledged a personal afterlife.

Finally, in July 1948, an important survey concerning the way in which the French celebrated their most important civic and religious holidays was conducted. Only 26% of those interviewed said that they had attended religious services on the Sunday prior to being questioned. Midnight Mass on the previous Christmas Eve had drawn 24% of the respondents and Easter morning services had attracted a large 35%.[88] On one holy day of obligation, the Assumption of the Virgin Mary, the 15th of August, only 22% had gone to mass and 4% had gone to church in the afternoon. On the other hand, 47% maintained that they had participated in religious services on All Saints' Day, the Holy day of Obligation which precedes All Souls' Day, when the French customarily commemorate their departed loved ones. A large 72% said that they had visited a cemetery. These figures contribute toward a clarification of French religious habits. On a given Sunday and on a peculiarly Catholic feast day, the Assumption, one-fourth at most went to religious services. On the great holiday of Easter, when many Christians throughout the world make their annual public appearance in church, perhaps over two-fifths of the French sample participated in corporate worship. The Christmas celebration, the other great magnet for church-goers, was not adequately investigated, for Christmas Day mass attendance data are needed to supplement Midnight Mass figures if a true picture of the situation is to be realized. The information on All Saints' Day observance was in a special category and would seem to attest to the power of sentiment and custom and to the conviction that obligations of prayer are owed to the dead. It is interesting to note here that the power of custom and tradition was also reflected in a survey taken in May, 1946, in which about seven-tenths of the parents interviewed claimed that their children who had reached the proper canonical age had made their first communion. This parental group amounted to approximately 45% of all the respondents.

In this survey the rate of habitual mass attendance was clearly differentiated from occasional or even fairly regular participation in religious services. Very obviously the majority of those who believed in both God and the immortality of the soul did not attend church every Sunday or religious holiday and barely a majority of these people went to church with regularity. Again the French, although revealing a higher incidence of atheism than the other nationalities surveyed, could boast a better than average record of church attendance among believers, a fact which suggests that the faithful quarter of the French made up a strong core of religious affiliation and observance. An equal number might be classified as resistant to traditional Christianity to the degree that they espoused atheism or indifferentism. The largest segment of the French—nearly one-half—was evidently somewhere in between, believers of a sort but not devout according to the criteria used.

Breakdowns of religious observance according to political preference add a new dimension to this information. No other sources can currently furnish data on the association of religious practice and political party choice. The surveys indicate that even among the so-called clerical parties like the MRP and various rightist formations, only about 50% were *pratiquants*. Also, at the extreme, among non-Communist anticlerical groups like the Socialists and Radicals, probably 10% to 15% were fairly faithful church-goers. In the November 1947 inquiry, for example, total church attendance on one or both of the two previous Sundays stood at 37%. On the Left 2% of the Communists but 12% of the Socialists and 15% of the Radicals said that they had been to a religious service.[89] On the religious Right 73% of the MRP, 53% of the PRL and 50% of the RPF followers participated in divine worship on one or both of the previous Sundays.[90]

When, in 1948, 26% of the respondents said that they had attended religious services on the Sunday before, 3% of the PC, 10% of the SFIO and 16% of the RGR voters were among them. Fifty-one per cent of the MRP, 50% of the PRL and 43% of the RPF followers also affirmed attendance at that time. The difference in the record of the electors of the reputedly clerical parties—and it is real—in the two surveys is probably accounted for by the inclusion of "or the preceding Sunday" in the first so that that inquiry represented the extremes of fairly regular religious practice and the second probably reflected habitual observance.[91]

RELIGION AND POLITICAL ACTION

The third major question raised at the beginning of this discussion was: what sort of information may be obtained regarding the influence organized religion should exert in political and other pursuits? The disagreements regarding the political role of the Church are fundamental, for they are among the cardinal reasons for French "disorder and . . . divisions." [92]

Catholic efforts to inject church influence into certain aspects of public activity are rooted in dogma and the logical developments of that dogma. Similarly, the anticlericalism of the Left is dogmatic in origin and expression and Marxism itself has been dubbed "the truth of God seen through the eyes of the devil." [93] The Catholic complex, although it has diminished somewhat since the "time when the separation of the profane and sacred, the opposition between the church, guardian of true values, and the state, charged with base necessities, counted for a great deal in the contempt for the state and the obligations of the citizen to the state," [94] may yet under certain circumstances come forth with renewed vigor to exercise a vital—and perhaps decisive—effect on French political fortunes.

In modern France the chief controversial facet of this church-state relationship has been the symbolic, emotionally charged issue of educational freedom, that is, the existence of free, largely Catholic, schools and, more particularly, state subsidization of them. In its desire to weaken if not destroy the power of the Catholic Church the Left has created and sustained a national educational system designed to replace private facilities. Nevertheless, private schools and Catholic influence in education have continued to exist on a variable and modified scale in the post-revolutionary epoch. At base this dispute involves, in the minds of the clerical elements, the right of competent citizens to conduct private schools and the right of parents to send their children either to private (free) or state institutions. On the other hand, the anticlericals hold that freedom of instruction means that schools should be free of Catholic religious and political influence and that children should be allowed to develop mentally without interference by the clergy. The freedom to maintain private schools, although not "constitutionalized" in 1946 as the MRP wished, has been maintained since the Second World War despite Communist and Socialist majorities on the side of state monopoly. Essentially not a major postwar problem, this dispute has been kept alive by many Frenchmen who apparently retain their suspicions that the Church is not sympathetic with either republicanism or democracy. In this way divisions which have been termed "fifty years out of date" [95] retained their timeliness and political usefulness.

The granting of state subsidies to private schools did provoke virulent disputes throughout this period. For the Catholics the freedom of education was barren unless implemented by official grants which would permit the church schools to pay their faculties appropriately and to minimize the extra financial burdens on parents who enrolled their children in these institutions. Moreover, the Catholics contended that the rise in the birth rate rendered a private educational system mandatory, since neither an adequate number of teachers nor satisfactory facilities could be provided by the public schools.[96]

The secular tradition was tenaciously adhered to by the Left. Under the Third Republic the lay laws of the 1880's became sacred and inviolable and when they were set aside for the first time by the Vichy Regime, their symbolic character was reinforced.[97] In the early spring of 1945 the lay laws were reinstated and all Vichy-instituted subsidies were withdrawn. This action placed the free schools in a difficult financial position, for the war had substantially reduced the wealth of those groups which previously had in large measure defrayed the cost of private institutions. In the succeeding years under present survey the Popular Republicans fought to rectify this situation but failed.[98]

It is evident from various IFOP inquiries that up to the beginning of 1949 popular feeling ran against state subsidies. Only about a third of the respondents looked with favor on government grants and from one-half to three-fifths opposed it. By the middle of 1948 nearly all the PC (92%), SFIO (81%) and a majority of the RGR voters (65%), making up the old anticlerical Left, were ranged against public assistance to the free schools. Yet the other electors were not all advocates of subsidies. Seventy per cent of the Popular Republicans approved aid but 17% disapproved it. Among PRL supporters 75% favored monetary grants to private schools and a small minority of 10% rejected them. The RPF voters were somewhat less enthusiastic over this policy: 65% for state aid and 22% against.[99]

The foregoing data provide the researcher with an interesting hypothesis; namely, that the disparity between the religious Right and the non-Communist, anticlerical Left was generally greater on this matter of principle than on the matter of church affiliation and religious practice. In the PRL and RPF especially far more people advocated a clerical policy in regard to education than attended Sunday mass even fairly regularly. While these surveys indicate a relationship between religious fidelity and endorsement of free schools, they fail to explore in detail the reasons for opposing private schools or for rejecting governmental aid to them. Although this again calls attention to the superficiality of much of the information at hand, the fact that these data exist at all should not be dismissed lightly. In themselves they possess some value but they are especially worthwhile as the point of departure for investigations into underlying convictions which may yield a rich future harvest to the historian.

V. Political Attitudes and Values

It has been virtually impossible to disentangle basic religious and economic convictions from the political pattern of postwar France since all are integrated in a rounded whole. Some value-schemes, however, display somewhat more highly developed and more exclusive political connotations. Among these are the values associated with freedom. What is liberty? Does it have more important and less important aspects? Is it the right to elect one's governors who remain responsible to the electorate? Is it the privilege of speaking one's mind openly and without fear of reprisal? Is it the freedom to earn one's living and to operate in the economic sphere with only a minimum amount of state interference? Is it rather the right to worship or not to worship, to believe or not to believe as one's conscience dictates? Is parliamentary government a luxury in times of national crisis and division? Is authoritarianism preferable in the interests of efficiency, order and stability? These are questions which are not new in French history; in fact they have been debated with great vigor for the last two hundred years. Therefore, any survey data available on these significant issues are not only helpful to an understanding of the contemporary spirit of France but may also provide an inkling concerning the attitudes of the past.

In molding France into the first of the great modern European states the Revolution created a tradition of political liberty that was to be periodically challenged by its enemies, among whom republicans would normally place figures like Napoleon III and General Boulanger. Indeed it has been said that the modern French parliamentary system was primarily conceived as a guardian of that liberty against the encroachments of autocratic power. After 1875, the government of the Third Republic, responding to demands from the Right for a stronger executive and to actual threats to the regime from that quarter, almost imperceptibly brought about the subordination of the executive arm to the legislative.[100] Control by parliament "in the name of the sovereign people" became equated with the republic.[101] With this experience in mind, contemporary leftist leaders, championing traditional republican ideals, attempted in 1945 and 1946 to establish complete government by assembly and, failing this, laid the groundwork for the modified government by assembly which has occasioned many of the parliamentary problems and weaknesses with which the Fourth Republic has become identified. By 1947 some voters, even of parties which were pledged publicly to uphold republican political principles, came to think that a parliament which reflected so closely the unyielding antagonisms and divisions in the body politic did not benefit France. Still more took cognizance of the worth-while character of parliament, although at the same time nearly a majority of the electors considered a strong man necessary to lift France from the quicksand into which she had stumbled. Political liberty and free speech were regarded as of primary importance by nearly three-fifths of the respondents but the rest were more inclined to see religious and economic freedom as fundamental.

The questions asked by IFOP in April 1947 were the following: "Do you believe things would be worse or better if there were no parliament?" The choices offered were: "worse, the same thing, better." "Do you feel that to get out of the present difficulties it would be necessary for an energetic man to take power, by force if necessary?" "To which one of the following freedoms are you most attached? Political, religious, economic (that is, of commerce and prices) or speech?" The answers to these questions on the basis of political affiliation have been divided into two groups of indices, one of leftist and one of rightist thought. Table II puts in capsule form the responses that things would be worse without parliament, a strong man was not necessary, political liberty was primary and freedom of speech was paramount. Table III features the answers of those who maintained that things would be better without parliament, an energetic man was needed, religious liberty was fundamental and economic freedom was of first concern.

Table II—Attachment to Liberties—Indices of Leftist Thought
(percentages of voters)

	All Voters	PC	SFIO	RGR	MRP	PRL
Championed parliament	33	64	49	37	15	8
Opposed strong man	37	67	56	37	20	3
Political liberty #1	32	59	45	31	21	15
Free speech #1	26	26	30	26	23	14
Total: Political liberty and Free Speech		85	75	57	44	29

Table III—Attachment to Liberties—Indices of Rightist Thought

	All Voters	PC	SFIO	RGR	MRP	PRL
Opposed parliament	21	8	9	21	31	50
Favored strong man	49	26	33	50	70	94
Religious liberty #1	24	4	9	18	44	46
Economic liberty #1	17	11	16	25	12	25
Total: Religious and Economic liberty		15	25	43	56	71

In respect to parliamentary attachment both the PC and SFIO voters were conspicuously identifiable with the old political Left and the MRP and PRL electors with the old political Right. Just as the Socialists were not so extreme as the Communists, the Popular Republicans were not so extreme as the Rightists. The major distinction between the Communists and Socialists was that more of the latter asserted that conditions would be neither worse nor better without a national legislature [102] and refused to answer the question.[103] Few of either party could visualize an amelioration of the general situation if the National Assembly were suppressed.

In both tables the Radicals and their allies are in the center, with a score at or near the average for the entire sample. Nevertheless, their basic pattern on these symbolic and practical issues was leftist rather than rightist. The MRP voters, while tending toward the Right, produced the greatest amount of hesitation and uncertainty (25%).

A majority of both the Communists and Socialists quite expectedly scouted the need for a strong man. The Radicals again occupied

a centrist position with average percentages on each side of the
question, a condition which made the Radicals, like the entire sample,
lean more to the Right than to the Left. Manifestly on the Right
were the MRP and PRL supporters, large majorities of whom hailed
an energetic leader. Again the difference between the two groups
was one of degree not of kind, for one fifth of the Popular Republicans, but only a handful of the PRL voters were hostile to authoritarian rule. The results of the foregoing questions suggested that
strong man allegiance of itself did not, in the view of many respondents, necessarily imply discarding parliament. Nearly one
fourth of the PC voters and one third of the SFIO partisans, most
of whom would have looked to an energetic leader other than De
Gaulle, saw some value in the proposal to install a strong man, but
these respondents were at the same time unconvinced that the suppression of parliamentary institutions was a key to the betterment
of the political situation. There was in general, however, a high
positive correlation between the two sets of attitudes.[104]

A primary devotion to political liberty existed among a substantial majority of the PC followers and among the largest numbers
of SFIO and RGR supporters, too. Freedom of expression ran high
among all three. The PC and SFIO patterns were essentially the
same in their expressed preference for political freedom, free speech,
economic freedom and religious freedom in that order. The pattern
of the Radicals was somewhat divergent. Their attachment to political liberty and speech freedom coincided with the average of the
complete sample. Political liberty came first and religious liberty
last, as among the Marxists and in accordance with nineteenth century republican tenets. But very different from the PC and SFIO
was the RGR partiality to economic freedom. Strong adherence was
offered by the Radical voters to the primacy of free enterprise in
numbers relatively the same as among those who selected the PRL.
The tone of the MRP and PRL electors was religious, the biggest
individual bloc—over two fifths—of each having selected religious
liberty as of basic worth.[105] With this aspect as fundamental there
were important distinctions between the MRP and PRL outlooks.
Fair-sized MRP minorities selected free speech and political freedom
as their chief concern and, with the Communists, the Popular Republicans were the least impressed by the first-rate importance of
economic freedom. On the other hand, the second greatest segment

of PRL voters, along with the Radicals, ascribed primacy to economic liberty.

The foregoing indices uncover several fundamental attitudes and suggest a four-fold division: (1) The Marxists; (2) The Radicals and their allies; (3) The Popular Republicans; (4) The PRL voters and other rightists. In a majority the Marxists were the defenders of the parliamentary system, the enemies of executive authoritarianism, the proponents of the fundamental worth of political freedom and freedom of speech. The voters of the RGR, in larger numbers than not, espoused the cause of parliament while strongly inclining toward an authoritarian solution to the crisis conditions. A majority of them endorsed free political practices and free speech, although a very substantial minority of them looked first to economic and religious liberty. The followers of the MRP (this before the RPF was organized) were more apt than not to question the value of parliament, although they were particularly uncertain on the issue. They strongly favored energetic executive rule and were attached primarily to liberties associated with rightist thought, despite a sizeable minority which was drawn to one or the other of the freedoms associated with leftism and the "Great Revolution." The PRL electors and other voters of the Right strongly questioned the value of a parliamentary regime and nearly all of them championed the cause of a strong executive. They were also powerfully behind the primacy of religious and economic liberty. In schematic form one might, on the basis of historic political tradition (the issue of whether Communism unavoidably brings a dictatorial form of government aside), put clear majorities of the PC on the Right. The RGR voters would fall somewhere in between, but would lean toward the Left. On the clerical issue, which has been the line of Left-Right demarcation in the past and which cuts across political and social divisions in dramatic form,[106] one would find the same groups fundamentally opposed to each other. But if one approached the matter of orientation from the economic angle, he would see the MRP aligned with the PC and SFIO on the Left, and the RGR with the PRL on the Right. Thus the ambiguity of the positions of the Popular Republicans and the Radicals can be seen fairly lucidly. Political orientation or the determination of Left and Right depends, then, not on one set of values but on several. There are, as Raymond Aron has written, "various rights and various lefts.[107]

VI. Alterations of Attitudes and Values

Basic values neither originate nor thrive in a vacuum; they are stimulated, refined and reversed by a complex variety of influences. Institutions such as the home, the church, and the school together with instruments like newspapers, motion pictures, television, radio, advertising, books and cartoons figure prominently in the process of value creation and change. Psychological studies indicate that direct personal influence occupies a key role as well. And just as fundamental convictions are the end-products of an indeterminable number of influences, so are the specific opinions which rise out of these convictions.

Once formed, these attitudes are subject to alterations which may be gradual and imperceptible or sudden and obvious. A study of the ways in which these changes occur is clearly within the province of the historian, for a knowledge of them is prerequisite to a more accurate understanding of the changes in the behavior of individuals and in "the behavior and organization of things and institutions which condition changes in human behavior," [108] with all of which the historian is properly—even unavoidably—concerned. Since old ideas and patterns, as the late J. G. Randall observed in his presidential address to the American Historical Association in 1952,[109] regularly become outmoded, the historian as a seeker of causal relationships is bound to investigate the nature and effect of the alterations and the circumstances surrounding their occurrence.

But the problem of explaining changes in attitudes is an extremely difficult one and the "methodology in causal analysis is still relatively crude and speculative." [110] A case in point is Randall's generalization that outmoding of old ideas might well be ascribed to "the passing of time . . . or the coming of fresh air." [111] But even more serious attempts to grapple with the problem often fall short of what might be accomplished with new data and new methods. For example, in an appraisal of English development between 1910 and 1935 Sir Ernest Barker describes the diminution of social intolerance during the reign of George V. He styles the early twentieth century a period of "truceless war" between the social classes and recalls his own unsuccessful efforts to get a hearing at Oxford for Keir Hardie, founder of the Independent Labor Party. By 1935, Barker observes, this situation was so radically different that labor leaders could probably have secured hearings anywhere. This alteration in the spirit of the age, according to the author, resulted from "a growth of social equality and of mutual respect of class for class, in the years since 1910." [112] This statement restates but does not explain the phenomenon under scrutiny.

Let us for purposes of illustration cite some of the questions which the historian ought to put to Barker's conclusions. After the fact of a change has been established—how did this transformation come about? What groups were most responsible for this shift in opinion? When did the shift take place? Was it gradual or was it sudden? Was it discernible or was it imperceptible to its contemporaries? How widespread was the new social tolerance? Which social groups were most clearly affected? Which least affected? What events helped to extend this tolerance, what events helped to restrict it? It is beyond question that, were they available, answers to these and addititional queries would create a clearer, more precise impression of the type of social transformation Barker explored.

Up to this point the IFOP data bearing upon changes in attitudes have been meager. Most of the data fall under the major headings of the role of newspapers and the role of events in molding attitudes. Only examples of the second will be examined in this essay because the French material on newspaper influence is less satisfactory than that on the importance of events. It may be observed in passing, though, that two tentative hypotheses are derived from the IFOP data that has been analyzed: first, it would seem that the readers of papers published by political organizations were more politically minded than the readers of other newspapers; and, secondly, it would appear that these people who read party dailies normally possessed more highly structured political opinions than the other voters of their party. But these findings are susceptible of several interpretations which could not in the present state of the French data be pursued further. The surveys that are framed to probe into the effect of events on the French opinion during the same period are somewhat more enlightening.

Historians and political scientists frequently examine events as end-products of public opinion. But events can be regarded not only as results but as causes of public opinion. Hadley Cantril has pointed out that "opinion is generally determined more by events than words—unless the words are themselves interpreted as an 'event'." [113]

Two examples of the way in which events have altered French public opinion in the postwar years have been chosen. The first deals with French views regarding monetary assistance which might be expected from the United States to help France in her recovery program. The second is concerned with the alteration of French opinion on German zonal unification.

INFLUENCE OF EVENTS

Financial Help from the United States. Public reaction to a changing situation finds expression in the results of the trend question, "Which nation will aid France the most in her recovery?" In the fall of 1944 about seven tenths of the Paris sample named the United States, but after General de Gaulle's December visit to Moscow during which a Franco-Soviet Alliance was concluded this figure fell among the enlarged sample to about one fourth and another fourth cited the Soviet Union. Over a year later, in April 1946, no real assistance having come from the U.S.S.R., estimates of aid from that quarter stood at only 17% and expectation of help from the Americans rose to 50%. Immediately thereafter, in the wake of Léon Blum's successful fund-seeking trip to the United States, anticipation of aid from America increased to 63% and hope for assistance from Russia decreased to 12%.

The announcement of Secretary Marshall's ideas for European recovery in the summer of 1947 did not greatly affect French anticipation of American help. In September 64% thought that the United States would assist France the most and only 8% named the U.S.S.R. At about the time that the American Congress was approving interim aid at the end of January 1948 70% of the French respondents believed in the primary assistance of the U.S.A. A good prospect of Russian monetary help could be seen by a mere 7%.

The oscillations in these figures can probably be accounted for by an early belief that the U.S.A. would immediately send financial aid to the French; disillusionment when this American assistance did not arrive; a foundationless hope that the Soviet alliance would bring substantial material and financial benefits for France; and the rewarded hope that Blum's mission to Washington for financial credits would meet with success. It was clear that only the positive action of the United States, beginning in the late spring of 1946, brought a substantial majority to the belief that the American Republic would aid France most in her recovery.

Zonal Fusion. The alteration of opinion on zonal unity in Germany in the fall and winter of 1947-1948 seemed to reflect the alteration of official French policy in the light of changing circumstances. Between September and February, it will be remembered, French opinion changed from an almost even threefold division on the subject—35% for, 31% against and 34% Don't Know to a majority favor of merger (47%). Hostility was reduced to 24% and the Don't Knows fell to 29% as French leaders seriously began to ponder the advantages of a trizonal establishment in western Germany. As has been observed earlier, there was a clear alteration of opinion among all groups of voters, but especially among those who supported the parties in the government.

THE "FAIT ACCOMPLI"

In regard to the influence of events themselves on opinion some consideration should be devoted to the "fait accompli." Challenging indeed is A. V. Dicey's generalization in his Harvard lectures on law and public opinion in nineteenth century England that a "fait accompli," i.e., the passage of a law or the official acceptance of a policy, creates opinion.[114] Especially captivated by legislative opinion, Dicey held that the body of public opinion in England in the last century was central in bringing about the passage of laws conformable to it and that this body of opinion was in turn affected by the passage of laws. In short, public opinion creates events and events create public opinion. Many refinements of the process by which public attitudes influence events in general and legislation in particular are certainly desirable, but since these can be achieved only through an excursion into propaganda analysis, only the second belief that a "fait accompli" is "à faire approuver" will be considered.[115]

The public opinion literature of modern democracies contains relatively few data that can be brought to bear in an attempt to prove the validity of this thesis. Among these the alteration of views concerning Franklin Roosevelt's effort to enlarge the Supreme Court in 1937 is well known.[116] There are, however, three good illustrations of how accepted fact has influenced French public opinion during the period under survey: the selection of De Gaulle as Provisional President; the imprisonment of Marshal Pétain; and the conclusion of the Franco-British alliance. In all of these cases the net approval of the event or action increased noticeably after the event or action had taken place.

De Gaulle's Election. Public approbation of General De Gaulle's assuming the presidential duties was markedly increased by his formal election in November 1945. Between July and November the desire to have De Gaulle as President of the Provisional Government fluctuated slightly but was never below 65% and was at a high of 75% just before he was designated. At this point 10% of the respondents were unwilling to express an opinion, thus leaving an opposition element of about 15%. After the Assembly's action, 81% of the sample indicated approval, 13% expressed opposition and 6% failed to answer. It thus appears that the "fait accompli" converted nearly half of those who had previously hesitated and had reduced opposition by a small percentage.

Pétain's Imprisonment. The fate of Marshal Pétain was considerably more controversial than the election to the Provisional Presidency of General de Gaulle. In April 1945 seven tenths of the sample wished to see the ex-Chief of State condemned and approximately one fifth registered opposition to such action. Of those urging a sentence the largest group (34%) proposed no specific penalty for Pétain's alleged crimes; however, 28% asked for capital punishment, 19% for imprisonment and 10% for degradation. The next month three fourths of the respondents favored punishment for the Marshal, with 40% advocating death, 17% prison and 6% degradation. At the beginning of the trial in late July, attitudes toward condemnation stood at the same level as in May and remained fairly stable during the course of the trial in August. The court's verdict was death tempered by a recommendation for clemency, a decision which did not affect the opinion structure regarding the prisoner's guilt but apparently did alter opinion regarding the proper sentence. Still about 35% championed capital punishment without leniency but a significant 27% upheld the action of the court, revealing the existence of a new current of opinion among an important minority. The Don't Knows and demands for other types of punishment both dropped off noticeably.

About a year and a half after Pétain's final sentence of life imprisonment on the Island of Yeu had been rendered, 63% of the sample were of the opinion that he should be left on Yeu and only 10% asked that he be executed. Thirteen per cent now felt that he should be freed. In this instance Dicey's point that a "fait accompli" not only stimulates its own acceptance but also engenders acceptance of the general principles on which it is based seems to be borne out. By this time most of the respondents who had previously demanded Pétain's condemnation seemed satisfied with the punishment meted out and about two thirds of those who had formerly urged his execution now seemed to accept the mitigation decreed by the government. Only one third of those who, in September 1945, had wished Pétain shot still considered such an action proper and just.

The Franco-British Alliance. As the European phase of World War II was nearing its finish the French were first asked their views on a political and military alliance with Great Britain. The idea was approved by a great majority (79%) and rejected by only 11%. By September endorsement of an alliance had declined to 72% and opposition had risen to 14%. Only 68% of those interviewed in April 1946 were partisans of such an alliance but at the same time antagonism was voiced by only 9%. Indifference was expressed by 15% and 8% volunteered no opinion. A month or so before the treaty was signed on the 4th of March 1947, 59% of the sample spoke in favor of an agreement and 21% spoke against it. The "fait accompli," the Treaty of Dunkirk, increased net approval and reduced net opposition: 63% were satisfied with the alliance (up 4% and only 12% were dissatisfied (down 9%). More indecisiveness, however, existed in April than in January (up 6%). Although, on the basis of net change, the largest movement was away from disapproval to hesitation, the positive effect of an accepted fact on the current of opinion cannot be dismissed.

WORDS AS EVENTS

A third category of events which influence opinion might be those words which in Cantril's statement "are themselves interpreted as an event." An example of this type showing the influence of a respected individual's announced viewpoint on an issue over which there is some public disagreement and uncertainty has been selected. In this instance the individual was General de Gaulle, the time was the fall of 1946, and the occasion was the referendum campaign. By the late summer of that year De Gaulle's convictions on the constitutional problem were widely publicized but it was not until just before the referendum of October 13th that he struck out against the revised draft in unmistakable terms. Before this pronouncement IFOP had asked its sample about referendum voting intentions and predicted that 65% would vote Yes and 35% No. Yet the possibility of a De Gaulle announcement could not be dismissed and the influence of a forceful plea for rejection by De Gaulle could not be omitted when essaying a forecast. Therefore, IFOP asked the following question in anticipation of the General's statement: "If General De Gaulle recommends a vote against the constitution, will you vote for or against the constitution?" Twenty-nine per cent said they would support the document; 28% said they would vote to defeat it; 33% did not respond and 10% said they would abstain. In the first week of October, after a speech by De Gaulle at Epinal on September 29, IFOP presented the following question: "All in all, do you approve or disapprove of what General De Gaulle said in this speech?" Approval was voiced by 28%, disapproval by 32%. A large 31% were unfamiliar with the statement and 9% lacked an opinion. On the basis of these two inquiries IFOP estimated the influence of the positive announcement made by De Gaulle for rejection on the 10th of October. This influence was gauged as considerable, for now IFOP predicted that 36% would abstain rather than 20% and that 54% of those who cast their ballots (against a previous 65%) would vote affirmatively and that 46% (against a previous 35%) would vote negatively.[117]

This inquiry uncovers the possibility that De Gaulle's last-minute statement was responsible for nearly one half of the abstentions and a 10% increase in the opposition vote and a corresponding decrease in the favorable vote. This is a moderately lucid exposition of the influence which is apt to be exerted on public attitudes by men whose following is large and whose prestige is great. True, De Gaulle did not turn the trend of thought on a controversial political issue but there is reason to believe that his words did affect the trend of thought substantially.

EXPECTATIONS

A final aspect of the study of events as an influence on opinion is a consideration of expectation as a historical force, that is, the anticipation expressed by men that contemporary events will have a certain outcome. In the past, historians have been able to ascertain the existence of this type of expectation and to isolate some of its facets as they were represented in groups and, more particularly, in individuals. Perhaps as public opinion data become more refined and more abundant the historian will be enabled to learn more about expectation and its relationship to present decisions. Very likely he can come closer to ascertaining why certain results are widely anticipated and do not come about, why others are not generally expected and do eventuate, why some movements collapse in the face of failure, why others persist and play a continuing role, whether major or minor, successful or unsuccessful, in history. Even at this moment some bits of information are ready for discussion.

Studies by polling agencies, for example, revealed that a substantial number of people will support a candidate who, because majority sentiment appears to be against him, seems destined to lose. This situation is particularly apparent when public opinion seems almost evenly balanced, with one candidate or side popularly given the better chance of winning. A distinguished French example is produced by the referendum of May 1946.

After the first constitutional referendum IFOP posed the following questions: "Did you expect a majority of Yes or a majority of No in the referendum?"; "How did you vote in the referendum?" A cross-tabulation of the results of these two questions discloses that 90% of those who voted for the draft expected to be on the winning side, and that only 4% expected to be on the losing side.[118]

On the other hand, there was less certainty on the opposing side which actually triumphed. In this group nearly 40% thought the draft would be defeated and 42% believed that their ballots would be cast in vain.[119] Definitely the side of adoption was the more popular according to the anticipation of those who voted as well as of those who abstained. Since all predictions—public opinion poll and other—signalled the adoption of the constitution, a last-minute increase in the affirmative rather than in the negative forces would have been natural if a strong band wagon effect had been operative.

The band wagon theory is "one of the oldest delusions of politics," [120] and neither a large scale band wagon movement nor one important enough to alter election results has ever been proven.

VII. Conclusion

Although many problems have been left unsolved, the purpose of this study has been to indicate what is possible of achievement, what types of material the historian may legitimately demand in public opinion surveys, what types of questions he might ask of a people or of a period. In the case of the French between 1944 and 1949 some answers to a few queries have been supplied; others have been hinted at and await more material.

For example, there are in the French surveys the faint beginnings of what may eventually become, along with data gathered on subsequent occasions, the basis for a tentative study of the RPF as a defeated movement. Customarily the source data of defeated movements are not so carefully preserved as those which have been crowned with success. The very fact that certain groups have satisfactorily accomplished their ends and that other groups have failed to attain their objectives confronts the historian with a serious interpretative challenge. Would it not be of some moment to learn, for instance, how long and how strongly people cling to certain attitudes despite the failure of those aspirations to triumph? Public opinion polls may, in the future, provide the historian with such data as one of their major services. Surely the entire question of defeated groups and their attitudes is worthy of speculation if one assumes that historical development would be obviously, and perhaps adversely, affected if those groups threw in the sponge when defeat was first threatened or when initial setbacks came.

Past histories of defeated ideals and groups have been rich in conjecture but understandably poor in factual information regarding the operation of influences. Two of the many studies of the middle class revolutions of 1848-1849 serve to illustrate this condition, particularly in their discussions of the reasons for the failure of the German movement and the general results of that failure in the following century. How influential was the *Communist Man-*

ifesto, for example, in this lack of success? Valentin believes that "to all practical purposes it at first attracted no attention," although it did much "to bring about the failure of the middle class revolution." [121] How pervasive and strong was the spirit of inferiority and "filialism" among the proletariat during the revolution? Did great numbers lack, as Mrs. Robertson suggests, "the sense of personal independence" which democracy requires? [122] And, granting that many members of the middle classes forsook the revolution out of fear of the rising proletarian forces, which groups tended to retire or ally "themselves with the older powers?" [123] For what reasons did they do this? How important were "emotionally strong appeals to religion, patriotism, morality and loyalty to the traditional ruling house?" [124] Which elements sank into indifferentism? What was the inferiority complex of the Germans which Veit Valentin claims antedated the revolutions? How was the "widespread belief in its own political inefficiency" implanted in the German people? [125] And by what processes was this complex made more acute after 1849 to bring about indifference to the public welfare and "the final dissolution of the German middle classes?" [126] No one would question the fact that more sharply determined answers to these and similar questions would enhance our appreciation of the modern history of the German people which reached a catastrophic climax under the Nazis.

In the post-liberation epoch in France the star of Charles de Gaulle rose to great heights and then fell. His political creation, the *Rassemblement du Peuple Français,* was born only to collapse five years or so later, apparently a defeated movement. A consideration of this failure—if it persists as a failure—should be one of the most fascinating facets of the postwar era in French history. The results of numerous surveys confirm the belief that De Gaulle's personal following in the years under study could be ascribed less to any unique personal attributes of the general or to a "Boulangist-Napoleonic mystique" than to De Gaulle's association with firmly planted, long existing French attitudes and policies pertinent to such matters as executive authority, Marxism-Communism-Socialism, the German problem, etc. Indeed the RPF was seen by many chiefly as a lesser evil than the PC and "as Communism receded, so Gaullism lost much of its *raison d'être.*" [127]

In defeat the RPF should attract investigators, for, in Williams'

words, "a volcano remains interesting when the eruption is over." [128]
The IFOP survey data up to the end of 1948, the terminal date of
the present investigation, report the public's expectation of De
Gaulle's possible resumption of official duties and responsibilities;
i.e. the Premiership or the Presidency of the Republic, an area that
is important to the comprehension of the rise of De Gaulle and
the RPF as well as to their subsequent decline. True, in the 1945-1949
period IFOP scarcely began to exploit the possibilities inherent in
the Gaullist movement, but it did investigate in very limited and
suggestive fashion the relationship between the support proffered
General de Gaulle and the expectation of his return to power. While
the data are scanty, they have the tendency to demonstrate that at
the time when objective evidence or what passed for such evidence
darkened the Gaullist hopes a small number of about 5% of the
general's champions held that he would not come back to the seats
of the mighty. Obviously, the Gaullists' faith in their cause and in
their hero was not easily shaken at this point. Unhappily, however,
there was no attempt to conduct more refined inquiries into the
attitudes of these voters as they contemplated the possibility of
defeat. The need for closely articulated survey planning by a team
of historians and pollsters is thus reemphasized, for the possibility
of an eventual Gaullist defeat would have been one of the "futures"
contemplated by the historians in 1948 and, if fully aware of the
value of public opinion polling, they could undoubtedly have laid
a fairly comprehensive survey network for the coming years to
explore various facets of the attitudes connected with General de
Gaulle, the RPF, hopes and expectations, etc.

There are, then, areas of historical concern in the IFOP poll
results which are neither noted nor discussed in this study. The
exploitation of all these areas is hardly necessary in order to achieve
the modest objectives of this investigation, which is by no means
an "ipse dixit" or definitive treatment of public opinion and historiography but is rather an early probing into a field which has
not yet been fully recognized. The possibilities for fruitful cooperation between the polltaker and the historian are indeed vast.
The results of collaboration will in the long run serve to benefit both
disciplines and will, though aspiring to furnish only auxiliary data
to history, improve the likelihood of depicting a people, its thoughts
and actions, with hitherto unrealized precision.

HISTORY AND PUBLIC OPINION
RESEARCH: A DEBATE

THE HISTORIAN AND THE POLLSTER

Paul F. Lazarsfeld

During the last twenty years public opinion agencies have built up rather reliable techniques for describing attitudes of people on public affairs. One would think that historians would welcome this way of obtaining information which in previous periods was available only indirectly, if at all. However, there is little collaboration between historians and "pollsters." The difficulty seems to be the problem of significance; pollsters ask questions meant to furnish headlines in the newspapers instead of using their techniques for the collection of data which have lasting value. As a result, the historian does not pay attention to their work; he does not give them the benefit of a broader view which would lead to the selection of more significant topics. Consequently, a vicious circle sets in which keeps separate two professions which could co-operate to mutual benefit. This paper tries to remedy the situation by inquiring into the various ways in which the historian and the pollster could aid the future historian to interpret our times.

It might be instructive to begin with an example in which a famous historian was confronted with this exact problem of explaining the past to his contemporaries.

We adopt in this paper a derogatory term to describe a profession which we intend to defend, and, in a way, represent in its academic form. This shouldn't be a surprising procedure for historians, who should remember many similar examples; for instance, the party of Dutch Protestants who called themselves "Beggars" after the lady lieutenant of the Spanish king had tried to deprecate them by this word. See footnote 7 on p. 6.

242

In the 15th century Machiavelli wrote what is probably one of the first examples of modern and careful analysis of political behavior. And yet, for several centuries afterward, "Machiavellian" stood for everything evil in public affairs. At the beginning of the 19th century a reaction set in, and in 1837, the English historian and statesman, Macaulay, wrote an essay to set the matter straight. He wanted to explain why Machiavelli was so misunderstood. His answer was that "The Prince" was written at a time and in a social setting where people had a very different way of looking at things. His argument runs about as follows: At the end of the Middle Ages the Italian cities had developed a middle class culture of artisans and merchants, while the countries north of the Alps, like England, France, and Germany were still in a barbarous state. In the north, courage was the main means of survival; courage to withstand the hardships of life and courage to repel hostile hordes which were incessantly threatening each other with war. In the Italian cities, ingenuity was the most cherished ability; ingenuity in improving the protective value of the community, and ingenuity in meeting the competition of their fellow citizens in an essentially democratic society. "Hence while courage was a point of honor in other countries ingenuity became the point of honor in Italy." The pertinence of this passage to Macaulay's main topic is obvious. He feels that a great thinker living in what we today would call "an ingenuity culture" was judged by people who lived and are still living in the aftermath of a "courage culture."

From our point of view it is important to see what evidence Macaulay tried to adduce for his thesis. The great English historian struggles hard to make his point clear and convincing to his reader. First of all he compares an English and an Italian hero. Henry V was admired by the English because he won a great battle, in spite of his personal crudeness and cruelty. Francis Sforza was admired by the Italians because he was a successful statesman, in spite of his personal treachery and faithlessness.

And still, Macaulay is not yet quite sure that the reader has seen the matter clearly. He finally hits upon what seems to him a useful literary device, and what today we can consider probably the first projective test recorded in the literature. He writes:

We have illustrated our meaning by an instance taken from history.

We will select another from fiction. Othello murders his wife; he gives orders for the murder of his lieutenant; he ends by murdering himself. *Yet he never loses the esteem and affection of Northern readers.* His intrepid and ardent spirit redeems everything. The unsuspecting confidence with which he listens to his adviser, the agony with which he shrinks from the thought of shame, the tempest of passion with which he commits his crimes, and the haughty fearlessness with which he avows them, give an extraordinary interest to his character. Iago, on the contrary, is the object of universal loathing. . . . *Now we suspect that an Italian audience in the fifteenth century would have felt very differently.* Othello would have inspired nothing but detestation and contempt. The folly with which he trusts the friendly professions of a man whose promotion he had obstructed, the credulity with which he takes unsupported assertions, and trivial circumstances, for unanswerable proofs, the violence with which he silences the exculpation till the exculpation can only aggravate his misery, would have excited the abhorrence and disgust of the spectators. The conduct of Iago they would assuredly have condemned; but they would have condemned it as we condemn that of his victim. Something of interest and respect would have mingled with their disapprobation. The readiness of the traitor's wit, the clearness of his judgment, the skill with which he penetrates the dispositions of others and conceals his own, would have ensured to him a certain portion of their esteem.

It is clear what Macaulay is striving for. He wishes someone had conducted attitude studies in Florence and in London of the 15th century. Let us suppose that a polling agency existed at the time, and was hired by Macaulay to test his hypothesis. In a somewhat facetious way, we can imagine how they might have proceeded. The Othello story could have been written up in one or two paragraphs, without giving either Othello or Iago any advantage. Pretests could have been conducted to make sure that the wording was quite unbiased. (Perhaps they might have concealed the fact that Othello was a Negro because that might bias some respondents.) The crucial question would have been: How many Florentines and Londoners, respectively, approve of Iago, how many of Othello, and how many say "don't know"? Nothing less, but hardly much more, would have been needed to provide empirical evidence for Macaulay's brilliant conjecture.

Few historians will make such elaborate efforts to document their statements about public attitudes. It is much more likely that we shall find statements which read like a Gallup release, except, of course, that the tables are missing. See, for instance, the following account from Merle Curti's, "The Thrust of the Civil War into Intellectual Life."

A growing number of men and women in both sections, distrustful of their leaders, sympathetic with the enemy, or merely war-weary, preferred compromise or even defeat to the continuation of the struggle. The fact of war affected the thinking not only of these dissidents but of the great majority of people who accepted it as inevitable and hoped that good would come from it.

Here are all the ingredients of a statement on the distribution of attitudes. We find quantitative statements like "a growing number" or "the great majority of people." There are suggestions for comparisons between men and women and between different sections of the country. The passage which we have quoted even implies certain cross-tabulations between attitudes toward the war and attitudes toward other issues of the day.

No wonder, then, that the historians of a later period for which polls were already available would eagerly incorporate them into their writings. Dixon Wecter writes about "The Age of the Great Depression." At one point he discusses the growing acceptance of birth control. To document this trend, he first uses the traditional, indirect methods of the historian, trying to derive attitudes from their manifestations. He points to the change in terms from "race suicide" to "birth control" and finally to "planned parenthood." Then he goes at his topic more directly.

A poll among Farm and Fireside readers early in the Depression showed two to one for giving medical advice on planned parenthood, and during the thirties the Sears, Roebuck catalogue began to list contraceptive wares. A straw vote of subscribers by the Protestant Churchman in January, 1935, revealed almost unanimous approval for birth control, while in the next year, among all sorts of conditions, a Gallup poll agreed with a Fortune survey in finding two out of three favorable. This majority, moreover, rose steadily in later years, with women outranking men in the warmth of their indorsement.

We could cite other similar examples to show further the place of attitude and opinion research in historical studies; but it might suffice instead to point out that some of the most enduring works of historiography, such as Taylor's "The Medieval Mind" and Weber's "The Protestant Ethic," are those which dealt with the attitudes, value systems, and prevailing beliefs of the period. By the historian's own testimony, there is a place for attitude and opinion research in their field, but this still leaves open the question of what kind of polling data the future historian will need. How can we fit at least some of our findings into the stream of intellectual work as it extends into the future?

We can expect guidance from three directions. For one, we can study historical writings; secondly, we can turn to certain works on the contemporary scene; finally, we can scrutinize existing speculations on the probable course of the future. It should be helpful to illustrate briefly each of these points.

The Pollster Reads a Book

It would be worthwhile for a scholar to review typical historical texts from our point of view. Where do competent writers show, either explicitly or implicitly, the need for attitude material of the kind a sampling survey can furnish? Short of a careful scrutiny we cannot know the prevailing modes of analysis. Furthermore, the specific need for opinion data will vary according to the topic under investigation. But a few expectations are rather obvious.

In at least three areas the historian will be confronted with the need for opinion data. The most obvious, of course, is when "prevailing values" are themselves the object of his study. There are a number of classical investigations of major changes in the climate of opinion such as the transition from medieval traditionalism to the individualistic thinking connected with the Protestant Reformation. During the first half of the 19th century a countertrend started, stressing public responsibility for individual welfare. This trend could be observed in the United States as well as in other countries. Curti, for instance, points out that, before the Civil War, there was considerable resistance against accepting tax supported public schools.

Men of power and substance frequently argued that education had been, and properly so, a family matter. . . . What could be more potent than the certainty that if free schools were granted, the concession would not end short of socialism itself? To provide free schooling for the less well-to-do would result in the loss of their self-respect and initiative.

Today, hardly anyone feels this way. But how did this shift of public opinion come about? Among which groups did it start and how did it spread? How long did it take for the initial resistance to disappear? What external events precipitated or retarded the development?

Such knowledge would be of considerable practical importance today. If we substituted the words "housing" for "schooling" in the preceding quotation, we would describe the way in which many people feel about public housing projects. It is probable that this sentiment is now in the process of historical change. So far as public health insurance is concerned, the resistance is still very great. More detailed knowledge of such developments in the past would help us to predict better what turn our contemporary problems are likely to take. If we know better the patterns of past change, we can perhaps extract from them some recurrent paths of development. Therefore, incidentally, we can expect that those historians who look at history as one sector of a general social science will be most likely to welcome attitude data.

This leads to a second area in which the historian would undoubtedly need public opinion data. Wherever a new type of institution or a major legislative development was investigated, he would be greatly helped by data on the interaction between the diffusion of attitudes and the sequence of social actions. One of the most thoroughly investigated phenomena of this kind is the turn from laissez-faire to social legislation, which took place in England during the second half of the 19th century. Karl Polanyi has pointed out that the free market system never really worked well in any event. He summarizes Dicey's famous investigation of "Law and Public Opinion in England" in the following way:

Dicey made it his task to inquire into the origins of the "anti-laissez-faire" or, as he called it, the "collectivist" trend in English public opinion, the existence of which was manifest since the late 1860's. He was surprised to find that no evidence of the existence of such a trend could be traced save the acts of legislation themselves. More exactly, no evidence of a "collectivist trend" in public opinion prior to the laws which appeared to represent such a trend could be found.

Here is a challenging suggestion that major legislative events may not be preceded, but rather followed, by changes in public opinion.

Before one could accept such a conclusion one would certainly want to know how safe it is to make inferences of this kind merely by examining newspapers, pamphlets and recorded speeches. Could it not be the case that there was an undercurrent of public opinion in the direction of social legislation which did not find expression in the kind of material available to the historian, but which would have been caught by systematic public opinion research at the time?

A third area of overlap between the historian and the pollster ought to be those writings in which specific events are to be explained. There is virtually no American historian, for example, who has not tried at one time or another to explain the outcome of some presidential election. Robert Bower has collected a whole folklore of stories which have arisen in connection with elections of major importance, such as those of 1840, 1882, and 1896. He analyzes these explanations of election outcomes and shows that all of them imply the type of knowledge about issues and personalities of the day which might have been obtained through polls. Even with poll data it is not easy to arrive at safe conclusions. This is known by everyone who followed the efforts to understand Truman's election in 1948. Bower's "Opinion Research and Historical Interpretation of Elections" shows how much more tenuous the conjectures are for previous periods.

Historians themselves are, of course, aware of this task. A group of medievalists started, in their professional journal, "Speculum," to appraise the status of their work. The first article, by J. L. LaMonte, was called "Some Problems in Crusading Historiography." It was of interest to read there that "the decline of the crusading ideal in spite of papal propaganda is a little known subject." One is reminded of the studies of returning veterans reported in "The American Soldier" when the author deplores how little is known about "the social effects of the change in material status of such crusaders as returned after considerably bettering their position in the East."

In such a reappraisal of historical writings, we should be sensitive to the effect which opinion surveys have had in changing the notion of a "fact." There was a time when only political documents found in archives were considered appropriate evidence for the historian. That made him focus on political events; everything else was interpretation. Then the "new history" centered attention on data such as economic and social statistics. This enlarged considerably the area of what were considered facts. Still, sentiments and attitudes remained a matter of interpretation. Now, however, they too have become facts. The result of a public opinion poll is as much a fact as the content of a political document or the crop and price statistics of a certain region.

In turn, the term "attitude and opinion research" should not be taken too narrowly. Let us remember that we have always known and discussed among ourselves that much more than simple "yes-no" questions belongs in our equipment. In connection with the historian's problem, two techniques in particular will certainly need considerable refinement on our part. One derives from the problem of saliency. The fact that a respondent answers a question which we put to him still does not tell us whether he would have asked himself this question or whether the matter is of particular concern to him. The historian will certainly want to know what issues were in the foreground of attention at various times and in various sectors of the population. Published polling material does not contain enough of such information; as a matter of fact, considerable methodological progress on this point is still needed. The diffusion of opinion in time and social space is a second problem which we do not yet handle with enough emphasis or enough technical skill. In many more of our surveys we should find out where people get their ideas and how they pass them on. All of this has thus far been a matter of conjecture for the historian; we are supposed to turn it into an enlarged array of "facts." Thus the study of historical writings will not only be a source of significant topics; it could also be a spur for methodological improvements.

Signs of the Times

A second source of ideas, interesting hypotheses and leads for significant field surveys may be found in many efforts to understand the meaning of what is going on around us right now. It has been said that each generation must rewrite history, because hitherto unconsidered aspects of the past become interesting in the light of the changing present. But there is certainly a limitation to this rule. If there is no data at all on certain aspects of the past, not much can be done, even under the impetus of a strong new curiosity. The pollster as a contemporary historian thus takes on considerable importance. What he considers worthy of a survey will, in later years, influence the range of possible historical inquiries.

Therefore, the question of where the pollster can get leads for significant investigations is an important one. Again, we cannot exhaust the possible choices, but a few clear avenues suggest themselves at the moment. There is, first, the critic of the contemporary scene. There are always social commentators who are especially sensitive to the shortcomings of our times; it is not unlikely that they hit on topics about which the future historian will want to know more. Let us quote passages which are characteristic of the type of statement we have in mind.

Much too early do young people get excited and tense, much too early are they drawn away by the accelerated pace of the times. People admire wealth and velocity. Everybody strives for them. . . . Here they compete, here they surpass each other, with the result that they persevere in mediocrity. And this is the result of the general trend of the contemporary world toward an average civilization, common to all.

We can visualize translating this social comment into a research program. It would not be too difficult to develop an index of competitiveness, and to study at what age individuals exhibit a marked increase in their average scores. But that would not be enough. We are also called upon to follow the consequences of such developments for broader areas of society; for "not the external and physical alone is now managed by machinery, but the internal and spiritual also. . . ."

Has any man, or any society of men, a truth to speak, a piece of spiritual work to do, they can nowise proceed at once and with the mere natural organs, but must first call a public meeting, appoint committees, issue prospectuses, eat a public dinner; in a word, construct or borrow machinery, wherewith to speak it and do it. Without machinery they were hopeless, helpless. . . .

Here a more sociological type of data is required; number and types of meetings, attendance figures, etc. Most of all we will want to study the statistical interrelationship between attitudes and kinds of social participation in intellectual enterprises.

Most interesting about these quotations, however, are their dates and their sources. The first is from a letter which Goethe wrote in 1825. The second is a characteristic portion of an essay written by Carlyle in 1830. Here are two leading minds in two different countries voicing the same apprehension in terms which might well be used today. Undoubtedly experts could provide us with similar statements for any other century, for we are always likely to find evidence of a feeling that matters were very different sometime ago. There are certain standbys which recur in many discussions: the tensions of daily living have become so much worse; people are now more apathetic politically than they were previously; the cultural taste of the country has been depraved. We shall not be able to decide the truth of such issues in retrospect, but we can at least lay the ground for more responsible discussion of the problem in the future.

The social critic will focus our attention primarily on certain contents and subject matters which are important for our times. There is another group of analysts who are more concerned with the kinds of dimensions which are useful in describing the social scene. They are likely to be interested mainly in comparisons between various countries, for instance, or between social groups. It should never be forgotten how difficult it is to make the social scene "visible." When we deal with nature, many objects, like trees or stones or animals, force themselves on us visually. Social entities are much more the product of creative intelligence. The notion of a clique, for instance, or of a reference group, the inner gallery for which so many of us play the drama of our lives, or the distinction between an introverted and an extroverted personality are real conceptual inventions. In social observations we are often in the position of a bird which flies across the sky with a flock of other birds. For the external observer, the flock has a clearly visible geometric shape; but does the bird within the flock even know about the shape of his "group"? By what social interrelations among the birds is the form of the group maintained?

When we translate these sketchy considerations into problems of survey research, we meet them in a familiar form. Every self-respecting pollster will report his findings nowadays "sub-classified by age, sex, and socio-economic status." We know from our findings that these are useful classifications. But are they the most significant ones? Wouldn't we be helped in the work of today, and wouldn't we help readers of the future if we were alert to additional variables according to which we might classify our samples and analyze our findings?

It is on such an issue that we can get guidance from writers who have tried to obtain the best possible view of the contemporary scene. Let us turn for a moment to the patron saint of modern public opinion research, James Bryce. He makes an effort at one point to compare the political scene in England and that prevailing in this country. To this end he distinguishes "three sets of persons, those who make opinion, those who receive and hold opinion, those who have no opinions at all." After elaborating on this distinction, he comes to the conclusion that the first group is somewhat larger in England than in the United States of 1870, while the proportion in the second group is very much larger on the American continent than in Britain. From this he draws a number of interesting conclusions. The "power of public opinion in the United States," for instance, seems to him related to the inordinately large ratio of opinion holders to opinion makers.

To find significant variables for political classifications continues to be a challenge for writers of this kind. It is quite possible that an index of political participation and interest might prove a useful instrument for a great variety of surveys, on a national as well as an international scale. As a matter of fact, some research organizations are reported to be working on the development of just such devices.

In the writings of contemporary social scientists, the pollster will find other classificatory suggestions which are worth pursuing. David Riesman, for instance, has just published a book centered on the distinction between three types of social character. One is the tradition-directed type; the person who behaves as he thinks his social group expects him to, does not believe he should change anything in his environment, and feels shame if he violates any of the rules under which he lives. The second is the inner-directed type; the person who is guided by strong moral standards, has a kind of psychological gyroscope which controls his conduct, and who feels guilt if he does something which is not right. Finally, there is the other-directed type; the backslapper who wants to get along with everyone, who has few convictions of his own, and who feels general anxiety if he is not successful in receiving all the signals which he tries to catch on his psychological radar system. In chapter after chapter of "The Lonely Crowd" Riesman tries to spell out the political correlates of these three types. He is especially interested in the other-directed type, which he considers characteristic of modern American life. Riesman discovers in him a dangerous kind of political apathy. He wants to get all the inside dope on politics just as on baseball, but he has lost all belief that he, individually, has any influence and therefore refrains from giving public affairs any serious thought or any active devotion. A careful reading of Riesman's chapters on politics will show how much empirical research could and should be geared in with such speculations.

Finally, the literature of the so-called cultural anthropologists belongs here. They are not only concerned with singling out significant topics or finding variables which would be useful to make more clearly visible the main character of the contemporary scene. They also want to uncover the mechanisms by which the scene develops. Distinguished equally by brilliance and by irresponsibility of factual evidence, they challenge the pollster to try to bring about effective cooperation. But the challenge is worth accepting, for from an interaction between the two groups could develop really new insights into human affairs. No newspaper reader can be unaware of the writings on "national character." The main thesis is that each society and each national sub-group develops its own way of looking at the world, and its own way of giving satisfaction to basic needs. It is the function of the family to raise children in such a way that they "want to act in the way they have to act as members of the society or as a special class within it." Like a group of expert ball players giving a public exhibition, the anthropologists toss their variations on the basic theme from one to the other. Margaret Mead describes in great detail the small American family with its lack of tradition and its uncertain goals in a quickly changing world:

. . . while the child is learning that his whole place in the world, his name, his right to the respect of other children—everything—depends upon his parents . . . he also learns that his own acceptance by these parents, who are his only support, is conditional upon his achievements, upon the way in which he shows up against other children and against their idea of other children.

Gorer picks it up from Mead. He agrees with her that there is a strong element of uncertainty in the emotional life of the American family. The parents do not quite know what is right and therefore can love their children only if they are successful in their own peer group, the school class or the gang. But Gorer does not think that ambition or success drive develops in children as a result; he has a different notion:

> The presence, the attention, the admiration of other people thus becomes for Americans a necessary component to their self-esteem, demanded with a feeling of far greater psychological urgency than is usual in other countries. . . . The most satisfying form of this assurance is not given by direct flattery or commendation (this by itself is suspect as a device to exploit the other) but by love.

The two writers, if confronted with their statements, would probably say that there is a strong relation between ambition and the desire to be loved. Yet how do they know that these desires are more frequent or more intense among Americans than among other people? They give many examples from Rotary meetings and from double dates in colleges which make their idea plausible. We pollsters are accustomed to asking for a better definition of terms and for more precise evidence; so we are inclined to criticize these anthropologists. But are we fully justified? Have they not seen here topics which are considerably more worthy of investigation than the rating of movie stars or even the attitudes of voters toward a local candidate?

Here are writers who have challenging ideas on the structure of our social relationships and their effect on attitudes and opinions. Does this not suggest that we have neglected the first link in this chain? To cite one specific example: in the writings of the social anthropologists, the authoritarian structure of the family plays a large role. Who among us, either in this country or abroad, has collected answers to questions like these: To what extent do young people make their own occupational choices and to what extent do their parents influence their decisions? In what countries and in what groups does a young suitor still ask the girl's parents for consent to marriage? How are conflicts between father and son resolved when they both want the car or both want to use the living room? Where do children still spend their holidays with their families, and where do they go off on their own? How much visiting of relatives is there, how frequent are family reunions, and so on? What would adolescents consider the main complaints as to the way they are treated by their parents? What activities are parents most eager to forbid in their young children and what principles are they most anxious to inculcate in their older ones?

Useful contributions along such lines could be made, especially by those among us who conduct international polls. But in this discussion we are not interested in the present for its own sake; we want to look at it from the point of view of tomorrow. What should we watch as the present slowly turns into the future?

Glancing into the Future

Scrutinizing writings on the past will give us an idea of the kinds of data which historians have missed prior to the appearance of the pollster on the scene. Studying the literature on present-day society will give us a chance to confront theoretical thinking with empirical data. A final, and probably the most important, possibility develops when we make efforts to guess what the future will want to know about today. Quite a number of political scientists feel that the best way to study the present is to see it as a transitional stage to future events. Harold Lasswell has emphasized the need of "developmental constructs."

In the practice of social science, . . . we are bound to be affected in some degree by our conceptions of future development. . . . What is the function of this picture for scientists? It is to stimulate the individual specialist to clarify for himself his expectations about the future, as a guide to the timing of scientific work.

We should form expectations of what major changes might come about within the next decades. It is in connection with these changing conditions that the historian will expect that we, today, have initiated a series of trend studies. This is undoubtedly the most difficult task. It not only requires of us pollsters that we translate more or less vague ideas into specific instruments of inquiry; there is so little thinking along this line that we shall even have to assume some responsibility for guessing what will be of importance a few decades hence. The best we can do in the present context is to give a few examples of the kind of effort which will be required.

There can be little doubt that the history of the next decades will be centered around the effects of the rapidly increasing industrialization characteristic of our times. Perhaps the reaction to contemporary mechanization will be found in strong religious movements. If this is the case, what will the future analyst, in retrospect, wish that we had ascertained today? An interesting lead for this is found in "The American Soldier." The importance of this work lies in the fact that, for the first time, we really know something about the experiences and feelings of an important sector of the population. As far as religion goes, the following observation is reported. About three-fourths of the soldiers said that prayer was a source of strength in battle, but the minority who did not find this so had certain interesting characteristics: they experienced less fear, laid more stress on their relations with other soldiers, and seemed, in general, to be what modern psychologists would call better adjusted personalities.

Here, in one result, may lie the seeds of an important bifurcation. Increasing industrialization may lead to a compensatory dependence on religious beliefs. Or, it may create a new type of personality, differently adjusted to new social demands. We cannot tell in which direction the future will tend; as a matter of fact, we do not even know whether any really new developments will take place in the religious sphere; but general considerations and bits of research evidence seem to indicate that systematic work is called for.

At the same time that we try to answer these more general questions about the intensity of religious beliefs, we should analyze the specific character of religious movements as they develop. In this connection Julian Huxley has provided an impressive set of predictions. In his essay on "Religion as an Objective Problem," he distinguishes between the "old" religion and the "new." According to him, the old one developed as a result of fear and ignorance of the external physical environment. Modern science has given us enough insight into and control over the forces of nature so that religious beliefs as we have known them so far are likely to fade away slowly. Now we are faced with a new set of problems emerging from what he calls the "internal environment"; the disorganization of our economic and social life, war, poverty, and unemployment. New religious movements are likely to develop, centered less around the worship of a supernatural being than around the worship of a single solution for social evils.

The process, of course, has already begun. Many observers have commented on the religious elements in Russian communism—the fanaticism, the insistence on orthodoxy, the violent "theological" disputes, the "worship" of Lenin, the spirit of self-dedication, the persecutions, the common enthusiasm, the puritan element, the mass-emotions, the censorship.

The new religion is now in its most primitive forms, with Communism and Fascism as typical examples. But just as the old religion moved from simple paganism to a refined monotheism, so will the new religion outgrow its present crudeness.

Accordingly, we can prophesy that in the long run the nationalistic element in socialized religion will be subordinated or adjusted to the internationalist: that the persecution of minorities will give place to toleration; that the subtler intellectual and moral virtues will find a place and will gradually oust the cruder from their present pre-eminence in the religiously conceived social organism. We can also assert with fair assurance that this process of improvement will be a slow one, and accompanied by much violence and suffering.

Here, indeed, is a research program. First we must find appropriate indices for the various shades of belief which Huxley distinguishes. Then we shall want to get our information separately from a large number of social subgroups. Trend data will have to be assembled over a long period of time; and wherever possible, these trends should be linked with external events. If a special movement starts somewhere, if a related book becomes a best-seller, if some special legislation is passed or a voluntary association established, we shall want to study the pertinent attitudes "before and after."

This is not the place to propose a concrete study design, but we should warn against oversimplifying the whole problem. The attitudes in which the historian will be interested are certainly complex in nature; and, in order to cover one single concept, it may be necessary to employ a whole set of interlocking questions. As a matter of fact, it might very well be that future trends will be different for different dimensions of the same notion. To exemplify what this means in terms of our work, we shall choose for our second example the problem of class tensions.

There is an abundance of prophecies in the literature which can be loosely labelled as Marxist. Conflicts of interest between the working class and the influential business groups will become more acute. The workers will become more class conscious, and more aggressive towards the privileged groups. The latter, in turn, will defend more strongly their class interests and more and more neglect the democratic forms of politics. These ideas are too well known to need further elaboration. Instead, let us pick out of this whole complex the notion of class consciousness, and see whether we can develop a kind of barometer by which to measure trends in the next few decades.

In recent years, a large number of business companies have conducted surveys to determine their standing with the public, but this by no means meets the task. There could very easily be an intensification of class conciousness among workers which does not express itself immediately in invectives directed toward General Motors or Standard Oil. Not even the recently increased interest of social psychologists in this problem covers it fully. Richard Centers, in his "The Psychology of Social Classes," has developed a set of questions pertinent to two elements: readiness to accept the government as an agent in economic affairs; and a feeling that avenues of economic advancement are closing up, that social rewards are not fairly distributed.

The total picture has many additional aspects, however. We should study whether workers have a feeling of identification with their class. If a worker's son becomes a lawyer, should he work for a union rather than for a big corporation? Is there an increased interest in reading stories about workers rather than about movie stars? Is there an increased interest in leisure-time associations especially designed for workers? Another aspect of the problem would be whether workers are concerned with the power structure in the community. Do they think that the courts handle poor and rich alike? Do and can the councilmen in the city represent both poor and rich? Do they feel that the rich have special influence with the police? Even if there is growing uneasiness on this score, the question still to be raised is whether it is channeled into political reactions. Does "going into politics" become a more respected and desirable pursuit? Is voting the "right" way something which becomes an important criterion for judging people? Do political issues become a factor in one's own personal plans?

This example, incidentally, raises a serious problem of strategy for the pollster. Topics relevant to the work of the future historian are likely to come from the area of social change. Polls dealing with such areas can easily become suspect as "subversive" or "inflammatory." It will therefore be important to make clear, both to the general public and to specific clients, that the public opinion researcher is not taking sides when he focuses part of his attention on more unconventional issues. As a matter of fact, it might very well be that some of the work suggested here might best be done under the joint sponsorship of several agencies or perhaps under the aegis of a professional organization like the American Association for Public Opinion Research.

What Should Be Done?

We pollsters cannot be expected to tackle the whole problem by ourselves. We should seek the assistance of a "commission for the utilization of polls in the service of future historiography," whose specific task it would be to furnish us with appropriate ideas. This commission should consist, on the one hand, of historians and other social scientists who have given thought to questions such as those we have raised, and, on the other hand, of research technicians who can translate research suggestions into actual study designs.

There certainly will be no scarcity of topics. There is much evidence to show that people in this country were inclined to shy away from concern with international relations. Suddenly we are thrust into the position of being the leading power in the world. How will people in this country adjust to this change, and what will be the mutual interaction between the distribution of attitudes and the actions of our policymakers? At what rate will Americans really become aware of the existence of the Far Eastern people? When will they notice that the famous destruction of the "human race" by the atomic bomb might really mean the replacing of the Western sector of humanity by their Asiatic fellow men? Another element of our tradition is the belief that one man is as good as another. But in a society which becomes ever more complex, the expert plays an increasingly important role. How will this proverbial anti-authoritarian tradition adjust to the increasing, and probably unavoidable, "bureaucratization" of the modern world? Or one might turn from the political to a more personal sphere. Increasing amounts of available leisure time will force more people to review their "designs for living." How will they use the time over which they themselves have control: will they use it to have a richer personal life, to equip themselves better for competitive advancement, or will they just fritter it away? There is certainly an obvious interrelation between these questions and new technical developments such as television.

Whatever topic we select, the procedure for research will always be the same. We must first formulate clearly a number of alternative assumptions about future developments. Then we must decide on the kind of indices which are pertinent for the problem at hand; this is where the research technician can make his main contribution. To set up the machinery for collecting the data is a matter of decision and funds. As to the selection of respondents, a certain flexibility will be necessary. For some problems a national cross-section will be most appropriate. For other problems very specific population groups will have to be sampled. When it comes to studying the diffusion of attitudes, attention will have to be focused on elite groups. In other cases specific occupations or special age groups will command our interest. And at all times we shall want to collect "background information": documentation on major events, on the activities of organizations, community leaders, etc.

At this point, we should warn against a possible misunderstanding. Previously we stressed that attitude surveys provide a new type of "facts" for the historian. But this does not imply that they are more important than the more traditional kind of data. It is just the interplay between the "objective" facts and attitudes which promises a great advance in historiography. If for a given period we not only know the standard of living, but also the distribution of ratings on happiness and personal adjustment, the dynamics of social change will be much better understood. Let us add that sampling surveys will enlarge our ideas on social bookkeeping in still another way. Nothing is more characteristic of this trend than what has happened in the decennial census of the United States. As long as we thought only in terms of complete enumerations, we could afford to include only a few questions. Now that we use five percent and one percent samples on specific items, we are able to cover a much wider range of topics. This is undoubtedly only a beginning. Since small sample designs have been perfected, there is no reason why sociography should not develop on a much broader scale. Cultural activities and other living habits may soon be added to the more conventional trends in the birth rate or export trade. It is certainly no coincidence that the Kinsey reports did not appear before 1948.

As early as 1908, in his "Human Nature in Politics," Graham Wallas pointed to such changes in what he called the methods of political reasoning. He compared the reports of two Royal commissions, both of which were concerned with the reform of the English poor laws. One was established in 1834 and the other in 1905. The earlier one dealt with "a priori deduction, illustrated, but not proved by particular instances." Now (in 1905) things are different.

Instead of assuming half consciously that human energy is dependent solely on the working of the human will in the presence of the ideas of pleasure and pain, the Commissioners are forced to tabulate and consider innumerable quantitative observations relating to the very many factors affecting the will of paupers and possible paupers. They cannot, for instance, avoid the task of estimating the relative industrial effectiveness of health, which depends upon decent surroundings; of hope, which may be made possible by State provision for old age; and of the imaginative range which is the result of education; and of comparing all these with the "purely economic" motive created by ideas of future pleasure and pain.

As can be seen, Wallas did not want to replace, but to complement, principles with social surveys. And so we too do not suggest that attitude data are better than "hard" facts, but that they add, so to speak, a new dimension.

There is one more suggestion for the work of the new commission on polling and historiography. We are all aware that prediction is one of the touchstones by which a science can justify itself. So far our predictions have been confined mainly to the outcomes of political elections; many have felt that this is a rather insignificant pursuit. There is no reason, however, that we should not predict future sentiments and then, later on, study whether we were right. One of the most impressive chapters in "The American Soldier" is that on "The Aftermath of Hostilities." In the summer of 1944, the Research Branch prepared a document predicting what attitudes they expected among soldiers at the end of the war. In 1945, many of those predictions were tested: At some points the predictions were correct, and at others, wrong. But no person reading this chapter can escape the feeling that here might be the substitute for laboratory experiments, so often impossible to carry out in the social sciences. Interestingly enough, without knowing about the experience of the Research Branch, an historian, Helen Lynd, saw this very link between her field and ours. In writing about "The Nature of Historical Objectivity," she stated:

> . . . we know surely . . . that the future which lies ahead will become present, and that hypotheses which we may now make can be tested by the course of events. If we are in earnest about historical objectivity, why do we not more often frame precise hypotheses about what may be the course of events in a given area in a given time? . . . With all that can be said against the recent opinion polls in this country there is this to be said in their favor: they at least made their errors public so that they could be subject to the verification of events.

It may be faint praise to say that pollsters at least make their errors public. It would also be helpful if the historians became more aware of their lack of data on matters about which they often write with considerable confidence. The present paper does not mean to claim that another "new history" is here just because public opinion data are now available. As a matter of fact, the main purpose was to point out that the historian has always wanted pubilc opinion research and has used whatever best substitute he could find for it. By more collaboration the sophistication and the significance of polls could be improved. The historian of the future would be better served.

HISTORY AND PUBLIC OPINION
RESEARCH: A DEBATE

THE HISTORIAN'S CONCEPT OF PUBLIC OPINION

Joseph R. Strayer

Historians have been talking about the importance of public opinion for several generations, longer perhaps than any other professional group. This early start meant that they had to develop their concept of public opinion without much assistance from other disciplines. The nature of the historical record meant that they had to apply their concept to situations in which the evidence was far from satisfactory. Little is known about anybody's opinion for the larger part of recorded history and even when letters, diaries and periodical publications become common they reveal the opinion of only a small, articulate group. Though convinced of the importance of public opinion historians could seldom study it directly. They had to deduce its existence, its weight and its direction from political perturbations, much like astronomers trying to prove the existence of a new heavenly body which they have not yet seen. They had to develop flexible techniques in order to make the most of evidence which varied widely in nature and reliability; there was no standard operating procedure. It is not surprising that the historian's concept of public opinion, developed under these circumstances, is somewhat different from that of experts in opinion and attitude research. The differences are important because they have caused misunderstandings between the two groups and have made it difficult for the historian to use the results of public opinion research.

The first and most striking difference is inherent in the nature of the historian's profession. He is looking backward, not forward; he is trying to explain what has occurred, not to predict what will occur. This does not mean that the historian is merely an antiquarian. He believes that his learning is useful in meeting new situations, not because it provides a basis for prediction but because a full understanding of human behavior in the past makes it possible to find familiar elements in present problems and thus makes it possible to solve them more intelligently. Still, there is a difference between the historian's interest in public opinion and that of the polling expert, and this difference is reflected in methodology. The historian starts with the act, the accomplished fact, and deduces from it the opinion which made the act possible. The student of public opinion starts with an expression of opinion and tries to predict from it a future act.

For most periods of history, the historian's method is the only possible one; he must "derive attitudes from their manifestations," to quote Professor Lazarsfeld (*POQ* XIV, 621), because there is no other way to operate. But even for the twentieth century with its numerous polls, even for the twenty-first century when polling techniques should reach an unbelievable stage of perfection, I doubt that the historian will ever rely entirely on the results of polls. He believes that action, not verbal expression, is the real test of opinion— or, to be more accurate, he believes that an opinion which does not result in, or modify, action is not very important. He could give you some rather striking examples to prove this point. To take one case, which is familiar to all of us, from the twelfth century down to the present day juries have had the disconcerting habit of giving verdicts which do not agree with the verbal expressions of opinion of the groups from which juries are drawn. Most societies have agreed that murder deserves the death penalty and most jurors presumably share this opinion. Yet when a juror realizes that he must give, not an opinion, but a verdict which leads to a death sentence, he often develops scruples, seeks extenuating circumstances, or votes acquittal in the face of the evidence. Ancient kings were so annoyed by the behavior of some of their juries that they put them in jail. Modern lawyers, deprived of this satisfaction, argue for the abolition of juries, but no one has ever found a way to achieve full harmony between general expressions of opinion and the actual decision of a jury in a specific case. Another example, from the period which I know best, shows a similar reluctance to translate opinion into action. As far as any surface manifestation of opinion goes, Crusades were just as popular in 1300 as in 1200. Able writers prepared countless tracts urging Crusades, the best preachers demanded Crusades in popular sermons, popes and councils planned Crusades, and kings and nobles took Crusade vows. Yet in the years immediately after 1200 there was a Crusade about every ten years; in the years immediately after 1300 there were none. Obviously an important change in attitude took place during this period but I doubt that it would have been revealed by any of the polling techniques which are now used.

In the second place, the historian doubts that for most periods the shifting day-to-day opinions of most people have any significance in modifying events. This is demonstrably true for any period in which the mass of the population consists of uninformed peasants. It is less true of periods in which the urban population is large and in which the structure of government approaches democracy. Yet, even in a period like our own, surface manifestations of opinion are not controlling factors. Within certain limits, leaders in all fields have a great deal of freedom of action. When they settle on a policy, lukewarm, loosely-held opinions are easily modified or overridden. The historian therefore would like to see more emphasis on the opinions of leaders, or at least more of an effort to find what opinions are strongly held. This would be more useful for his work than a mass of detail about opinions which are not strongly held and which have little influence. The historian is especially suspicious of polls which try to reduce the number of "don't know" or "no opinion" answers to a small percentage. He believes that demanding an answer from uninformed or uninterested people creates a false picture of real opinion and that really accurate polls would show that the majority of respondents have no opinions on most issues. It would be more useful to him if the minorities who have strong opinions were identified clearly, even if this meant that the no response category were greatly increased.

In the third place, as has already been suggested, the historian is interested in basic beliefs rather than in superficial expressions of opinion about current events. It is in this field, rather than that of short-term policy, that the opinion of the mass of the population

is important. The opinion of the general public does not immediately control policy, but it sets limits within which the men who
make policy must operate. The historian would like to know what
those limits are. What are the basic convictions and desires of the
people which cannot be opposed without the risk of serious dis-
turbances? What are the common ideas which hold society together,
the areas of basic agreement which lie below the surface issues
on which individuals disagree? What, to use Becker's famous phrase,
is the "climate of opinion" of the present age? It is difficult for
anyone to describe this climate in purely scientific terms—it cannot
be measured statistically and most people find it hard to put their
basic beliefs into words. Yet the climate of opinion is one of the
most important factors in history; it favors some activities and
represses others; it sets the limits of the possible. To take another
example from early history, the change from a climate in which
the basic loyalty was to the Church, to a climate in which the basic
loyalty was to the State, was one of the most important shifts in
Western European history. We know that it took place, but we
are still trying without much success to explain how and why it
happened. If a similar shift should be starting today, does anybody
have the techniques by which it could be brought under observation?

In short, to satisfy the needs of the historian, public opinion
research would have to change direction and emphasis. There should
be fewer polls of the election-prediction type and more studies
which try to cut deep and find influences which are important over
a long period. There should be less effort spent in securing snap
judgments on issues about which the public knows little, and more
attempts to discover the basic convictions or beliefs which influence
action. There have been some studies which attacked the problem
at this level; there have not been enough of them to satisfy the
historian.

To make specific suggestions, very often it would be better to
ask questions after an event instead of before. The predictive element in public opinion research is not very useful to the historian
because no prediction can ever be as accurate as the record of the
event. What he is interested in is why this particular event took
place. For example, Cantril's investigation of the "invasion from
Mars" is useful to the historian because it explains actual behavior.

It is hard to imagine a set of questions based on a hypothetical future invasion from space—or anywhere else—which would have the same value. Another possibility is the type of question which has been used in some experiments with the Army. The respondent is given a picture showing an approaching crisis and is asked what he would do in that specific situation. In either case, there is a concrete act to be explained and evaluated and not a mere expression of verbal opinion.

In the second place, as was suggested above, the historian would like to see a distinction made between the makers and the followers of opinion. He would like to find a way of segregating the leaders, the men with strong opinions who will act on them and influence others. This would throw a great deal of light on social change, which is one of the most important and least understood parts of the historical process. Do leaders develop new opinions or change old ones because one or two striking events shake their old convictions, or do these changes occur gradually due to slight shifts in the daily routine? The difficulty here would be in discovering the real leaders. A group selected, like the *Fortune* executive poll, on the basis of present prominence would include some of the real leaders, but by no means all of them. I doubt, for example, that anyone would have included Lincoln in a list of leaders of opinion in 1856. It would probably require a number of careful preliminary studies to find out who are the leaders in various types of activity. Once they were discovered, a continuing set of interviews might be a more effective way of discovering their opinions than the conventional poll. Even this technique, however, would not give entirely accurate results; the mere asking of the question for the record might make the respondent too cautious or too logical in his answer.

In the third place, the historian needs information about the "climate of opinion," the basic beliefs of the mass of the population which set limits and goals for the leaders of opinion. As I said before, this is the most difficult of all inquiries, since these basic beliefs are so deeply buried that often they have never been clearly formulated by the respondent. In this case the question-answer technique is especially dangerous, since the mere asking of the question inevitably shapes the answer and probably makes it both clearer and more conventional than the real belief. Here the technique suggested above of asking questions after the event would probably be helpful. If the respondent is asked why he did something, how he felt about a given event, he might give an answer which would reveal his basic convictions. But obviously this kind of questioning cannot give answers which can be easily reduced to statistical form. I suspect that in this field the historian will have to rely, as he always has done, on other indications such as investigation of the books and periodicals which are most widely read and the movie, radio, and television programs which are most popular. These sources are far from satisfactory; they do not touch all, or even all important beliefs and they give only indirect indications of what basic beliefs are. But they do demand some commitment; the act of buying a book or paying for a movie is a more positive sign of approval than answering a question.

Finally, we must find some way of reconciling the difference between the time-span of historical thinking and that of public opinion research. The historian must deal with decades and centuries and millennia, while the public opinion expert tends to think in terms of weeks and months. A great deal of public opinion research will seem completely unimportant to the historian of the year 2400. He might sum up the polls on presidential elections for a century in a single sentence like this: "Americans of the twentieth century were much interested in politics and enjoyed trying to predict the outcome of elections." Even if we take a shorter period, it is likely that the historian of 1984 (to use Dr. Lazarsfeld's example) would find most current public opinion research less important than an analysis of the movies, or of publications like the *Saturday Evening Post* and *Life,* though probably more important than newspaper editorials. It is hard to find a way of overcoming this difference, since it is inherent in the nature of the two professions. Certainly, continuing studies, repetition of the same questions or the same types of investigation over a long period, would come closer to giving the historian the material which he needs. But I doubt that any technique will be entirely satisfactory and I am sure that the future historian will find that public opinion research is only one of many sources which he will have to use in establishing his own idea of what public opinion was in the twentieth century.

HISTORY AND PUBLIC OPINION
RESEARCH: A DEBATE

OPINION RESEARCH IN THE SERVICE OF THE HISTORIAN

Henry David

The relationship between opinion research and history is a particular aspect of a larger problem: the relationship between history and the disciplines of the social sciences.

Dr. Lazarsfeld examined what may be called the service function of the opinion researcher to the historian from the vantage point of the former. Thus, he asks whether the historian of 1984 might not reproach the pollsters of today "for not having given enough thought to what he would want to know about 1950?" This query may strike the historian as curious, if it appears to suggest that the opinion researcher should try to forecast the specific historical problems that will engage the attention of historians three decades hence who are studying mid-twentieth century developments. The inquiries which future historians will conduct will in part be shaped by their own cultural setting and by what appear to be the compelling social, economic, intellectual, and political issues of their day. These will give some distinctive character to their views of the past, and, therefore, influence the identification of problems worthy of study. The work of the historian turns on rendering a judgment about the past from his own peculiar position in time and space. But the inquiries of the future historian will also be conditioned

269

by the traditions of historical scholarship, the wealth or the poverty of source material, and other factors. In any case, the behavior of contemporary opinion researchers will stand as evidence, whether or not they are moved by the desire to serve the interests of the historians of the 1980's, for those historians concerned with developments in the field of opinion research.

A future historian could conceivably reproach today's opinion researchers not because they failed to give "enough thought to what he would want to know about 1950," as Dr. Lazarsfeld suggests, but because they were remiss on other counts. One of these might be inadequate concern with the preservation of their primary records. Another reason for reproach might be found in a failure on the part of opinion researchers to make effective use of the historical data currently available to them and relevant to their investigations of opinion problems. Where opinion researchers also operate as historians, as they do in offering explanations for alterations and continuities in opinions, some future historian might take them to task for having performed this function poorly.

Neither contemporary nor earlier historians have been inhibited from investigating problems in mass attitudes simply because they have not had access to the published findings of opinion research. On the other hand, the historian of the future whose inquiries grow out of the existence of polling data will, in a literal sense, need them because his inquiries will result from their availability. The historian may render judgments—and sometimes quite respectable ones—about matters of mass attitudes without the findings of opinion research to support his seemingly quantitative statements. Such assertions about what most people thought, felt, and did, or about the manner in which a body of opinion influenced the behavior of a group or class, are the product of unstated (and sometimes unconscious) processes of evidence sampling. Qualitative evaluations of evidence permit the historian a certain range of quantitative assertions. The historian who has developed a sense of what evidence means, as distinguished from what it merely states, can reach highly satisfactory conclusions about the kind of issues which the opinion researcher regards as his special province. The manner in which the historian is likely to state his conclusions, moreover, provides him with some measure of protection against criticism. When he speaks of "most of the people," "substantial numbers," "a growing majority," and the like—the very vagueness of the terms he employs makes him an elusive target.

I am persuaded that some historians have reached conclusions about opinion and attitude problems which cannot be responsibly queried, even though they employed a method which an opinion researcher might dismiss as "unscientific." The formal validation of such conclusions in opinion research terms would not be possible, but they remain, nevertheless, valid historical judgments. I suspect that some qualitative statements made by historians about the attitudes or opinions of a society or a class are far more accurate than many quantitative statements, based on respectable statistical data, about such matters as trade, wages, unemployment, and the like. There is a case in point in the brilliant, and properly famous, opening chapters of Henry Adams' *History of the United States during the Administrations of Jefferson and Madison,* which survey the American scene a century and a half ago. What Adams has to say about the American "mind" and about the shape of opinion and dominant attitudes is probably no less—and may well be more—reliable than the documented, quantitative information he offers about certain aspects of economic activity.

Perhaps the historian of today is too relaxed about the crude answers he provides to such questions as the distribution of opinion in the South over secession, or the number of Loyalists during the American Revolution, or the extent of public support for the strikers during the long drawn-out Homestead conflict of 1892. Yet, more often than not, such answers are adequate in the light of the questions he has raised and of the materials at his disposal. Veblen is credited with replying to many queries from troubled students that the things which bothered them did not worry him. The historian cannot really be worried, as is the pollster, because he is compelled, in dealing with such questions, to employ in his work what Dr. Lazarsfeld regards as indirect means. They are the only means at his disposal.

It is true, as Dr. Lazarsfeld observes, that the opinion researcher, in his role as a contemporary historian will affect the writing of history in the future. His investigations will obviously encourage the writing of particular kinds of history. The concern of earlier historians with political and legal history was at least in part a result of the volume and accessibility of pertinent documents. If there is available to the future historian a fair run of data on American attitudes towards the United Nations, he will be stimulated to make this kind of problem the subject of inquiry. But this is not an unmixed blessing. The historian may be led by the mountains of polling data which will pile up over the years to undertake the easiest kind of historical inquiry. He may merely turn to the description of changes in opinions or in attitudes between selected points in time as they are recorded in survey reports. This may be expected because the historian, like other investigators in the social sciences, sometimes pursues the line of easiest advance, or of least resistance, in fulfilling minimum professional requirements.

In remarking that, in recent years, so-called non-political "facts" have acquired respectability and importance, Dr. Lazarsfeld calls attention to changes in style with respect to the subject matter of historical inquiry. Economic, social, intellectual, and emotional "facts," he observed, are now grist for the historian's mill. It hardly has to be pointed out that attitudes, sentiments, and opinions were dealt with as "facts" by historians long before James Harvey Robinson gave his paper on "The New History" before the Philosophical Society in Philadelphia in 1911.

There are, I believe, five distinct respects in which opinion research, in the broadest sense of the term, may be pressed into service by the historian. To begin with, the work done within the opinion field provides a body of primary source materials which differs somewhat from, but basically resembles, the kinds of documents which the historian normally uses. From the latter's viewpoint, opinion research serves to enrich the store of documents which are at his disposal. For the historian, more significant than the published findings of opinion research are the primary data upon which these are based. The raw questionnaire returns are a form of primary source material which the historian, as distinct from the opinion researcher, has yet to exploit directly. Thus far, the historian has used what he would describe as secondary accounts of opinion history, as, for example, when Dixon Wecter, in *The Age of the Great Depression* shows broad public approval of New Deal measures designed to regulate the economy by reference to *Fortune* and other poll data. The reworking of the primary materials by the historian in the light of his own inquiries and for purposes different from those of the opinion researchers opens up a new dimension of investigation.

From this point of view, opinion research performs a task similar to that accomplished by the historian when he turns up, as a result of diligent search, hitherto unused letters or diaries. Take, for example, the responses to open-ended questions covering almost any kind of contemporary domestic or international issue. If he has access to the schedules, the historian may undertake to code such responses in quite a different way from that of the pollster. He may examine them with quite different objects in view. He may, for example, be concerned not with the distribution of opinion, but with the use of language. Or, to take a concrete illustration provided by Samuel A. Stouffer's *Communism, Conformity, and Civil Liberties*, the historian could examine the responses to such a question as "What kinds of things do you worry about most?" not to secure information about the sources of personal insecurity, but about the characteristics of women in paid employment or, more broadly, about the meaning of work in present-day America.

Opinion research can also serve the historian by sensitizing him to sampling problems present in his own work. Broadly speaking, the historian always faces certain sampling problems with respect to sources and to evidence. For example, in the writing of recent history it is frequently impractical to attempt to exhaust all the materials available. Some sense of the manner in which available materials can be properly sampled so as to avoid undue distortion becomes essential. This is quite patent in any historical study of press opinion of which, of course, there were many before the days of opinion research. Clearly, the influence of opinion research will not be to transform the historian into a sampling expert. It will, rather, help him to realize in what kind of context his sampling problems are really determining, and it may facilitate his solutions of these problems.

The third respect in which opinion research can serve the historian has already been suggested. It will open up a new series of subjects for historical inquiry simply by providing information. When opinion surveys report on everything from the numbers of Americans who believe in God to the degree of ignorance concerning leading public figures, new kinds of information become available. Nobody knows what the historian of the future will make of the fact that many Americans were not able to identify correctly Molotov or General Marshall, or that some believed Picasso to be the head of the Italian government. He will, however, be able to undertake, if he so desires, studies of public understanding and ignorance of a character quite different from those feasible for his ancestor. Of course, the most obvious kind of subjects which will be opened up by the mere presence of opinion research will be histories of various polling organizations, research institutes, and the like, and of the relationship of their work to various aspects of the American scene. It is not difficult to imagine the future doctoral dissertation which will be titled: "The Role of Public Opinion Research in the Decline of Racial Prejudice."

In two other respects the work done in the larger field of opinion research can be of even greater service to the historian. First of all, the work in that field has produced and will in the future continue to produce findings which the historian may use as hypotheses in structuring his inquiries. Take, for example, the central finding of *Votes in the Making*, to the effect that presidential campaigns in recent years—at least up to 1948—are over before they even begin. For the historian, it does not really matter whether this holds as well for the elections of 1936 and 1944 as for that of 1940. What is significant is that it provides a hypothesis for an investigation of any presidential contest. If it is employed in the re-study of elections, including those already studied in painful detail—such as 1860, 1884, and 1896—it can conceivably lead to fresh findings.

Some of the findings reported in *The American Soldier* permit the formulation of hypotheses for the study of historical problems which have nothing to do with the soldiers of World War II. This has already been suggested by Dr. Lazarsfeld, who has noted the broader implications of the effect of the new situation upon army replacements. It should be possible, using hypotheses drawn from *The American Soldier*, to re-examine the problem of westward expansion in terms of the relationship of the individual and of family groups to a new situation. This would exploit a different socio-psychological point of view from that employed by Frederick Jackson Turner when he developed the "Frontier Thesis." The use of hypotheses drawn from opinion research may stimulate those border-line studies between history and social-psychology which have long been viewed as promising rich returns, but have been infrequently undertaken.

It is difficult to draw a firm and clear line between its contribution through the suggestion of fresh hypotheses and the fifth service which opinion research can perform for the historian. Nevertheless, there is some warrant for distinguishing between hypotheses which emerge from opinion research and the body of findings of that research concerning the behavior of man in society which the historian may use as assumptions in his work. In this respect, of course, opinion research has a relationship to history no different from that of psychology, social psychology, economics, sociology, or anthropology.

Historians frequently like to believe that the fundamental rule of their craft is that nothing must be taken for granted. This is a canon which the historian, as a mere mortal, cannot fulfill. Every act of historical inquiry rests upon presupposition and assumptions, only some of which are generally explicitly recognized by the historian. Some of these involve the nature of historical knowledge. The historian is likely to take it for granted—rather than satisfy himself as a result of rigorous intellectual demonstration—that knowledge is possible; that he knows what the nature of his subject matter is; and that he can deal meaningfully to himself and others with that subject matter in the sense that he can make significant judgments about events that happened in the past without having an immediate first-hand relationship to them. When he deals with evidence and makes judgments of validation or verification, the historian assumes that a logic of probability is applicable in his work, although he may not master that logic. Where the historian is more sophisticated in this respect, it may be noted, he is likely to be more sensitive to the important distinction to be made between obligatory inferences and those which are, by contrast, permissive.

It is a commonplace that another group of assumptions made by the historian reside within him, so to speak, as a reflection of his culture. His beliefs about desirable ideas and ideals, good or appropriate behavior, and worthwhile experience mean that he carries about with him a system of values which are not the outcome of his controlled and purposeful thinking about the past, but which affect his behavior as historian. Through conscious self-examination he may come to know what these values are, how they are hierarchically ordered, how he came to hold them, and how they influence his work as historian. Opinion research is relevant in this context, for the more light it casts upon the cultural setting within which the historian operates, the easier that exercise in self-examination becomes.

The most important operational assumptions made by the historian are the things he takes for granted about man and society. Human beings and human life stand at the center of the historian's work. He cannot operate at all without assuming that he knows something about what moves people to behave in the way they do, either as individuals or in social groups. He has to have some notion of the kind of relationships which obtain between their activities and interests on the one hand, and among their interests, outlook, and behavior on the other. The historian, in short, has to act as if he is a psychologist, social-psychologist, and sociologist.

It is extraordinarily difficult "to prevent most men," as J. A. Hobson put it, "from finding reasons for believing anything they want very badly to believe." Historians are human, and some of them have wanted to believe some very odd things about memory, man's motives, race, and national character, to mention only a few items, with very striking consequences for the kind of history they have written. It can be demonstrated from the work of even the great historians that, for those who believe, the substance of things taken for granted becomes the evidence for things not seen.

Distinctions can be made among the historian's assumptions about man and society. First, there are assumptions which take the form of underlying conceptions of man's nature, the character and purpose of social organization, and the overall direction of social movement. Then, there are varied assumptions of more limited scope, generally spoken of as theories, bearing on the role of environment and heredity, the nature and constitution of cultures, the character of social classes or of racial, ethnic, or national groupings, individual and group motivation, and the like. Finally, there are many more or less carefully stated propositions concerning man and society, growing out of empirical research and supported by persuasive evidence, which the historian accepts and relies upon in his work. These involve such subjects as the nature and function of memory, the learning process, rational and non-rational behavior, leadership, and the determinants of morale, among a host of others.

Such conceptions, theories, and propositions are normally not put to examination or test by the historian when he utilizes them, either knowingly or unknowingly. He would, in fact, be deflected from engaging in his own labors if he felt under obligation first to investigate all the assumptions about man and society which penetrate and shape historical writing.

Most historians leave it to other disciplines to determine the status and validity of the assumptions about man and society which they employ. Nor does the historian have much choice about his behavior in this respect. Either he assigns to his assumptions a validity which makes them immune from examination; or he employs them with doubts and reservations, but knows that he is unable to submit them to test within the limits of his own operations.

The state of the historian's knowledge about man and society has frequently produced high dissatisfaction both within and outside the historical guild. In the preface to *St. Joan*, George Bernard Shaw tartly remarked that "the variety of the conclusions" reached on Joan's voices and visions demonstrate "how little our matter-of-fact historians know about other people's minds or even about their own." Henri Davenson in "La Tristesse de l'historien" observed that explanations of human conduct offered by the average historian take the disappointing form of cautious and off-hand suggestions grounded in elementary psychological notions about the motive power of ambition, patriotism, fear and greed. The English philosopher-historian, R. G. Collingwood, found the field of historical writing tragically weak in its analysis of people and in dealing with the human personality, and pointed out that novelists have been far more successful than historians in treating human nature.

This kind of charge against the historian can be easily documented. The great Taine started with the assumption that there were basic racial types and fundamental characteristics of an age. These he invoked as final and permanent causes "explaining" the character of English literature. Research could not carry him beyond his "man of the North." The character of the work of nineteenth century Liberal historians, both European and American, was profoundly affected by a fundamental assumption concerning the rationality of man. A contemporary eminent English historian conditions elements of his work by assuming that racial stock counts heavily. Even James Harvey Robinson fell back upon something called the French temperament in order to explain the "perpetual partisanship" of revolutionary France. Dubious assumptions, cast in the form of "scientific" theories of racial inferiority and superiority, led distinguished American historians to give a peculiar shape to the treatment of immigration in the history of the United States. Important facets of Burckhardt's work were in part fashioned by his assumption that man is unchanging. In consequence, his interest in historical development was limited, and his attention was largely focused on what he held to be the "constant factors" and the permanent forces at work throughout history. Biographical studies invite research by the scholar who would like to demonstrate that historians have been attracted by simplistic and outmoded conceptions of human nature.

Interestingly enough, historians have been relatively indifferent to the manner in which elementary assumptions about man and society shape the outcome of historical inquiry. They have, however, been aware that there are virtually no limits to what they should know about the central object of their concern—human beings and the terms of human life in all its fullness. And it is precisely in this respect—that is, in what it may enable him to learn about man and society—that opinion research may perform its most significant service for the historian.

PART II

Economics

and

Sociology

Clark Kerr
and
Lloyd H. Fisher

PLANT SOCIOLOGY:
THE ELITE AND THE ABORIGINES

The differences between the sociologist and the economist represent one version of the modern form of the debate about the nature of man and the nature of groups. In many of their tasks and interests, the conflict between sociologist and economist is neither manifest nor important. When, however, they both enter the work place and factory, when they both ascribe function to plant managers, unions and workers, the conflict in viewpoint and vision is evident and acute.

Until very recently it has been the task of economics, among the social sciences, to examine the role of the director of the business enterprise. Ordinarily, the economist viewed him as an entrepreneur and derived his social justification from the creation of wealth for the society and productive employment for the workers. To the entrepreneur went the task of combining and recombining scarce resources in a free market governed by self interest and the promise of gain. The worker was equally governed by self interest, ordinarily in the form of higher wages. The model of the business enterprise was that of a voluntary association. The test of performance was efficient production.

Within the past two decades, economists have watched the growth of a new and vigorous competitor, equipped with a different view of the nature of man and a different vision of human welfare.

The authors gratefully acknowledge the active and intelligent assistance of Ruth Deutsch in the preparation of this paper.

During this period a group of sociologists has arisen to take the industrial community and its subdivisions as its province. For these sociologists also, the manager is a key and crucial figure, but the role to which he is assigned is markedly different. The test of performance is not efficiency, but stability. The industrial plant is not a voluntary association but a social organism. The view of man is that of the dependent part within the social whole. The task of the manager is to produce coherence, stability and a sense of community. For the economist, the obligation is the efficient management of productive resources; for the sociologist, the obligation is the harmonious management of social systems.

This group of sociologists has grown steadily in size and influence during the past few years, bringing with it certain charges against the intellectual apparatus with which the economists have worked. For those with a sense of the history of ideas, there is a haunting familiarity to the charges. For they are the charges levelled by the church and aristocracy against the abstract, individualistic conception of the *philosophes;* they are the charges levelled by Burke against the French Revolution in the name of the prior rights of society and group as against those of the artificial conception of reasoning man, by the German romantics of the 19th century in the name of the greater reality of the folk, by the Nazis against "liberalism," and by the Communists against cosmopolitanism; by the exponents in all times and all places of the virtues of the coherent and cohesive rural society against the disintegrating individualism of urban life. This is the most modern episode in the attack on reason in the name of harmony, cohesion and a traditional culture.

To identify an intellectual tradition, however, is not to prove it wrong. But this identification does help to define the issue. In the industrial context, the economist must meet the charge that individual reason is an index of group disintegration and that an intellectual system which bases its explanations upon calculating, reasoning man can at best explain only the pathological manifestations of a society and perhaps not even those. For the economist is undoubtedly addicted to rationalism and atomism. He has a certain trained incapacity for dealing with the non-logical. He has also a certain scepticism about ideals of group solidarity and its opposite, anomie. Most particularly he would be reluctant to accept individual reason as an aberration and therefore as a poor guide for human affairs. There persists the notion that although reason, highly enough developed to serve as a guide for behavior, does not exist among all men, it surely exists among some. It is perhaps only an article of faith that the uncertainty of its distribution is so great that it may turn up among members of a factory work group as well as in the managerial elite.

If the issues between the industrial sociologist and the economist could be settled empirically, their genealogy would be a matter of interest only to the historian of ideas. If they turn out to be, as indeed their predecessors were, value judgments, then we may regard ourselves as reasonably free to plot our course by the values we hold and make our judgments accordingly. What we must do, then, is to examine the arguments and the evidence upon which the propositions of plant sociology rest.

Plant sociology is a remarkably coherent body of doctrine. A thorough review of the literature as it now stands does not support the observation of William Foote Whyte that "So much has been done since Mayo's pioneering research that arguments over what he did and thought are out of touch with present-day realities." [1] Techniques have altered, to be sure, and case studies have accumulated but along a path clearly laid out by the founders of the school. Values which were explicit with the teachers have sometimes been muted in the students, but it seems to us they have not altered. It has, therefore, appeared necessary for both completeness and coherence to treat the founders, their critics and their disciples and then to examine expressly the question of whether in fact so much has changed that it is appropriate to distinguish the founders from their disciples.

We have used the term "plant sociology" to designate the subject of this paper. It is, so far as we know, a new coinage and perhaps of doubtful value. But since it has no accepted usage, it is important to state with some precision the territory we propose to cover. More commonly, the authors discussed here are designated as industrial sociologists. But the term "industrial sociology" has no accepted meaning either and contains diverse enterprises and conflicting traditions. We shall also attempt, therefore, to define our subject in the context of industrial sociology and differentiate it from other branches of industrial sociology so that there may be no more generality given to these remarks than is intended.

Industrial Sociology and Plant Sociology

Industrial sociology has been variously defined as covering almost everything or nearly nothing. At its grandest, it is said to include the study of "the industrial way of life" [2] or the "industrial community." [3] In the Western World, where industry has come to dominate economic activity, industrial sociology would thus become virtually synonymous with sociology. To the non-industrial sociologists would be left the under-developed territories, presumably to be shared with the anthropologist. At its most modest, industrial sociology is viewed as the investigation of "the interaction of two bureaucracies" [4] (unions and companies) or of the "mass interaction of work groups." [5] This definition limits industrial sociology to the study of certain aspects of collective bargaining and excludes the work of many if not most "industrial sociologists."

More serviceable appears to be the definition of the field as the study of "institutions of work as forms of social organization," [6] or somewhat more broadly as "all work relations." [7] This definition carves off work relations from the many other kinds of relations of people in society.

"Work relations" and the "institutions of work" may be and are studied at several levels: the job, the plant, the community, and the society. Different people interested in distinct problems work at each of these levels and frequently they have little more in common than the use of industrial materials.

This suggests that the term industrial sociology confuses more than it clarifies and consequently should be discarded: The actual research products can better be grouped according to a different system of classification. The "sociology of work relations" constitutes all or a significant part of these four fields: the sociology of occupations, the sociology of organization, community sociology, and political sociology. [8]

1. *Occupational Sociology.* Occupational sociology takes as the relevant environment the job. It is concerned with the effect of the job on status and on political and social attitudes; the routinization of work and its consequences; the social environments and the social requirements of jobs; inter-job mobility; occupational career patterns; the social adjustment of the worker to his job;

and a number of other aspects of life which are heavily influenced by the specific and associated characteristics of jobs. The occupational sociologists emphasize, in general, the importance of work to man, and, in particular, the significance of his job to his way of life and to his view of himself and of society. Their studies are closely related to the investigation of social stratification and class alignments.

2. *Organizational Sociology.* The universe for the organizational sociologist is the organization under the microscope. The organization is a social system with lines of authority, channels of communication, a status hierarchy, individual and institutional goals, human and physical resources, an arsenal of rewards and punishments, a constitution or charter, and so forth. While the organization exists in an external environment, it is to the internal life of this small society that the organizational sociologist turns his interest. Exogenous forces are of concern primarily as they compel the organization to make internal adjustments. The entity studied may be a trade union, a corporation, a government agency, or a small work group. The minimum requirement is an informal structure peopled by several individuals.

Among the organizational sociologists, the *plant sociologists*, during the past two decades, have made the most influential contribution. The plant sociologists have had a clear focus for their studies, a methodology of sorts, and a well-developed value system. Out of the myriad organizations in our society, they have selected the work place, whether factory, office, or shop, for their investigations. Through the interview and participant observation, they have become intimately familiar with the life of the work place. In addition, they have developed a systematic view of society which raises to a position of pre-eminence the small work group and its leaders. It is to these plant sociologists that we shall shortly return.

3. *Community Sociology.* The community sociologist takes the rural or urban locality as the social system to be examined. He is interested in the labor force, the ethnic groups, the power structure, the voluntary associations in this locality. If the community is an industrial one, he may study the place of the factory in it, or the relations of the unions to large and small business, the church and the workers, or the effect of social groupings and attitudes on the course of a strike. He may treat with the process of industrialization

of a community or its restructuring with the advent of unionism or the arrival of new ethnic groups. In method and orientation, the community sociologists and the cultural anthropologists have much in common.

4. *Political Sociology.* The political sociologist, in the grand tradition, takes no less than the total society as his frame of reference. He is interested in mass power conflicts, competing ideologies, class divisions and the like. In an industrial society, the organizations of workers and employers, as well as the state and political groupings, comprise the salient materials with which he works; and he thus has close affinity to the political theorist.

While scholars in each of these four fields study the phenomena of "industrial life" and "the institutions of work," they are such different people, with such diverse interests and methods and systems of thought, that it is quite misleading to group them together as "industrial sociologists." Their points of distinction overwhelm their points of similarity, and a useful system of classification should group the like rather than the unlike.

The conflict between economist and sociologist is least evident at the level of political sociology where the sociologist, the political theorist and the economic historian, at least, share many concepts and points of view. They are united by the importance which they ascribe to the idea of "interest" and ultimately of self interest as a motivating force in human affairs. They may, indeed, deal with group action and group interests; individual reason may become joint purpose; self justification is convertible to ideology; but however broadly the units of social action may be defined, the intellectual tradition of the political sociologist and of the economist is rational and secular.

The occupational sociologist, on this scale, stands between the political sociologist and the community sociologist, and the plant sociologist at the farthest remove from the secular rationalism of economic explanation. The plant sociologist meets the issue of rationalism and universalism squarely with a tribalized society, the unity of man with the diversity of culture, the force of reason with the force of tradition, the idea of purpose with the concept of function, and the mechanical model with the organic analogy.[9] It is, therefore, in the writings of the plant sociologist that the economist finds his indictment most comprehensively expressed.

Plant Sociology

It is an understandable and common error to identify plant sociology as though it were the entirety of "industrial sociology." For the plant sociologists have not only produced a "school" with substantial output to its credit, but a school whose findings, if not its ideology, have greatly influenced both academic thinking and professional practice. "Human relations" is the transforming phrase which divides the new teachers and executives from the old. The course in personnel administration has become one in human relations in industry; and the epitomizing symbol is now Chester Barnard with his doctrine of implicit "consent" instead of Frederick Taylor with his "incentives."

The founder of this school was the late Elton Mayo. His chief laboratories were a Philadelphia textile plant and the Hawthorne works of the Western Electric Company; and his chief intellectual forebears were two: Pareto and his preoccupation with non-logical action and the role of the elite, Durkheim and his persistent concern with the anomie of industrial society. Early advocates, before Chicago began to rival Cambridge as the intellectual center of the school, were T. N. Whitehead and F. J. Roethlisberger. In the writings of these three men are found the essential doctrines of the school.[10] At Chicago, Burleigh Gardner, Lloyd Warner and William Foote Whyte [11] established the western branch of the human relations school, although with a substantial dilution of the original *weltanschauung*.

Two recent books by William Foote Whyte [12] and George C. Homans [13] afford an opportunity to examine the development of the school, where it stands currently, and what can reasonably be guessed as to the course of its future development.

The Founders

1. *Their Discoveries.* As Darwin evolved the theory of natural selection out of a few homely observations, so Mayo and his asso-

ciates made their basic discoveries by examining several small groups of employees. These discoveries have worked their way into a large volume of research, teaching, and practice.

Two findings were basic: that the small work group is the elemental building block in the plant structure and that this group and its members are motivated by "sentiments." Up to that time supervisory practice was largely founded on the two opposite assumptions of the social isolation of the worker and of the primacy of economic incentives. The clearest case of the inadequacy of the earlier assumptions and the policies which grew from them was the restriction of output in the face of an incentive plan. Instead of each worker producing to capacity and thus maximizing his own income, it was found that the workers informally set output limits for the sake of the security of the group and its members. The worker's view of his social relations with fellow workers and with managers was thus held to be more significant, than not only economic motives but also physical conditions of work and the physiological condition of the worker.

While most business leaders would now stipulate that workers are social beings, this obvious fact was not so obvious in the personnel practices of earlier decades. The growing prominence of the human relations expert is the institutional expression of this insight. This new kind of engineering, following the Hawthorne discoveries, has been concerned with the informal structure of the organization and the segmentation of this structure, with the development of effective work teams, with the adequacy of upward and downward communications, with the manipulation of status and symbols to evoke constructive worker response, and with the easing of changes into the work group to avoid the normal negative reactions which spring from the essential conservatism of the group. Perhaps the best practical exposition of these discoveries, without their ideological overtones, is that of Burleigh Gardner,[14] for whom they remained largely tools and techniques of rational industrial supervision. With Mayo and some of his followers, however, the Hawthorne findings intermingled with an older social philosophy and a more modern cultural anthropology, overwhelming the humanitarian implications of the study with a feudal vision of unity, order and a stable society.

2. *Their Ideology.*[15]   The ideology of Mayo and his original

followers may be parsed into three parts: a view of man, a conception of industrial society, and a solution to the problem of man (as they see him) in an industrial society (as they see it). These three elements are woven together into a system of thought.

Man. Man is a uniquely social animal who can achieve complete "freedom" only by fully submerging himself in the group. Mayo believed that traditional societies with their emphasis on ritual, conformity, and social codes were "very compatible for the individual." [16] While critical of the force used by those primitive societies, Mayo thought their close-knit life a satisfying one: [17]

> Amongst the Australian aborigines their method of living involves almost perfect collaboration drilled into the members of the tribe. . . . Each member knows his place and part although he cannot explain it.

Mayo added that in modern societies it is often forgotten "how necessary this type of non-logical social action is to achievement and satisfaction in living." [18] The industrial worker is no different from primitive man in his longing for group solidarity: "The industrial worker wants . . . first, a method of living in social relationship with other people, and, second, as part of this an economic function for and value to the group." [19] He added later: [20]

> Whether as anthropologists we study a primitive race or as industrialists we study some part of the modern complex and chaotic scheme, we find, either in the natural wilds or in the modern city, groups of individuals who find their happiness and such sense of personal security as may be in subordination of an individual to a common purpose. The solitary who works alone is always a very unhappy person.

Whitehead also expressed his preference for an "orderly society" which is "based upon routine, custom and historical association" [21] and believed that loyalty to society is the source of liberty: "The only social liberty which is possible depends upon the loyalty of the individual to his society, and is proportional to that loyalty." [22]

Industrial Society. Industrial society annihilates the "cultural traditions" of established societies and leads to "social disorganization." [23] "At no time since the industrial revolution has there been, except sporadically here and there, anything of the nature of the effective and wholehearted collaboration between the administrative and the working groups in industry"; [24] and Mayo considered "the chief difficulty of our time" to be "the breakdown of the social codes that formerly disciplined us to effective working together." [25]

The sources of this social disruption are two-fold: Industrial society destroys the group solidarity of the church, the small community, the guild, and thus increases "the number of unhappy individuals," while simultaneously the number of "pressure groups" increases.[26] In the face of these unhappy individuals and conflicting pressure groups, industrial society can easily disintegrate.

The state is "too remote morally and spatially to possess anything of the living reality of active collaboration for individuals." [27] Instead it is the plant, under the leadership of its manager, in which order can be established even in the midst of anarchy outside. Dean Donham in his preface to *The Social Problems* stated this very succinctly: [28]

> Mayo gives us instances where industrial administrators have succeeded in making factory groups so stable in their attitudes of group cooperation that men in the groups explicitly recognized that the factory has become for them the stabilizing force around which they developed satisfying lives . . . in spite of . . . social chaos in the community outside.

A skilled administrative elite can win the "race for stability, security and development" [29] and "very many of our difficulties would dwindle to the vanishing point." [30] There is one clear road from industrial chaos to group solidarity, if the managerial elite would only see it in time—human relations in industry. These "human relations" could substitute for the "simple religious feeling of medieval times." [31]

The Critics

The Mayo school has not lacked for critics.[32] The criticisms have been directed mainly at four aspects of the approach:

1. The plant sociologists virtually ignore the external environment and in doing so, while not neglecting all the important variables, do neglect most of them. They are relatively unconcerned

with the impacts of ideology, of the business cycle, of external associations, to mention only a few. As a result, they are better at describing a group than at analyzing the important differences among groups; and, by ignoring the surrounding and changing environment, they are more likely to present a static picture of the group at a moment of time than its rise, or fall, or metamorphosis.

2. Mayo and his close associates have a most egregious bias. They begin by saying that man dislikes isolation and end up by consigning him to the care of the managerial elite for his own salvation. In heading for their chosen solution they overlook a number of alternatives. Assuming that man dislikes isolation, which to a degree may be quite true, does that necessarily mean that he is happy only when he loses his identity in group life? If he is happy only after having lost his identity in group life, does it follow that he must lose his identity in only one group rather than several? Finally, if he must lose his identity in only one group, must it be the plant?

The answer to all of these questions appears (to Mayo and his associates) to be in the affirmative, for they prefer the plant to the church or the state or the trade union or the family; single-minded loyalty to divided loyalty; "social collaboration" to "competition." They accept the goals of the managerial elite and advise it how to reach these goals in an efficient manner. It is not to the dictator, however, that they address themselves, but to the benevolent despot who manipulates his subjects in the interests of his own security and their welfare.

3. Some of the critics contend that the Mayo-ites ignore the important problems of society. While looking at status in the plant, they ignore power in society; while examining the face-to-face relations of supervisors and the supervised, they overlook the dominant role of group bargaining; and while concentrating on day-to-day contacts at the work bench, they cannot see the sweep of history.

4. Finally, certain of the critics attack the empirical methods of the school [33] and claim that even if a long series of case studies eventually results in a theory, this approach violates the law of parsimony.

The Disciples

From the point of view of intellectual influence, the two principal descendants of Mayo and Whitehead are William Foote Whyte and George C. Homans. Whyte's *Pattern for Industrial Peace* and Homans' *The Human Group*, the two most recent volumes by "plant sociologists," provide an opportunity to judge whether the school has advanced in any significant fashion since Mayo. Specifically we shall be concerned with whether there are any new discoveries, or a changed theoretical structure, and whether the objections of the critics have been met.

Whyte. Pattern for Industrial Peace is a detailed study of interpersonal relations in the Chicago plant of the Inland Steel Container Company over the period 1937 to 1950. Industrial relations there passed through the three stages of "disorganized conflict," "organized conflict" and "organized cooperation." These stages are defined and identified by the pattern of communications. The first is characterized by downward communications in the management and upward in the union hierarchy; in the second, upward channels open on the management side and downward channels open on the union side; and, in the third, management can initiate action for the union—communications take place freely up and down and back and forth. The method of study is the counting of contacts and the analysis of their content.

"It has been possible to tell the story of that plant almost as if it were a completely independent unit."[34] This statement is almost literally true. At only three points is reference made to exogenous forces: the sit-down strikes of 1936-1937 which encouraged the workers in the plant to resist a dictatorial management; the assumption of ownership by Inland Steel in 1939 and the introduction of new managerial personnel; and the boundaries set to local relationships by the absentee owners (Inland Steel Company *and* the United Steelworkers of America)—the parent company, for example, did not permit a closed shop or strict seniority rules, and the parent union insisted on local imitation of the national steel wage pattern. No reference is made to the war, or the Taft-Hartley Act, or the cost of living, or the tightness or looseness of the labor market, or the profitability of the industry.

Yet a very great change did take place—from a sit-down strike to union-management cooperation—and an explanation is both required and rendered. The explanation is quite a simple and not unexpected one—good human relations. With time and self-conscious effort, good face-to-face relations were developed—the attitudes of the leaders toward each other became more friendly and they developed greater skills in handling personal relationships and problems. While the individual heroes of the story are the leaders on both sides, the real, although impersonal hero, is time—the passage of years in the relationship and the passing of hours in personal contact. "Disorganized conflict," "organized conflict" and "organized cooperation" are not types of labor-management relations but stages on the highway to industrial harmony—a highway paved with time.

Whyte makes the union an integral part of the human relations structure of the plant, and his technique is instructive, since Mayo and Whitehead had difficulty working the union into their system of thought. It is not true, as often alleged, that the "human relations" school ignores unions; rather, it has not always known whether to reject them completely or embrace them tightly. Mayo expressed three views on unions. He saw the British unions engaged in "the resistance of a dying social code to innovation," [35] but this was a special case. In the more general case, the unions brought "not discipline and collaboration but disorder and resistance." [36] They "imposed upon the workers a low level of human organization from which social participation and social function were excluded." [37] The International Ladies Garment Workers Union was another exception, for it maintained cooperation between "the union and the management" [38] while most unions organized "for warfare against management." [39]

Thus unions were bad if they opposed management and good if they cooperated—but in the latter case, as Whitehead pointed out, they were probably unnecessary. To Whitehead, the rise of unions reflected the broadest problem of man in society—it was a revolt not against bad conditions but social isolation.[40] Were this social isolation to be overcome by good human relations stemming from changed managerial policy, then the unions would either disappear or be greatly changed: [41]

. . . these unions are not adequately led and have no great traditions of collaboration with management, and the future history of human relations in industry might be an unhappy one.

On the other hand, the executive ranks in business contain many of the best brains of the country, and it is very possible that they will prove adequate to the task of adapting the organism of industry on lines more satisfactory for those involved; if this happens, trade unions may lose their members, because they find in direct collaboration within the factory all they need in the way of personal self-expression and of adequate consideration.

However, institutions die hard, and it is more likely that in such a case the unions would insensibly change their functions and become more exclusively a means for collaboration.

Whyte, in his earlier work, had the same difficulty in treating with unions as Mayo and Whitehead did and for the same reasons. At first he viewed unions as the fault of the workers or of the society in which they were reared—too many workers were not good industrial material since they were subject to emotional upset and discontent. Workers who had been raised with close parental contact but otherwise in social isolation and who had worked at an early age were less likely to join unions than their opposites [42]—thus the farm boy resisted unionism and the gang member was the organizer's delight. Later, unions were taken to be, in part at least, the outgrowth of bad management: [43]

While it is impossible to generalize for all workers, we may say in general that the worker wants security in his job. . . . Now, top management may make decisions that disrupt the informal organization of workers, lower the status of many individuals, and destroy the workers' sense of security. . . . Union organization functions, in part, to build up a new equilibrium through establishing communication with top management and through resisting decisions that would upset relationships at the work level.

The trouble is that "the personnel man and the executive have been misled by the individualistic point of view, which has been so popular in our society" [44] when they should have been building a "system of human relations."

In *Pattern for Industrial Peace*, there is no longer any effort to explain away unions as the consequence of malfunctioning workers or society or managers, but instead the union is accepted as making an important functional contribution. It does this essentially by accepting the goals of management—industrial harmony and productive efficiency—and helping management achieve these goals. When "organized cooperation" is reached "management is now utilizing two channels to get things done" [45] since it can originate "action directly for the union." [46] This is possible, in part, because "the union officers are now originating action for their subordinates with greater relative frequency than heretofore" and "the union officers . . . are in a greatly improved position to plan and control the activities of the rank and file." [47] The parties, instead of opposing each other, join forces against the "small minority" causing trouble.[48] When they have reached this point in their development, the parties are "no longer seriously concerned over powers and prerogatives." [49] It is absolutely essential to industrial peace that management "originate action directly for the union. Only in that way can management get away from its defensive frame of mind. Only in that way can the union leaders play a responsible role in the development of the enterprise." [50] Union leaders are now part of the elite charged with maintaining harmony in society and, along with the business executive, "must know how to deal with the sentiments and emotions of men." [51] The union, once it collaborates with management in striving for harmony through human relations, can be worked into the system.[52] It no longer need be either ignored or castigated.

Homans. *The Human Group* is a more complex book than *Pattern for Industrial Peace.* Whereas Whyte adopts the role of exhaustive and systematic reporter, Homans is concerned with generalization. Whyte reports a single case study; Homans draws on five earlier studies [53] so that he may offer hypotheses and draw tentative generalizations about the behavior of human beings in small groups. *The Human Group* offers Homans' view buttressed by quotations from Francis Bacon, Wilard Gibbs, and A. N. Whitehead of the nature of hypothesis, experiment and the relation of the parts to the whole. From a different tradition in intellectual history he also draws through Mary Parker Follett upon a Hegelian construction of the unity of "the interacting, the unifying and the emerging." [54] It is perhaps captious to note that Homans has been no more successful than anyone else in devising experiments within the framework of Hegelian metaphysics for it is not clear that he intended to. Given his endorsement of both intellectual traditions as preconditions for the development of a science of society he ought, perhaps, to have attempted the reconciliation, but obligation and intent are not the same thing.

It is not easy to come to terms with Homans because he appears to alternate between several views. If they are contradictory and if the reader chooses one as the more representative, a rebuttal is readily available from another section of the book.

Thus Homans' initial rule of theory building requires the study of "the obvious, the familiar, the common." [55] Further "we shall need, first, the innocence of the child, not the good little boy or girl but the *enfant terrible* who stops the conversation by asking the wrong questions. For we shall have to ask, 'What do I actually see?' and, as we have said, no question is more devastating." [56]

From this it might be presumed that the social scientist should cultivate simple perceptions. But he must also "make use of the past experience of the intellectual disciplines in dealing with problems of complicated fact." [57] He must have sophistication as well as simplicity, a sophistication which includes a clear understanding of Mary Follett's dictum that "we should be interested not merely in the totalness of the situation but in the nature of the totalness." [58]

But how is one to know whether a situation is total and what the nature of that totalness is? Is a less than total situation conceivable? Obviously it is; it is virtually inevitable. Is a more than total situation conceivable? Obviously it is not. Yet the boundaries of the situation will be defined differently by different social scientists and, in general, the plant sociologist working with the smallest group is the most committed to totality.

How does this apparent paradox come about? There appear to be two answers offered by Homans. One is at the technical level and the other has the character of an *a priori* truth. The technical answer is that no science can work with all of the variables which may influence the phenomena it studies. What is true of advanced and mature sciences is certainly equally true of an infant science. Therefore one deals with the small group and takes the environment [59] in which the group resides as given. The other answer is that the group will be shown to be an organic whole. If the small group can be shown to be an organic whole then it may be taken as a legitimate universe for study because the organism is a self-contained system.

Now a notion like that of the organism cannot be established as valid in the social sciences because it has proved useful in biology. Yet Homans seems to have no doubt that the small group is an organic whole. He says, "We do not want just to get the feel of this whole. We want to be men and understand." [60]

This is the kind of perception that develops more readily from the innocence of the adult than from the innocence of the child. But Homans will not let it rest as an article of faith, nor even as a broad analogy. "This," he says, "is a book on social theory, the theory will show the group to be an organic whole; and the theory will be built up through careful examination of the link between social concept and social observation." [61] This involves an offer of proof. The method appropriate to the proof is the case method and the case method is appropriate because it deals with connected facts.

We must now ask whether connectedness is the test of an organism. The question answers itself in the asking. Obviously the connectedness of parts is a necessary condition of the organism. Equally obviously it is not a sufficient one. Mechanisms also meet the condition of the connectedness of parts. Any engine will display functional relationships between its parts and yet in most nomenclatures be regarded as the virtual opposite of organisms. To establish the existence of an organism it is necessary at least to demonstrate in a quite literal sense that it has biological life *and* that this life is of such a character that an event befalling any part of the organism communicates itself to the entire organism. Additionally the term connotes conventionally that the major parts are not replaceable and that the organism changes by slow evolutionary processes. It is true that by miracles of modern surgery major parts of the "human organism" may soon be replaceable but to this extent even the biological fastnesses of organic theory are being rapidly invaded by mechanistic notions.

It is difficult to believe that Homans proposes to prove so much, and the insistence upon the human group as an organic whole had better be taken as a broad analogy,[62] and his use of the term cell as a synonym for individual taken as a bit of biological license. But even with this adjustment there remains the question of why this analogy. If the image is simply one of the connectedness of the parts, why not the simpler mechanical model?

Still another analogy suggests an answer of some plausibility. Some political theorists have employed the organic analogy in contexts clear enough to permit a confident statement of their purposes. One of the oldest similes in the history of political thought pictures the state as a human body writ large. This has been one way of answering the classic question of political theory "what justifies political authority?" The answer of the organic theorist is that this is a nonsense question, as nonsensical for instance as the similar question "what justifies the hand in obeying the brain?"

Homans is not unaware of the uses for which the organic analogy is employed. He cites Myrdal's warning [63] with apparent approval but remains essentially unmoved. The danger is conceded but thought greater in discussions of large groups than of small. It is then disposed of in a few sentences which deserve to be quoted in full, for they are among the most curious in the literature:

> We shall try not to allow hidden emotional evaluations to creep into our discussions by this entrance, but we may not succeed, so let no one say he was not warned! Myrdal says that the mere use of the word equilibrium, and of another one, *organization*, that is scattered through these pages, may encourage conservative thinking both in the author and in the reader. So beware! For dangerous as it is, we shall use the concept anyhow. Myrdal would not have had to stretch his list much further to show that there is no concept that may not let in an evaluation. If we are evaluators—conservative or radical—we will evaluate, and nothing shall stop us. It would be intolerable to let this melancholy fact divorce us from conceptual thought. So we shall work with *equilibrium* and may even learn in time to find its terrors delicious.[64]

At night all cats are black.

Yet it is also true that the inductions which Homans draws from the five case studies do not depend in any important way upon his predisposition to organic explanations. If he can develop valid empirical principles to explain group behavior, it may matter very little whether he is skilled in the definition of organisms and wholes. It is at this point that we revert to canons of simplicity. If Homans has not succeeded in his quest for Bacon's middle level generalizations he has at least rediscovered his innocence. The rules which he derives from the behavior of successful leaders include such generalizations as: the leader will maintain his own position, the leader will live up to the norms of his group, the leader will lead, the leader will not give orders that will not be obeyed, the leader will take into consideration the total situation, the leader will listen, the leader will know himself. Since by leader is always understood successful leader, these maxims are unexceptionable.[65] It may readily be conceded that major discoveries have often rested on the most commonplace foundations. It does not follow, however, that obviousness is in itself adequate proof of value.

There are also rules governing individual relationships within groups. For instance, "the relationship between two persons, A and B, is partly determined by the relationships between A and a third person, C, and between B and C." [66] Or, "the more frequently persons interact with one another, when no one of them originates interaction with much greater frequency than the others, the greater is their liking for one another and their feeling of ease in one another's presence." [67]

Finally, there are a set of propositions which are neither obvious nor trivial. These are the deductions from the rise and fall of civilization. In his summary chapter Homans observes that "the appalling fact is that, after flourishing for a span of time, every civilization but one has collapsed. The ruling class, if there was one, has lost its capacity to lead; the formal organizations that articulated the whole have fallen to pieces; the faith has no longer commanded the allegiance of the citizens . . ." [68] In accounting for what he calls "the cycle of civilization and decay," Homans offers this summary:

> Our own theory, in its main lines, would run as follows. At the level of the tribe or group, society has always found itself able to cohere. We infer, therefore, that a civilization, if it is in turn to maintain itself, must preserve at least a few of the characteristics of the group, though necessarily on a much expanded scale. Civilizations have failed in failing to solve this problem. In fact the very process by which civilization emerges has, up to now, made failure inevitable.[69]

This process has had three main features, technical change, economic expansion, and warfare, each resulting in "breaking up old social units without putting anything in their place." [70] Among the principal results was the growth of great cities whether they be Detroit or Los Angeles or the teeming metropolis of the Near East, "filled with traders, artisans and slaves." [71] Thus man is uprooted, wrenched from his primary group life, prone to "develop disorders of thought feeling and behavior. His thinking will be obsessive, elaborated without sufficient reference to reality . . ." [72]

Deprived of the stable relationship provided by the small group, man is lonely and unhappy, on his way to a meaningless and inconsequential atom in a society reduced to a dust heap. This is also the dust heap of Elton Mayo; it is the rabble of the rabble hypothesis with which Mayo attacked the classical economist; it is the forerunner of despotism and tyranny to which, if necessary, man will turn to escape individual responsibility.

Founders and Disciples—The Common Thread

Despite a very considerable measure of confusion in Homans' writings, a simple pattern persists, one which is to be found also in the works of other members of the group. Whyte notes in his preface "how closely my theoretical statement parallels that of George C. Homans in *The Human Group*." [73] This is not so surprising since the analytical framework of each of them is almost identical with that of Whitehead. The central core of group behavior is made up of three elements: activities, interactions, and sentiments. [74] The nature of the activity affects the frequency and content of interactions and these in turn affect sentiments. When group norms are added, the dynamics of group life emerge from the interrelations of each with every other. While this analytical framework is not rigorously used by any of these authors, it is considered to be the central theory by each of them.

The parallels do not stop here but run the whole way through. Whyte and Homans, like Mayo and Whitehead, stress the importance of the small group to society and of sentiments to the small group. They all concentrate on the significance of the informal structure, the flow of communications, and the dominant importance of status.

Their presuppositions are almost identical. Man is a social animal who wants security more than freedom as ordinarily defined. Homans states that the "isolated individual is sick" [75] and "a society is free so far as the behavior it makes appropriate and natural for its citizens—the behavior they feel is good—is also the behavior its controls demand of them." [76] If a slave enjoys his slavery, he is free, while a free man who wants more freedom is a slave. "If freedom is to mean no more than emotional isolation, it will not survive. Men will do any mad thing, even merge in a mass under the sword of a tyrant, to escape freedom of this kind." [77]

One of the sources of distress in industrial society is this emotional isolation; the other is the growth of pressure groups. Mayo groups these tendencies under "social disorganization" and "social conflict." Society can be destroyed by both isolated individuals and isolated groups. Homans repeats the central query of Mayo: "How can a social order change without either dissolution into a dust heap or cleavage into hostile camps?" [78] Whyte sees as the essential problem of industrial society the trend toward centralization—its demand for consistent policies, leading to a large bureaucracy, clogged channels of communication, and, as a final consequence, destruction of consideration for the individual.[79] Simultaneously "with the rise of industrial society we see a decline in our ability to live and work together in harmony." [80]

The solution is always the same: better human relations by the leaders of society. This is true whether it is a restaurant [81] or an industrial plant or a warship.[82] The heroes of *Pattern for Industrial Peace* were a union leader and a manager who learned to get along together. Homans, in his study of wildcat strikes, spoke of the need for skilled foremen and shop stewards who could "make the men a clan." [83] He found one man, "K," who kept his men from striking on Christmas Eve in 1943 by good communications and appealing to the solidarity of the informal work group: [84]

It was evident that in K's department the accepted members, largely old-timers and supervisors, held together. Cooperatively these people maintained their integrity against what they felt to be the troublemakers of the department. There was no great split based on worker-management distinction; rather the distinction was between insiders and outsiders, conformers and nonconformers . . . our industrial society is held together by thousands of men like K.

The new leader guides the workers from individual isolation and group conflict back to the womb of group solidarity.

The orientation continues to be toward the problems of management: harmony and efficiency. While Whyte does bring in the union, it is less as a new social force in society than as a hand-maiden of management. Notwithstanding the claim that much has changed since Mayo's pioneering research, the changes have been remarkably slight. The focus is on the same range of problems, the solutions are now as they were then, the methodology is not significantly different.

The Essential Choices

The Mayo system flows automatically from two crucial decisions. Once these decisions were made, the methods, the area of focus, the prescriptions for behavior, the selection of problems to be investigated were all given. These decisions contain within them the totality of the ideology and methodology of the human relations school. If they are accepted, one can only quibble about the detail; if they are rejected, then the detail becomes too unimportant to quibble about. Consequently it is important to see what these decisions were, why they were made and the results which depended upon them.

The Plant as Society.   The isolated individual is lost. He is not truly free and can never be happy. Only in social life does the individual find satisfaction. This social life cannot be afforded by the State, for it is too impersonal and far removed. It can only be contributed by the relatively small group. Now there are many small groups which possibly could develop an intimate social life but most of them are eliminated because they do not meet an additional qualification. The limiting requirement is that the group must be a work group; for man in addition to being a social animal is pre-eminently occupied with work.

Thus are rejected both individualism and socialism in general, and the church, the community, the fraternal lodge, and other associations in particular. The plant or the work shop is the decisive unit for human activity. It is Society; and if there is to be a Good Society, it must be found within the plant.

The Plant as the Good Society.   Men like security. They dislike change. They need a strong group around them which will have customs which they can follow and goals to which they can contribute. Such a group needs a leader or leaders. Above all else the group must be stable and give its members a sense of security. To this end the members should know their position in the status hierarchy; there must be an effective system of communications so leaders and led may understand each other and become properly adjusted. The leaders should be "natural" leaders but they must also be skilled; there should be free lines of communication; and the led should consent to the leadership.[85]

It is sometimes said that good human relations aid efficiency as well as stability, but efficiency is not the real purpose, for our society is being destroyed by disorganization and not by inefficiency or a low standard of living. If the "logic of efficiency" and the "logic of sentiments" are in conflict, it is obviously the second which must be preferred, although good human relations may mitigate any such conflict.

This stability in plant life is not only desirable but possible. There is no basic conflict between the managers and the managed. There can only be misunderstanding. The managed like to be managed and get their satisfaction from being well-managed—liberty is proportional to loyalty.

Human Relations in Industry. If the Plant is Society and if stable and secure plant life is the Good Society, then several things fall into place as a matter of course:

1. The plant manager is the key person in our society. He is the proper source of authority and the proper object of loyalty. However, the plant manager, when conceived as entrepreneur, is also the key individual for the liberal economist. In his economic function he is charged with combining scarce resources efficiently to satisfy the desires of consumers. For this he needs authority but not loyalty. If he is unskilled, the standard of living is lowered, and thus to encourage him to be skilled markets are kept as competitive as possible.

The Mayo-ite view is quite different. The manager is combining men to save society by making them into the modern counterpart of the tribe, or clan, or guild. If he is unskilled, measures of efficiency will have little meaning, for the survival of society itself rides on the manager's skill. It is human relations training, rather than competition, which will avoid the debacle. The worker's primary contribution is his loyalty, and only secondary are his production skills.

"The manager is neither managing men nor managing work . . . he is administering a social system." [86] Since the manager has the all-important task of developing a satisfying social life, those who help him are to be praised and those who deter him are to be castigated. Thus unions which aid management carry out its functions are supported and those which fight management are condemned.

2. The external environment is either inconsequential or subversive. The internal life of the plant is of such overwhelming importance that almost everything that goes on outside it can be ignored, whether one is studying wildcat strikes in Detroit or a manufacturing plant in Chicago. Even if all the important problems do not arise in the plant, they are at least settled there. The environment is important as it creates problems to which the plant must adjust, but it is the process and nature of this adjustment which is significant rather than the originating factors.

The external environment, however, can be disturbing. The union or the church or political parties or ethnic groupings may pull the interests of workers outside the plant or cause conflicts within it, and consequently it is desirable for the plant environment to be as comprehensive as may be necessary in order that it may be exclusive and self contained.

On such a view of society it is possible for the plant sociologists to ignore questions of class, of ideology, of power. From this view of society flow the characteristic methods of study—the examination, day by day, of face to face contacts in the plant.

3. The operational proposals of the human relations school are directed at increasing the social skills of the plant manager, who must have the insights identified with "human relations" and come to realize the significance of his role in society. Basically he should develop good face to face relations with his employees. He should embrace the workers into his family. Specifically he should encourage participation in decision making, a smoothly running flow of communications, a satisfying status system, a harmonious functioning of work teams, a counselling service which will help employees themselves settle the grievances they do not know they have, and an undisturbing method of introducing changes.

Moreover, the plant should become the focus of as many of the worker's interests as possible. It should substitute "welfare capitalism" for the "welfare state." It should care for the security, the health, the welfare, the recreation and even the psychological problems of the employees. If all this is done well, "the Rights of man can be made just as safe in corporate hands as they were in individual hands." [87]

Caveat Emptor

The Value System. The chosen world of the plant sociologists is peopled by non-rational workers who desire security under the leadership of skilled plant managers. The workers have a strong sense of group interest, welcome control, and feel loyalty toward their leaders. The society is a relatively static one. The workers are manipulated for their own welfare by a benevolent leader. This is a fairly accurate description of traditional societies which flourished before the industrial revolution. The aim is not to preserve the status quo but rather to create a status quo which this time can maintain itself. The great triumphs of the liberal era—individualism, liberty, competition—are viewed as the great disasters which will result in social disorganization. The great apologists of liberalism—such as Ricardo—are reviled.

The liberal economists have an almost opposite view of heaven on earth. Man is a reasoning being and is primarily motivated by a desire to maximize his individual welfare. Competitive markets are used to spur on managers to greater efficiency. Reliance is primarily placed on regulated self interest, and freedom of choice as consumers, workers, and voters is considered essential. By the nature of things, loyalties are divided—to self, to family, to state, to employer, to union—and in this division is seen the guarantee of freedom. The society is a progressive one. Instead of the visible hand of the elite, the invisible hand of the market assures the achievement of group welfare. Organizations, particularly economic organizations, are viewed with considerable suspicion. This is the open society to which the Western World has been dedicated for a century and a half. It is a society of accommodated conflict rather than universal collaboration. It is the world of Adam Smith rather than that of Plato.

The Theoretical System. The human relations school offers two theories—one a theory of societal development and the second a theory of group behavior. The first states that modern industrial society tends toward disorganization owing to the isolation of individuals (social disintegration) and the isolation of groups (social conflict), and that this can only be overcome by making industry "a socially satisfying way of life."

The second theory says simply that good group life results from good human relations and vice versa; and further that good human relations are always possible. The first half of this statement is good so far as it goes, but it does not go very far; and the second half is almost certainly not true.

It is probably a truism that good group life results from good human relations. It then becomes important to ask, not only what are good human relations, which the plant sociologist does, but also under what circumstances they are most likely to develop, and this he does not do. Environmental influences are largely ignored. The theory of plant behavior employed does not require this oversight since their analytical system (activity, interaction, sentiments) admits of the introduction of the environment through the notion of "activity" as a basic conditioning factor. Much of the surrounding environment—the nature of the job, the size of the group, the fluctuations in group size and membership, the location of the enterprise, etc.—could enter the system by this channel.

In the *Pattern for Industrial Peace,* as we have seen, Whyte detailed over a decade of industrial relations history with almost no reference to external factors. This was possible, in part, because of the very nature of the environment within which the plant operated. The Inland Steel Company and the United Steelworkers of America removed one of the most outward looking issues from discussion at the plant level—the settlement of wages. There was full employment and profits were good. If, for example, the company had been a marginal one, or there had been a period of mass unemployment, or the union Communist-dominated, or the work casual, it would not have been possible so to ignore developments outside the plant society. Or if the case had been one of a break-down in union-management relationships, then, presumably, the external environment would have been the source of the deterioration.

There are some environments where good industrial relations

are unlikely to develop—such as the coal and maritime industries—and others where they almost always emerge—such as pulp and paper and garment. It seems unlikely that leaders with social skills should always be absent in one set of industries and always present in another. Rather the environment must be the essential determinant. It is most doubtful that the contrast between the waterfront and garment district can be explained by so complete an attention to internal affairs as in the Inland Steel Container case. Which environments are more and which less conducive to good human relations and thus good industrial relations? This is a question to which the plant sociologist has not yet addressed himself; and it will be difficult for him to do so without altering his concentration on the plant as a largely self-contained society.

If he did, it would probably develop that there are types of industrial relations and not just stages. In discovering types of industrial relations, it would be found that some are not open to improvement by an increase in social skills but only by an alteration of the external environment. By adding important independent variables, the school would become more analytical and less descriptive.

The Program. Let us assume for the moment that the great problem of society is the one the Mayo-ites consider it to be, social disorganization, and that the best solution to it is the one they propose—the creation of an enveloping and satisfying plant life. Now ask whether the proposed solution is adequate to the stated problems. There are at least three unanswered questions: (1) How can managers be forced to develop good human relations if exhortation is not enough? The liberal economy relies on the whip of market competition to force managers to perform their assigned tasks adequately. What enforcement machinery is there within the plant? Might the workers be allowed to vote out of office managers who did not develop a satisfactory plant life, or should the unions strike, or should government step in, or is there no method of enforcement?

(2) What should be done about the farmers, the unemployed, the self-employed, the aged—in fact, the bulk of the population—if a work community cannot provide a socially satisfying way of life for them? Can any other acceptable institution provide them with a socially *satisfying* way of life? (3) What of the groups which

may conflict with management? What "central control" [88] should be exercised over combative organizations so that they may be made to contribute to "the life of organized society"? [89] If the unions insist on "disorder and resistance," what should be done about them?

Conclusion

No research in the social sciences can be free of value assumptions, and the claim that is sometimes made that the social sciences must eschew values if they are ever to rise above the level of ethical exhortation is always naive.[90] It is seldom a difficult task to discover the implicit values held in a theoretical system. Even when an antipathy to value premises is carried to the lengths of denying theory any explanatory role, the problems selected by the empiricist as worth worrying about carry a core of value judgment within them. Even if this were not demonstrable there would remain, as ultimate and unprovable, the faith in the value of empirical research itself, variously called science or truth by empiricists.

It is not, therefore, a meaningful charge that Mayo and his followers are moralists. So are economists. What is more disturbing in economist and plant sociologist alike is the effort to disguise these moral judgments as truths objectively deduced from observation or research and the prescriptions which follow as the inevitable consequences of a neutral set of facts. For Mayo and Whitehead these prescriptions are deducible from the true nature of man and the true nature of society, and the research of Mayo and his followers only counterfeit a pervasive eleaticism. Empiricism becomes a series of case studies revealing the "essential" organization and structure of small work groups as small scale analogies to society.

That these studies are only analogies rather than representative situations might be conceded by those who have made them. For the argument runs not so much that these plant societies are true samples of the universe of industrial environments but rather that the universe of industrial environments could become like the case histories, given a skillful managerial elite in charge. The case for the prescription of the plant sociologist is not, therefore, that the facts compel the prescription but rather that the vision of the plant sociologist is not impossible of achievement if we want it badly enough. The charge against those who do not share the vision cannot be, therefore, that they are blind to facts but rather that they are of the wrong religion and worship false gods.

There is a modest area in which the plant sociologist has had a contribution to make but this has not been in the domain of social policy. Divorced of its medieval vision, the school has advanced the diagnosis of certain not unimportant plant problems such as absenteeism, turnover, and increased worker efficiency. Happily this is also the area of its greatest influence, since the findings have humanitarian implications and ought not to be made unusable by exacting as a price for their employment the remaking of society in a corporate image.

Certainly the lot of modern man is not an altogether happy one. He is doubtless lonely, of divided loyalty and often discontented. But loneliness may be the cost of the struggle toward rational self development; divided loyalties the surest guarantee against totalitarianism; and discontent the price of progress itself.

Conrad M. Arensberg
and
Geoffrey Tootell

PLANT SOCIOLOGY:
REAL DISCOVERIES AND NEW PROBLEMS

Another article of this volume presents modern studies of the world of work made by followers of the behavioral sciences in the light of economists' concern with public policy and the nature of man. It may be of interest, therefore, to present the same studies in another light. Let us grant that like Eddington, who turned from physics, about which he knew a great deal, to God, about whom he knew no more than you or I, some industrial sociologists have let themselves go in sweeping introductions or final paragraphs. Let us grant that some of them have unguardedly, like other human beings, betrayed their identifications with the political trends and cultural climates of their times. One might wish that economists, a little calmer about defending a former monopoly of the description of men at work in our civilization, might have displayed enough intellectual sophistication to distinguish between *obiter dicta* and empirical generalizations.

Granting all these things, let us turn from lofty debate about the nature of man and public policy and instead see what humbler describers of behavior in workroom and factory and union have thought they have learned. Students of behavior have been willing to dirty themselves by looking hard and long at these grubby things so far from the tidy bookshelves of theory and statistics.

Most behavioral scientists are busy with their tasks of observation and interpretation. Theirs is the problem of learning about the processes at work in a concrete human situation like a workroom torn with distrust over a sour incentive scheme, or a factory swinging from industrial strife to release of workers' initiative through a viable union grievance procedure. They make a workaday distinction between their task, exacting enough in itself, and the grand defense of economic theory, of the Manchester tradition or of values of individualism and freedom which they inherited in the West just as much as have the more vocal of the economists.

In point of fact, of course, industrial research in the behavioral sciences is merely the body of fairly systematic observation that has accumulated out of Western Man's long-term naturalist concern with his post-Industrial Revolution "problems of labor unrest." There are, of course, real troubles in the industrial apparatus of our civilization, in the connections between Man and The Machine apart from the effects of industrialization upon society as a whole.[1] If that body of observation about the human failings of machine industry yields something new or useful, it is not to the grand policy makers. It is rather to ordinary working citizens suffering through jobs or choosing work, union officials, engineers, pastors, doctors, wives, and even (oh, shameful admission!) industrial managers and personnel men. If the body of observation contributes to theory and values, it is less likely to be to the Grand Ethical Management of Human Society than to more modest and piecemeal theories of group process, emotional adjustment, motivation and performance, good and bad organization. Such piecemeal contributions might as often illuminate sociology, anthropology, psychology, whence some of the researchers came, as economics or politics. Nevertheless, since even the Grand Economic Theorist and the Liberal Philosopher may eventually want to ground his theories in the facts of experience, it may be that the economist, sparing a moment for the narrow world of Production Shop no. 465 from his usual contemplation of the Laws of Supply and Demand and of World Policy, can find something of fleeting interest.

Robert Merton [2] has pointed out that social science is in need of partial generalizations, based on studies already achieved, rather than of further scheme-building. The need today is not so much for concepts aiming at a wholesale reconciliation of existing theories of man, society, and human interaction as for what he aptly calls "theories of the middle range." Such theories serve to unite single cases and gross observations into meaningful summary and comparative hypotheses.

Industrial sociology, in studying plants and their problems, has begun to fashion a few of these. Rather than deal with all of them, let us examine four main lines of development within industrial sociology. If we do not choose more than four main lines it is because, after all, our purpose is exemplary and our space limited.

The Mayoite Middle Range Theories

The Mayoites, Mayo himself, Roethlisberger and Dixon, Lombard, Scott and others of the Harvard Business School group of institutional inheritors of Mayo's mantle, have been amply discussed. We can treat them here first because their eponym came first, historically, among the lines of development we shall cite. They retain the distinction of having demonstrated again and again the crucial role of teamwork in the creation of work morale and in the productivity of workers. They show that morale and output depend, not on individual incentives alone or directly, but upon the "informal organization" of interpersonal relationships and small-group sentiments within the immediate working force (fellow workers and immediate supervisors both). We need not review here the continually mounting evidence of their carefully studied cases. Nor need we dignify with an answer the recurrent criticisms that such a discovery of the role of informal organization in altering behavior (discoverable and documented as well for prisons, armies, churches, cities, etc., etc.) glorifies a medieval past or surrenders free workers in chains to morale-building managers. Such debate is better addressed to individuals in their human rather than their scientific capacities. In fact, it is just possible that some people may like rural parishes better than urban barracks and that some managers might want, for their organizations, to use knowledge of human beings just as they might want to use knowledge of good materials. Rather the point for us is: how good is the discovery for further growth of understanding of work, men, and groups? The discovery merits discussion on the level of social science, where it was made.

On that level, Roethlisberger, Lombard, and associates treat work groups as "situations." They aim at finding skills for use against misunderstanding and conflict.[3] They use a "clinical approach" to the real-life practice of responsible persons and expect science to develop, here as elsewhere, from such materials. They have found it useful to treat their work groups as complex ongoing processes of human relationship in which the participants' dominant assumptions (*not* those of the observers, note), their overt behavior toward one another, their sentiments, and their judgment of these things in one another all figure. A work group, they find, moves *away* from misunderstandings and conflict under certain conditions. It moves so *both toward* managerially set or otherwise "common" goals and *toward* wider personal satisfactions. Its officers, from manager to foreman, function *thus* the better, when those officers, abandoning many logico-secular assumptions (e.g., that work gets done through forceful authority and clear logic of communications, or that people accept emotionally what they are told logically, or that individual hedonism is their chief motivation, etc., etc.), deal with their organizations as the emergent "social systems" which they are.

The Mayoites continue to find it useful to deal with work groups, including large factories, as such social systems. They have learned that these must be understood *in addition to* their rationalist formal-institutional elements for their non-logical (symbolic, sentimental, not *il*logical) informal organization, their rites and accumulated customs and interpersonal adaptations. They have thus learned from experience that paper-based, rationalist authority, acting in ignorance or violence of these things, is both humanly and organizationally less effective than a supervision which encourages informal solidarity, free communication and initiative from below, stability of identification beyond (*not* in place of) self-enhancement and recognition of status (as well as monetary reward).

One can, of course, ask the dark question whether these discoveries are a mere humanization of a once savage industrial discipline. Some critics hold these findings to be simply a shift of managerial advantage. Under quasi-monopoly conditions of bigness, modern management may find it pays to move from competition by price and volume to competition through friendly work forces and appeased unions. But, even then, these discoveries raise interesting behavioral-science issues.

For one, the conclusion that work groups, from shops to multi-plant companies and companies-cum-unions, are social systems needs re-examination. Elsewhere a social system implies or is accompanied by a cultural system. Elsewhere a social system is usually encrusted with a body of custom and belief, in which common goals, common views, norms, values (the rationalist economist, surer about these things, thinks he need only reckon with "interests") find embodiment in sentiment-supported moral sanctions. Yet it is clear even from the internal evidence of the Mayoites that such a body of common custom, a cultural system, does not exist. The shop may have its customs, but the office has others. Workers and managers share very few if any common goals. The informal organization which exists is paralleled by a policed enforcement of the rationalist disciplines. Certainly neither workers nor even white-collar ranks (foremen, engineers, accountants) are in agreement about goals with management.

The goals of good pay and high profit are not the same; "security" and "success" may be opposite motives instead. What culture exists in common comes from outside the shop, from the community as a whole. It represents agreement only on means, at the most. Many of the particular findings and recommendations of the Mayoites, indeed, address themselves to coping with such divergences of goal, assumption, and value. These aim at a viable *modus vivendi* among them, that is, at a mutual and realistic recognition of diversity rather than at a forging of common agreement.

In this sense the "social system" the managers are to cope with is less a cultural or emotional unit, like a tribe or a church, than a political one. Far from making the managers patriarchs of a tribal unity, the Mayoites ask the managers to abandon their beliefs that workers must agree (except on means) with managers. To tell managers, as the Mayoites do, that efficiency is not the greatest good in their factories, nor individual incentive the most effective, to get managers to countenance team loyalties that skirt "restricting output," or to persuade them to work toward "cooperative industrial relations" with unions who enforce production decisions on grounds of protection and seniority rather than efficiency and low cost, is to push them *away* from doctrinal social unity *toward* political wisdom and constitutional monarchy. It is by no means to make them priests of a common cult, mesmerizing workers into accepting the values of a "community." The new managers are at best practical politicians compromising with what their fellows must still feel is evil.

Thus it is doubtful, even from internal evidence, that factories as social systems are cultural units. It seems more useful to treat them, as more and more industrial-sociological writing does, as political equilibria where clashing "interests" find temporary resolutions.[4]

For social science, then, more work is needed on the nature of the "system" which individual work groups make up. What is the process by which agreement on limits arises but divergent interests remain? What is the connection between cultural values (property rights, morals, ideals of fairness, concern for "law and order," etc.) from outside and motivations from within the work group and the supervisor-employee relationships? How far can a shift of supervisory practices influence group spirit and individual morale; and these in turn determine change in productive output? [5] Under what conditions do personal goals and organizational ones bolster one another or tear an organization asunder? These indeed are the questions which the early Mayoite "teamwork" theories raised, for good or ill, and the ones to which some at least of the subsequent work of industrial sociology has given us better-based answers than those of former speculation. If they are not answers to Grand Questions of Public Policy, they are at least useful additions to workaday knowledge.

Beyond Teamwork to Processual Analysis

That some sort of organizational process is at work in occasions of industrial "teamwork," "increased morale," and productivity seems to be established. The many reanalyses of the original Hawthorne Plant Relay Assembly Test Room as well as subsequent work on other industrial workrooms and on such non-industrial performing groups as airship crews concur on the point. What has emerged from the reanalysis is less a decisive weighing of the role of any factor, like "good supervision," or take-home pay, or an efficient grievance machinery, than the outline of an unfolding process with laws of growth of its own, in which factors appear not only in great or small degree but also in a necessary order of occurrence.[6]

As we shall see, it was the later "interactionists," Whyte, Chapple, Homans, Arensberg, not the Mayoites of pure descent, who discovered this process and have gone on to study it. But their discovery had to rest upon the Mayoite teamwork hypothesis and the cases supporting it. The Mayoites worked with doctrines of "equilibrium," social and personal, already discussed (though only for their societal implications, not for their relevance to in-plant data) by the economists in this volume.

But the Mayoites seem to have misread their own data. Reanalysis shows their "teamwork" and "informal organization" are less multi-factorial results, or even steady states, than emergent results of prior and continuous managerial and flow-of-work changes. The process took the form of this definite order of developments: (1) an increase of managerial initiative, (2) followed by an increase of inter-worker communication, (3) followed by an increase of re-dressive up-the-line action of the workers upon foremen or spokes-men, (4) which resulted in further changes of rewarding sort in managerial action, (5) changing individual attitudes, (6) reaching expression as new group attitudes or morale ("the norms" of Homans), (7) which won informal sanction by the workers on one another, (8) and stimulated further releases of individual output productivity. To check this order, one had only to note carefully that each and every departure from it (in other cases) brought a different processual end-result, as for example, where at point 4 a blockage rather than a carry-through of redressive new managerial action occurred, a devolution toward walk-out or strike brought a different processual result.

It is worthwhile reiterating the discovery of the "interactionists" that this process, and the gain in productivity it brings about, seems to have very delicate and narrow limits. The Mayoites were content, and are still, to leave the cultivation of the process of building teamwork an art. But other workers have dared to look at it closer. In Whyte's "Bundy Tubing Case," [7] one of the few well-documented stories of the real workings of an incentive scheme, incentive failed as soon as management's own enthusiasm with the scheme prompted management to take initiative for setting performance goals out of workers' hands. Indeed, present evidence suggests that the release of productivity is not so much limited by human capacity or by "diminishing returns" of maximization, as older efficiency doctrines have it, as it is dependent upon some "feedback" between worker initiative and managerial facilitation. A next advance in our understanding will come when we work out the empirical characteristics of this process.

Such a finding about process and its effects on individual behavior is subject matter of much experiment and speculation in social psychology today.[8] For many students of the matter, both hedonist-rationalist economic theorists and grubbier natural science observers, the limits to which any one individual participates in such a process like "teamwork" is another point of inquiry.[9]

Here the Mayoites are admittedly only indirectly informative. They have been criticized for not noting that their own data showed workers to have been sensitive to informal-group pressures only within well-defined personal limits of background custom and private interest. But such critics have been too eager, like our fellow authors, Kerr and Fisher. They reëcho twenty-year-old blasts against Mayoite failure to bring in the outer world, or the societal and institutional matrix, or the swings of the employment cycle, as if experimenters were not entitled to isolate a field of close observation and, furthermore, in ignorance of the record. Roethlisberger, like Mayo, had been after all a practicing clinical psychologist. In "Management and the Worker," [10] in discussing the famous boy W7 whose work output fluctuated with his sex life, and in speculating why the Mica Splitting Room did not develop the teamwork of the Relay Assembly Test Room, he treated us to a careful juxtaposition of "personal" and "social" equilibria, a formulation which did much to stimulate Chapple's [11] later more precise work on the interconnections of these states. It accords so well with continuing psychiatric understanding in mental hygiene of the connections between personal and work "problems" that it is a pity more is not done.

As for the role of common cultural (and institutional) backgrounds in setting limits within which teamwork operates, that is, after all, the burden of the work of Collins, Roy, etc., on the "rate-buster," which we will discuss a little further along. It is little wonder that our Manchester-school Grand Economic Theorists do not recognize this work for what it is. Caught as they are within economics in a debate between Classical Economic Doctrine and Marxism, between profit motive and exploitative class power as the only possible dynamic forces of human affairs, steadfastly turning their backs on institutional explanations even in their own economic field, they cannot see the extent to which social science is documenting proof that American workers of the twentieth century follow in practice neither the doctrines of rational maximalization of individual gain nor the calculus of class power advantage.

For these workers, certainly, other motives prevail. That is not to say that twentieth century American workers do not know the rationale of maximizing gains and class interest. It means rather that only the "ratebuster" conforms to the ideal of the "economic man." The ratebuster, rugged individualist that he is, is a lonely figure. Neither his fellow workers nor his managers seem comfortable with him. In fact, in America today, his ideological brothers seem to be found oftener in university departments of economics than in factories.

The kernel of the Mayoite discovery stands confirmed. We can remind the economists that the older counterpoint between large-scale economic forces and the individual motives is no longer adequate. The social factors in the factory can no longer be overlooked. Whether the classical economists or the Marxists like it or not, real people structure their responses to stimulation (here managerial incentive or "driving") in situational (social) reaction to one another. There are discoverable processes by which this structuring occurs.

The efficacy of teamwork for productivity stands. But it operates within the limits and in response to other situational changes of workroom and factory. Teamwork comes not from managerial good will but from changes in managerial action. What the Mayoites saw as a simple correlation we now see as a complex process whose laws are still to be worked out.

What remains to be discovered about the process of group "facilitation" of achievement is, unfortunately, still nearly everything. Naturally industrial sociology's (or applied anthropology's, since some people prefer that phrasing) contribution from observation of work relationships will feed into other studies in social psychology, sociology, organization theory, and labor economics, and will be further sharpened by cross-cultural and international comparisons. But studies of work groups even today can help with these major questions: (1) What degree of fusion or amalgamation must come to exist in this process, what degree of convergence must there develop between the goals (values) of the led (here the workers), and the goals of those planning and commanding? (2) What leadership starts this convergence growing? (3) How is this process affected by values held by the manager and the management? (4) Once it starts, what is the action that keeps it growing: what are the laws of its unfolding and the laws of its destruction?

1. THE PROBLEM OF FUSION OF GOALS

Little organized empirical work in industrial sociology seems to be addressed today explicitly to the first question. Yet we have raised it theoretically ourselves in asking in what way a "social system" also includes a cultural system, and rests on "common norms."

Wight Bakke, of Yale, has formulated a theoretical model for a "fusion" of such individual goals, the conditions of its emergence, and its necessary connections with ongoing organization.[12] His formulation is like that of much of organization theory, which is stronger on the need of organizations to condition members to acceptance of organizational goals than it is on the necessity of an organization's reflecting in some way the "consent of the governed."[13] Organization theory today is well aware that some mutual accommodation of organization and individual values is indispensable, but it has little as yet to say about the process by which such accommodation develops. Nor do its theoretical explanations get much beyond the far too simple polarity of organization and individual, group and person, as if groups had neither internal structure nor organizations any complex unit-combining institutional politics.

It is of more interest, therefore, to turn to the formal sociological speculation about the process by which interaction systems among human beings acquire common norms and come to share the "culture" of common goals. Here we are indebted to Parsons, Merton, and Homans.[14]

Following them one might view the complete coincidence of

a social and a cultural system as an end state toward which the process of productivity release, once triggered off, might tend. In such a system, relationships among members should be highly stylized ("structured"). Behaviors in these should be faithfully reciprocal with high correlation between stimulus and response in the one party and the other. To protect this agreement and insure against divergences, there should be strong "role segmentation." That is, members' roles inside and outside the organization should be kept firmly apart so that nothing outside affects their behavior within their group.

But such socio-economic cultural systems with norms well-integrated and universally shared are empirical rarities. If the Mayoite workrooms had been real examples of "socio-cultural systems," there should have been in the teamwork cases a large amount of enduring agreement about solutions to problems. There should have been values common to both management and workers deeper than mere agreement upon limits or "rules of the game." But even the workgroup of the Mayoite literature showing the most perfect correlation of teamspirit and high productivity, the famous five girls of the Bank Wiring Room of the Hawthorne Plant, reached such a state of goals presumably shared with management only after long evolution of their group's existence and acceptance (both by themselves and by management). Even they lost it quickly as soon as it became apparent that management's goals included possibly laying them off in the coming depression.

But if such socio-cultural systems are rare, enough evidence of them exists in the record of beleaguered armies, martyred sects, isolated kingdoms, and dedicated bands. The yield of human self-sacrifice, effort, and emotional exaltation they give is so immense that man has never given up his search for the alchemy that may produce them. The danger is that the newer social science, on the track of that alchemy, be perverted before we learn its laws, its dangers, its appalling costs. Some masters of organizations have always tried to force men into a yield of such devotion, for their own ends. They tried to dictate coincidence of value and role long before business sought to "manipulate" and indoctrinate its employees, and long before Big Brother thought to impose the world of 1984. The message of social science, whether in Mayoite workrooms, or tyrannies, is a simple one; the "fusion" process may perhaps someday be cultivated according to the laws of its own growth. It cannot be forced.

If "fusion" is an end-result of process, and trend to it is a matter of degree, what is the reverse process? What is the downward trend through organizational coercion to a group's dissolution in strife, or in revolt of its members? Here again we have precious few empirical studies, though, as we shall see, industrial sociologists are now documenting industrial strife, the causes of tensions and strikes, and the internal (not the external) dynamics of good and ill "industrial peace." They are trying to document the theorist's perception that an organization, even where culture and social system are coincident, can degenerate into discordant behaviors producing "dysfunctional" [15] norms and cumulative conflict. When, then, does absence of shared values alter relationships, and lack of agreement make for breakdown? When does "role segmentation" become so incomplete, and when do outside interests intrude so far, that forces outside the organization alone move the members, and their group either splits or loses its autonomy? All this is still to be learned and the dynamics of the processes are still to be worked out. The critics' fears about perversion of the knowledge seem a little premature.

Let us now consider the connection between this "fusion" of goals appearing when social and cultural systems coincide and modern social-psychological treatment of "communication." The common possession of values by members of a group is today often treated as if it more simply were the result of "communicating" or even propagandizing such values from some members of the group to others. This is not so, since the acquisition or loss of common values is a much more complex process. Nevertheless, the concept of communication is useful in studies of organization. If it is through communication that any interaction (social) system is built up, then the longer and the smoother, the more satisfying and the less blocking and frustrating the communication, the more common norms appear. "Two-way" communication, then, might afford the link between a social system and its possible eventual creation of common values. The question arises as to what interaction and communication leads to what norms, to what individual new behaviors and attitudes, to what new group behaviors and beliefs? [15a]

The contribution of the Mayoite empirical in-plant studies lies in the very separation of these things. They related analytically such action variables as concrete supervisory behavior, or informal job-swapping and "binging," to such measures of performance as output and bogie figures. They separated such attitudinal matters as the Relay Assembly Test Room girls' erroneous belief that lighting had been changed or a girl's expression, "we have no boss" from the changes in supervision and the achievement of common work rhythm in clique partner output. Without a separation of the evidence of what men do and what men say, without a clear separation of interpersonal and individual behavior (e.g., binging and output), without a firm grouping of kinds of behavioral events, no comparisons of group to group and process to process can be made. With their taking over from anthropology of observational methods, the Mayoites marked a clear advance in social science research and set the groundwork for correlating behavior and attitude. Without such separation of the data into clearcut workable categories, communication study falters. Without it there is no separating what is communicated from prior information nor general, "public," or formal messages from restricted, "private," and informal ones. Without it, too, there is no identifying who communicates and who receives, no establishing the directions in which communications flow. Again, as we shall see, it was not Mayoites who refined these discriminations and made discoveries with them, but it was the Mayoites who paved the way.

Now the sociologists already know something about the fate of communication in large-scale organizations and the process of devolution which perverts organization means to personal ends at variance with organization goals. They call this "bureaucratization." They know less about the other, upward trend. Their information deals with the reverse of the process of the social release of productivity.

Indeed a bureaucracy can develop, or better "devolve," some peculiar features of communication within its social system. Mayo, as we know, felt that in-plant informal groups offered some of the primary attachments lost, according to Durkheim and many others, in the growth of industrial cities. But he never compared the work group's effect with the manner in which a bureaucracy regenerates such attachments. Merton [16] has re-outlined the "dysfunctions" of bureaucracy: (1) inflexibility under changed conditions, (2) emphasis upon rigid conformity (since bureaucracy is effective as it is reliable, predictable, regular, faithful to statute and law), (3) buttressing of its members' performance by sentiments beyond technical need, (4) a trend whereby goals are likely to be displaced and means substituted for ends, (5) a resulting stereotyped impersonality, (6) a discrepancy between a member's place in the bureaucratic hierarchy and his position in the broader outside social system which is likely to give rise in him to "unjustly" domineering attitudes, and (7) lastly a conflict between the needs and norms of the organization, the bureau as a rational whole, and those of the clique groups that emerge out of an inevitable informal organization of the favorably situated long-term members. Beyond all this, of course, there is a "cultural system" produced, a set of mechanisms enforcing this developing conformity (point 2), like overweaning pride of craft and stuffy sanctification of the bureau's symbols. And the rich informal organization of cliques (point 7) comes to embody, guard, and enforce these, as strongly as in any Mayoite Bank Wiring Room.

Because Merton's work represents an initial descriptive attack on the problem of bureaucratization, he gives us all this only in static terms. Consequently we hear only a little of performance, except in the effect that conformity and inflexibility can have on the work and careers of bureaucrats. When such norms as we have just heard about develop, they guide the rising young man; he is also assured that merely by conforming he may one day attain an important post. So far so good. But what downward course might further devolution bring?

What of those for whom, for various reasons, there are no "promising" careers? What of those who, while formal members of the bureau, are isolates rather than members of its dominant informal groups? How can they learn the inner-core norms? If they cannot acquire them outside, by family or class, and they are not subject to the internal "fusion," what then? To begin with, we should guess such bureaucratic "culture"-building interaction to be greater within such dominant cliques than across clique lines. As more "bureaucratic" norms developed, so would the barriers between the cliques which act them out and those which did not. Only a periodic shake-up, a "reorganization," might revivify organizational goals or force a lowering of such barriers. If upward redress tempered such reorganizing drives for the informal core-groups, who might learn to "ride them out," or for other reasons barriers were not reduced, then we should expect cross-group contacts further to decline. Then shared values might well go forgotten, mutual disagreements and divergences of goals mount up. Communication would devolve into conflict and disruption.

The parallel with industrial exploitation, with interworker conflict and management-worker strife is too good to be missed.[17] It remains only to quantify and regularize the conditions and the steps of such processes.

2. PERMISSIVE LEADERS, PARTICIPATION, POST-LEWIN

Let us turn next to Kurt Lewin and his followers who have contributed to our knowledge of the role of leadership in social productivity-release. This contribution to plant sociology comes from those who think of themselves as psychologists. It is addressed to the problem: "What sort of leadership sets our process off?"

This is not the place for a comprehensive review of the "field theory" of Lewin.[18] Suffice it to say that Lewin occupies the position for the industrial social psychologists that Mayo occupies for the sociologists. Lewin, however, seems to have escaped so far the tender ministrations of the economists and Grand Policy Makers. Yet, *mutatis mutandis*, Lewin used a conceptual scheme of quite different language but much the same content, and he and his followers have sought out relationships among much the same variables in the work room. For "morale" they say "climate"; for "management," "leadership"; for "informal organization," "participation"; for "output," "performance"; for "social system," "group life"; etc. At many other points, however, they use a magnificently resounding if woefully imprecise jargon of psychologisms. Their great strength, of course, is the same as the Mayoites'. They have given us a small body of carefully documented experimental and observational cases of real change in real work rooms in real plants.

Combined with other work on leadership at Ohio State,[19] by Shartle and his group, at Carnegie Tech by Simon, Guetzkow and others,[20] and by Argyris at Yale,[21] this body of cases confirms the existing discoveries that the leadership which sets off our process is that which somehow combines coordination toward common goals with receptivity toward, even stimulation of, initiative from among the led. Following the original famous Iowa study of "autocratic," "democratic," and "laissez faire" leadership of a group of children executing a task under three styles of direction, the Lewinians have gone ahead to tie up high morale, fusion of goals, and performance with "democratic" and "people-minded" (rather than "production-minded") supervision.[22] And they connected these and other variables of workroom attitudes, like acceptance of change,[23] with increased employee participation in goal-setting created by "permissive leadership." [24]

The Lewinians are much to be congratulated that they have almost from the beginning seen these relationships as more than correlations, as a "group dynamics" (a term they claim an unjustified monopoly upon). They have the further merit of exploring the primacy of leadership (management) changes in the dynamism involved and in focussing attention upon the up-the-line inclusion through "participation" of the needs and values of the led. Their psychological orientation, while seemingly blinding them to the problems of quantifying action and limiting them to attitudinal scales, does make for a sharper concern with individual perception and understanding of the changes in the process. Thus Viteles is quite just when he summarizes their work as a discovery of a "feedback" of new information uniting personal and organizational goals in "group decision." "Participation," says Viteles about their viewpoint, "is an experience wherein attitudes favorable to change are taken on by the workers. The group-determined decision, according to Lewin, provides the link between motivation and action." [25] We can learn, thus, a good deal more about the need for contact, discussion, and growth of new understanding between the parties, leader and led, in our process, and see these things as part of the fusion of goals leading to immediate new results in performance. But we learn little more about the leadership action which permits such contact nor of the necessary contents of the communication it entails. Nor do we learn anything deeper about limits of the process and the connections of external and internal values. Only the note that somehow the "permissive" or "democratic" leader must "best fulfill the needs of the led" (Argyris on Gordon [26] reporting the Bethel experiences) suggests where an answer may lie.

All this must alarm our economist critics of plant sociology. Not only empirical sociology but empirical psychology is flirting with knowledge which someone might pervert to "manipulating" man for his own ends! Too bad that the heirs to 18th and 19th century Liberal Rationalism should fear, like the Marxists, the very Science their spiritual ancestors gave rise to! What irony it may well be when we finally learn, with empirical proofs rather than moral homilies, that the best way to manipulate man to organized goals is the very representative democracy these economists think they are defending!

The nature of the "democratic" leadership, then, which triggers our process off, like the limits of the process itself, is still very little known. Despite the Lewinians, we know little, in action terms, about what to do when, or about what leaders' acts bring what responses with what chain of further consequences. Nor is there much promise in the work of social psychologists in general. Until they turn from exclusive concern with broad statistical variables and correlations, as in the survey techniques, and record personal acts instead of broad and ill-defined "variables" like "supervision" or "participation," they will take us little beyond broad correlations. Until they correlate action of known persons with consequent actions of others, until they relate attitude changes with progressions of interpersonal action and thus bring their psychological terms down to operational definition in the concrete, they will go on merely documenting what we already know: the historically and experientially obvious. They must learn with the other social and psychological disciplines (sociometry, institutional sociology, social anthropology, animal sociology, reinforcement theory) how to connect behavior and attitude through time and one person's doings with another's. Only then will we learn what it is to "lead democratically" and what it really is to "participate."

Take for example the matter of the leader, the successful "permissive manager" of a human organization. Is he a doormat? Or a martinet? If neither, as this work proves again, when, how, on what issues does he dictate, initiate, stand firm, help or refuse help to a subordinate, redress or refuse redress to a complainant, encourage ideas not his own, or judge them down? What is the balance in time of compromise and strength, of alert receptivity and personal sway? To label leadership after the fact "democratic"

which avoids one extreme or another is only a little better than
to say with the Mayoites that a successful leader "diagnoses right"
and has the needful "social skills." Nor is it any help to take note
with Weber and students of fascism that some leaders sometimes
have a charm, a *charisma*, that carries them through the most oafish
blunders and the most blind arrogance *for a time*. These excellent
perceptions must next be turned into common comparative measures
and must be checked, watched, and generalized by all the scientific
observers.

No, the Lewinians are no help here, good as their work is. Even
in their own cases their leadership techniques are not made explicit.
At Harwood Mfg. Co.[27] we are told that the observational groups
led by Bavelas showed the most marked recovery of production
after a machine change, while French's did less well until a year
later when French had gained more experience in leadership. It
would be interesting to know these fateful differences of leadership.
What precisely is the process by which workers are made to commit
themselves to the programmatic goals (here management's)? How's
that done? The Lewinians imply the group as a whole swings over.
Are there no dissenters, no exercisers of *liberum veto*, no majority
and no minority reservations? Presumably the manager (leader)
must use only what influence he can get away with, within the
norms upon which they, the workers, agree. Presumably he must
leave them to convert or control one another to decision. To get
them to include his goal (more productivity) among theirs (pay-
check, pride, or assurance of security) he must trade off his acceptance of their goals for his. The Lewinian findings change nothing;
they merely document further the leader's part of our process and
leave its other details as dark as ever.

The extent to which the norms of the work group carry over
into other spheres of life is another matter which should receive
further study. Our Liberal Economists fear that a more humane
work discipline might destroy free citizenry or end the class
struggle outside. And yet at Harwood, not much time after the
successful cultivation of "group life," the workers went out on
strike over a unionization drive.

How did the experimental groups behave? Like all the others.
Word of mouth reports showed all groups to have been equally
pro-union. Perhaps the participation in the experimental rooms was

ended "too soon." Possibly the values and interests from the working-class subculture were too deeply imbedded for any such process to replace them.

Once again we learn that in-plant sociology works within the limits of institutional and organization relationships. There need be no fear that a fusion of goals in a workroom pushes Man to a fusion of goals outside. Plant sociology teaches about Man and Industrial plants, not about Man and Society. The connections between experience in one institution and that in another are matters for objective study of societal functional integration. They are not matters for hasty speculative extrapolation.

A good parallel exists in current studies of race relations. After the war, we have found that brotherly attitudes toward racial minorities won in common combat dangers did not long survive the return to normal, prejudiced communities.

3. CLASS VALUES AND MOTIVES FOR WORK

Let us turn, now, to another line of development in plant sociology. This line gives some answers to our third major question. We asked about the process of social productivity release: within what values of the parties, manager and managed, can it grow?

The third line of development connects plant behavior and attitudes with class differences. Two things may be said right off about those who have used class as a factor in industrial sociology: their reports have had the great verisimilitude of first-hand observation and first-hand interview; these men have talked *with*, not merely *about*, modern workers. Yet they have used the class factor only to treat difficulties rather than strengths in modern industrial society. They have attended to the old "problems of labor unrest" rather than labor's general compliance in industrial discipline. The divergence of point of view immediately separates them from the economists.

Thus Collins, Dalton, and Roy have treated the ratebuster and restriction of output by relating them to different class, ethnic, and religious values.[28] Warner and Low based their Yankee City strike on changes in class and community relationships.[29] Allison Davis has probed the motives of lower-class urban workers and the norms of their class "subculture." He noted the lack of fit between these norms and the rewards offered by institutions.

This line of development has something to tell the economic critics of industrial sociology. Both on theoretical and empirical grounds the data challenge easy assumptions that values of market-capitalism, either embodied in classical economic doctrines or (after Weber) consecrated in older Puritanism, are more than the particular and dominant norms of particular institutions or dominant classes. They suggest that the struggle to win other institutions and other classes to conformity with these norms is ever-repeated. The best that we can hope for, perhaps, is not to theorize away the non-conformant values, nor to mould every one alike to the conformant ones, but to cultivate intelligent conciliation, accommodation, and balance.

To get a more detailed look at work in which class differences have figured, let us cite the work of Allison Davis as a background to the factory situation. In the United States there are many aggregates of persons (sects, ethnic groups, etc.) who approach to greater or lesser degree the theoretical state of a pure social system, a closed group with its own norms. But the isolation of perfect closure is a rarity for any of our population aggregates. Two such imperfectly closed groups are the middle and lower "classes" of our urban, industrial, metropolitan regions, white collars and black collars of the East and Middle West.[30]

Davis is one of many persons documenting such differences in the social and cultural life of middle and lower classes.[31] Where other persons find them in sex, courtship, recreation, consumption, saving, he finds them in their work behavior. Pride in self-sufficiency, "self-reliance," taught in middle class childhood, seems to be replaced by obligations of emergency generosity. Belief in getting ahead is replaced with belief in "the breaks"; competitive best effort with giving a fair stint; compulsive regularity of punctuality and effort with spasmodic effort and bouts of enjoyment; anger suppression before authority with aggressive revolt. He thus leads us to see, once again, that the motivation such workers bring to a factory situation is not that of white-collar persons, let alone managers. His thesis is that the rewards projected from middle class values into the incentive schemes and the disciplines of the factory are inappropriate in the lower-class workers' case, a finding for the factory much like that of his colleagues for the school.[32]

But the two class subcultures or value systems may not be

simply different. It may not be outlandish to diagnose the lower-class subculture to be, in great part, a mass withdrawal [33] from that of the middle class. If this be so, workers can be said to have withdrawn their allegiance to formerly general cultural values of success and independence because institutional means have proved inadequate to get them such goals. In support of this Toynbeesque "secession of the internal proletariat" is the presence of some defiant "contrast phenomena" in the outcasts of lowest class: some hate-driven inversions of respectable values. But here we are in the dark, even theoretically. What is secession in these divergences of class values and what is "normal" structuring of antithetical values in any complex and multigroup society is entirely unknown today. The social scientist is always damned a cynic when he points out that some criminals are necessary to any society, just as some danger and ill-health are needed for the tonus of any organism. "Scape-goating" the unsuccessful in an achievement-oriented society may perhaps be one of the unpretty functional necessities of such a society's existence, a necessary cost. Nor do we know how much the different values of the people who "do not get ahead" are a socially necessary consolation prize.

Thus it is plain that the process of productivity release through cultivation of "group life" in an organization works somehow *within* the cultural limits imposed by a society which puts middle class values higher than lower-class values, while it still permits both to coexist and offers some reward for individuals who choose one or the other. Were the classes and their values completely foreign to one another, or intransigently unbridgeable, there could be no compromise leadership and partial fusion of the kind we are discussing. There is a great deal to be said for the "open society" of America and the industrializing West. With so much still to learn, it's a pity to waste our intellectual efforts on internecine polemics among the nascent social sciences.

In the light of these class differences in values, it is interesting to look more closely at the "ratebusters" and "restricters" of Collins, Dalton, and Roy, industrial sociologists already referred to above.

Collins, Dalton, and Roy used the notion of this cleavage of values as their central concept in explaining such phenomena as restriction of production. They studied both the workers who "restricted" and others who did not conform to the prevalent norm of restriction.

They discovered that non-conformists were typically from rural backgrounds and of independent farm families, often of Protestant origin, with very different cultural values than the workers of urban origin. Their differences extended broadly to many other attitudes, such as those regarding the New Deal, private property and unions. In matters of motive, the workers from the country had, in the old tradition, come to the city "to get ahead," whereas the city-born workers did not aspire so to higher status. Though the non-conformist "ratebusters" led in output, their relations with their fellow workers were so bad that the foreman characteristically thought them to be "trouble makers" and would not back them for promotion. Here we have the case of the worker whose values are the same as those of "management" and indeed the same as those which management in large part imputes to all workers. We should expect these workers to have motive patterns leading to maximization of output. And, in this case they did, but these motives were not rewarded. These non-conformists received no social rewards which could sustain their cultural values of hard work. They do not get ahead. They do not receive compensatory rewards from any peer group within the factory. This case still demonstrated that productivity is related to the values held by workers, but it leaves unanswered why these workers retain values that they are penalized for having. We can only hypothesize certain explanations: (1) that in the face of frustration they have become fixated on their existing behavior patterns, (2) that they regard the "urban" work groups as hostile and are thus exhibiting a defiant non-conformity or defense of traditional ideals. Although these two notions are not mutually exclusive, we are tempted to emphasize the first. These "rural" workers remain isolated even from each other; they are the real isolated and depersonalized victims of the machine. There is no "symmetrical" ("two-way") communication between them and anyone in the factory. Such isolation from alternate stimuli is one of the classical conditions for fixated behavior.

In general, in industrial sociology, as elsewhere in social psychology today, the accounting for differences between the scores of different groups on the same performance calls for specifying the motivating values of each group. Work performance like psychological test performance might be expected to vary not so much with individual capacity, where training is equal, as with the meaningfulness of the work to the performer. The manager (leader) would be smart to choose workers who already value the work he wants done, just as the psychological tester is now learning that disinterest may explain some children's inferior performance better than "low intelligence." But since we know it is the world outside (class, religion, etc.) which gives the workers their values, there seems little ground for fear that managers, however skilled in one-way employee communication, will improve performance by persuading the workers of their own, the managers', values. The matter is different if the skills should include tapping the values of the workers themselves. Many critics of plant sociology have attacked just such successfully painless and beguiling "manipulation." With the critics of the influence of advertising on the mass taste of today, they think the manager need only give the "contented cows" what they want and he may drive them where and how he will.

Yet that is specifically not the burden of the evidence from "plant sociology" itself. This fear disregards the finding that the process of the social release of productivity, in the empirical studies so far made, is not a matter of offering rewards alone. It is also always a matter of the balancing of initiative. It is not only what is given but who gives it or gets it that must be reckoned with. Performance is related not only to reward, but to the exercise of one's own initiative. We must remember that a plant is not only a place of performance tests and output scores. It is a power situation where a lesser-powered group is performing a test imposed and surveyed by a higher. Even if the management with consummate skill learned to use all the goals of its employees there is both theoretical and empirical reason to doubt that human "contented cows" stay contented under continuous driving. A "strain" is likely to develop. Such a strain is likely to show up in an increase of aggressive, fixated, or withdrawn behavior on the part of the lesser-powered group. If, however, for any reason the cumulative process of changes in interaction, initiative, and accommodation which we are discussing gets under way, a different outcome may ensue. In that case, such a process might move the relevant social systems comprising the two groups *towards* some "fusion," so that a common system of shared values might develop about the performance in question. This process might thus effect a reintegration of the expectations of both groups vis-à-vis performance. Only in this sense of a brittle, unstable end-result of a trend is this "fusion" of goals and maximization of effort which some fear and others seek likely at all.

4. PROCESSUAL DYNAMICS, INTERACTION, AND THEORY

We can turn now, at the end of our review of the real contributions of industrial sociology, to a last main line of development. This is the line that gives some hope for answers to the questions of process we have raised continually and have just now finished discussing abstractly. It is the line, also, that at least searches for an answer to our fourth grand question about the processes of social release of initiative.

Once the process starts, we asked, what keeps it going, what is the course of its unfolding toward its end? It is a happy state of affairs to be able to report that some empirical industrial sociology (even if by other names) exists which, often unwittingly, unites its practitioners with labor economists and critics of "plant sociology." Thus we can report recent studies of "industrial peace." Now complete in thirteen cases, these explore both external and internal factors and give ground for reconciling those who study only the one or the other.[34] Harbison and Dubin show acute realization of the impact of national forces in their study of General Motors and Studebaker[35] while attention to internal politics of company and union is evidenced in studies of Whyte or Sayles and Strauss.[36] A comparative analysis of these studies would do much to clear the air.

But our concern here is invested in the internal picture. There a last main line of development shows in interesting convergence of findings in the work of two quite different theoretical foundations. The studies of industrial organization by interactionists, both in companies and in unions, stress a growing awareness that the process in question is in fact a matter of the progressive inclusion of every party's needs, as and when these are put forward in the stream of ongoing organizational activity. The work of the abstract sociological theorists about Parsons at Harvard pushes toward a similar awareness that group goal fusion and heightened unified activity depend upon a growing mutual conciliation by the parties of one another.

Just as industrial sociology has been little understood and bitterly resisted in the wider scholarship about man, society, and the
machine, so in sociology in general, a theory and methodology,
originated by Chapple and Arensberg, the present senior author,
in the 1940's and fairly widely represented in the work of Whyte
and others in industrial studies since, has been very little understood.[37] The theory held that, beneath the symbolism of human
speech and the norms and meanings of human culture, patterns of
social action, made up oftenest of recurrent events in time of interaction of pairs of persons or sets of one person in the lead of
several, occur in nature, are subject to third-party observation (as
well as to description and introspection by the actors), and that
these are the independent subject matter of speech, symbol, and
meaning, including feeling, of human culture and society. Such
interpersonal action, like the symbiosis (from predation through
parasitism to commensalism and cooperation) among all animals,[38]
provides the principal matrix for human psychological and physiological adaptation, for cultural symbolisation, for institutional structuring of human affairs, for the projection of individual experience
and emotion in speech and thought. Changes, steady states, and
interconnections of these time-bound recurrences of specific events
of specific interaction among specific persons are the dynamic factors of culture and society, in interplay with the physiological
states of the persons and the conditions of the external natural
environment. For good or ill, the theory was an attempt at a
unification of the sciences about men, a model for the complexities
of human behavior. It is relevant here because it gave, and still
gives us, a hope of exploring unfolding social processes like the one
before us now.

The methodology this unified sociology, biology, and physiology
of social action required was rigorously operational. Since speech
has its referent in action, interviews were, as in anthropological
field work, to be analyzed for the identification of the actors. Their
roles and activities were to be used for stating the order of initiative
and response among these actors. The contexts of situations, techniques, and sentiment were to be related to such roles and such
orders of actions, and the connections among all these in the events,
taken as unique configurations, to be counted for their recurrence
in time and place. Action itself, in events directly seen by the

observer, ideally thus a "participant observer" (again in the field work tradition), was to be treated in the same manner. Thus the evidence of the ear (interview) and that of the eye (observation) could be compared and correlated and any record of social history be treated as a summarization and comparison of events in time. In strictest inductive manner definitions of categories, forces, and institutions must be re-created from the observed and documented data of this record.

The method dealt squarely with recording of personalities in action, with the effect of one person's doings on another in ongoing situations.

Whatever one may think about all this, interaction theory was in its way a codification of some of the emerging research methods of the new empirical social science, or at least of the non-scale building and non-statistical aspects of it. And it had definite fruits in the study of smaller groups, in industry and outside.[39]

In industrial studies the theory and methodology of interaction led to a re-examination of prior work and to discovery out of extant case observations of the process we are discussing.[40] It led on to an analysis of union-management relationships which discerned in events of negotiation the pattern of balanced mutual concessions which is described in Whyte's *Pattern for Industrial Peace*, already mentioned by our economist critics. In Whyte's *Human Relations in the Restaurant Industry*[41] it figured in Whyte's interpretation of the "crying waitress" as a person caught between pressures from customers and from countermen. In Richardson and Walker's study of an IBM plant it gave an insight into crucial connections between work flow and human relations problems of supervision,[42] just as it had earlier proved the key to distinguishing real from fictitious organization in an early study by Arensberg and McGregor[43] and the key to informal organization and leadership in a shoe factory study by Horsfall and Arensberg.[44] Chapple has reported his own use of the concepts in various papers[45] where he refined the method into a diagnostic for mental illnesses, with the psychiatrist Lindemann,[46] and into a personality and performance prediction instrument, with Donald[47] and alone. C. W. M. Hart, sympathetically alerted, found that the theory distinguished for him the pulling and hauling currents among unions, the church, and the older voluntary associations in modern industrial city life beyond work hours, in a superb study of Windsor, Ontario.[48] And Sayles and Strauss, already named, found the inner structure of unions to be a similar balance of pressures from officers, rank-and-file and out-side forces. Most recently, on a smaller scale, Rubinstein has tested out other sociometric devices, like the Bales categories of kinds of interaction in problem solving,[49] to report the "content-less" inter-action measures quicker and more reliably.[50]

Now the point of all this is not to argue the merits of one theory and method over another, a rather barren intellectual exercise. The point is rather that the theory of interaction gives a tentative mastery of relationships in the data which we did not have before. It has a predictive force, in that, by uniting descriptions of social system and "group life" to measures of individual action, by turning processes of attitudinal change and creation of "norms" into pres-sures of persons upon persons, it lets one dare a guess that here, with these persons, the next action is likely to be a walk-out, wildcat strike, failure of incentive, crying fit of a waitress, or emergence of a new leader. The theory is bound to time, is a counterpoint between individual and group, and treating process for itself, stands or falls in proof against predictions. Right or wrong, it walks the path toward a knowledge of the dynamisms within human social relationships.

It is in this light that one must read studies and comments from interactionists about industrial relations. To search for a "pattern for industrial peace," as Whyte called his book, in a course of ongoing concessions of management to union and union to man-agement, concessions which "get something for the boys" through their union officers' efforts when the boys want it, concessions which let management do its job, and avoid merely holding it up for spite, and yet do not turn a conceding union into a pusher for management's goals, is not to write a How To Do It Manual for Managers. It is to come to grips with the movement of a social system. The critics do not look deeply enough. Our aim is to turn the homely lesson of this practical case into a dynamic model of such a social process by charting the sequences of pressures up, down, and across the line and by recording accessions to and refusals of such gambits of the parties pushing forward their needs. It is a long way yet to good measures comparable from case to case, to realistic and detailed summaries of rates of change and degrees of effect. But the model is a good one and the sharpening of the measures comes later on.

The interactionist, then, stands at the point where such dynamic structural models for human groups and their processes, and the counterpoint of those processes with individual situation and external force, are shaping up. We believe with Levy-Strauss [51] that the ones that will eventually prevail will be structural-processual ones, much more complex, definite, and operative than current statistical factor analysis. The interactionists are on the right track. Even the economists are beginning to be aware that an endless weighing of factors must eventually be superseded by some right guess as to the way relevant factors fit together.[52]

Thus the interactionist position, beginning in a few abstract premises, developing in close appeal to concrete events, has matured to give a description of a "fusion"-devolution process which has parallels far beyond the factory.

It is very hopeful that the interactionist has reached a model of a process (through many-sided mutual conciliation, with the servicing of the parties' own needs to resultant incremental initiative-release) with his empirical studies of grubby workrooms, companies, companies-cum-unions at the same time that some "purer" theorists in sociology seem to have proposed similar models of action "pressure" as most needed in advancing the sciences of human behavior.

It will require another place than this chapter to point out these convergences between the findings of plant sociology and those of theoretical sociology. Suffice it for us to say in closing that plant sociology is not merely an applied "manipulative" sociology. It is instead in the main line of our continuing efforts at building a scientific knowledge of man and his social action. If it opens Pandora's box, as all science does, we can only hope man is strong and brave enough to survive the self-knowledge.

Robert Lekachman

THE NON-ECONOMIC ASSUMPTIONS
OF JOHN MAYNARD KEYNES

I

The Keynesian explanation of the size of national income and employment is clothed in severely technical language, addressed originally to economists, and applied in explicit form to situations of brief duration only. Yet, this novel doctrine has altered the actions of politicians, trade union leaders and even bankers; for the problem of full employment upon which Keynes concentrated the full powers of his intellect has fascinated every political party and every organized economic group. Keynes' ideas are taught in the schools and debated in the Parliaments of the West and from them has been derived not only a whole set of short run policies but a diagnosis of the ills of capitalism as well. The problems which his analysis poses have stimulated and channeled research in economics and increased the need for cooperative research by sociologists, psychologists and economists, at the same time as the difficulties of such research have been multiplied. Surely Keynes has been the most influential economist since his illustrious predecessor, David Ricardo, and like Ricardo's, Keynes' triumph was compounded of intellectual virtuosity and supreme relevance to the events of his own day.

This essay makes no effort to criticize the formidable logical structure of Keynes' thought, a task accomplished many times over. It proposes to demonstrate instead that Keynes' new engine of analysis depends upon a set of psychological and sociological insights which appear to demand much combined research by social scientists. This research in itself involves many difficulties, the most important of which is the relationship between theory and empirical findings. We also shall suggest that Keynes' conception of social change and the policies which flow from it, shows the effects of a limited historical judgment. The remainder of this section offers a précis of Keynes' theory of employment. In Section II we outline and briefly criticize the psychological and sociological elements implicit in the theory and deal with some of the research problems which arise. Section III centers on Keynes' longer term judgments of society.

The impact on the imagination produced by the simplicity of Keynes' system and the momentous policies he infers from it, is tremendous at first sight and scarcely diminishes as summary proceeds. For from the interactions of a very few variables, Keynes derives both the size of national income, a way of forecasting change in this huge aggregate and a technique for enlarging national income. In an economy subject to frequent spells of painful depression, both economists and other citizens are prone to esteem the size of national income and the number of persons employed as the most important indices of social welfare. Since, for Keynes, income and employment run parallel courses, what is learned of income will apply as well to employment. What follows is a condensed account of the pure theoretical structure of Keynes' analysis.

There are two ways of classifying national income. National Income may be the sum of the salaries, wages, rents, interest and profits which individuals receive for services performed. People either save or spend these incomes. National Income from this point of view is equal to Consumption plus Saving. National Income is also the value, or the prices paid, for total new output. Output is divided into goods and services destined for the individual consumption of individuals, and those machines, buildings and inventories used by businessmen in the production of other commodities. Regarded in this manner, National Income is the sum of Consumption plus Investment. Since Consumption and National Income appear in both classifications, Savings and Investment, the residual items, must be equal in equilibrium.[1]

This definitional identity neither implies that savers and investors *plan* to save and invest equal amounts, nor explains the size of the national income out of which savings and investments are made. Savers and investors are different individuals with different aims.

The divergence in their views has important consequences to the economic system, by causing an economic process which reconciles the plans and determines a new level of income. An arithmetic example will illustrate this process. Assume an economy in which the starting national income is 100 and that out of this income, consumers spend 90 and save 10. Investment must also be equal to 10. Now a change occurs: investors increase their commitments to 20, for reasons which will emerge later. For the moment a contradiction threatens: investment apparently exceeds saving. The contradiction is resolved in this way. Increased investment entails increased spending by businessmen and increased incomes for their employees. Out of these increased incomes, individuals increase both consumption and saving. For the sake of simplicity, assume that for every additional dollar of income, consumers increase consumption and saving by 50¢ each. The sums which consumers spend become income to other individuals who in turn spend and save equal shares. Thus the original increase in investment fosters a series of increases in consumption and saving as follows: 5, 2½, 1¼, etc. The sum of each set of increases is 10. The ultimate result is a new national income of 120, out of which consumption is 100 and saving 20. Saving is once more equal to investment and this new level of national income will last just as long as investment remains 20.[2]

The account thus far proves that the total spending of the community can be enlarged by the activities of investors. Can it not also be enlarged by additional spending by individuals out of the same incomes? Although the answer numerically is clearly affirmative, Keynes attached little theoretical importance to this type of change.[3] For him consumer behavior in the short run is rather stable and alterations in consumption derive from alterations in the size of the national income. Consumers react to, rather than initiate, new levels of national income. Disturbing circumstances aside, their tastes are stable. Should their incomes increase, their actions are also predictable: their consumption will increase but by an amount smaller than the increase in their incomes.[4]

The central issue consequently discloses itself as the determination of investment, for if the consumption function is stable, changes in investment must occasion changes in national income and employment. Keynes describes the mechanism of investment in the following manner. Business (or entrepreneurs) who make investments compare as well as they can the rate of profit [5] expected from the use of a machine during its productive life with the rate of interest which must be paid to acquire the funds needed to purchase the investment.[6] An investment will appear profitable only when the marginal efficiency of capital, the profit expected, exceeds the rate of interest. In promoting investment a drop in the rate of interest brings the same result as an increase in the marginal efficiency of capital.

The result so far is simple but incomplete. Investment dominates national income and is in turn dominated by two groups of influences, summarized in the marginal efficiency of capital and the rate of interest. An explanation of the rate of interest and the marginal efficiency of capital completes the account. Once more Keynes' answers can be made concise. The expected rate of profit (the marginal efficiency of capital) depends on one objective cause, the price of capital assets, and on one subjective factor, the expectations held by investors of the total dollar profits their investments will earn. A shift either in the dollar amount of profits expected or in the price of an investment alters the marginal efficiency of capital.

The rate of interest remains. Once more two forces account for its shifts: the existing stock of money, an objective influence, and individuals' attitudes toward the holding of money for speculative purposes, a subjective influence.[7] Individuals who speculate on the prices of securities divide their liquid assets between cash and securities.[8] Where all of them are satisfied with this division, no change in interest rates occurs. But, if speculators expect interest rates to drop and security prices to rise, they will attempt to shift from cash to securities. Should this expectation be general, security prices will rise and the rate of interest will decline *in the present*. Similarly, if speculative expectations are of higher interest rates, security prices will decline and the rate of interest rise *in the present*. In Keynesian language, liquidity preference has declined in the first example and has increased in the second. This is an explanation of changes in current interest rates as caused by shifts in market expectations of future interest rates.

The entire apparatus is now in our hands. To recapitulate briefly. Investment determines income and employment and is itself determined by the marginal efficiency of capital and the rate of interest.

The price of capital assets and the state of long term expectations combine to explain the marginal efficiency of capital; and the stock of money and the state of liquidity preference explain the rate of interest. The spare, logical structure which rises from this pairing of the objective and subjective elements compels admiration and satisfies the esthetic sense.

Not the least of the charms of the construction is in its consequences. A simple example will demonstrate how one change introduced into the system can produce large results. Assume a downward shift in liquidity preference. Then the rate of interest falls, investment increases, income increases by some multiple of the change in investment, and the multiple itself can be found by examining the consumption function. The same effect on income will follow from a drop in the price of investment goods, an increase in the supply of money, or an upward shift in the marginal efficiency of capital.

The economic forecaster has found in this array of concepts ideas profitable in his business. If he can form an enlightened estimate of investment plans through business surveys, he is able to forecast investment. Then, in this unsophisticated example, he is also able to predict the size of national income, consumption and saving very easily. Saving must equal investment. The level of national income with which such an amount of saving is associated can be deduced from the consumption function. Subtract saving from national income and the remainder is consumption. If the predicted level of national income will not provide full employment, a whole range of policies can be applied, as the political orientation of the forecaster suggests. A conservative may urge tax relief for the business community, hoping thereby to increase the marginal efficiency of capital. Others may prefer to increase investment by government deficit spending, while another school advocates remission of personal taxes, and consumer subsidies as a way of raising the consumption function. Variable tax rates, variable government spending and programs of incentives to various groups may all in one situation or another increase the national income.

II

At three critical points Keynes' insights into human nature dominate the movements of the economic variables within his system. The expectations of speculators and investors if created in ways other than he describes would produce other rates of interest and other marginal efficiencies of capital, just as more active individual attitudes toward spending would lessen the stability of the consumption function. From these changes quite different policy recommendations would flow. This section discusses the group characteristics which Keynes actually imputes to consumers, investors and speculators; it continues with an account of the research methods used by his followers; and it concludes with a discussion of some of the difficulties encountered, especially as they center on the relationship of empirical research and macroeconomic theory.[9]

The strategic economic groups in Keynes' universe are large and few: investors, consumers, and speculators. Although motivations differ by group, behavior within each group is taken as homogeneous. Keynes conceived of the typical consumer as stable in his tastes and as, therefore, unlikely to re-examine his pattern of purchases very often or very lightly. In the short run, he alters the rate and the pattern of his spending only as his income changes. If his income increases he will increase his consumption by a lesser amount; and if his income declines, he diminishes his consumption by a smaller amount. Spending is largely a habit which varies, after a time lag, as income varies.

What is true of the individual consumer is equally true of consumers as a group. "The fundamental psychological law" in which Keynes conveys his conviction is famous. "The psychology of the community is such that when aggregate real income is increased, aggregate consumption is increased, but not by so much as income." [10] Keynes was quite aware of the complexity of individual motivations and of the numerous influences which control spending. He simply believed that individual differences tend in the short run (the only period of interest to him) to cancel and that the only important force remaining to account for changes in spending was changes in income. The consumer, then, seldom if ever initiates economic changes by spontaneous action of his own. Only gradually, as the time horizon widens, do other forces influence his action, "those psychological characteristics of human nature and those social practices and institutions, which, though not unalterable, are unlikely to undergo a material change over a short period of time except in abnormal or revolutionary circumstances" [11] —but again it is the short run situation which Keynes prefers to handle.

The consumer who emerges from this description is a representative type of much the same breed as Alfred Marshall's representative businessman. He is tailored for easy generalization into the aggregative relationships of the consumption function. As in Marshall, the dynamic activities of entrepreneurs shape the tastes and the attitudes of consumers—wants must wait upon activities. Since in the short run Keynes abstracts from this innovating activity, consumer spending becomes no more valuable than National Income, and it follows that each level of National Income induces a predictable amount of aggregate consumption.

It is not surprising that this theory of consumption stimulated an enormous burst of economic research. The theory intrigued the imagination and stimulated the mind by its sweep and its simplicity. It suggested policy implications to a world wracked by depression and these policies were easy to apply and well calculated to soothe. Perhaps best of all, the important variables seemingly could be measured, as the crucial cost and demand magnitudes of ordinary price theory could not. Did not Keynes concentrate his attention on saving, investment, consumption and income and were there not, especially in the United States, abundant data measuring these variables over many years? Did not the two sets of concepts, empirical and theoretical, come to the same thing? No wonder that numerous empirical consumption functions were constructed on the basis of national income statistics. Apparently these functions summarized the behavior of income and consumption over varying periods of years. At the simplest, the analyst plotted a scatter diagram of consumption and income values (suitably deflated) and fitted a line to them, either visually or by least square techniques. Not surprisingly, excellent correlations were found between income and consumption,[12] although they were much worse between saving and income. Some economists concluded that the relationships were stable enough to assume that a repetition of any historically observed national income would carry with it the same level of consumption, within a rather small margin of error. In other words, these investigators generalized Keynes' short run theoretical consumption function into a longer run historical relationship and imputed to income a truly dominating actual as well as theoretical role in the determination of consumption.

The growing confidence of many economists in this framework of analysis persuaded them to depend heavily on it for forecasting. Indeed in the interval between V-E and V-J days, a popular Washington sport was the forecasting of postwar income and employment.[13] Most of these forecasts relied on Keynesian methods and in most cases they predicted for the spring of 1946 much lower income and much higher unemployment than actually ensued. Although there are many reasons why these forecasts went wrong, one is especially relevant: forecasters assumed stability in consumers' tastes. If tastes were stable, then consumers would, it followed, continue to plan their expenditures in the prewar pattern, dividing them in historically set proportions between durable goods and non-durables. But, argued the forecasters, fewer durable goods would be immediately available than consumers planned to buy. What would consumers do? They could increase their savings or they could spend more on clothing, amusement and other non-durable goods and services. Most forecasters made the strategic assumption that consumers would increase their savings and that the prewar ratio of spending on non-durables to income would be restored. Because they considered tastes stable, they concluded that these efforts to increase saving would decrease employment, and cause a recession.

Events proved the forecasts wrong. Consumers spent a larger portion of income than past relationships made it plausible to predict, and, since durables were scarce, their spending was concentrated on other items. Consumers would not be balked in their desire to spend more of their incomes. One clear moral of the story lies in the evident ability of consumers to alter their tastes spontaneously [14] and to assume the active role allotted to investors. Obviously the economy is a great deal more complicated than a naive Keynesian is likely to suspect.

But this unhappy forecasting experience suggests something more important than this moralistic observation: a certain confusion of saving, investment, consumption, and income as part of the static equilibrium relationships of the initial Keynesian formulation with the statistical concepts used in National Income measurement. For as soon as investigators either applied the correlation techniques already mentioned or resorted to the survey techniques to be discussed, they encountered what Marshall considered the principal difficulty of economic analysis, time and its effects.

Marshall, himself, provides an example of the importance of this hurdle. It was comparatively easy for one of his intellectual powers to formulate the pure theory of demand and of the individual firm; it was much harder to derive an empirical demand function based on price and quantity data which pertained to varying points in time; for adjustments had to be made for all changes of importance in the surrounding context. Under the circumstances rather few empirical demand studies have been made and none at all by Marshall himself.

The Keynesian analysis is in technique an extension of the Marshallian and shares in its difficulties: where Marshall dealt with the demand curve of the individual consumer Keynes treated the aggregate demand of all consumers for all commodities. Keynes matched Marshall's concern for the production of the individual business firm with his own emphasis on aggregate supply of all firms in the entire economy. In part their differences are in what is treated as a datum and what is treated as a variable. Keynes considered prices as data and incomes as variables and Marshall precisely reversed this procedure. But the emphasis on timeless relationships and the search for equilibrium characterizes the work of both men and proves once more that Keynes was Marshall's aptest pupil.

Perhaps it is unfortunate for the ultimate fruitfulness of the Keynesian line of economic research that the Keynesian concepts were so formed that there appeared to be available these masses of data suitable for statistical generalization and that the policy uses of these generalizations were so very tempting. In their eagerness, researchers did not immediately perceive the analogy we have advanced between the problems of computing a relationship between income and consumption over time and of deriving a simple relationship between price and quantity over time while ignoring shifts in tastes, incomes, and the kinds and prices of competing goods. The simple relationships between income and consumption contained in an aggregate demand curve, the consumption function, purported to represent the same set of underlying conditions while actually they represented a series of points, each one of which actually appeared on a separate and distinct short run aggregate demand curve. As economists became increasingly aware of this difficulty, they attempted to surmount it by breaking their data down into relevant subperiods, but if the subperiods become too short the explanatory and predictive value of the construction correspondingly diminishes.

Considerations of this kind: the desire to identify additional variables which influence consumption, the need to characterize strategic subgroups in the population, have led to increasing use of survey data. The hope has been that economic surveys will increase understanding of the factors which influence individual economic units and it has been believed that to understand macroeconomic relations it is first necessary to understand microeconomic behavior. Surveys are one method of breaking down the consumption total and searching for the amount of homogeneity which exists within it.

Probably the most important of these surveys and the most widely cited is conducted by the Survey Research Center at the University of Michigan under the direction of George Katona, himself a psychologist as well as an economist. This annual survey of consumer finances is both a description of expenditure and saving broken down in various ways and also an analysis of the reasons why spending and saving change. The Survey Research Center has found that a number of forces in addition to income help to explain spending and saving, among them assets, debts, home ownerships, occupation, size of family and expectations. The value of these surveys in increasing our knowledge of consumer behavior is not at issue: it is very great. Among other uses, these surveys have facilitated short term prediction and the construction of annual income distributions.

But we immediately encounter some major difficulties in assimilating these results to the structure of Keynesian theory summarized in the first part of this essay. If we seek to construct an empirical consumption function out of these data collected in successive years, we are brought up short by the problem of time. The families questioned have been selected from a universe which has undergone significant change, the longer the period the more important the change. Our construction is all too likely to give us once more a collection of points on various short run aggregate demand curves.

Another problem may be hardest of all to solve. Survey research develops many interesting relationships between pairs of variables, which we can term low level generalizations. The curious can learn a great deal about who saves, what affects saving, who spends and what is purchased. What he doesn't learn is how to move from these low level generalizations to the macroeconomic equations of the Keynesian system. To make this journey necessitates the evaluation of the significance of these low level generalizations, the discovery of how they modify the original Keynesian equations, and a method of incorporating them into these equations. All kinds of correlations may be found. The need remains for a theoretical rationale to identify those which are strategic. Regrettably it must be said that it is far from clear how Keynesian theory can integrate survey findings which all agree are significant, but no one seems able to incorporate into the theory proper.

This is much the same thing as saying that economists find their theory of consumption somehow unsatisfying, admit that other social disciplines have much to offer, express pious hopes that the practitioners of the various subjects can usefully combine their knowledge, but can point to no mechanism which links the diverse findings.

We have spent so much time on Keynes' theory of consumption partly because stable consumer behavior is an essential part of Keynesian theory, but largely because this portion of Keynes' analysis has attracted a disproportionate amount of attention from economists. Just as important to the theory and just as demanding of extension are Keynes' explanations of the actions of investors and speculators. As can easily be proven, most of the difficulties raised by our examination of consumer behavior apply as strongly to these groups.

A good starting point is Keynes' own description of the investor, the dynamic figure in his economic system. There is no one concept of the investor in Keynes, for his views altered over time. In 1920 [15] he described a collapse of self-confidence:

> We are thus faced in Europe with the spectacle of an extraordinary weakness on the part of the great capitalist class, which has emerged from the industrial triumphs of the nineteenth century and seemed a very few years ago our all-powerful master. The terror and personal timidity of individuals of this class is now so great, their confidence in

their place in society and in their necessity to the social organism so diminished, that they are the easy victims of intimidation.

Later in the 1920's Keynes changed his views and it appeared that the capitalist became no more than a "Schumpeterian 'manager'— head of some semi-monopolistic, trustified, 'rationalized,' well-entrenched English firm with ample internal funds." [16]

The entrepreneur of the *General Theory* is the focus of diverse influences. His expectations as investor are potent in determining the marginal efficiency of capital and hence the rate of investment. But, here is the rub, expectations deal with the future and the future is always uncertain, perhaps more uncertain now than ever before in the history of capitalism. Developments in consumer tastes, new kinds of equipment, the height of effective demand: all of these and more are unknowns. Obviously investors make up their minds, for investments are made. How closely can they calculate in the face of so much uncertainty? How rationally can they compare expected profits with known costs? In Keynes this uncertainty engenders a convention and explains an emotion. The convention is reliance on the rule that the future will resemble the present. [17]

The present at least is solid and this solidity induces an habitual adjustment which itself influences expectations. Uncertainty about the future also explains the grip which emotion in the form of waves of exaltation achieves over the business community, that pervasive optimism often unrelated to economic events which Keynes dubbed "animal spirits." It is well-known to the financial community as the "state of business confidence." Thus into the last home of rationality in economic affairs, Keynes introduced two interlopers, convention and emotion.

This was a brilliant tour de force, an imaginative and an analytical triumph of the highest order, but it is scarcely a satisfactory theory of the investment process. A satisfactory theory would identify the relevant factors in a variety of investment situations, explain their relationships and eventually assign quantitative weights to them. It would necessarily provide a consistent explanation of these waves of animal spirits in terms of measurable, identifiable phenomena. Eventually also such a theory would facilitate accurate forecasts of investment and income.

The work that economists have done in investment theory is

excessively vague as a guide to empirical investigation. For example, economists in the Keynesian tradition have tried to analyse the structure of expectations held by different groups of investors, although nothing aids them in identifying the significant groups. They have carefully examined the institutional environment in which investment proceeds and tried to discover who plans investments, what influences plans, how firmly they are made and what causes them to be changed. Part of the difficulty in all such undertakings is that the theory applicable to such researches is not Keynesian and is scarcely economic at all: relevant concepts are more likely to be found in psychology or sociology. The findings of the survey methods used are as difficult to assimilate into a theory of investment behavior on the Keynesian level of abstraction as it was to combine the various low level generalizations made from the Survey of Consumer Finances into a theory of consumer behavior.

One example of the way economists have examined investment will illustrate this point. Dr. Franco Modigliani at the University of Illinois has applied elaborate statistical techniques to the studies of business plans made by Dun and Bradstreet and by Fortune Magazine. Both sets of surveys cover the investment anticipations of various samples. Using these samples rather than collecting one of his own, Dr. Modigliani has attempted to prove or disprove the usefulness of investment anticipations in economic forecasting. That his conclusions are tentatively optimistic is less important to us than the observation that Keynesian theory provided him with no guide at all to research beyond the vague indication that "expectations" are important. It is evident that research into investment behavior is at an even earlier stage than consumer research. In this area economists lack even the low level generalization available to them in consumer theory, despite numerous studies made by them and by business analysts.

Changes in investment and in national income reflect changes in the expectations of speculators as well as investors. And the role of the speculator is the more important to the Keynesian because it is easier for a government to manipulate the rate of investment via shifts in the volume of money than it is to alter the marginal efficiency of capital by influencing the tricky attitudes of investors. As described by Keynes, the professional speculator is a shrewd individualist whose single desire is to profit by alterations in the prices of securities. His is a short run view. He does not care how sound a security is over a period of time: he much prefers to know what its price will be tomorrow. Since the prices of securities tomorrow or next week are the result much more of shifting, uncertain views held by the speculating group than they are of more stable economic tendencies, the professional speculator expends his energy on "foreseeing changes in the conventional basis of valuation a short time ahead of the general public." [18] Professionals may profit from the contributions of amateurs, but the game can be played as well by professionals alone.

Economists have done very little research in the theory of speculation. They have not gone much beyond the feeling that the expectations of speculators are in some manner important to the determination of the rate of interest, the level of income and the size of employment. Early studies suggested that the rate of interest was less important than Keynes had assumed in the calculations of businessmen when they came to make investments. Nothing conclusive was found and the survey techniques used were far from satisfactory. The sociology as well as the economics of speculation remains exceedingly obscure and the speculating group itself an ill-defined mass.

III

The formal economic theory advanced by Keynes is limited as to time by the array of assumptions already cited. But the appearance of the *General Theory* in 1936, its emphases, and the policies which Keynes derived from it, all emerge from a distinct historical vision and a definite conception of social change. It is impossible to understand completely even the pure theory in Keynes without a conception of the problems he felt compelled to solve in behalf of the England he loved. The warning implicit in this statement is that England's problems are not inevitably our problems and that we should be wary of easy generalization to our own circumstances from Keynes' policies.

The better to appreciate Keynes' intellectual outlook, this section of the essay ranges over many of Keynes' published writings, from 1920 to 1936. On occasion it emphasizes Keynes' asides and random opinions, not with any intent of unfair criticism, but with a view to understanding the stable elements in Keynes' social vision.

Keynes perceived that in the making of current institutions, current problems and current policies, many irrational forces participated, among them emotion, wrong-headedness sanctioned by tradition, insensate greed, and sheer stupidity. But he would never admit that these influences are controlling. Nor does the reader discover in Keynes that perception of "inevitable" trends, hardly to be altered by human will, that is the quality of a Marx or even of a Schumpeter, a Sorokin or a Toynbee. If post-World War I England suffered from unemployment, dwindling markets and an unfavorable trade balance, it was not because long run changes had fatally undermined her economy, nor was it because the tenuous balance of English class relationships had been wrecked. Rather her problems were the result of "muddle," of unclear thought and hesitant action.

Here is the clue to Keynes' historical outlook: history at its simplest presents to the intelligence a series of problems, some of them economic, some of them social, and all of them intellectual. At least for the England which he addressed, Keynes never entertained the hypothesis that the failure of intelligence might be symptomatic of other failures in a society. The line of causation ran in the opposite direction for Keynes.

Keynes was a man happily wedded to an intellectual heritage, that "English tradition of humane science," which included Locke, Adam Smith, Hume, Jeremy Bentham and John Stuart Mill. To its past practitioners he attributed a controlling influence in English history. In their descendants, the "educated bourgeoise," Keynes reposed his hope of English progress and rational social control. They alone can be expected to formulate policies at once clearheaded and disinterested, novel enough to cope with new circumstances and reverent enough to respect useful tradition.[19]

This vital intelligence is unevenly distributed among Keynes' major social groups. Consumers are guided in their spending by habit and income in the short run and by a set of unanalysed institutional shifts in the long run. "Animal spirits" are often decisive in the case of investors. As for manual workers, they suffer from an aggravated case of "money illusion" which persuades them to combat reductions in money wages but to submit to rising prices which have the same effect on their real incomes.[20] Even capitalists are guided less by the economically rational motive of enjoyment than by the desire to achieve prestige or to pass on a fortune. Amid all this unreason, Keynes remained confident of the manipulative ability of that small group which does guide its actions by conscious intelligence. "Soon or late, it is ideas, not vested interests which are dangerous for good or evil."

Because Keynes trusted in the power of truth to overcome error, he was not disheartened by his own gloomy diagnosis of the state of capitalism. Keynes argued that the nature of capitalism has changed from the apparent durability of the nineteenth century to the growing instability of the twentieth. In 1920, he commented that "very few of us realise with conviction the intensely unusual, complicated, unrealiable, temporary nature of the economic organization by which Western Europe has lived for the past half-century." [21] As he saw them, many of Europe's troubles were institutional: they included maintenance of a precariously balanced gold standard and the growth of increasingly complex division of labor and national specialization. But Europe's greatest instability was psychological. Here is Keynes' own description of it:

> While there was some continuous improvement in the daily conditions of life of the mass of the population, Society was so framed as to throw a great part of the increased income into the control of the class least likely to consume it. . . . This remarkable system depended for its growth on a double bluff of deception. On the one hand, the laboring classes accepted from ignorance or powerlessness, or were compelled, persuaded or cajoled by custom, convention, authority and the well-established order of Society into accepting a situation in which they and Nature and the capitalists were co-operating to produce. And on the other hand the capitalist classes were allowed to call the best part of the cake theirs and were theoretically free to consume it, on the tacit underlying condition that they consume very little of it in practice. [22]

"This remarkable system" operated in part spontaneously. Its success depended also on the astute men who sat at the central banking controls in each nation and played an economic game according to a set of rules which they completely understood. It was a different game they had to play after the first World War. The gold standard disappeared for a decade and returned only as a ghost of its former self. The complex division of labor in which

Germany took an indispensable part, was distorted by the Peace of Versailles. That same treaty, born in emotion and nurtured in stupidity, fostered an inflation which destroyed the incentives to accumulate and revealed the nature of the double bluff which had supported prewar capitalism.

From such a picture the faint-hearted might conclude that the case of capitalism was hopeless. Keynes, on the other hand, remained steadfastly confident of the creative potentialities of the human mind. There was nothing here that intelligence could not mend, he stoutly affirmed, and so during the 1920's he proposed a whole armory of ingenious expedients. If inflation threatened, then the currency should be managed. If the gold standard impeded English recovery, then we should either dispose of the gold standard or amend it into tractability. And, if the Treaty of Versailles threatened all Europe, then as men of reason, let us revise it. The enemy was unclear thought, muddle, not revolution.

As the 1920's merged into the even more troubled 1930's in England, Keynes' diagnosis deepened. He became convinced that the great disease of English capitalism was over-saving. Partly it was England's time of life: "Great Britain is an old country . . . The population will soon cease to grow. Our habits and institutions keep us, in spite of all claims to the contrary, a thrifty people." [23]

In his last major work, the theme is unmistakable:

> Today and presumably for the future, the schedule of the marginal efficiency of capital is for a variety of reasons, much lower than it was in the nineteenth century. The acuteness and the peculiarity of our contemporary problem arises, therefore, out of the possibility that the average rate of interest which will allow a reasonable average level of employment is one so unacceptable to wealth-owners that it cannot be readily established by manipulating the quantity of money.[24]

This is the germ of the celebrated secular stagnation hypothesis, much amplified and applied to American conditions by Keynes' followers here.[25] As in 1920, Keynes pointed to a massive structural change in capitalism, a shift which occasioned new difficulties and demanded new solutions. Nonetheless, he curiously limits the effects of the development. He perceived no substantial changes in class relationships and no mortal wound to the institutional structure within which capitalism has lived. No one was to conclude with the Marxists that capitalism's irreconcilable conflicts were ending as they must in proletarian triumph; nor with Schumpeter that socialism would win by default and capitalism disappear without even a whimper. Even the more moderate view of the English Labor Party was suspect.

Keynes could accept none of these easy inferences, for they all smacked to him too much of intellectual abdication in favor of a rigid creed. His attachment to nineteenth century individualism was far too strong, in addition, to permit purchase of security with the price of variety. Witness this passage:

> Let us stop for a moment to remind ourselves what these advantages are. They are partly advantages of efficiency—the advantages of decentralization and of the play of self-interest. The advantage to efficiency of the decentralization of decision and of individual responsibility is even greater, perhaps, than the nineteenth century supposed; and the reaction against the appeal to self-interest may have gone too far. But, after all, individualism, if it can be purged of its defects and abuses, is the best safeguard of personal liberty in the sense, that, compared with any other system, it greatly widens the field of personal choice. It is also the best safeguard of the variety of life, which emerges precisely from this extended field of personal choice, and the loss of which is the greatest of all losses of the homogeneous or totalitarian state. For this variety preserves the traditions which embody the most secure and successful choices of former generations; it colors the present with the diversification of its fancy.[26]

"Purged of its defects and abuses": this is the key phrase. Perhaps we can have our cake and eat it too; perhaps we can save all that is good in capitalism and destroy all that is bad. Keynes sketches a program. The enlightened capitalist state must assume a responsibility for the welfare of its citizens. It must maintain full employment within a framework of liberty and individuality. Never resorting to physical compulsion, it may vary governmental spending and tax policies in order to produce surpluses in inflation and deficits in deflation. Via control of banking policy, this state will manipulate the quantity of money and the rate of interest. In order to combat the evils of secular stagnation, it will socialize investment, although "this need not exclude all manner of compromises and of devices by which public authority will co-operate with private initiative."[27]

Grave doubts arise as this carefully rational program unfolds. Did Keynes see all the implications of these measures? The prosperity, the social efficiency and the self-confidence of a capitalist class derive from a rising schedule of the marginal efficiency of capital. It is the lure of riches which fosters the initiative and the fertility of imagination which characterized capitalism in its best days. Now Keynes tells us we face a secular decline in the marginal efficiency of capital. Instead of more opportunities for profitable investment, there are fewer. More and more investments fail to fulfill even the diminished expectations held for them. Can such a change leave unaltered either the economic or the political position of capitalists as a class? As their social performance grows increasingly less satisfactory, would it not be reasonable to expect that the tide of criticism directed against them will rise and that other groups will seek the dominant role they had once enjoyed? If the future is as Keynes sees it, it may be rash indeed to expect a few judicious reforms to preserve the freedom of choices and the capitalist led culture of which Keynes was so fond.

If ever the possibility existed, surely Keynes' own program of socialized investment would destroy it. One of the most important defining characteristics of capitalism is the free use of capital by private citizens who reap the rewards of success as they suffer the losses of failure. Take away from the capital class the right to invest and you alter at the same time the very meaning of capitalism. The consequences which flow from the declining schedule of the marginal efficiency of capital will surely be strengthened and hastened by socialization of investment.

These might be the results of the Keynesian prescription. But how likely is it that any western industrial community will adopt the prescription itself? Many social scientists have come to regard political economy in the western world as the study of the conflicts of increasingly powerful economic groupings: of trade unions, farmer's organizations and associations of businessmen. Each such group, influenced by rivalry with the others, seeks its own economic advantages as narrowly construed. How very easily indeed can the public interest be disregarded.

Yet it is the characteristic of the Keynesian program that it appeals to no doctrinaire grouping, to no vested economic interest. All too probably the owning groups will see neither the need nor the desirability of the sacrifices they are asked to make. As for the working classes, Keynes' nostalgia for a nineteenth century individualism which was rather hard on them, might have little appeal. They might readily distrust Keynes' cool detachment from their immediate interests and resent some of his comment on their leaders.

Keynes' description of capitalism's troubles and his remedies from them thus suffer from limitations which concealed from him the strength as well as the irrationality of group pressures, the shifts in class structure and the real changes in social outlook, to all of which many would turn for a completer explanation of historical change and a more useful guide to social control. Yet, all of this scarcely diminishes our intellectual debt to Keynes for the technique which his social vision and his anxious desire to solve England's difficulties, caused him to create.

George Katona

THE FUNCTION OF SURVEY RESEARCH
IN ECONOMICS

Many of us who conduct scientific sample surveys believe that the survey method is a basic tool of all behavioral sciences. Through this method quantitative data are collected about what people, and groups of people, do and think in a variety of fields such as politics, economics, labor-management relations, public health, or education, and it is determined what kind of factors are or are not associated with diverse forms of behavior.

The survey method is of particular importance in economics. Much of the present-day discipline of economics deals with theoretical models which indicate what must be done in order to achieve certain objectives (e.g., to maximize profits) and is therefore of a normative rather than a behavioral character. Much of economic statistics deals with production, prices, profits, and similar financial data which are viewed as if they were independent of the decision makers—businessmen or consumers—and their behavior. Economic surveys turn to these individuals and attempt to discern the objective as well as the subjective factors responsible for their behavior. The surveys make no use of restrictive, a priori assumptions about goals and means. Variables often excluded from economics because of their alleged non-economic nature—striving for power, prestige or approbation, group belonging, uncertainty and ignorance, etc.— are studied in the same manner as financial variables. By considering a greater variety of factors economic surveys are intended to advance our understanding of economic developments and improve our predictions of forthcoming trends.

One function of survey research in economics is widely accepted by now. Economic surveys represent a technique of fact-gathering. In discussing this function of surveys, we shall show that the kinds of fact collected in surveys—micro-economic distributions—differ from the ones most commonly compiled in economic studies. Then we shall point out that fact-finding is not the only, and not the most important, function of surveys. Surveys are used to study the relationship between two or more variables and to test hypotheses. Among the relationships studied in economic surveys those between attitudinal and financial variables are particularly relevant. Through such studies surveys became the most important methodological tool of a new discipline, "economic psychology."

Fact-Finding Through Surveys

Those who believe that economic surveys are just another technique of fact-gathering think, first of all, of what has been called budget studies. In this area the need for interrogating samples of consumers, by mail and in person, is widely acknowledged by now. The usual statistics on retail sales show the total amounts spent on, say, food, clothing, or automobiles (in a given period and country), but surveys are needed to determine the share of income expended on these goods by different income groups. National income statistics, compiled from payroll data and similar information on money disbursed, show the total amount of income received by all people and the changes of aggregate income from one period to the next. These statistics do not indicate, however, what proportion of families receive more than $10,000 or less than $1,000 income, or what proportion of families had an increase or a decrease in income from one year to the next. Similarly, nationwide statistics on total assets and debts, or on amounts saved each year, need to be supplemented by survey data on the micro-economic distributions of these amounts.

Even if the function of surveys were completely described by providing such statistics, there would be good reasons to discuss economic surveys in a book dealing with common frontiers of the social sciences. The survey method has been developed by scientists with a variety of affiliations. Mathematical statistics is the basis of sampling, which is necessary to supplant complete enumeration (census) that has proved not only expensive and cumbersome but also inappropriate for some purposes requiring lengthy questioning on complicated matters. The considerable recent progress in such aspects of surveys as question formulation, interviewing, and avoidance of bias is due primarily to the efforts of psychologists and sociologists.

The contribution of social scientists to economic surveys may be illustrated by a reference to a survey of that type which is customarily accepted as fact-gathering. The Bureau of the Census conducts sample surveys every month to determine the number of employed and unemployed persons in the United States. Before interrogating a representative sample of people about their employment status it was, of course, necessary to define the terms employed and unemployed. It was further necessary to formulate a series of questions which satisfy the definitions and transmit their contents to the respondents in a way understandable to them and not biasing their answers. Findings about the size of the labor force and the number of unemployed are dependent not only on the statistical treatment of part-time workers, seasonal workers, those looking for work, the old, the housewives, etc., but also on the way the questions are asked.

Fact-finding through economic surveys is, however, not restricted to compiling statistics on unemployment, or the distribution of income, assets, and expenditures. From the point of view of survey methodology there is not much difference between finding out about employment status or income, and about the subjective feeling of well-being or distress, or expectations of future income. Both types of data are obtainable in an unbiased and reliable way, they are quantifiable, and contribute to the description of the situation as it exists at a given time. Both types of data are subject to sampling and reporting errors, and if there is a difference between them then it is that interviewing directed toward collecting attitudinal data is simpler than that directed toward collecting financial statistics.

One illustration of the process of collecting attitudinal data may suffice. Suppose we conduct a survey about U. S. Government Savings Bonds. Two types of questions may then arise. We may want to know how many American families, and what kinds of families, own such bonds and have recently bought or cashed such bonds. Therefore, we may ask the heads of a representative sample of families whether they have any Savings Bonds. If the answer is in the affirmative, we may ask them about the amount of money they have in bonds, when they have purchased them, and whether they have redeemed any bonds. Those who do not have any bonds should be asked whether they ever owned bonds. A second type of data we may want to collect refers to the level of information about bonds, and to motives for purchasing or cashing them. In this connection, among many other useful questions, we may ask people to tell us in what form they would prefer to invest money they do not need for current expenses. Which would they choose, savings accounts with banks, U. S. Savings Bonds, common stock, or real estate? What speaks, in their opinion, for and what against each of these forms of investment? Do they believe that people who had bought Savings Bonds during the last war fared well or not too well?

The task of formulating easily understandable, non-suggestive attitudinal questions may be more difficult than that of formulating questions about bond ownership. But the questions about owning, buying and cashing bonds often appear to the respondents as concerned with their private affairs. Such financial questions are willingly answered—though the answers are subject to memory errors—provided close rapport has been established and the respondent understands and appreciates the purpose of the survey. The best method yet discovered to obtain detailed answers to such questions as those concerning the amount of bonds owned and bought is to introduce them by attitudinal questions. People in all walks of life readily give their opinions about the advantages and disadvantages of different kinds of investments, and following a pleasant conversation about such problems it is easier to ask factual questions. Thus attitudinal questions have a function even if we were not interested in attitudes.

But the thesis of this paper is that as social scientists or economists we are interested in attitudes. Why? Because attitudes matter. They influence behavior.

Establishing Functional Relations

To provide evidence for the last statement, it is obviously not enough to conduct surveys that collect statistical data about people's economic behavior and other surveys that collect data about their economic attitudes. It is necessary to study the relation between the two. Our previous discussion was introductory and needs to be extended. To establish the relationship between ownership of U. S. Savings Bonds and preferences for bonds over common stock was a major purpose of the bond studies previously mentioned. Similarly, surveys of unemployment need not be restricted to the measurement of the number of unemployed. They may extend to the determination of the relation of employed or unemployed persons to age, occupation, willingness to work, and other characteristics.

We recognize in these areas the principal objectives of surveys—of economic surveys as well as surveys in other fields of social or political behavior. The aim of surveys can be expressed by such terms as establishing functional relationships, arriving at empirically validated generalizations, or testing hypotheses.

How relationships between several variables are studied in economic surveys, and what may be accomplished by such studies, will be discussed by presenting the rationale and some major findings of three investigations. The first example concerns the effects of income change and the second the effects of liquid asset holdings on spending and saving. Studies of factors relevant for economic fluctuations represent the subject matter of the third example. In these examples we shall try to show the complexity of studying relationships between behavior and attitudes, as well as the function of a theoretical framework and hypotheses in deciding which relationships to study.

EXAMPLE 1: EFFECTS OF INCOME CHANGE

The studies of the factors relevant for fluctuations of spending and saving have been made on the basis of the Surveys of Consumer Finances (conducted by the Survey Research Center for the Federal Reserve Board). Each of nine consecutive annual surveys contains a multitude of data on factors that may be related to level and change of different kinds of expenditures and savings. These factors include income level, assets, debts, home ownership, age, occupation, number of people in the family, as well as various kinds of expectations. One variable of special interest in any attempt to understand changes in rates of spending or saving is change in income. In economic theory, and especially in Keynesian theory great emphasis has been placed on this variable and the following principle has been advanced: If income increases amounts saved increase and if income decreases amounts saved decrease.* A corollary to this principle is the one about a time lag in adjusting one's expenditures to changes in income. It has been frequently assumed that shortly after an income increase families will save more, and shortly after an income decrease families will save less, than families with stable income (and similar income level).

The first attempts to confirm these assumptions from survey data yielded ambiguous results. The only clear conclusion drawn from these studies was that the situation must be more complex than described by the principles cited above. It became necessary to compare spending and saving behavior of more than three groups (the families with rising, declining, and stable income). Psychological considerations helped to distinguish further groups and to formulate new hypotheses about the probable effects of income changes under different conditions on the following lines:

1. The manner in which a given income change is perceived may influence its effects. Specifically, an income gain (or decline) which is considered to be temporary (is expected to be followed by a change in the opposite direction) will have different effects on spending and saving than one which is considered permanent or followed by a further change in the same direction. Therefore, income expectations must be studied in conjunction with past income changes.

2. Favorable and unfavorable developments need not have symmetrical opposite effects on behavior but may exert, like reward and punishment, qualitatively different influences. Specifically, adaptation of expenditures to higher income may be an easy and quick

---

* This principle was either presented on a priori grounds or was derived from the empirically established fact that high-income people save more than low-income people.

process while adaptation to lower income may be a difficult process which involves, under certain circumstances, a considerable time lag.

Only a few results of survey analysis carried out in an attempt to test these assumptions will be reported here. Among all kinds of income changes temporary income declines were found to have the most pronounced effect on saving. Families who experienced a decline in income but expected their income to go up again saved a smaller proportion of their income (and therefore spent a larger proportion) than families in other situations. The influence of permanent income increases—to mention just one more group which was numerically important during the last few years—on the rate of saving was found to be rather small; but this group was found to spend a disproportionately large sum on the purchase of durable goods (automobiles, furniture, electrical appliances, etc.).

Research is not completed with such findings. It appears necessary to take further variables into account in studying the effects of income changes on spending and saving. In addition to temporary and permanent changes, gradual-small as against large changes and expected as against unexpected changes need to be distinguished. Of greater importance still may be the distinction between income changes that are (or are felt to be) in accord with the trend of one's group, community or country and income changes that are contrary to those trends. Regarding the last problem, only fragmentary information is available up to now. Our data on the effects of income declines were collected in the United States in the years 1946-1953, in which the general trend in the country was toward higher and higher incomes. In years of depression the effects of income changes might be different. It is possible that in periods in which the incomes of the majority of families decline expenditures are adapted to reduced incomes faster than in periods in which only a relatively small minority experiences income declines. This hypothesis cannot be tested except in times of economic depression. Therefore as citizens, rather than scientists, we must hope that we shall not be in a position to test the hypothesis soon.

EXAMPLE 2: EFFECTS OF LIQUID ASSET HOLDINGS

We turn to a second example to illustrate the function of survey research in economics. The problem of the effects of wealth, and of increase in wealth, on spending and saving has been long recognized as an important one in economic theory. At present the problem is of great practical significance in this country because during World War II a substantial proportion of the American people accumulated sizable amounts of liquid assets (bank deposits and Government savings bonds). Theorists formulated almost unanimously that the larger the liquid assets (of a family or a country), the larger will be the proportion of income spent and the smaller the proportion of income saved. They came to this conclusion, first, by adhering to what may be called the "principle of saturation." It is obvious, so we read in some theoretical papers, that the larger the assets the smaller the needs and incentives to add to them, that is, to save. Closely related to this principle is the thesis that "money burns holes in one's pocket." By definition, it was asserted, liquid assets have no other purpose than to be available for investments or the purchase of consumer goods. If liquid assets are invested, spending and saving are not affected (buying a house out of bank deposits represents a transfer from one form of saving to another); if they are used for the purchase of consumer goods, spending is increased. The larger the liquid assets the more probable are some effects in the latter direction.

In regarding economics as a normative discipline which describes how people should behave if they were fully rational, one may not be interested in the verification of these principles. Or one may disregard findings contradicting the principles by arguing that they must constitute temporary deviations due to irrational influences which cannot endure.

If the principles presented above are viewed as hypotheses, to be tested through empirical research, the difficulties on the macro-economic level (comparison of total assets with amounts spent in several periods or countries) are almost insurmountable because the economies compared usually differ in many respects in addition to differences in asset holdings. Survey research, testing the hypotheses on the micro-economic level, enables us to hold many other factors constant and to test modifications of the hypotheses if they are not verified in their original form.

The first few studies, made on the basis of early Surveys of Consumer Finances, did not show any effects of liquid asset holdings on spending and saving. In each income level families with small liquid assets saved about the same proportion of their income as families with large liquid assets. Instead of concluding that liquid assets do not have any effects the hypothesis was advanced that they have different effects which tend to cancel out. The following assumptions were made:

1. For some families availability of liquid assets will increase spending because such assets represent "enabling factors" which make larger expenditures possible.

2. For some families large liquid assets will be associated with high rates of saving; substantial liquid asset holdings are, most commonly, results of high rates of saving in the past years, and the habit of saving large proportions of income may continue. Psychological studies in diverse non-economic areas indicate that quite commonly levels of aspiration rise with achievement, rather than that incentives weaken when proximate goals have been attained.

The influence of diverse motivational forces has been confirmed. For some families large liquid assets were found to be associated with spending much and for others with saving much. Thus among holders of substantial liquid assets both high savers and high spenders were found more frequently than among holders of small liquid assets. Further multivariate studies established such principles as "people with income declines and large assets spend more than people with income declines and small assets."

Establishment of such principles of behavior represents progress but does not suffice. The principles do not enable us to predict what will happen to the economy as a whole. To make the transition from micro-economic principles to macro-economic generalizations the relative strength of the different motivational forces must be determined. This task has not yet been accomplished although new investigations which study the effects of the factor "ratio of liquid asset holdings to income" instead of those of "size of liquid assets" seem to be promising.

EXAMPLE 3: STUDY OF INFLATIONARY FORCES

In the two examples just discussed no use was made of trend analysis which is an important feature of survey research. Through surveys we may attempt to discover the changes in the strength of variables over time. Studies of business cycle developments may serve as examples. In the period 1950-52 these studies took the form of measuring the strengthening or weakening of inflationary forces.

In order to indicate the function of attitudinal data in such studies we may again begin with a brief reference to traditional economic principles. According to the usual textbook formulations, such objective factors as the level and trend of national income, of Government receipts and expenditures, and the quantity of money in circulation, fully account for fluctuations in production, sales, employment, and prices. We may contrast this thesis with what has happened in the United States during the Korean war. In the fall and winter of 1950-51 prices rose rapidly although Government receipts far exceeded Government expenditures; there was hardly any rearmament as yet and income increases followed rather than preceded the price increases. In the last nine months of 1951, on the other hand, national income increased and Government surpluses gave way to deficits, while production and sales of consumer goods declined and prices remained relatively stable.

To explain such discrepancies we find in the literature references to the erratic, irrational, or unpredictable behavior of businessmen and consumers. We read that people sometimes do not do what they should do because of their ignorance, prejudices, or emotions. People's attitudes are thought to be independent of economic events. Frequently it has also been assumed that psychological factors are not susceptible to scientific investigation.

We hold not only that human behavior is in principle lawful and determinate and that attitudes of businessmen and consumers influence their behavior, but also that these attitudes are not independent of economic events. Nevertheless, it is not permissible to substitute so-called objective factors for the psychological ones. Not the events themselves but their perception by consumers and businessmen matters. The objective situation is, quite often and especially in crucial situations, not such that it can elicit just one kind of perception. We cannot rely on the opinion of experts to determine the economic developments to which people, and different groups of people, react. We use survey research to determine (1) the perceptions, and the changes in perceptions, of different groups of people and (2) the factors that explain differences in perceptions and their changes.

The Survey Research Center conducted three nationwide economic surveys in 1951, the Survey of Consumer Finances for the

Federal Reserve Board in January and February and two smaller ones in June and November of that year.* In these surveys changes of perceptions and attitudes in several different areas were studied. Among them six will be singled out for discussion:

1. Evaluation of one's financial situation. All through the year 1951 the proportion of families who thought that their financial situation improved was much smaller than in 1950. Increases in family incomes continued to be much more frequent than decreases in incomes, but people in all walks of life were greatly concerned with the rising cost of living and connected it with unfavorable conditions. Expectations of income increases were likewise much less optimistic in 1951 than in 1950.

2. Buying intentions. At the beginning of 1951 the proportion of families, and also the proportion of upper-income families, who expressed an intention to buy automobiles and other durable goods was smaller than at the beginning of 1950. (Expressed buying intentions are not exact indications of people's future purchases but reflect attitudes held at the time of their expression.*)

3. Evaluation of buying conditions. Somewhat more people said at the beginning of 1951 that these were bad times to buy household goods (mainly because prices were high) than said that these were good times (mainly because prices would go up). In June the adverse judgment about buying conditions was much more pronounced than in January; in November the relation of favorable to unfavorable judgments was similar to that in January.

4. Price expectations. In January 1951 most people expected prices to go up during 1951; in June the number of those who expected stable or even falling prices was as large as the number of those who expected rising prices; in November expectation of price increases again predominated but to a smaller extent than in January. At all these dates, however, only relatively small price increases,

---

* The developments in the second half of 1950 will not be discussed here since they have been studied in much less detail than those in 1951. On the basis of a few survey questions it appears that the unexpected military reversals in Korea (in summer 1950 and again in winter 1950 after the intervention of the Chinese) shocked the people and aroused strong expectations of shortages and rapid price increases.

* See on this point the author's article, "Expectations and Decisions in Economic Behavior," in *The Policy Sciences*, edited by Daniel Lerner and Harold D. Lasswell, Stanford University Press, 1951.

which would not last longer than a year or two, were considered probable.

5. Expectations of shortages. In June 1951 fewer than one out of every three consumers expected that some consumer goods would be short during the next 12 months; in November the proportion was slightly higher. The official announcements about forthcoming curbs on civilian production were widely mistrusted.

6. Investment preferences. In 1951 expressions of choice between U. S. Savings Bonds and common stock as well as other indications of investment preferences showed no distrust in the future purchasing power of the dollar except among a small minority. Yet the proportion of upper-income people who favored investment in common stock was much larger in 1951 than a few years earlier and rose slowly during the year.

In analyzing survey data great reliance is placed on the consistency of different opinions and attitudes. Opinions about changes in one's financial situation, about buying conditions, forthcoming shortages, or investment preferences need not necessarily influence each other. The thoughts of individual respondents about these topics may be inconsistent, and the same may be true at certain times of all people (the entire sample) or some important groups of people (such as the high-income people or the businessmen). In 1951 this problem did not arise. A consistent picture emerged which provided an explanation for the prevailing trend in production, sales and prices that was characterized at that time by most economists as a "spending lull." From January to June evaluation of one's financial situation, income expectations and opinions about buying conditions worsened, while price and shortage expectations became less inflationary. In November 1951 all these indicators pointed toward a slight increase in the "inflationary fever," but the thermometer reading was still low (lower than in January 1951, for instance).

Understanding past developments should serve the purpose of enabling the investigator to make predictions. The scientific problem involved in making predictions from attitudinal studies may be summarized in the following question: Are attitudes and opinions advance indications of forthcoming behavior or do they lag behind and represent expressions of past developments? We are not in a position to give a definite answer to this question although more and more evidence speaks in favor of the first point of view. In 1951, for instance, predictions derived from the survey findings presented above proved to be correct—sometimes in sharp contrast to the most common economic predictions. (In June 1951 it was concluded from the survey data that the so-called spending lull was not a temporary interruption of the inflationary trend but would endure for quite a while.)

To be sure, the transition from survey findings to predictions is a matter of interpretation. Also, unexpected events of great import—outbreak of war, for instance—may change people's attitudes rapidly and invalidate the predictions. Finally, attitudinal data should not be studied in isolation; they must be considered together with the so-called objective data (trends of national income, Government deficits, money volume, etc.) which they are intended to supplement. Yet it appears that the joint use of attitudinal and financial trends makes our diagnosis more complete and therefore enables us to make better predictions than the exclusive reliance on non-attitudinal data.

Values and Limitations of Survey Research in Economics

In the preceding discussion the emphasis was placed on what the author believes to represent the most important single contribution of survey research to economics, namely, the integration of attitudinal and motivational data with the study of economic processes. Several other generalizations about the function of survey research may also be derived from the examples cited earlier and will be summarized here briefly. We may thus try to clarify the limitations of survey research as well as its positive contributions.

1. Survey research is a method of quantitative measurement. It purports to determine the frequency of different forms of behavior and of different motivational factors. Yet qualitative research and case studies also have a function in economics. From them hypotheses may be derived which are to be tested by quantitative measurement. Moreover, qualitative research can indicate the manifold complex variations of economic behavior.

2. Survey research is a method of empirical science. Its use,

however, should not contribute to empiricism. Speculative theories and models are necessary and useful. Empirical research cannot be fruitful without guiding principles and hypotheses that it is intended to test, and its results must be integrated in a theoretical framework.

3. The first aim of survey research is the development of micro-economics, which deals with the behavior and attitudes of individual decision makers. However, we also need to understand and predict macro-economic trends, that is, the trends of such aggregates as the entire American economy. If it were true that individual variations in spending, saving, and investing always cancel out, there would be a somewhat greater justification in excluding the human factor from economics and in relying on past relationships between such variables as national income and aggregate amounts saved or spent. Even though this is not the case, the reverse mistake must also be avoided. In studying variations among small groups, or the effects of motivations and attitudes held by small groups of people, we must not lose sight of the macro-economic goals. The transition from micro-economic principles of behavior to macro-economic regularities, or the integration of survey data with the economic budget of a country, is often difficult but definitely possible.

4. The main function of survey data is to understand and predict short-term changes in economic behavior. Generalizations derived from survey research refer usually to a specific country at a specified time (e.g., the United States in the 1950's). In other words, survey research is concerned with human behavior under specific conditions rather than with basic features of human nature. It is conceivable that in the future survey research may contribute to the understanding of long-term changes and differences between cultures, but as yet there has been little progress in this direction.

5. Survey research is concerned primarily with motivational patterns of a relatively superficial or surface character. To be sure, analysis of the presence or absence of correlation between different conditions or attitudes and ensuing behavior, on the basis of survey data, may shed light on motivational factors of which the actors themselves are not aware. It remains to be seen whether such studies suffice and whether and how a study of deep-seated, elusive motives may enrich economics.

Research Tasks

Although much work has been done during the past ten years in an attempt to integrate economics with other social sciences and to develop adequate research tools to study economic behavior, we are still at the beginning of our endeavors. Many more scientists and research organizations need to be engaged in this undertaking, each applying and testing its own theoretical framework and methodology. The number of unsolved problems, of importance for either theory or practice, and usually for both, is very large. After having cited some examples of progress in analyzing economic behavior through surveys, it is fitting to list research tasks regarding which only scanty results have as yet been achieved.

We may begin with a reference to the problem of economic motivation. Perhaps because the theory of motivation is in an unsatisfactory stage or because the methods used were not adequate, findings about why people purchase homes or life insurance, or why businessmen build new plants and buy new equipment, resemble lists of factors positively or negatively correlated with behavior without presenting an integrated picture. The same is true of our knowledge about the role of the profit motive and its interaction or conflict with other motives that influence people in conducting their businesses. Still less is known about what is called speculation and, specifically, about the factors motivating people in their stock market investments.

Progress may be sought in these respects by linking the survey approach with studies of individual psychology, especially an analysis of personality. Some questions that might be studied by means of interviews of the more clinical type are the following: Are there differences in the personality traits of people who engage in different kinds of economic activities? What environmental factors, or crucial experiences of the decision makers, are responsible for these personality traits?

These questions lead into, and are of course not independent of, problems of social psychology. Far too little is known up to now about the influence of face-to-face groups on economic behavior. Do neighbors, colleagues, club members think and behave uniformly and do they influence each other? Concerning what kinds of economic ideas and actions is this usually the case, and under what conditions are divergencies more common? What is the role of leadership in economic behavior? And what are the cultural patterns which shape current American economic behavior differently from what was prevalent 50 to 100 years ago and from what prevails in other societies at present?

A set of unsolved questions, somewhat different from those relating to economic motivations, is raised by inquiring about stability or variability of attitudes and behavior over time. Data have been collected about how spending or saving of young people differs from that of old people. But many crucial problems cannot be answered unless we follow a large panel of families over several years. What makes years of adding to one's reserves (saving) and years of drawing on one's reserves (dis-saving) alternate? Are there any economic attitudes and aspirations which are maintained over many years and which shape our attitudes toward issues that come up at one time or another? If so, what accounts for differences in these long-range attitudes?

The ultimate goal of economic psychology is the development of a theory of social action. Theory construction proceeds in two closely related ways. On the one hand, attempts are made to integrate low-level generalizations (functional relationships among variables) in a theoretical framework. On the other hand, theories and hypothetical constructs developed in fields other than economic behavior are tested and, if necessary, modified. In closing, a few words may be said about the general theoretical framework of survey research in the field of economic psychology.

Situational and attitudinal factors jointly determine social behavior. Changes in the environment are sometimes compelling or overwhelming—in which case changes in attitudes may lag behind changes in behavior—while sometimes they are filtered through attitudes. In the second case, businessmen and consumers have some latitude, and what they perceive as having happened as well as their reactions are a function of their sets and expectancies. Although socio-cultural norms, group belonging and reinforced past experience influence, and sometimes determine, people's attitudes, attitudes may also change radically under the impact of strong motivational forces and social facilitation. This is true not only in the sense that an individual businessman or consumer may change, for instance, his spending and saving pattern in consequence of changed attitudes and feelings. Changes in attitudes may also have an influence on social action and on economic fluctuations because substantial similar changes in attitudes may and do occur among very many people at about the same time.

Economic psychology draws both on economic theory and on social-psychological theory. In setting up its hypotheses economic psychology is indebted to Keynes (the preceding discussion of the effects of change in income represents just one example for that indebtedness), to Pigou (regarding the effects of assets on spending) and to classical economic theory about rational behavior and utility preferences (this is particularly true of studies about the presence or absence of deliberation and of weighing alternatives). Psychological theories of learning, habit formation, and problem solving have been of great importance in analyzing routine economic behavior as well as sudden changes in behavior. Theories of motivation and of groups have been utilized in studying such problems as levels of aspiration or saturation and their dependence on past accomplishments or failures and reference groups. Integration of empirical findings with these and other theoretical assumptions represents the most important research task for the years ahead.

Bibliographical Note

The book by the author, *Psychological Analysis of Economic Behavior* (McGraw-Hill, New York, 1951), presents some of the ideas expressed in this paper in greater detail and contains an extensive bibliography. It also contains a discussion of the non-economic assumptions by Keynes (pp. 133-149).

A rudimentary theory of economic behavior and quantitative data on the influence of different variables on spending and saving are presented in *Contributions of Survey Methods to Economics* by George Katona, L. R. Klein, J. B. Lansing, and J. N. Morgan (Columbia University Press, New York, 1954, edited by L. R. Klein).

The references to economic surveys of the Survey Research

Center of the University of Michigan apply primarily to the Surveys of Consumer Finances, conducted for the Federal Reserve Board and reported in the *Federal Reserve Bulletin* since 1945.

The business cycle surveys conducted during the Korean war have been presented in *Consumer Attitudes and Demand, 1950-1952* by George Katona and Eva Mueller (Survey Research Center, Ann Arbor, Mich., 1953).

Earlier relevant articles are those by the author in the *Review of Economics and Statistics* of 1949 and the *American Economic Review* of 1949, by L. R. Klein in *Econometrica* of 1951, and by L. R. Klein and J. N. Morgan in the *Journal of the American Statistical Association* of 1951.

Concerning the use of survey methods and techniques in economics—problems of sampling, interviewing, questionnaire construction, survey errors, etc.—the reader is referred to Chapter 15 ("Economic-Psychological Surveys," pp. 302-335) in G. Katona's *Psychological Analysis of Economic Behavior*, to the article "Methods of the Survey of Consumer Finances," *Federal Reserve Bulletin*, July 1950, and to the chapters by A. Campbell and G. Katona, by Leslie Kish, by C. F. Cannell and R. L. Kahn in *Research Methods in the Behavioral Sciences*, edited by L. Festinger and D. Katz (The Dryden Press, New York, 1953).

*   *   *

After completion of this manuscript multivariate analyses were carried out on the relation of financial, demographic, and attitudinal variables to consumer spending; panel studies were set up to study origin and effects of changes in economic attitudes, and the predictive value of economic attitudes was subjected to tests under different conditions (see George Katona and Eva Mueller, *Consumer Expectations, 1953-56*, Survey Research Center, Ann Arbor, 1956).

KEYNESIAN THEORY AND EMPIRICAL INQUIRY

A NOTE ON MICRO- AND MACROECONOMICS

William S. Vickrey

The central methodological problem raised by the foregoing two papers is that of the relation between macroeconomic and microeconomic theories and studies.

The Keynesian explanation of the size of the national income and employment is an example of macroeconomic theory. The variables are aggregate economic phenomena, such as national income, level of employment, and of savings, etc. Individual decision makers are supposed to be influenced by these magnitudes in determining the economic behavior which in turn results in these magnitudes, relatively independently of other "exogenous" influences. Keynes imputes certain simplified patterns of motivation to the three categories of economic agents: consumers, investors, and speculators. These motivations however are largely in terms of responses to current phenomena, and are thus static in nature, leaving out of account (at least in the simpler forms of the analysis) the more complex patterns of responses that may be generated by the relation of current to past experience, and by expectations about the future. Usually the psychological factors in individual behavior are viewed as passive responses to economic forces rather than initiators of change. Motivations of consumers in particular are so viewed. In the case of investors, whose fluctuating "animal spirits" are held

significant for the understanding of changes, Keynes professes ignorance of the determinants of these psychological moods. He, therefore, uses them as givens in tracing the workings of the economic
process.

Keynes not only points to certain variables as crucial but postulates a strategic set of determinate relations between them.

Keynesian theory offers an example of the kind of contribution
which a macroeconomic theory can make. It provided a new way
of thinking about economic phenomena. It singled out a new set
of processes held critical in reaching an equilibrium.

A basic assumption of classical theory is that a market economy
possesses automatic mechanisms that are constantly tending to bring
it to a stable state of full-employment equilibrium. The classical
view is one of a full-employment economy. Classical economists
were able to conceive of temporary deviations from this state, but
reasoned that automatic corrective devices would immediately come
into play and wipe out any excesses of either under- or over-employ-
ment, of either deflation or inflation. The fact that deviations from
the full employment equilibrium situation were considered to be
only temporary meant that fluctuations were viewed, not as oscillations of constant or ever-increasing magnitude, but as oscillations
always tending to converge toward full-employment equilibrium.

Keynes, undoubtedly disturbed by the world's economic ills of
the 1920's and 1930's, made an entirely opposite assumption about
the major characteristics of a market economy, namely, that there
is no automatic corrective mechanism in a market economy restoring
full employment after the occurrence of any deviation from that
state. He went even further, however, in his assumption and posited
that an *under*employment equilibrium could exist.

In the Keynesian system, decisions to save and decisions to
invest, each made by independent groups of people, can be out of
balance at full employment levels of activity. Keynes reasoned that
the situation in the early 1930's was such that intended savings out
of incomes that would have been generated by full employment
levels of activity exceeded intended investment, and that the level
of income fell to a less-than-full employment amount in order to
bring these two sets of basic decisions into balance. This, in fact,
is the automatic mechanism that Keynes considered to be at work
in the market economy in contrast to the classical theory which

assumes that interest rates (not amounts of income) fluctuate so as to balance saving and investment decisions at full employment. The interest rate, in the Keynesian framework, is related to preferences of individuals among financial assets instead of to their savings-investment intentions.

A feature of the classical system, consistent with the balancing of savings and investment flows at full employment via interest rate fluctuations, is the balancing of supply and demand for labor via fluctuations in the "real" wage rate, i.e., the money wage rate corrected for changes in its purchasing power over goods. Keynes originally found his less-than-full employment equilibrium to be stable because unemployed workers would not bargain in terms of "real" wage rates to wipe out existing unemployment. Keynes first considered the supply of labor to be dependent on the money instead of the real wage rate; therefore, his critics were able to level the charge at him of introducing market imperfections ("money illusion") in order to explain underemployment equilibria. They argued that if he retained the market perfections of classical economics he would not find underemployment to be a position of equilibrium. This is not purely an academic point to be dismissed by the observation that markets are far from ideally perfect. The policy implications are far reaching. The Keynesian analysis has motivated those types of liberal reform which aim at pushing the economy towards full employment by vigorous use of fiscal policy and deficit financing. On the other hand, the classically minded thinker has tended to look towards policies of removing market imperfections and stabilizing the money supply in order to restore the automaticity of full-employment equilibrium.

Post-Keynesian thinking has pushed ahead on both sides. Some followers of Keynes have argued that imperfections of the labor market, such as a tendency to bargain in terms of money rather than "real" money wage rate, are not essential to the logic of the system. They argue that full-employment equilibrium does not necessarily exist in an automatic sense and that the money fluctuates in an internally consistent pattern but not about an internally consistent equilibrium level. No static equilibrium generally exists for them, either of full- or underemployment. Theirs is inherently a dynamic system and not the static model of Keynes.

On the other hand, an attempt has been made to rehabilitate the classical system in response to the Keynesian attack by assuming that savings depend upon "real" wealth as well as income.

Precisely because Keynes' theory postulated relationships between variables which were measurable it stimulated tests in the form of forecasting levels of income and employment. The extrapolations on the basis of Keynesian theory did not prove satisfactory.

The failure of the forecasts did not strictly speaking prove the structure of the theory wrong, but it did indicate that the relationships used to apply the structure to a concrete case were too simplified to provide a close enough approximation to the real world. The theory asserted relationships between selected variables with other variables held constant.[1] "We have taken," said Keynes, "as given the existing skill and quantity of available labor, the existing quality and quantity of available equipment, the existing technique, the degree of competition, the tastes and habits of the consumer, the disutility of different intensities of labor and of the activities of supervision and organization, as well as the local structure including the forces other than our variables set forth below, which determine the distribution of the national income."

The failure of forecasts showed that a theory which in static terms could provide insights into the functioning of the economic process, and even provide prescriptions as to what to do in order to shift the course of the economy in a desired direction, was not, without the introduction of essentially dynamic elements, capable of making predictions in a world in which circumstances were in fact changing rapidly.

In contrast to the macroeconomic approach, Katona's paper deals with survey research. As Katona suggests, survey research studies individual behavior and attitudes, is prepared to include non-economic variables, and, in consequence of the first two characteristics, often calls for direct investigation of individuals and groups.

In considering the interrelations of the two approaches we may first note that the broader theory can and has contributed to the survey research by directing the latter to certain areas of study, and, even more specifically, to certain variables within the area. Katona's study of the relations of income and savings, Mack's study of income-consumption relationships, Duesenberry's work on saving, draw their inspiration from the importance of these relationships in Keynesian theory. This is true even when these and other investigators did not deliberately set out to test or modify Keynesian theory.

Conversely, what is the significance of the survey research for the broader theory? The most general answer is to say that microeconomic research has pointed to additional factors variously related to the few which compose the Keynesian model. These will be illustrated from the research on the consumer. We shall include not only confirmed relationships, but also suggested hypotheses provided they call for microeconomic studies.

In the earlier and simpler versions of the Keynesian theory, consumption was postulated to depend almost exclusively on the current or immediately preceding level of disposable income. Microeconomic studies are expected to provide a more complete explanation of determinants of consumption in four different ways: attitudinal, dynamic-historical, dynamic-expectational, and distributional.

1. ATTITUDINAL

Since the relationship of income to consumption postulated by Keynes is mediated by attitudinal factors, studies of attitudes towards saving and spending should improve the accuracy of prediction. This would be the case even if the analysis is not pushed back to investigate the factors which in turn affect attitudes. Insofar as changes in attitudes precede changes in behavior—to isolate relevant attitudes and to recognize changes in them would in itself improve prediction. Attitudes are not in general capable of being studied by aggregative methods, and microeconomic methods must be employed.

2. DYNAMIC-HISTORICAL

Past history (other than the income of the immediately preceding period) may exert a considerable effect on the level of consumption. In particular, survey research has suggested that the relationship between income and consumption, while in general following the Keynesian pattern, is more complicated than a mere linear relationship subject to a time lag. For one thing, it has appeared that adjustment of consumption to an increase in income is more rapid than adjustment to reduced income, and that a standard of living once achieved is given up much more slowly for a lower one than for a higher one. These relationships can be studied by macroeconomic methods, but survey research provides a far greater richness of data from which to discern these relationships.

3. DYNAMIC-EXPECTATIONAL

Anticipations concerning future incomes, prices, and other economic phenomena also can be considered to have a significant influence on consumption. These anticipations can in turn be generated by other phenomena than the strictly economic ones of past prices and incomes. Survey research can shed light both on the influence of such expectations on consumption and on the sources of these expectations themselves, in a manner that macro-analysis is powerless to emulate.

4. DISTRIBUTIONAL

The Keynesian convention of treating consumers as a homogeneous group has been questioned. That convention is based on the assumption that the great variety of individual attitudes affecting consumption operate independently and will balance themselves out.

But different economic groups are often found to react to economic change in significantly different fashion, so that the aggregate response cannot be reliably inferred solely from the aggregate figures but will depend to a considerable extent on the distribution of income, for example, among economic units. That differences of individual income levels might produce differences in the marginal propensity to consume was early recognized by Keynesian writers. "Cross-section" data in terms of families at different income levels was used to provide the necessary information for filling out the consumption function. More recently it has come to be recognized that differences in the propensity to consume occur systematically for other reasons than size of income and that it is not safe to rely on an assumption of equipartition of aggregate income changes among such groups to keep the aggregate relationship unaffected. Survey research has become necessary to search out these relationships.

So much then for refinements and modifications in the Keynesian theory suggested by the findings of consumer survey research. What bridge, if any, can be built between these findings and the original theory?

A pessimistic view of the prospects of such integration is taken by some because of the unwieldiness of a theory which takes too many factors into account. Insofar as psychological factors are introduced, their use requires in turn a valid theory of their determination.

But the choice does not lie between, on the one hand, the Keynesian theory in its present form, and, on the other, the incorporation of every correlation uncovered by the survey research. The optimum complexity may lie somewhere between the two extremes. Such "middle range" theories are the subject of the following section.

KEYNESIAN THEORY AND EMPIRICAL INQUIRY

A NOTE ON "MIDDLE-RANGE" FORMULATION

L. R. Klein

Business cycle theory and formal business cycle models are customarily developed in terms of a few main principles and variables. As an extreme example, the simple multiplier-accelerator model involving aggregative consumption and investment functions together with simple accounting definitions, represents a neat pedagogical device for demonstrating the cyclical mechanism through the interrelationships of a few macroeconomic variables. Interestingly enough, Keynes and other inspirational thinkers who have constructed such global theories have been thoroughly trained in classical economics of the individual consumer and producer. How has their formal and early training helped them in constructing highly aggregative systems and can a bridge, with sound construction, be built between micro- and macroeconomics? These are provocative questions taken up indirectly and in different form, in the contributions of Katona and Lekachman. The latter in discussing the necessity of such bridge construction, pictures the task as hopeless, at least in its present state of development. Katona, on the other hand, sees great potentialities in the application of microeconomic survey methods and results to business cycle analysis. I shall try to take up concrete situations which show how we might build a "middle-range" theory of obviously greater applicability to real life situations than the purely pedagogical models, yet much less complex and complete than the Walrasian type network tying together all the fine details of microeconomic behavior. The "middle-range" theory will rely heavily on the use of sample survey data of the type discussed by Katona.

In sample surveys of American households, both the family budget inquiries of 1935-36 and of 1941 and the postwar Surveys of Consumer Finances, we note differential patterns of spending and saving behavior by age classes, family size classes, racial characteristics, city size classes, income change classes, occupational groups (especially farm *vs.* non-farm and business owners *vs.* non-owners). In addition, new dimensions have been studied in the postwar surveys, namely, consumer assets, debts, and attitudes. How can this large number of interpersonal differences and possibly more, as yet unexamined, be integrated with macroeconomic business cycle theory in a systematic way that does not confront us with a hopeless maze of details?

In the first place, some of the empirical findings in consumer surveys throw direct light on bothersome amendments to the aggregative consumption function of Keynesian economics. Keynes, as well as his critics, recognized the need to assume a given distribution and dynamic pattern of income in order to postulate the simple relation between aggregate consumption and aggregate income known familiarly as the "Keynesian consumption function." If each individual in a society regulates his expenditures or his saving by an identical linear function of income, we observe readily that aggregate consumption or saving and aggregate income will be connected by the same linear relationship.[1] The Surveys of Consumer Finances show a nonlinear relationship between individual savings and individual income of a type that aggregates into a macroeconomic function dependent on the distribution of income. At this point, it is possible to show how the empirical findings on occupational differentials in saving behavior are related to the question of income distribution and contribute to a definite practical result.

The functional distribution of income among wage earners, farmers and recipients of property and entrepreneurial income (the latter hereafter referred to as *businessmen*) is closely associated with the size distribution of income. Essentially businessmen receive relatively large incomes (with great dispersion) and wage earners receive relatively small income. The farm-nonfarm distribution is not a distinction between low and high incomes but a distinction between functional types that accounts for differences between city and rural modes of life and for the fact that farmers, like business-men, must rely to a large extent on their personal savings for productive capital formation.

Kalecki's model of the business cycle and some direct macro-economic refinements of Keynesian theory make aggregate consumption a function of aggregate wage income and aggregate prop-erty income. As a superior refinement, we may envisage aggregate consumption to be a function of aggregate wage income, aggregate farm income, and aggregate nonwage-nonfarm income, with three separate coefficients of the marginal propensity to consume—highest for wage earners, lowest for farmers, and between these extremes for businessmen. The nonlinearity of the savings—or expenditure—income curves found in sample survey data and the occupational differentials observed in the savings or expenditure-income patterns in these same data can be used to direct advantage in aggregative business cycle models.

Suppose that we want to make use of the usual social accounting aggregates for estimating the three marginal propensity coefficients mentioned above in a single linear consumption function with four separate variables (consumption expenditures and three income types). Intercorrelations of time-series estimates of these three in-come types is usually so high, that the separate marginal coefficients cannot each be estimated with a reasonable amount of precision. On the other hand, in sample survey collections of data we have separate statistics on the savings or expenditure *and* incomes of the three types of individual consumers—wage earners, farmers, and businessmen. We can estimate three separate functions, one for each, and use the *relative* magnitudes of their separate marginal propensities as estimated constants in the aggregative relationship and then estimate the entire aggregative relationship without chances of intercorrelation.

A similar linkage between time-series aggregates and sample survey data can be used to remove the restrictive assumption made by Keynes concerning the dynamics of income fluctuations. The time-series aggregates of our economy are known to have high serial correlation; thus income in one period is highly correlated with income in the previous period. The high serial correlation of income makes it difficult to assess, with high degree of reliability, the separate contributions of current and past income in the statistically estimated aggregate relationship. From sample survey data we can make an independent estimate of the joint effects of current and past income. Substantial agreement has been found between the estimates from time-series and sample survey data; therefore, we are led to attach more confidence to the former estimates even though reliability measures based on time-series data alone are not high. Analogous considerations are involved in the estimation of a separate coefficient of liquid asset holdings in an aggregate consumption function. Prewar time-series data, because of high intercorrelation and small variation, did not produce a reliable estimate of the relation between liquid assets and consumer expenditures. Sample survey data, on the other hand, provide a firmer estimate because the variability of liquid asset holdings is great in a cross-section sample, and these holdings are not too highly correlated with income.

The records of historical income aggregates do not provide us with an adequately large sample for making distinctions between income increase and income decrease. The modifications of the Keynesian consumption function, popular a few years ago, suggested by Modigliani and Duesenberry, claimed distinctive effects of income increase and income decrease.[2] They implied that people would resist decreasing consumption as a result of an income decline and would, although with a lag, be willing to increase consumption as a result of an income increase. In the formulation of an aggregate consumption function, they constructed a relationship between savings on the one hand and income and highest previous income on the other.

Their underlying arguments can be more carefully checked by examination of sample survey data, and Duesenberry, in fact, built much of his theory from this source of information. More recent sample survey data than those considered by Duesenberry show that there are significantly different behavioral effects on saving of income increase and income decrease, but they show also that a further distinction must be made in a psychological dimension, namely, that between changes perceived to be permanent and changes perceived to be temporary.[3]

In using sample survey data to specify, more accurately, the relationship among certain variables known to be of interest to economists in their aggregative models, many seemingly irrelevant variables must also be taken into account. As mentioned just previously, psychological perceptions of income change must be considered, and to meet Lekachman's point that individual expenditure-income data may actually be observations drawn from as many separate expenditure functions as there are individuals, we must use numerous demographic variables in our relationship estimated from microeconomic data. An adequate version of a consumption function estimated from sample survey data may include as separate variables: consumption expenditures, income, income change, functional income type, assets, debts, age, family size, marital status, urbanization, race, income expectations, price expectations, general economic outlook, and other variables. Compared with the usual macroeconomic formulations, such a relationship may appear to be cumbersome, full of irrelevant variables and dependent on variables with an unknown tie to the economic mechanism.

Both survey data and time-series aggregates suggest that the simplest version of the Keynesian consumption function has no more than pedagogical significance, yet they do not suggest, either, that an empirical consumption function useful for practical purposes must contain one hundred, one thousand, or one million variables. Something of the order of magnitude of five, ten, or possibly twenty variables would be adequate and manageable. Although the number of variables needed to explain inter-individual variation in sample survey data may be large, e.g., as many as ten, all such variables are not relevant in short run business cycle analysis. Many of the demographic variables which positively must be taken into account for the study of microeconomic data are, so to speak, "averaged out" in associated macroeconomic analysis. A macroeconomic consumption function will depend on the average age of the population, the average family size, the percentage of non-whites, the percentage of homeowners, average population density, etc. These average demographic characteristics may change gradually over time and make only a modest trend contribution to the explanation of aggregate consumption variability. In a long run theory, these demographic factors are endogenous, but for short run analysis they may be assumed as given; thus it is comparatively simple to include them in aggregative business cycle models.

One of Duesenberry's main points in support of his particular aggregative consumption function was the observed fact from sample survey data, that Negro families appear to save more than White families at comparable income levels. Further study of these survey data and extensive analysis of the more recent Surveys of Consumer Finances, in which numerous income, asset, attitudinal and demographic differentials by social classes could be examined, cast considerable doubt on Duesenberry's theory and therefore helped toward a sharper formulation of macroeconomic theory.[4]

The psychological or attitudinal variables discovered to be important as a result of analysis of survey data are less satisfactorily assumed to be given, or classified as exogenous. We should be involved in a much expanded chain of relationships if we had to treat psychological together with conventional economic variables as endogenous in a completely closed system, yet a step forward is taken if we can at least make numerical measures of psychological variables and quantify their effect on economic behavior. With the use of time lags we attempt to do this with sample survey data. We first determine the empirical relationship between beginning-of-period expectations or attitudes and subsequent economic decisions from sample survey data. These are actually empirical relationships involving many variables such as expenditures, income, income change, assets, debt, age, family size, income expectations, price expectations, general economic outlook, etc. We then use statistical distributions of these psychological measures in conjunction with the estimated relationships to predict the course of economic activity in situations independent of the original sample.

In developing an aggregative consumption function for use in an econometric model of the economy as a whole, one that is to be used for practical analysis of the actual situation, findings from survey data have been put to work. In the first place, marginal propensities to consume out of wage, farm, and nonwage nonfarm (property) income were estimated from time-series aggregates by first obtaining estimates of the *relative* marginal propensities from survey data. Secondly, the level of liquid asset holdings was introduced as a variable in the consumption equation on the basis of survey findings concerning the relevance of this variable in the saving-spending process. The order of magnitude of the coefficient estimated from time-series data is reconcilable with that estimated from survey data and can be used with more confidence than would be justified on the basis of its sampling error alone.

In forecasting economic activity by econometric methods, the performance of the aggregative consumption function just prior to the forecast period and survey measures of consumer attitudes are considered together for possible adjustment of the consumption function in making the forecast. From survey data we estimate the net relationship between savings and consumer attitudes after taking income, liquid assets, age, family size, and other variables into account. We are not in a position to introduce explicit attitudinal measures in the aggregative consumption function because we do not yet have a sufficiently large sample of years in which attitudinal data were obtained.

No explicit use has been made, in the aggregative functions, of various demographic factors found to be significant in estimating coefficients from survey data. Insofar as these variables are nearly constant in the short run, we need not be concerned about their exclusion from the aggregative functions. If, however, average age, family size or frequency of marriage status change radically, survey data will provide one of the few sources of information of their effect on economic decisions.

While this discussion has centered around the consumption function as an interesting example, similar procedures have been followed in using the investment function for forecasting. Sample surveys of intended expenditures on plant and equipment have been used to adjust aggregative investment functions—equations relating investment expenditures to profits, stock of fixed capital, liquid assets, interest rates, etc.—in forecast situations. In actual practice, if aggregative functions appear to be consistently in error for a number of recent periods and if surveys of intentions to spend on capital formation indicate continued error in the same direction, we adjust the aggregative equation by the amount of recent errors for purposes of forecasting. In making predictions for 1954, it was found that survey intentions resulted in a modest drop in expected outlays for plant and equipment; therefore, the aggregative investment function *was not* adjusted for the amount of error found to be prevalent in recent years.

Microeconomic data in the form of statistics on individual firms can be used to estimate patterns of business behavior in much the same way that consumer survey data are used to estimate consumption functions. Investment functions (for both fixed capital and inventories), production functions, and corporate savings functions have been the object of much study on the basis of accounting records. These statistical calculations go far in providing new data on financial and physical operating variables and do not usually involve the expense of collection in field surveys as do corresponding data for household consumers. However, if we want to obtain proper estimates of the aggregative functions from microeconomic data, we must include variables responsible for interindividual variation, namely measures of attitudes and psychological characteristics of business entrepreneurs. Personal interviews conducted in the framework of scientific sample surveys seem to provide a natural source for these data. Having them, we shall be better able to "homogenize" individuals and thus obtain more refined estimates of the propensity to invest, save, etc., for the business equations of an aggregative model.

Seymour Martin Lipset

and

Martin Trow

REFERENCE GROUP THEORY
AND TRADE UNION WAGE POLICY

Until recent years, two distinct schools of American economists concerned themselves with labor problems. On one hand the institutional economists—Commons, Hoxie, and Perlman were the most prominent—laid the groundwork for labor studies through their collection of primary materials, histories of labor organizations here and abroad. Out of these historical data came several theories of the labor movement. On the other hand, there was a group of more or less orthodox economists who dealt with labor problems in the traditional categories of classical economics.

More recently a younger generation of labor economists has emerged whose system of analysis differs distinctly from either of the above schools. Giving their closest attention to concrete cases of industrial relations, these writers attempt to account for the *actual* behavior of trade unions and business enterprises over the wide range of circumstances in which these two institutions (and the state) interact. For their purposes, the macroscopic theories of Perlman and Hoxie are too wide-meshed to contribute much to understanding the great variety of trade union behavior observable today.[1] At the same time, contemporary labor economists are almost unanimous in agreeing that orthodox economic theory is inadequate for explanation of actual conditions. At present, these younger labor economists are engaged in detailed studies of unions in action. They have not yet presented a theoretical framework which could make these investigations coherent and cumulative, point up gaps in the data, and direct further research in the field.

In the course of their studies, some of these men have noted the considerable influence of "non-economic factors,"—such as worker sentiments and union politics,—on collective bargaining relationships. Several of them have begun to deal more fully with these "non-economic" variables and to explore their background and their consequences for bargaining relationships.

One approach to the analysis of trade unions conceives of them as political as well as economic institutions. Simple though this newer perspective may seem, it suggests the fruitfulness of studying trade unions in terms of the concepts and research methods that have arisen through study of other political institutions.

For example, conceiving of union behavior as political behavior suggests an analysis of the decision-making process within trade unions. Some labor economists have recently asserted that many strikes, wage demands, and other union behavior cannot be understood solely in the logic of economic bargaining; instead it is recommended that we also see them as power struggles between different unions, or between different groups and factions within a single union. If this is true, then the need arises for a theoretical structure which can deal with the bases for such behavior. As a step in this direction, economists have begun to use the concept of "equitable" or "coercive" or "invidious" comparisons as a possible determinant of collective bargaining patterns. This concern with comparisons stems from attempts to explain the oft-noticed fact that unions frequently make "uneconomic" wage demands and settlements supposedly because of feelings that given wage adjustments will establish "equity" among groups of workers, who believe that they ought to receive the same wages.

Arthur Ross, one of those most responsible for this new concern in labor economics, has suggested that the forces of the "labor market," as described by traditional wage theory, do not have "compelling significance," but rather, that "in collective bargaining determination the strongest equalizing tendencies emanate from the force of organization and the force of ideas. Organizations are established for the very purpose of achieving mastery over market factors. The ideas are concepts of equity and justice which move in an orbit different from that of supply and demand." [2] He points out that, "comparisons play a large and often dominant role as a standard of equity in the determination of wages under collective bargining." [3]

In the essay in which the concept of "equitable comparison" received its first clear formulation, Ross contends that the traditional treatment of wages by economists is no longer adequate. The orthodox formulation simply cannot explain why "a union behaves as though it had ends in view other than the maximization of the wage bill, when strikes are resorted to which by any monetary measure will not be worth their costs, when some differentials in wages are borne without protest and others occasion bitter attack, . . . when the standardization of rates or of increases is pursued at the expense of a larger total wage bill. . . ." [4] A number of questions current economic analysis cannot answer are:

1. "Why, in a bargaining process, is the size of the wage adjustment often more crucial than the amount of the wage which results?" Apparently, "equalizing tendencies in collective bargaining are directed toward equalization of adjustments as often as equalization of rates." [5]

2. What are the mechanisms which tend to make for equalization of wage rates, and what are those that tend to sustain differentials?

3. How does it happen that "work stoppages frequently occur when the difference between the parties has been reduced to minute proportions?" [6]

4. Why do many unions insist upon a uniform wage rate throughout their jurisdiction when "there is little doubt that a union could achieve a higher average wage rate, and a greater total wage income for its members, if it were to extract from each employer the most that he could be made to pay." [7]

5. Why is it "that unions often press for consolidated bargaining structures, as represented by multiunion and multiemployer bargaining," when "it is highly probable that total wage payments are less under multiemployer bargaining than would be true if separate bargains were negotiated between the union and each employer." [8]

Ross notes that "all these questions are addressed to the relationship between one wage rate and another, or between one wage bargain and another. They involve the structure and function of equalizing tendencies in wage determination." [9] Comparisons are important to employers, workers, and union men. The employer does not want to "get out of line," the worker wants "what is coming to him," and the union leader wants security for himself and stability for the administration.

Reference Group Theory and Economic Problems

The sociologist and social psychologist will recognize that the economist's concern with comparisons appears similar to problems developing within the new and rapidly expanding field of reference group analysis.[10] Reference group analysis is concerned with the "determinants and consequences of those processes of evaluation and self-appraisal in which the individual takes the values or standards of *other individuals and groups as a comparative frame of reference*."[11] The economist's concern with the role of "coercive" comparisons in collective bargaining is clearly a special case of this more general area of social psychological interest. The reference group analyst asks, what are the forces shaping the comparative evaluations that individuals make of their own situations and those of others, and what difference do these comparative evaluations make on the ensuing sentiments and behavior of those making such comparisons?

The major difference between current efforts to develop reference group analysis in social psychology and sociology and the discussion of the "comparisons" in labor economics is that the sociologist approaches the problem with a body of theory designed to deal with group behaviors of all kinds, while the labor economist, entering the province of "non-economic" factors without any previously developed system of integrated concepts, tends to formulate ad hoc hypotheses. In the absence of interplay between theory and research there is no clear building of one study on the findings of another. A concept like "equitable comparison" enters succeeding works in its original form, collecting around it additional illustrations and implications, but is not further developed or reformulated. Yet the small set of empirically warranted propositions and the larger store of theoretically posed questions in sociological reference group analysis hold promise of fruitful incorporation in related studies by labor economists. In this paper we will examine a few of the problems generated by the juxtaposition of reference group concepts and generalizations from recent works in labor economics, concluding with a set of suggested research directives.

Ross's recognition that "comparisons play a large and often dominant role as a standard of equity in determination of wages under collective bargaining" may be fruitfully respecified in terms of reference group concepts. Ross, in his primary concern with the factors involved in wage determination under collective bargaining, has in fact been led to raise questions similar to those he might raise if he were directly concerned with identifying the effective reference groups of participants in the bargaining process.

Since groups with which one identifies can determine an individual's attitudes and behavior, the first problem is the discovery of the processes shaping the selection of these groups. What are the conditions which affect the choice of the groups? Do some individuals have conflicting reference groups? If so which reference groups take precedence over which others—and for whom?

Four categories of possible reference group determinants may be suggested here:

(a) *The social structure itself* may pattern common frames of reference for individuals in a given social category.

(b) *The institutional definitions of the social structure* may focus the attention of individuals on common reference groups.

(c) *The legitimacy ascribed to the social structure* may affect the choice of groups used for comparison.

(d) *The effect of conflicts within and between institutions* may focus the leadership's appeals in the direction of particular comparative references and thus help determine the meaningful reference groups.[12]

The following sections, based on analysis of collective bargaining, respecify reference group determinants in the above categories and are designed to illustrate the usefulness of these provisional categories in analyzing union behavior.

The Social Structure as a Reference Group Determinant

The *size* and the *scope* of a structure influence wage rates by directing the attention of its participants toward the making of certain comparisons rather than others. Ross suggests that *centralized collective bargaining* and the *common ownership of multiple employing units* create reference groups for the members and leaders of unions different from those which operate under the conditions of *local bargaining or bargaining with different firms*.[13] These structural variables act as reference group determinants because they lead union members to define as "inequities" certain differentials in wage rates when found among members of the same union or employees of the same firm.

Three general propositions may be drawn from this analysis:

(1) Individuals or groups who are subordinate to the *same* authority are more likely to use each other as reference groups, than if the reverse were true.

(2) Workers in a large "membership" structure are likely to use abstract status reference groups, such as class and steel workers. Workers in smaller membership structures are more likely to use face to face relationships such as bench-mates and neighbors as their reference groups.

(3) Workers who *see structural elements as general status categories* are likely to use these categories as reference groups. For example, workers are more likely to become incensed over wage differentials between the plants of one company than they are over the same differentials between different companies.[14]

There is some reason to believe that whether men use a highly *generalized category* such as class or occupation, or whether they use a specific set of individuals as their effective reference group for given appraisals, makes an important difference in their ensuing sentiments and behaviors. It should, therefore, be of crucial importance, in the analysis of workers' sentiments to ask the question: What factors operate to increase the effectiveness of general status categories over the "primary environment of opinion?" The size and the scope of the structure may be the factors which determine what reference group is used.

Institutional Definitions of Reference Groups

Labor economists have suggested that not only the structural form, but also the related norms presumably held by the participants affect reference group determination. For example, the norm of "equal pay for equal work" is assumed to generate pressures for wage equalities, particularly in situations where the structure of ownership directs the attention of workers to similar workers in other plants owned by the same firm.

In addition to a presumably widely held and diffusely defined norm or value prescribing "impartiality of treatment by government," [15] more specific government norms, in the form of administrative rules and decisions, tend to direct comparisons in some ways and not in others. An arbitrator's or government agency's "discovery" that a group of industries are related so that a given decision may cover all provides a good example of this.

Some effects of government participation in the bargaining situation may be suggested here:

(a) The imposition, by the government or other effective agency, of norms which are inconsistent with existing norms will lead to dissatisfaction, resistance and possibly abandonment of the prescribed norm.

(b) The effectiveness of an imposed norm will depend on the extent to which it conforms to more general norms of equity.

(c) The permanency of an imposed norm will also be dependent upon its consistency with norms already existing in the group.

(d) An imposed change in a group will have unanticipated consequences for other groups.

Though governmental wage policies operate as *institutionally prescribed norms* in the determination of workers' reference groups, these policies, which may be functional for the bureaucratic or political needs of the administrative agency, do not always coincide with the frames of comparative reference used by the affected workers. The rationale behind different government wage decisions *can be* diverse. In one decision, the Wage Stabilization Board approved a general pattern for the electrical, steel, and auto industries on the grounds of similar wage movements in the past, common job classifications, a " 'considerable degree of geographic relationship,' " and the " 'limited interrelationship in terms of products.' "[16] On another occasion a presidential fact-finding board "brought forth a new category of 'fundamentally basic industries,' " which involved steel, iron ore mining, aluminum, and non-ferrous metals.[17]

There is evidence that some government orders have upset traditional differentials among different industries and groups of workers, thereby engendering considerable dissatisfaction with the workings of the government agencies. Ross himself provides a case in point:

> The two-day strike of the Locomotive Engineers and the Railway Trainmen throughout the nation's railroad system in 1946 resulted from the mismanagement on the part of the government officials involved as much as from arrogance on the part of the union leaders. Considerable dissatisfaction had developed among the railroad workers over the deterioration of their relative earning status. Once they were "the aristocrats of labor." By 1945, their annual earnings were surpassed by those in the automobile, shipbuilding, machinery, rubber, and petroleum industries.[18]

This is an interesting illustration of the unanticipated consequences of a governmental decision, which ignored the actual operation of the social structure. The norms of equity underlying government decisions may assume that machinists in the railroad industry should not receive higher wages than machinists or equally skilled workers in other industries. This "objective" skill basis of classification, however, ignores the possibility that the traditionally superior status of the railroad workers leads them to use workers in other manual occupations as "negative reference groups," and to regard wage increases for the other "inferior" industries as threats to the railroad man's status position. The attempt, therefore, to eliminate an "inequality" creates discontent among another group.

Consideration of the ways in which institutional (in this case, governmental) norms serve to define reference groups raises a number of additional questions. It is clear from the nature of governmental decisions that the norm "non-discrimination among employers and unions" is so vague as to allow an almost unlimited scope for administrative discretion. The war-time government agencies could and did choose to "relate" or "non-relate" many different industries and occupations. In their arguments before these governmental agencies, union leaders and employers frequently compare their own jurisdictions to those of others chosen for their usefulness in establishing a case for or against a wage increase. When faced with the decisions as to which comparisons (reference groups) it should accept as "valid" for a given case, a government agency is exposed to a variety of political and economic considerations and pressures. Probably the least important criterion to members of such government boards is the question of whether the different groups of workers involved actually use each other as reference groups for wage purposes. In the process of establishing official "patterns of relatedness," these governmental decisions may in effect be opening a Pandora's Box. Much of the labor unrest following upon decisions of the War Labor Board may be adequately understood as a consequence of the arbitrary superimposition of conflicting frames of reference upon patterns of comparison already operating among workers. One key area for further research, therefore, would be a study of the degree of comparative reference in given industrial situations and the consequences that flow from the contradictions between them.[19]

Seeing the policies of governmental labor agencies not only as sets of prescriptions enforced by the power of the state, but also as supplied frames of comparative reference, raises a question about the influence of such rules and decisions after the legal force behind them has been removed. To what extent, for how long, and under what conditions do administrative decisions continue to operate as "residual" determinants of worker's reference groups?

The authors of *The American Soldier* observed that:

Comparing himself with his unmarried associates in the Army, (the married man) would feel that induction demanded greater sacrifice from him than from them; and comparing himself with his married civilian friends he could feel that he had been called on for sacrifices which they were escaping altogether. Hence the married man, on the average, was more likely than others to come into the Army with reluctance and, possibly, a sense of injustice.[20]

In this case, the institutional norms embodied in the rules governing induction into military service apparently did structure the reference groups used by those affected. We do not know, however, whether the norms embodied in the wage decisions of governmental labor agencies are equally effective in shaping the reference groups of the workers to whom they refer. Among other things, this may depend on the extent to which affected individuals *are aware of and accept the institutional definitions of the situation*. In *The American Soldier*, the authors assumed that inductees were aware of and concurred in the justice of the institutional rules governing induction. A similar degree of awareness and acceptance cannot, however, be assumed for workers with regard to administrative decisions of government agencies. Although Ross treats government participation in collective bargaining in terms of the pressures this creates for "uniform treatment," he does not tell us very much about the workers' responses to the institutionalized norms thus supplied. Since we have raised the question not only of the immediate impact of governmental decisions on workers' sentiments but also of the *continuing* influence of governmental decisions and "patterns of relatedness" on workers' reference groups, we have additional reason for wanting to know how and to what extent the decisions, policies and other "institutional definitions" of government agencies filter down into the awareness of the rank and file and become a basis for their own comparative evaluations.

"Legitimacy" of the Social Structure and the Choice of Reference Groups

The degree of *legitimacy* which individuals impute to a given social structure may affect the choice of groups they use as effective bases of comparison. We may presume that among organized workers, the extent to which various wage relationships are felt to be *morally right*—either rationally justified or as part of a traditionally accepted hierarchy of occupations—will influence the choice of comparative appraisals of their own situations.

The relationship between concepts of legitimacy and reference group behavior as they affect collective bargaining may be approached two ways, by cross-cultural comparison or within a given society. We may ask how ideas justifying total social structures are related to the variations in reference group behaviors of strata within them; or, what are the differences considered legitimate in a given society?

These questions may be illustrated by discussing a comparative analysis of collective bargaining patterns in different countries. Ross and Irwin suggest that the reason strike rates in the United States and Canada have been considerably higher than those in Great Britain and Sweden can best be explained by the different political positions of unions in these countries.[21]

It is, however, possible to explain variations in strike rates either within or between countries by an alternative set of hypotheses:

(a) The more rigid the social structure the more likely it is that individuals will make intra-group rather than inter-group comparisons.

(b) Therefore, the less rigid the social structure the more the discontent that will be engendered.

An egalitarian, "open class" value system with its less rigid social structures may actually engender more immediate discontent among low socio-economic groups, than does a more rigidly stratified structure. An open-class value system leads workers to define inequalities in income and status between themselves and others as illegitimate more frequently than do workers in countries which have more sharply and rigidly defined social structures. Our egalitarian ideology, by more broadly and less clearly defining the range of reference groups with which American workers can legitimately compare themselves, may thus make for more free-floating discontent among workers here than in Europe, where more rigid systems of social stratification narrowly limit the range of legitimate reference groups.

In attempting to locate the determinants of variations in sentiments among workers in different countries, we are continuing to use the intervening variable of "effective reference group." We suggest the variations in the social structures and "legitimate" normative systems of different countries affect the kinds of reference groups used by workers and that these in turn affect workers' attitudes in and toward labor-management-state relations.

Shifting our attention from comparative social structures, we observe that labor economists take notice of the relations between the "legitimacy" of given social relations and collective bargaining *within a given social structure* by distinguishing between "differentials" and "inequities."

> Viewed in the large, what is euphemistically called our "national wage structure" is a maze of distinctions and differences. Some are more or less in accordance with commonly accepted notions of equity, such as distinctions between skilled and unskilled workers, or appear to follow economic geography or to correspond to the profit position of employers. These we call differentials. Others exist without apparent reason. These we call inequities." [22]

The legitimacy of such economic differences and their concomitant status implications are continually subject to challenge and strain in the give and take of collective bargaining. When relationships such as those which obtain between the wages of workers in given industries, unions, or communities, are held to be morally right, the workers included in those relationships have a standard frame of reference for appraisal of their own situation. When such sets of legitimate wage and status relations are called into question or disrupted, as through technological innovation, the groups used for reference by the participants in such relations may shift to include some that have not before been used. In turn, changes in the reference groups of given categories of workers, as a result of changes in the structure of ownership, efforts of union leaders, or new definitions of "patterns of relatedness" imposed by government agencies, may call into question wage relations previously felt by these workers to be legitimate differentials. [23]

The differential union strength of different occupations has often meant that the economic results of collective bargaining reflect not a legitimate hierarchy of occupations but the differential power of organizations. White collar workers now make less than many manual workers; miners have moved ahead of many other occupations in earning capacity; railroad workers have moved down the list of high paid occupations. Since the organization of the Newspaper Guild, journalists, who once earned less than the unionized printers, now earn more. What is the effect of such changes on the self-appraisal of each group of workers? Does the improvement in the position of the previously unorganized make them more likely to accept the existing set of economic relationships, or does it expose them to contact with new groups on this higher level, and simply leave them disgruntled because of their failure to reach equality with groups on an even higher level? Conversely, do the gains of previously low-paid groups lead to discontent among the workers who were formerly paid more?

Ross's problem—when, why, and by whom are some differentials seen as "equitable" while other differentials are not so defined—is peculiarly amenable to reference group research. Which reference groups individuals use, and how they use them, are questions intimately related to their feelings regarding the *rightness*, the legitimacy, of the comparisons made. A study of the reference groups used by groups of workers in their appraisals of their wages, status, or other aspects of their situations, could not avoid attempting to identify the nature, intensity, and bases of the moral sentiments lying behind specific comparative appraisals. Such a study might provide a systematic approach to the patterns of legitimacy (and illegitimacy) in a "national wage structure" which now "seems to consist of little islands of rationality in a sea of anarchy." [24]

The Effect of Conflicts Within and Between Institutions (The Manipulation of Reference Groups)

Earlier in this paper we have suggested how such factors as the structure of ownership, the scope of a bargaining relationship, and varying concepts of the legitimacy of different social structures may serve to "produce a sense of pertinent similarity between statuses" which are then used in other connections as "comparative contexts." We are now suggesting that political, union, and other leaders, in their efforts to manipulate the reference groups of their audiences, attempt to establish a "sense of pertinent similarity" between the statuses of an audience and other specific groups or strata, *so that the ensuing comparisons will engender sentiments strengthening and supporting the position of the spokesman.* The consequences that follow upon such efforts may or may not coincide with the intentions behind them; but in any case, such purposeful efforts to manipulate comparisons compose a class of reference group determinants that should be taken into account.

Union officials may point to an unfavorable wage differential in order to mobilize rank and file support for a strike. They may point to a favorable differential to demonstrate their own effectiveness to their members, or to unorganized workers. Labor leaders may also engage in multi-union bargaining to indicate the absence of differentials between their own contracts and those of other unions which are, for the membership, actual or potential reference groups. Under what conditions are union leaders likely to attempt to manipulate reference groups in this fashion? Ross in his essay suggests that:

> The more intense is leadership competition, the more certain it is that comparisons will be played upon for all they are worth. Practical politics and personal animosities combine to make this the one situation in which workers are assured of "full knowledge." [25]

Some implications of inter- and intra-union conflict on attempts to manipulate the reference groups of the members may be seen in a recent case. In New York City, the Transport Workers' Union, the union of subway and bus employees, began an organizing drive among the police force. Michael Quill, the president of the union, defended this drive by saying that the traditionally lower-paid transit employees were earning more than the police, and that the city officials were pointing to this discrepancy to justify refusing higher wages to the transit employees.

One would assume that transit employees and policemen are not ordinarily effective reference groups for each other. With the gradual assumption of transit services by the city, the two groups have the same employer, and this, plus the fact that the lower status occupation has a strong union while the policemen do not, created a situation in which the transit union leaders were driven to attempt to make these groups mutual reference groups. If Quill's tactics had succeeded, policemen would presumably have become increasingly dissatisfied as they were made aware of their lower pay. The failure of this attempt points up the existence of structural constraints against the extension of the reference groups.

As part of the struggle for power among competing leadership groups, their manipulations of comparisons tend to emphasize the importance of general status categories as over against the spontaneous use of face to face intimates as comparative references. It is a short step from the observation to the hypothesis that the *more active the internal political life of a union,* and the more *factional or competitive* is the propaganda to which the rank and file is exposed, the more the membership will tend to appraise comparatively its own wages and working conditions on the basis of general status categories.

If this hypothesis is true, further consequences for internal union politics may follow. For example, it may be that workers who come to use more generalized reference groups, perhaps initially as a result of the manipulation of comparisons during leadership fights, will continue to do so beyond or outside of the circumstances which gave rise to them. Union leaders may be able to generate specific patterns of comparisons among their membership, but they may be less able to end their use—their attention-directing efforts in any given union or factional fight may have unintended consequences for subsequent patterns of comparisons made by the rank and file.

It is important to note that the presence of conflict organizations in any situation often means the addition of a new channel of communication. A trade union, a faction within a union, or a political party will attempt to make people aware of "facts" that they would not ordinarily know about. It would be extremely useful for the sociologist to study the reactions of workers to such new knowledge. In situations like this it would be possible to test hypotheses about the factors relating to and the effect of the differential selection of reference groups.

Understanding what part manipulation plays in the determination of reference groups would involve dealing with propositions such as the following:

(a) The more active the political life of a union, the more leaders will attempt to manipulate the reference groups of workers.

(b) Inter- and intra-union conflict will lead toward the manipulation of reference groups in the direction of status categories and away from face-to-face relationships.

(c) Leaders who suggest the use of reference groups which do violence to existing concepts of legitimacy or are outside the meaningful experience of group members will have little success.

(d) The generation of patterns of comparison for specific purposes will probably alter the "permanent" frame of reference for a group—possibly in unanticipated directions.

Non-Economic Institutional Variables
Affecting Union Behavior

Although labor and product market conditions probably are the most important determinants of the collective bargaining policies of unions, it is true that economic variables cannot account for some of this behavior. It is important, therefore, to analyze the factors which affect policy decisions within given unions, and in particular, to distinguish between the goals and needs of the members and the leaders.

We are told, for example, that a transit workers' union in San Francisco prolonged a strike for four cents more an hour to gain equality with the going rate in Los Angeles after the transit lines in the two cities were brought under the same management.[26] Ross appears to assume that the workers in San Francisco really cared about this small difference, whereas it is possible that the San Francisco union leader, given his own values and reference groups, was attempting to match the gains of other comparable union leaders. The competition for greater salary increases among unions such as the U.A.W., the U.M.W., or the Steelworkers appears to be related to the struggle for power and prestige among their leaders, a struggle which directly affects few members.

The introduction of reference group concepts requires that at some point in the analysis of factors entering into wage determination under collective bargaining new questions be raised: What is the distribution of sentiments among members of the union with regard to the wage differentials or increases? How does this distribution vary between different statuses of union members, and as between leaders and rank and filers, and do these differences reflect the use of different reference groups by the several categories of union members? If we can only *tentatively suggest* that union leaders often select their effective reference groups in terms of their own position vis a vis *other union leaders* rather than in response to the values and orientation of their members, we can say even less with regard to how union members themselves select their own reference groups.

Challenges to a union leadership, either from within the union or from rival unions appealing to the same membership, apparently work to increase the direct influence of rank and file sentiment, often pushing the union in the direction of greater militancy. The influence of opposition factions or rival unions presumably works to force a group in power to be more sensitive to rank and file attitudes and to develop increased expectations among the rank and file.

One tendency working to minimize the direct influence of membership sentiments on the bargaining process, is the increasing role played by the international office. The increased importance of the international office is generally accompanied by the increased bureaucratization of labor unions. Not only are the international officials "better insulated from rank-and-file pressures," but they are also better equipped to deal with the professional economists on the other side of the bargaining table and to provide legal and administrative counsel and other special technical services. The shift in the locus of control in the bargaining relationship out of the local union to the international office serves to move the whole bargaining process beyond both the technical competence and the effective influence of the rank and file.

The level and intensity of union politics and the role of the international office are not the only possible determinants of rank-and-file influence on the bargaining process. Even where the absence of important internal political challenge would tend to minimize the effectiveness of rank and file attitudes, the ideology of the union and its leadership may prescribe a degree of sensitivity to membership sentiments beyond the minimum required to maintain themselves in office. The benevolent paternalism of the leadership of the International Ladies Garment Workers Union is a case in point.

We do not have the space here to discuss at length the factors that tend to make workers in certain industries more militant than those in others. Some of these factors seem to be related to the nature of the occupation and of the communities in which they are carried on. Neither miners nor maritime workers are integrated into the rest of society, since they usually live together and their occupations keep them both spatially and socially apart from other groups. Without attempting an adequate interpretation of the trade union militancy associated with specific occupations and industries, these illustrations do demonstrate that sentiments rooted in the specific social structure of different occupations affect the collective bargaining policies of "dictatorial" as well as "democratic" unions, and these sentiments may be closely related to the direction and intensity of reference group orientations.

The non-economic variables which affect the character and results of collective bargaining, need to be investigated. The following propositions suggest the direction that investigation might take:

(a) Challenges to union leadership increase the sensitivity of leaders to the sentiments of the rank and file.

(b) The effectiveness of membership sentiments on the rate of strikes and collective bargaining is minimized when the reference groups of the leaders differ from those of the membership.

(c) Increased bureaucratization of unions insulates officials against pressures from the rank and file.

(d) The ideology of a union may prescribe more sensitivity to member sentiments than would be required to maintain the organization.

Ross's concern with the reasons that "some wage differences persist indefinitely, others narrow gradually, and still others are eliminated entirely," cannot be answered solely by research on membership sentiments. As we have noted before, in the general effort to develop a theory of collective bargaining, membership sentiments are only one set of variables to consider. Ross correctly emphasizes the whole set of problems implicit in the view of the union as a political organization, and one might suggest many other factors. But these several problems need to be analytically distinguished if they are to be translated into research studies.

Conclusion

Labor economists, in their continuing efforts to come to grips with the real forces impinging on industrial relations, have been led to observe that among those forces are sentiments held by the union members, that these sentiments frequently arise out of comparisons made by the worker between his own situation and the presumed situations and standards of other individuals. Apparent congruities between this orientation and certain aspects of emerging reference group theory led us to consider (a) some of the structural and normative determinants of workers' reference groups, and (b) some of the factors, such as the presence and intensity of inter- and intra-union conflicts, and the locus of union control in collective bargaining, which affect the weight of influence these membership sentiments have on union behavior in collective bargaining.

The economist's task would seem to be to specify both the economic limits as derived from theoretical and empirical analyses and the types of situations in which "economic" factors do not have "compelling influence." The sociologist, taking these economic limits as given, can then explore the structural, organizational, and social psychological factors which are *also* present, and which have varying consequences for collective bargaining. Further research study might proceed along the following lines:

A. Instead of assuming the nature of rank and file sentiments, or inferring them from leadership behaviors, it would be valuable to study them directly. In the course of such a study we would want to determine not only men's sentiments and expectations with regard to their work situations, but also how these expectations were come by, and especially the composition and characteristics of the reference groups which the workers used.

We would certainly come upon situations in which given workers do not use directly identifiable reference groups, but if we think of reference groups as special kinds of frames of reference, we may raise the more general question: Under what conditions do men most frequently take the values and standards of other individuals and groups as their comparative frame of reference? The immediate social context in which evaluations are made may affect the character of the evaluation itself. Reynolds and Shister, who asked workers to evaluate aspects of their own jobs, elicited many evaluations seemingly couched in "absolute" standards.[27] Nevertheless, in contexts of collective bargaining, evaluations may far more frequently be made in terms of explicit reference groups in thinking about a wage *scale* or *pattern* rather than an *individual* pay envelope.[28]

Any systematic effort to study the reference group behaviors of organized workers that presumably have influence on collective bargaining relationships should answer the following sets of questions:

1. What groups or categories are used by workers as effective frames of reference? If more than one group is used, do they conflict? If so how is this conflict resolved?

2. What differences can be observed in the effective reference groups of different subgroups or statuses of workers? Are different reference groups used by older and younger, more and less educated workers?

3. What are the kinds of evaluations for which different reference groups are used? Do workers use the same groups for evaluation of their wages as they do for other aspects of their work situation?

4. What kinds of structural factors influence the composition of effective reference groups in the situation? Which are the reference groups that actually operate in a given situation?

5. What is the character of the norms which give the observed comparisons their moral force? By what groups and strata in the union are they held? Under what circumstances? With what consequence?

B. Assuming we know the nature of the sentiments of the rank and file and their effective reference groups, it would be valuable to study the conditions which inhibit or facilitate their direct influence on bargaining relations. What are the actual connections between the presence of rival unions, spirited intra-union politics, shifts in the locus of bargaining control within the union, the nature of the union ideology, and the direct influence of rank and file sentiments on bargaining relationships?

We do not yet know the answers but we can raise the question: What are the conditions within a union, industry, craft, or community, which make for and sustain different kinds and degrees of union politics and membership activity? [29] Labor economists ordinarily take union politics as a given, and are concerned primarily with its influence on the bargaining relationship. If the sociologist could contribute empirically grounded generalizations regarding the structural and normative conditions making for different types of union politics, the labor economist could predict developments in labor relations more accurately.

The diligent pursuit of any problem will sooner or later carry a student outside the boundaries of his own discipline (i.e., beyond the scope of the variables which he and his co-workers habitually take into account) and into the realm of factors which are or will be the daily concern of another discipline. Certainly the study of the role of equitable comparisons in collective bargaining has carried labor economists into the study of unions as social and political structures.

Research in labor relations oriented toward reference group theory, far from involving a "handing over" of the problem by economists to sociologists, makes possible cumulative and mutually instructive contributions by members of both disciplines. This paper should be viewed as a preliminary effort toward converting that pious hope into a working reality.

NOTES

PART I—History and Social Research

<small>THE DEBATE OVER ART AND POPULAR CULTURE IN
EIGHTEENTH CENTURY ENGLAND</small>

Notes to Pages 35–43

1. *qu.* A. S. Collins, *The Profession of Letters: Study of the Relation of Author to Patron, Publisher, and Public, 1780 to 1932* (London, Routledge, 1920), 83.

2. *qu.* A. S. Collins, "The Growth of the Reading Public During the Eighteenth Century," *Review of English Studies*, Vol. II (1926), 429.

3. William Lecky, *History of England in the Eighteenth Century* (New York, Appleton, 1888), 560 *ff.*

4. *qu.* Walter Graham, *English Literary Periodicals* (New York, Nelson, 1930), 35.

5. *Ibid.*, 59.

6. *qu.* George Sherburn, *The Restoration and the Eighteenth Century*, Pt. III of *A Literary History of England*, Ed. Albert C. Baugh (New York, Appleton-Century-Crofts, 1948), 1053.

7. Collins, "The Growth of the Reading Public," 289-90.

8. *Ibid.*, 291.

9. *qu.* Collins, *The Profession of Letters*, 96.

10. Ernest A. Baker, *The History of the English Novel* (10 vols., London, Witherby, 1934), V, 252-53.

11. Collins, *The Profession of Letters*, 98.

12. *Ibid.*, 65.

13. Sherburn, 1052.

14. W. T. Laprade, *Public Opinion and Politics in Eighteenth Century England* (New York, Macmillan, 1936), 13-14.

15. Samuel Johnson, *The Idler*, No. 30. *The British Essayist*, Ed. A. Chalmers (38 vols., Boston, Little, Brown, 1856), XXVII, 104.

16. A. Aspinall, *Politics and the Press* (London, Home and Vanthal, 1949), 6-7.

17. *qu.* Lecky, I, 561-62.

18. *qu.* Alexander Pope, *The Dunciad (A)*, Ed. James Sutherland (London, Methuen, 1953), 448. (Vol. V of the Twickenham Edition, General Ed. John Butt.)

19. Daniel Defoe, *The Review*, Aug. 30, 1709. *Defoe's Review in 22 Facsimile Books* (New York, Columbia Univ. Press, 1938), VI, Bk. 15, 253-54.

20. Arthur Y. Trace, "The Continuity of Opposition to the Theater in England from Gosson to Collier" (unpublished dissertation, Stanford University, 1955), 11.

21. *qu.* H. W. Pedicord, *The Theatrical Public in the Time of Garrick* (New York, King's Crown, 1954), 41.

22. *qu.* Lecky, I, 586.

23. *qu.* M. D. George, *London Life in the Eighteenth Century* (New York, Knopf, 1925), 288.

24. Pedicord, 14-15.

25. *Ibid.*, 16.

26. Ian Watt, *The Rise of the Novel* (London, Chatto and Windus, forthcoming), 37.

27. *Adventurer*, No. 115. *British Essayists*, XXI, 137-38.

28. Leslie Stephen, *English Literature and Society in the Eighteenth Century* (London, Duckworth, 1904), 37-38.

29. James Lackington, *Memoirs of the Forty-Five First Years of the Life of James Lackington, Written by Himself* (London, 1803), 250.

30. *qu.* Lecky, I, 165.

31. Collins, *Profession of Letters*, Ch. I (v), *passim.*

32. Lackington, 225.

33. *Ibid.*, 259.

34. Ralph Straus, *The Unspeakable Curll* (New York, McBride, 1928).

35. *qu. Ibid.*, 49-64.

36. Lackington, 224.

37. *qu.* Collins, 63-64.

38. *Ibid.*, 58.

39. J. M. S. Tompkins, *The Popular Novel in England: 1770-1800* (London, Constable, 1932), 7.

40. Tompkins, 10.

41. Lackington, 286.

42. Joseph Wood Krutch, *Samuel Johnson* (New York, Holt, 1944), 35.

43. Collins, "Growth of the Reading Public," 429.

44. James Boswell, *Life of Samuel Johnson* (London, Oxford Press, 1953), 217.

45. Oliver Goldsmith, *An Inquiry into the Present State of Polite Learning in Europe* (1759). *The Works of Oliver Goldsmith*, Ed. Peter Cunningham (4 vols., New York, Harper, 1881), II, 56-57.

46. Oliver Goldsmith, *The Citizen of the World*, Letter XCIII (London, Everyman, 1934), 255.

47. *Ibid.*, Letter LI, 142.

48. Thomas De Quincey, "Oliver Goldsmith." *The Eighteenth Century in Scholarship and Literature* (Boston, 1877), 335.

49. *qu.* Graham, 204-205.

50. *qu. Ibid.*, 208.

51. *qu. Ibid.*, 213.

52. *qu. Ibid.*, 224-25.

53. *qu.* Tompkins, 15.

54. *Ibid.*

55. *Ibid.*, 15-16.

56. Goldsmith, *Citizen of the World*, Letter XIII, 34.

57. John Dennis, *The Grounds of Criticism in Poetry, Critical Works of John Dennis*, Ed. Edward Niles Hooker (2 vols., Baltimore, Johns Hopkins Press, 1943), I, 338.

58. Sherburn, 826.

59. J. W. H. Atkins, *English Literary Criticism: 17th and 18th Centuries* (London, Methuen, 1951), 102.

60. Pope, *Dunciad*, 165 n.

61. Joseph Addison, *The Spectator*, No. 10 (4 vols., London, Everyman, 1950), I, 32.

62. Addison, *Spectator*, No. 10, I, 31-33.

63. *Ibid.*, No. 34, I, 104.

64. *Ibid.*, No. 63, I, 196.

65. Emile Legouis and Louis Cazamian, *A History of English Literature* (New York, Macmillan, 1933), 738.

66. B. Sprague Allen, *Tides in English Taste* (2 vols., Cambridge, Mass., Harvard Univ. Press, 1937), II, 36-37.

67. *qu.* Allen, I, 87.

68. Graham, 120.

69. *Ibid.*, 152 *ff*.

70. Laprade, 249.

71. Stephen, 219.

72. Henry Fielding, *The Covent Garden Journal*, No. 10. *The Works of Henry Fielding*, Ed. James P. Browne (10 vols., London, Bickers, 1903), X, 26.

73. *qu.* Pedicord, 31.

74. *qu.* Chauncey B. Tinker, *The Salon and English Letters* (New York, Macmillan, 1915), 177-79.

75. Sherburn, 1031.

76. *qu.* Tompkins, 47.

77. Pope, *Dunciad*, 49-50.

78. *Ibid.*, 192 n.

79. *qu.* Ian Jack, *Augustan Satire, 1660-1750* (Oxford, Clarendon Press, 1952), 119.

80. Pope, *Essay on Criticism, The Best of Pope*, Ed. George Sherburn (New York, Ronald Press, 1940), 64-65.

81. Fielding, X, 28.

82. *qu.* Allen, I, 243-44.

83. *qu.* James Sutherland, "Introduction," *Dunciad*, xlviii.

84. *qu.* Allen, II, 189.

85. Goldsmith, *Inquiry into the Present State, Works*, II, 57.

86. Goldsmith, *Citizen of the World*, Letter LXXXIV, 234.

87. Goldsmith, *Inquiry into the Present State, loc. cit.*

88. Goldsmith, *Citizen of the World*, Letter XCIII, 256.

89. Johnson, *The Rambler*, No. 2. *British Essayists*, XVI, 76.

90. Goldsmith, *Inquiry into the Present State, Works*, II, 47 *ff*.

91. Pope, *Dunciad* (B), 272-73.

92. *qu.* Baker, IV, 15.

93. F. W. Bateson, *English Comic Drama: 1700-1750* (Oxford, Clarendon Press, 1929), 8.

94. Johnson, *The Rambler*, No. 4, *British Essayists*, XVI, 82-83.

95. *Ibid.*

96. Johnson, *The Rambler*, No. 4, 84-88.

97. Mary Wortley Montague, *Complete Works*, Ed. Lord Wharncliffe (2 vols., Paris, 1837), II, 100-105.

98. Goldsmith, *The Bee*, No. 6. In: *Citizen of the World*, 399.

99. *qu.* Tompkins, 74.

100. Henry Mackenzie, *The Lounger*, No. 20, *British Essayists*, XXX, 124.

101. Johnson, *Lives of the English Poets*, II, 135.

102. Addison, *Spectator*, No. 44, I, 133.

103. Goldsmith, *Citizen of the World*, Letter XXI, 56.

104. David Hume, *Of Tragedy, Four Dissertations* (London, 1757), 198-99.

105. Goldsmith, *A Comparison between Sentimental and Laughing Comedy, Works*, III, 380.

106. Addison, *Spectator*, No. 37, I, 112.

107. *qu.* Francis Gallaway, *Reason, Rule, and Revolt in English Classicism* (New York, Scribner's, 1940), 115.

108. William Cowper, *The Progress of Error, Poetical Works of William Cowper*, Ed. H. S. Milford (London, Oxford Univ. Press, 1934), 24.

109. Richardson, *The Novels of Samuel Richardson* (20 vols., London, 1902), XIX, 15-16.

110. Jean Marie Arouet Voltaire, *Essay on Taste;* Alexandre Gerard, *An Essay on Taste; With Three Dissertations on the Same Subject by Mr. de Voltaire, Mr. d'Alembert, and Mr. de Montesquieu* (London, 1759), 220.

111. David Garrick, "Prologue," *The Farmer's Return from London, Poetical Works of David Garrick* (2 vols., London, 1785), I, 186-88.

112. Johnson, *The Idler*, No. 36 and No. 85, *British Essayists*, XXVII, 124, 297-98.

113. Goldsmith, *Specimen of a Magazine in Miniature. The Miscellaneous Works of Oliver Goldsmith*, Ed. David Masson (London, Macmillan, 1925), 288.

114. *qu.* Allen, II, 25-26.

115. *Ibid.*

116. Goldsmith, "Editor's Preface," *Citizen of the World*, 4.

117. Addison, *Spectator*, No. 44, I, 133.

118. *Ibid.*, No. 42, I, 127.

119. *Ibid.*, No. 5, I, 18.

120. Pope, *First Epistle to the Second Book of Horace, The Best of Pope*, 236-37.

121. Goldsmith, *Citizen of the World*, Letter XXI, 56-57.

122. *Ibid.*, Letter LXXIX, 219-20.

123. Goldsmith, *A Comparison between Sentimental and Laughing Comedy, loc. cit.*

124. *qu.* John A. Kelly, *German Visitors to the English Theaters in the Eighteenth Century* (Princeton, Univ. Press, 1936), 55.

125. Pedicord, 135-39.

126. David Hume, *The Rise and Progress of the Arts and Sciences, Philosophical Works* (4 vols., London, Tait, 1826), III, 152.

127. Voltaire, *loc. cit.*

128. Hume, *Of Simplicity and Refinement in Writing, Philosophical Works*, III, 223.

129. *qu.* Sutherland, "Introduction," *Dunciad*, x-xi.

130. Pope, *Dunciad* (B), 337-38.

131. Pope, *First Epistle to . . . Horace, The Best of Pope*, 233.

132. Sutherland, xlii.

133. *The Sylph,* No. 19, *qu.* J. T. Taylor, *Early Opposition to the English Novel: The Popular Reaction from 1760 to 1830* (New York, King's Crown, 1943), 43.

134. *qu.* Tompkins, 5.

135. Bateson, 145.

136. *qu.* Allen, I, 110.

137. Goldsmith, *Inquiry into the Present State, Works,* II, 58.

138. Fielding, "Prologue," *The Universal Gallant,* Works, III, 165.

139. Garrick, "Epilogue to Arthur Murray's *All in the Wrong,*" *Poetical Works,* I, 173-74.

140. *qu.* Pedicord, 119.

141. Theophilus Cibber, *Two Dissertations on the Theatres* (London, 1756), 5.

142. *qu.* Allen, I, 269.

143. *Ibid.,* I, 255.

144. *qu.* Collins, *Profession of Letters,* 96-97.

145. Taylor, 101 *ff.*

146. *Ibid.,* 97.

147. Robert Lloyd (satirist, poet, member of Trinity College) writing in *The Connoisseur,* No. 135, *qu.* Gallaway, 277.

148. Goldsmith, *Taste, Miscellaneous Works,* 313.

149. René Wellek, *A History of Modern Criticism* (2 vols. to date, London, Cape, 1955), I, 26.

150. Sherburn, 997.

151. Addison, *Spectator,* Nos. 411, 412, 416; III, 276-82, 290-93.

152. Goldsmith, *Citizen of the World,* Letter XXI, 55.

153. Joseph Warton, *An Essay on the Genius and Writing of Pope* (1756). In: H. A. Needham, *Taste and Criticism in the Eighteenth Century* (London, Harrap, 1952), 113.

154. Goldsmith, *Taste,* 314-15.

155. Fielding, *Covent Garden Journal,* No. 10, *Works,* X, 29.

156. Addison, *Tatler,* No. 165; *Guardian,* No. 19. *British Essayists,* III, 319; XIII, 162.

157. Edmund Burke, *Essay on Taste, Harvard Classics* (50 vols., New York, Collier, 1909), XXIV, 13.

158. Hume, *On Taste, Four Dissertations,* 215.

159. Burke, XXIV, 14-15.

160. Henry Home, Lord Kames, *Elements of Criticism* (3 vols., Edinburgh, Kincaid and Bell, 1762), III, 358-65.

161. Addison, *Spectator,* No. 70, I, 215.

162. *qu.* Gallaway, 53.

163. Hugh Blair, *Lectures on Rhetoric* (3 vols., Basle, J. Decker, 1801), I, 34-35.

164. Kames, *passim.*

165. Hume, *On Taste,* 228.

166. Fielding, *Covent Garden Journal,* No. 23, *Works,* X, 41-47.

167. Needham, "Introduction," 38.

168. Burke, *On the Sublime and Beautiful, Harvard Classics,* XXIV, 108 *ff.*

169. Richard Steele, *Tatler,* No. 173, *British Essayists,* III, 356-60.

170. Needham, 36.

171. *Ibid.,* 52.

172. Gallaway, 347.
173. *qu.* Sherburn, 1001.
174. Edward Niles Hooker, "The Reviewers and the New Criticism, 1754-70," *Philological Quarterly,* Vol. XIII (1934), 197.
175. Gallaway, 345.
176. Kames, I, 337.
177. Hume, *Of Tragedy, Four Dissertations,* 186-87.
178. Archibald Alison, *On Taste* (1790), *qu.* Needham, 181.
179. *qu.* Atkins, 173-75.
180. Pope, *Essay on Criticism, The Best of Pope,* 71.
181. Goldsmith, *Inquiry into the Present State, Works,* II, 31.
182. Sherburn, 841-42.
183. *qu.* Atkins, 312.
184. Goldsmith, *Inquiry into the Present State, Works,* II, 47.
185. Johnson, *The Rambler,* No. 92, *British Essayists,* XVII, 182.
186. Krutch, 497.

RESEARCH PROBLEMS IN AMERICAN POLITICAL HISTORIOGRAPHY

1. The study has been prepared under the joint direction of Professors Paul Lazarsfeld of the Columbia University Planning Project for Advanced Training in Social Research and Seymour Lipset of the Columbia Committee Conducting a Propositional Inventory of Political Behavior. Both advisers have contributed much to the final result, but I am particularly grateful to Professor Lazarsfeld for searching criticisms and fruitful suggestions. It need hardly be added that neither adviser should be held responsible for any short-comings.

I am indebted to Thomas C. Cochran of the University of Pennsylvania, Manning J. Dauer of the University of Florida, and James C. Malin of the University of Kansas for calling my attention to errors and questionable formulations in an earlier draft.

2. Subsequent to the completion of the present study, W. Dean Burnham's compilation of national election statistics was published. *Presidential Ballots, 1836-1892* (Johns Hopkins Press: Baltimore, 1955), is a praiseworthy example of scholarly resourcefulness and diligence. By presenting the raw voting statistics for American presidential elections in the nineteenth century, it makes a basic contribution to political historiography. It neatly supplements the pioneering works of Edgar E. Robinson, *The Presidential Vote: 1896-1932* (Stanford University Press, 1934), and *They voted for Roosevelt, the presidential vote, 1932-1944* (Stanford University Press, 1947). The publication of Mr. Burnham's volume increases the likelihood that some day we shall have verified statements of who voted for whom, when. When this indispensable task is accomplished, it will then be possible to tackle the more difficult questions involved in *explaining* American voting behavior.

3. Although the concepts employed here differ somewhat from those developed by Derwent Whittlesey, see his stimulating paper, "The Horizons of Geography," in *Annals of the Association of American Geographies,* 35:1-36 (1945).

4. Allan Nevins, *Grover Cleveland* (New York, 1947 printing), 187.

5. *Ibid.,* 145-188, 190.

6. *Ibid.*, 166-167. However, five other "special factors" affecting voting behavior were named "apart from the dominant issue of Blaine's integrity . . ." *Ibid.*, 169-175.

7. *Ibid.*, 145-146, 156-157, 159, 166.

8. *Ibid.*, 187.

9. *Ibid.*, 174-175.

10. The table is based upon the voting statistics given in the *Tribune Almanac* (New York) for the years 1881-1889, inclusive; the index in each edition lists the pages on which the New York election returns are found. As in all the election statistics cited below probably there are minor inaccuracies in the data, but cross-checking has failed to turn up any error of significant proportions. Besides the Prohibitionists, other minor parties received votes; the Prohibition percentages are of the total vote.

11. The discussion of Cleveland's election is based upon material in Lee Benson, *Merchants—Farmers—and Railroads* (Cambridge, Mass., 1955), 174-203.

12. Compiled from data in U. S. Bureau of the Census, *Historical Statistics of the United States, 1789-1945* (Washington, D. C., 1949), 293.

13. The table below is compiled from data in the *Tribune Almanac for 1885, 1889, 1893.*

14. See the tables in Stuart A. Rice, *Farmers and Workers in American Politics* (New York, 1924), 26, and Louis H. Bean, *How to Predict Elections* (New York, 1948), 181. For elections prior to 1852 I inspected the returns in Edward Stanwood, *A History of Presidential Elections* (Boston, 1892 ed.).

15. The data from which the table below is compiled is found in the *Tribune Almanac* for 1881, 1885, 1889.

16. Table V is based upon data found in appropriate editions of the *Tribune Almanac*, 1865-1901. In 1864 no Republican Party existed as such in Kansas and the vote in that election was for the National Union Party; it is not directly comparable with 1868 but it provides a crude basis for comparison. Although the same situation obtained throughout the nation, in some states, such as New York, the voting data for 1860-1868 indicates that the National Union and Republican parties received virtually the same support.

17. The data from which the table below is compiled is found in the *Tribune Almanac* from 1877 to 1885. Comparison of the 1884 Massachusetts Republican vote for President and Governor indicates that Blaine's percentage was 4.0 less than the state ticket. No doubt Butler's candidacy was not the only possible reason for the Republican 10.1 decline from 1880 in the presidential vote. As usual, the analysis here is illustrative rather than substantive. To indicate that a really intensive analysis is necessary to arrive at an explanation for the Republican presidential decline in Massachusetts; Blaine only ran 0.08 behind the Republican state ticket in Connecticut, like Massachusetts, a category H state.

18. Nevins, *Grover Cleveland*, 159.

19. Harry J. Carman and Harold C. Syrett, *A History of the American People* (New York, 1952), 2:248.

20. cf. Thomas Cochran, SSRC Bulletin #64, 1954, 158-164.

21. Arthur M. Schlesinger, Jr., *The Age of Jackson* (Boston, 1946 printing), 36. The quotation below is from p. 38.

22. Henry Jones Ford, *The Rise and Growth of American Politics* (New York, 1898), 191.

23. Stanwood, *A History of Presidential Elections*, 88.

24. These statements, and the table below, are based on the data found in *ibid.*, 88.

25. Population and voting statistics for 1824 and 1828 are found in U. S. Bureau of the Census, *Historical Statistics*, 26, 289-290.

26. Stanwood, *History of Presidential Elections*, 87. A later study claims that the North Carolina vote *was* primarily for Jackson. The point is, however, that the confused nature of the 1824 campaign makes it difficult to comprehend the real significance of the vote given in the name of a particular candidate. The Electoral College vote, cited below, is given in *ibid.*, 93.

27. *Ibid.*, 87. The same page gives the information for the Massachusetts vote cited below and indicates that the situation in the Bay State was not unusual.

28. The information concerning Pennsylvania politicians is found in a letter from Samuel R. Overton to Andrew Jackson, Aug. 1, 1821, in John S. Bassett, ed., *Correspondence of Andrew Jackson* (Washington, 1928), 3:105-106.

29. Marc Bloch, *The Historian's Craft* (New York, 1953), 35.

30. See in this connection the series of essays brought together in Frederick J. Turner, *The Significance of Sections in American History* (New York, 1932). The importance assigned to the election of 1896 for the frontier thesis is perhaps made most explicit in "The Problem of the West," in Frederick J. Turner, *The Frontier in American History* (New York, 1950 ed.), 205-221.

31. Arthur M. Schlesinger, Sr., *The Rise of the City* (New York, 1933), 302.

32. William Diamond, "Urban and Rural Voting in 1896," *American Historical Review*, 46:305 (January 1941). For Diamond's critical analysis of the "urban thesis" see his article "On the Dangers of an Urban Interpretation of History," in Eric F. Goldman, ed., *Historiography and Urbanization* (Baltimore, 1941), 67-108.

33. Diamond, in *American Historical Review*, 46:303-304.

34. *Ibid.*, 304.

35. *Ibid.*, 281.

36. *Ibid.*, 281-282.

37. *Ibid.*, 304. Certain voting groups were designated by Diamond in general terms, but the conflicts between them and the reason for their intensification by the Bryan campaign were only implied in a highly generalized fashion.

38. *Ibid.*, 282-283.

39. *Ibid.*, 283.

40. The table has been compiled from material in the *Tribune Almanac* for the years included in the time span covered. The 1892-96 comparison is slightly distorted because of the erratic fusion of Democrats and Populists in several states; however, the basic point is not affected. The national percentages, of course, exaggerate the degree of stability because they obscure the impact of counter-balancing changes on the state and local level.

41. The table is based upon unpublished data compiled by myself and various assistants in connection with a long term statistical analysis of New York voting patterns. The *Tribune Almanac* was the primary source of the raw data. The two urban counties selected were actually cities and contained an insignificant farm or rural population; all other urban counties show the same trend in 1896. Beginning in 1876, minor parties were on the ballot and hence the percentages above do not add up to 100%.

42. Based on data in the *Tribune Almanac* for 1893 and 1897.

43. Calculated from the *Tribune Almanac for 1897*, 226.

44. Samuel E. Morison and Henry S. Commager, *The Growth of the American Republic* (New York, 1947 printing), 1:637.

45. Adreas Dorpalen, "The German Element and the Issues of the Civil War," *Mississippi Valley Historical Review*, 29:55 (June 1942).

46. *Ibid.*, 29:73-74.

47. *Ibid.*, 29:75.

48. *Ibid.*, 29:75-76. I am aware of the considerable number of secondary studies concerning the German vote in 1860 but there seems little need to discuss them since the point here is illustrative rather than substantive. Of all the approaches taken to the question, Dorpalen seems to me to have adopted the most interesting and logical; it is the kind of approach applicable to studies of ethnic groups in all elections.

49. Paul W. Gates, *Fifty Million Acres* (Ithaca, New York, 1954), 72-105.

PUBLIC OPINION IN FRANCE AFTER THE LIBERATION, 1944–1949

1. Thomas C. Cochran, "The Social Sciences and the Problems of Historical Synthesis," in Thomas C. Cochran *et al.*, *The Social Sciences in Historical Study: A Report of the Committee on Historiography* (New York: Social Science Research Council Bulletin #64, 1954), p. 162. See also Russell E. Planck, *Public Opinion and Political Development in the Fourth French Republic, 1944-1949* (Ann Arbor, Mich.: University Microfilms Publication #6684, 1953), from which the author has borrowed, occasionally extracting quotations and repeating arguments. No other references to this doctoral dissertation will be made.

2. See above.

3. Herbert H. Hyman and Paul B. Sheatsley, "The Current Status of American Public Opinion;" in the *National Council of Social Studies Yearbook*, XXI (1950), as cited by Daniel Katz *et al.*, *Public Opinion and Propaganda* (New York, 1954), p. 46.

4. See the discussion of values and value systems in Thomas C. Cochran, "A Survey of Concepts and Viewpoints in the Social Sciences," in Thomas C. Cochran *et al.*, *op. cit.*, pp. 43 f.

5. Paul F. Lazarsfeld and Frank Stanton, eds., *Communications Research, 1948-1949* (New York, 1949), pp. xiii f.

6. For example, Herbert Luethy, *France Against Herself* (New York, 1955); Catherine Gavin, *Liberated France* (New York, 1955); Ronald Matthews, *The Death of the Fourth Republic* (New York, 1954); Dorothy Pickles, *French Politics: The First Years of the Fourth Republic* (London and New York, 1954); François Goguel, *France under the Fourth Republic* (Ithaca, N. Y., 1952); David Thomson, *Democracy in France; the Third and Fourth Republics*, 2nd ed. (New York, 1952); O. R. Taylor, *The Fourth Republic of France: Constitutions and Political Parties* (Oxford, 1951); Gordon Wright, *The Reshaping of French Democracy* (New York, 1948); Philip Williams, *Politics in Post War France* (Longmans Green, 1954). Many of these authors make use of IFOP survey results. Those who wish to know what French political scientists are thinking of the political importance of public opinion surveys can consult: Jean Pouillon, "Les Sondages et la Science politique," *Revue Française de Science Politique* II (Mai 1951), 83-106; and Raymond Aron, "Flecteurs, Partis et Elus," *ibid.*, V (Avril-Juin 1955), 245-266.

7. See the illuminating discussion of this by Luethy, *op. cit.*, p. 107, in which he states that the Communists, while claiming 75,000 shot patriots, could name only 176. Cf. also Matthews, *op. cit.*, pp. 119-155.

8. In the early summer of 1946 over two fifths of the respondents opposed De Gaulle's return to office, a number which rose to over a majority by the end of September. The largest portion of those who rejected De Gaulle— about four fifths—believed that the general aimed at gaining personal power. See IFOP, *Sondages,* 1946, #15, p. 180; #16, p. 196; #18, pp. 242f. Thomson says that De Gaulle's "naturally egotistical and brooding nature evolved certain Napoleonic characteristics." David Thomson, *Two Frenchmen: Pierre Laval and Charles de Gaulle* (London, 1951), p. 251.

9. Queuille was approved by only 28% of the sample in October; 50% wanted parliamentary dissolution and new elections; *Sondages,* 1949, #2, pp. 15, 17. Nearly two fifths of the respondents thought that on the whole 1948 had been for them a worse year than 1947 and over seven tenths would not venture to predict that the coming year would be better than the previous one; No. 4, pp. 39-40.

10. G. M. Trevelyan, *The English Revolution, 1688-1689* (New York, 1939), p. 214.

11. The question: "If elections were held today, for which party would you vote?"

12. Robert F. Byrnes, "The Christian Democrats in Modern France" in Edward Mead Earle, ed., *Modern France* (Princeton, N. J., 1951), p. 174, and Dorothy Pickles, *op. cit.*, p. 27.

13. In the interests of simplicity generally no specific references are made to *Sondages,* the official publication of IFOP, in the pertinent issues of which most of the survey results contained in the study will be found. The IFOP sample consisted of the following occupational divisions: (1) Workers, 24% of complete sample; (2) Salaried employees and civil servants, 11%; (3) Merchants and manufacturers (including Artinsans), 7%; (4) Members of the Liberal Professions, 3%; (5) Women without gainful employment, rentiers and retired people, 30%; (6) Farmers, both laborers and proprietors, 25%. In accordance with the poll findings of IFOP it can be determined that in round numbers the MRP had among its voters only about 300,000 workers category (1) above—at this time.

14. François Goguel, "Christian Democracy in France," in Mario Einaudi and François Goguel, *Christian Democracy in Italy and France* (Notre Dame, Indiana, 1952), p. 218.

15. Williams is very explicit in his statement that within the MRP workers occupied a more important position among the militants than among the party's deputies or electors. In 1950, Williams says, about one fifth of the party's members were from the working classes. Philip Williams, *op. cit.*, p. 84. It may be noted here that Williams very gratifyingly makes use of many IFOP data in his study.

16. The *Rassemblement des Gauches* consisted of the Radical Socialists and their allies.

17. This was organized about a year after liberation by elements of several prewar parliamentary groups, including the Democratic Alliance and Republican Federation. It is now defunct.

18. Byrnes, *op. cit.*, p. 174.

19. Raymond Aron, *Le Grand Schisme* (Paris, 1948), p. 187. See Gerard C. Thormann, *Christian Trade Unionism in France* (Ann Arbor, Mich.: Uni-

versity Microfilms Publication #3386, 1951), pp. 1, 124, 131, 151, for observations concerning the numerical strength and social character of the C.F.T.C. See also Pickles, *op. cit.*, p. 272.

20. See Jacques Fauvet, *Les partis politiques de la France actuelle* (Paris, 1947), p. 26.

21. Pickles, *op. cit.*, p. 94. These ideas are also noted by Williams, *op. cit.*, pp. 69 ff.

22. Henry W. Ehrmann, "The Decline of the Socialist Party," in Edward Mead Earle, ed., *op. cit.*, p. 188. In the spring of 1948 indices were developed by IFOP to determine the socio-economic groups in France. The sample fell into four principal divisions: Class A, the rich, comprising 10% of the total; Class B, the upper middle class, 30%; Class C, the lower middle class, 40%; and Class D, the poor, 20% of the complete sample.

23. François Goguel, *France under the Fourth Republic*, pp. 49 and 189; Charles Micaud, "The Third Force Today," in E. M. Earle, *op. cit.*, p. 146.

24. The adversaries were not specified.

25. The figures: 38% in April; 39% in July; 37% in October.

26. Very few were found in the lowest or D category.

27. See Survey #26, published Dec. 1, 1945, in which the PC Program was hailed by more people than any other reason for the Communist success. The two next most frequently noted were discontent, the occupation role of the party, together with the action of the USSR. See also Williams, *op. cit.*, pp. 58-59.

28. A. Rossi, *Physiologia du parti communiste français* (Paris, 1949), p. 381; Kenneth Douglas, "The French Intellectuals: Situation and Outlook," in E. M. Earle, *op. cit.*, p. 65.

29. *Ibid.*, p. 67.

30. The standard age groupings employed by IFOP are fourfold: (1) 20-34, composing 34% of the sample; (2) 35-49, making up 29%; (3) 50-64, comprising 23%; (4) 65 and over, composing 14%.

31. According to Thomson, "the nature and organization of the political parties . . . was the one new element in the Fourth Republic." David Thomson, *Democracy in France*, 2nd ed. (Oxford, 1952), p. 230. As for the electoral laws and their influence, the following explanation by Goguel may enlighten the reader: "The most important characteristic of this electoral system was the principle of the 'blocked list,' which denied the voter both the right to change the order in which the candidates were placed on the lists and the right to erase certain names and substitute for them the names of candidates on other lists. The principle of the blocked list reduced the voter's role to choosing one of the parties, leaving to the executive committee of these parties the choice of the men who would represent them in Parliament. Theoretically, this system was designed to prevent certain undesirable tactics. For example, it prevented one candidate from trying to increase his own chances of being elected by trying to harm the chances of other candidates higher up on the same list. It also would prevent one party from trying to 'decapitate' the lists of its opponents, by having a certain number of its followers vote for the candidates in the lowest positions on rival lists in order to elect them instead of their leaders.

"Actually the real purpose of the blocked list was to increase the authority of the parties over the members of Parliament and to reinforce their role in political life. In 1945 and 1946 the Socialists, the Communists, and the Popular Republicans agreed that the decadence of the Third Republic had been caused by its excessive individualism. They thought that democracy had to be 'organized' and that this could be done only through strong parties capable of maintaining direct discipline among their representatives in Parliament. The passage of an electoral law which made the deputies completely dependent on the parties for their re-election seemed to be one of the most effective ways to make individualism disappear from political life." *France Under the Fourth Republic*, pp. 58–59. See the treatment of electoral procedure in D.W.S. Lidderdale, *The Parliament of France* (New York, 1952), pp. 85 ff.

32. See D. Pickles, *op. cit.*, pp. 277 ff.

33. A. L. Lowell, *Greater European Governments* (Cambridge, Mass., 1918), p. 162.

34. André Siegfried, *France, a Study in Nationality* (New Haven, Conn., 1930), p. 30.

35. Jean-Marie Domenach, "The French Communist Party," in Mario Einaudi, Jean-Marie Domenach, Aldo Garosci, *Communism in Western Europe* (Ithaca, N. Y., 1951), p. 118.

36. Paul F. Lazarsfeld *et al.*, *The People's Choice* (New York, 1944), p. 37.

37. Also in favor of the document and equally distrustful of the views of General de Gaulle, the Socialists were more cautious in committing themselves, more at variance with their party's stand, or more individualistic. Over three-fifths of this group—20% under the PC figure—pledged support of the constitution on instructions from their party directors, but only two-fifths expressed a willingness to go against the document if the party executive advised them to do so. A cross reference of the two questions hints at the extent of discipline among the electorate as a whole: 36% tended to follow party recommendations; 10% seemed to be for the constitution regardless of party counsels and 8% against it; 10% were independent and 20% undecided.

38. In American presidential election campaigns, it appears that late decisions are much less than half of this French figure. In November 1940 the American Institute of Public Opinion asked: How long before the election had you made up your mind to vote for Roosevelt or Willkie? Most respondents made up their minds before or at the time of the nominating conventions: Roosevelt: 69%; Willkie: 66%. Some time in the last week, up to and including election day, 6% decided on Roosevelt, 5% on Willkie. Hadley Cantril, ed., *Public Opinion, 1935-1946* (Princeton, N. J., 1951), p. 620. In October 1944 the National Opinion Research Center found that only 8% had not decided for whom they were going to vote. *Ibid.*, p. 638. And in 1944 A.I.P.O. learned after the election that 4% chose Dewey in the last week and 5% decided in Roosevelt's favor. *Ibid.*, p. 641.

39. *European Recovery Program in France, 1948* (Economic Cooperation Administration, Special Mission to France, 1948), p. 130. See below pp. 79 ff. for a more detailed summary of the French postwar price and salary situation.

40. As for the recommendation of parliamentary dissolution and new general elections, that was received with favor by 40% of the entire sample and with disfavor by 33%. Among the Communists a highly structured opinion existed, over four-fifths being adverse to the RPF demand and 13% accepting it. Since the question was largely one of political tactics, implying a Gaullist challenge to the entrenched parliamentary power of the Big Three, the results are not considered of importance to the present discussion. The Communist minority who voiced approval of De Gaulle's proposals probably mirrored the general disillusionment with the existing parliamentary stalemate and the

desirability of trying anew to obtain a workable majority in the National Assembly.

41. Theodore White, *Fire in the Ashes* (New York, 1953), p. 105.

42. See Winston Churchill, *Triumph and Tragedy*, Vol. VI of *The Second World War* (Boston, 1948-1953), pp. 241, 256-258.

43. J. M. Domenach, *op. cit.*, pp. 130 ff.

44. On only one other proposition were the Communists unusually un-decided; namely, that of the electoral law. This was a question over which hesitation was widespread, for only 57% of the complete sample expressed an opinion, 35% favoring De Gaulle's ideas and 22% opposing them.

45. These questions were also asked of respondents in seven other coun-tries. Comparative figures demonstrate that among the Communist electors of the Netherlands, France, Italy and Sweden, the French were the most inimical to the United States and the Swedes were the most friendly; 33% of the latter thought the USA would fight only to defend itself.

46. Mario Einaudi, "Communism in Western Europe," in Mario Einaudi *et al., op. cit.*, pp. 33 f. In view of the new Soviet anti-Stalin line and the recent rapprochement between the Russian leaders and Tito, the expression "Titoism" to describe nationalistic tendencies in opposition to Soviet policy is probably no longer apt.

47. Vernon Van Dyke, "Communists in Foreign Relations," in E. M. Earle, *op. cit.*, p. 237.

48. That dissident ideas existed within the ranks of the Communist electorate was well-known to the PC leaders themselves and to all who studied French politics. These public opinion data are not needed to establish this fact; they do help, however, to clarify the areas in which such differences of outlook appeared and, sometimes, flourished.

49. Herbert Luethy, *op. cit.*, p. 117.

50. The material available on the East-West cold war demonstrates that after 1945 a majority of between one-half and three-fifths of the French were pro-American as differentiated from pro-Russian; that the same number fav-ored some type of European union and considered the Communist Party not a national party serving peculiar French interests. Contemporaneously, though only about 20% could be taken as pro-Russian by any stretch of the term, over 50% of the voters feared another war to the extent of rejecting any commitments which bade fair to aggravate the already strained East-West relations and hasten the day of conflict.

51. A seventeenth century phrase revived by Alfred North Whitehead.

52. Louis Gottschalk, *Understanding History* (New York, 1951), p. 154.

53. Carl Becker, *The Heavenly City of the Eighteenth-Century Philosophers* (New Haven, 1932), p. 31.

54. *Ibid.*, p. 7.

55. *Ibid.*, p. 9.

56. *Ibid.*, pp. 10-11.

57. *Ibid.*, p. 5.

58. Preserved Smith, *The Age of the Reformation* (New York, 1920), p. 6.

59. *Ibid.*, p. 688.

60. *Ibid.*, p. 693.

61. *Ibid.*, p. 695.

62. *Ibid.*, p. 648.

63. *Ibid.*, p. 651.

64. B. M. Trevelyan, *English Social History* (New York, 1942), p. 232.

65. *Ibid.*, p. 259.

66. See, for example, Hippolyte Taine, *The Ancient Regime* (New York, 1876), pp. 289 ff. or Alexis de Tocqueville, *The Old Regime and the Revolution* (New York, 1856), pp. 182 ff. for an appraisal of the religious climate of the 1770's in France.

67. A. Dansette, *Histoire religieuse de la France contemporaine* (Paris, 1948), I, 158.

68. A. Aulard, *Christianity and the French Revolution* (London, 1927), p. 14.

69. Quoted by H. Taine, *op. cit.*, p. 293.

70. *Ibid.*, p. 289.

71. P. de la Gorce, *Histoire religieuse de la révolution française* (Paris, 1917-18), I, 415 ff.

72. Dansette, *op. cit.*, I, 47.

73. Gabriel Le Bras, "La Religion dans la Societé" in André Siegfried *et al.*, *Aspects de la Societé Française* (Paris, 1954), p. 236.

74. Dansette, *op. cit.*, II, 30, 36; 557-8; 617.

75. *Ibid.*, I, 43.

76. Fourteen per cent Don't Knows compared with an average of 6% for all others.

77. In Britain alone a distinction between a Supreme Being or Personal God and an impersonal First Cause was proposed to the sample. About 45% saw God in the traditional Judaeo-Christian personal sense but a large 39% believed in an impersonal sort of force which might be termed God.

78. The first and last mentioned were in the only two predominantly Catholic countries outside of France in the survey, a fact which may stimulate speculation and should invite further investigation into patterns of belief for Protestant and Catholic nations, if such exist.

79. This question generally produced more numerous Don't Know and a greater amount of rejection than the first. The only exception was in the Netherlands, where the Don't Knows did not vary—6% for each.

80. The largest gaps were discoverable among the Australians (35%), Swedes (31%), Americans (26%), and Danes and Czechs (25% each). The average, Britain excluded, was about 20%.

81. One might mention the distinguished work of Gabriel Le Bras, *Introduction à l'Histoire de la Pratique Religieuse en France* (Paris, 1942-1945), as an example and the same author's contribution to *Aspects de la Societé Française*, already referred to.

82. Le Bras, "La Religion dans la Societé," in Siegfried, *op. cit.*, p. 225.

83. F. Boulard, *Essor ou Déclin du Clergé Français* (Paris, 1940); cf. Dansette, *op. cit.*, II, 614-639.

84. F. Goguel, *Géographie des élections Françaises de 1870 à 1951* (Paris, 1951), pp. 134 f.

85. Four per cent were not Catholics and 8% refused to answer the question. The Protestant population of France has been estimated at 800,000 or about 2% of the total population. André Latreille and André Siegfried, *Les Forces Religieuses et la Vie Politique* (Paris, 1951), p. 206.

86. Le Bras says that women outnumber men by two to one in their religious devotion except in areas where nearly all people are practising. "La Religion dans la Societé," p. 226. Among the occupational groups the farmers (47%) habitually went to Catholic services in greater numbers than others. Next came the merchants and manufacturers (40%) and members of the

liberal professions (37%). The rentiers and retired people (24%) and the workers (17%), whose dechristianization has been widely remarked, came last. On the basis of town size the lowest devotional figure was found among the residents of towns of 20,000 to 40,000 and of cities over 100,000 (25-27%). The power of the Catholic church in rural areas has been a standard emphasis of interpreters of French religious habits. Shortly after Liberation Canon Boulard estimated that 38% of the rural residents were *pratiquants* and 57% *conformistes saisonniers. Problèmes Missionnaires de la France* (Paris, 1945), 1, 136. To those occasions on which the latter attended church may be joined periodic assistance at All Saints' Day, Christmas, Easter and Assumption Day services. The true faithful or *pratiquants* make their Easter communion and go to Sunday mass or at least do one of these. Dansette, *op. cit.*, II, 30. Several years after the period of the current survey IFOP indicated that in the agricultural population 31% of the men and 35% of the women were devoted Catholics. See Gordon Wright, "Catholics and Peasantry in France," *Political Science Quarterly*, LXVIII (1953), 527.

87. Five per cent made no response.

88. Another 9% had gone to afternoon services.

89. Of those who would vote PC about 65% were atheists and 60% denied the immortality of the soul. Only 15% believed in God. Of the SFIO electors 30% inclined toward atheism and about 30% rejected personal immortality. Among the radicals 20% claimed to have no faith in God's existence and in life after death. In the two latter parties positive acceptance of a divinity of sorts ran between 50% and 60%. Of the SFIO and RGR supporters 22% and 32% respectively went to religious services on All Saints' Day; only 5% of the Communists did likewise.

90. Well over 90% of the MRP and PRL voters believed in God and between 85% and 90% of the RPF electors. Between 80% and 85% of the first two groups accepted the soul's immortality and over 75% of the RPF supporters also espoused this doctrine.

91. The most widespread participation was, as usual, in All Saints' Day services: 80% of the MRP, 74% of the PRL; and 69% of the RPF followers.

92. Jacques Fauvet, "Les partis et le pays," *Synthèses*, VIII (Dec. 1953), 100.

93. *Ibid.*, p. 101.

94. Eric Weill, "Complexes françaises," *Synthèses*, VIII (Dec. 1953), 35.

95. *L'Aurore* as quoted by *Le Monde*, May 25, 1951.

96. See "Propositions de Paix Scolaire," *Esprit*, XVII (March 1949) for a provocative discussion of the problem. In 1947-1948 about 18% of the elementary students and nearly 43% of the secondary school students were in private institutions. *L'Enseignement en France* (Paris, 1950), p. 14.

97. See Goguel, *France under the Fourth Republic*, pp. 123 ff.

98. Later, in the fall of 1951, Parliament passed two bills which extended aid to students in private schools.

99. After the two aid bills referred to above had been adopted, 45% of the public spoke in favor of subsidies and 42% against them. Was this alteration the effect of a "fait accompli"? See discussion of this in Section VI.

100. See the discussions in André Siegfried, *op. cit.*, pp. 97 ff. and in A. Soulier, *L'Instabilité Ministerielle sous la IIIᵉ République* (Paris, 1927), pp. 232-249.

101. Vincent Auriol in a speech in 1948 as quoted by Luethy, *op. cit.*, p. 164.

102. SFIO—27%; PC—19%.

103. SFIO—15%; PC—9%.

104. Fifty-three per cent of those who acclaimed a strong ruler wanted De Gaulle to be that man, 33% did not. Only 8% who considered a strong man undesirable desired De Gaulle's return. Most of the general's backers (84%) were naturally for an energetic leader but a minority (9%) was not.

105. Of this group 31% might be classified as anti-parliamentarian and 17% as parliamentarian; 68% favored a strong man and only 18% rejected one. This reveals a correlation between political and religious outlook which is, in regard to the retention of Parliament, by no means as close as some might have predicted or as it had been assumed to be in the late nineteenth century.

106. See P. Williams, *op. cit.*, p. 24.

107. Raymond Aron, "Reflexions sur la Politique et la Science Politique Française," *Revue Française de Science Politique*, V (Janvier-Mars 1955), 19.

108. Charles A. Beard and Sidney Hook, "Problems of Terminology in Historical Writing," in Merle Curti *et. al., Theory and Practice in Historical Study: A Report of the Committee on Historiography* (New York; Social Science Research Council #54, 1946), p. 117.

109. J. G. Randall, "Historianship," *American Historical Review*, LVIII (1953), 249-264.

110. Samuel H. Brockunier, "Problems of Historical Analysis," in Thomas C. Cochran *et. al., op. cit.*, p. 88.

111. J. G. Randall, *loc. cit.*, pp. 260 f. Randall, perhaps more than anyone else, has emphasized the importance of psychological factors in the background of the American Civil War.

112. Ernest Barker, "The Movement of National Life: 1910-1935," *The Fortnightly*, CXLIII (1935), 518.

113. H. Cantril, *Gauging Public Opinion* (Princeton, 1944), p. 226.

114. A. V. Dicey, *Lectures on the Relation Between Law and Public Opinion in England during the Nineteenth Century*, 2nd ed. (London, 1914), pp. 17-47.

115. Curtis MacDougall, who generally berates the pollsters and their accomplishments in his *Understanding Public Opinion* (New York, 1952), endorses this view by observing that "In many, if not most cases involving government, even in a democracy, the role of public opinion is restricted to approval or disapproval of a 'fait accompli' "; p. 670.

116. See Frank W. Cantwell, "Public Opinion in the Legislative Process," *American Political Science Review*, LV (1946), 924-935.

117. Actually 33% did not participate in the voting; of those who did the division was: 53%—Yes; 46%—No. The forecast, therefore, was very close.

118. Six per cent expressed no conviction.

119. Nineteen per cent lacked an opinion about the outcome.

120. George Gallup, *A Guide to Public Opinion Polls* (Princeton, 1944), p. 81.

121. Veit Valentin, *1848: Chapters in German History*, tr. Ethel T. Sheffauer (London, 1940), p. 150.

122. Priscilla Robertson, *Revolutions of 1848: A Social History* (Princeton, 1952), p. 417.

123. Valentin, *op. cit.*, pp. 150, 170.

124. *Ibid.*, p. 449.

125. *Ibid.*, p. 428.

126. *Ibid.*, p. 151.

127. David Thomson, *Two Frenchmen*, p. 229.

128. Williams, *op. cit.*, v.

Part II—Economics and Sociology

Plant Sociology: The Elite and the Aborigines

1. William Foote Whyte, "Framework for the Analysis of Industrial Relations," *Industrial and Labor Relations Review*, April 1950.

2. Wilbert E. Moore, *Industrial Relations and the Social Order* (2nd Edition), Macmillan, 1951, p. 3.

3. Mary Van Kleek, "Toward an Industrial Sociology," *American Sociological Review*, October 1946.

4. Wilbert E. Moore, "Current Issues in Industrial Sociology," *American Sociological Review*, December 1947.

5. Herbert Blumer, "Sociological Theory in Industrial Relations," *American Sociological Review*, June 1947.

6. *American Journal of Sociology*, January 1949 (Foreword).

7. Delbert C. Miller and William H. Form, *Industrial Sociology*, Harper and Brothers, 1951, pp. 14-16.

8. For other systems of classification see: Wilbert E. Moore, "Industrial Sociology: Status and Prospects," *American Sociological Review*, August 1948; Wilbert E. Moore, "Sociological Approaches to Industrial Relations," (Wayne University Lecture, February 1950); Delbert C. Miller, "The Social Factor of the Work Situation," *American Sociological Review*, June 1946; Delbert C. Miller, *American Sociological Review*, August 1948 (comment on paper by Wilbert E. Moore); and Miller and Form, *op. cit.*, p. 23.

9. A very different theoretical approach by a sociologist is taken by Reinhard Bendix: "Some Theoretical Implications of Industrial Sociology" (unpublished manuscript).

10. Elton Mayo, *Democracy and Freedom*, Macmillan and Co., Ltd., Melbourne, London, 1919.

————, *Revery and Industrial Fatigue*, Williams and Wilkins Co., Baltimore, 1924.

————, *The Human Problems of an Industrial Civilization*, Macmillan Co., New York, 1933.

————, *Teamwork and Labor Turnover in the Aircraft Industry of Southern California*, Harvard University, Graduate School of Business Administration, Boston, Massachusetts, 1944.

————, *The Social Problems of an Industrial Civilization*, Division of Research, Graduate School of Business Administration, Harvard University, Boston, 1947.

————, *The Political Problem of Industrial Civilization*, Division of Research, Graduate School of Business Administration, Harvard University, Boston, 1947.

T. N. Whitehead, *Leadership in a Free Society*, Harvard University Press, Cambridge, Massachusetts, 1936.

————, *The Industrial Worker*, Harvard University Press, Cambridge, Massachusetts, 1938.

F. J. Roethlisberger, and W. J. Dickson, *Management and the Workers*, Harvard University Press, Cambridge, Massachusetts, 1939.

F. J. Roethlisberger, *Management and Morale*, Harvard University Press, Cambridge, Massachusetts, 1941.

11. Burleigh B. Gardner, *Human Relations in Industry*, R. D. Irwin, Inc., Chicago, 1945.

————, *Man in an Industrial Society* (Human Events Pamphlets, #16), Chicago, 1947.

William Foote Whyte, *Industry and Society* (W. F. Whyte, editor), McGraw-Hill Book Co., New York and London, 1946.

————, *Human Relations in the Restaurant Industry*, McGraw-Hill Book Co., New York, 1948.

W. L. Warner and P. S. Lunt, *The Social Life of a Modern Community*, Yale University Press, New Haven, 1941.

W. L. Warner and J. O. Low, *The Social System of the Modern Factory*, Yale University Press, New Haven, 1947.

12. William Foote Whyte, *Pattern for Industrial Peace*, Harper and Brothers, New York, 1951.

13. George C. Homans, *The Human Group*, Harcourt, Brace and Co., New York, 1950.

14. Burleigh B. Gardner, *Human Relations in Industry*, *op. cit.*, also Revised Edition, Gardner and D. G. Moore, R. D. Irwin, Inc., Chicago, 1950. The best description of the Hawthorne studies is found in Roethlisberger and Dickson, *op. cit.*

15. See Reinhard Bendix and Lloyd Fisher, "The Perspectives of Elton Mayo," *The Review of Economics and Statistics*, November 1949, for a more detailed discussion of this ideology.

16. *Human Problems*, op. cit., p. 156.

17. *Ibid.*, pp. 179-180.

18. *Ibid.*, p. 180.

19. *Ibid.*, p. 18.

20. *Political Problem*, op. cit., p. 21.

21. *Leadership in a Free Society*, op. cit., p. vii.

22. *Ibid.*, p. 225.

23. *Human Problems*, op. cit., p. 166.

24. *Ibid.*, p. 179.

25. *Ibid.*, p. 188.

26. *Social Problems*, op. cit., Chapter 1.

27. *Human Problems*, op. cit., p. 149.

28. *Social Problems*, op. cit., p. viii.

29. *Human Problems*, op. cit., p. 178.

30. *Ibid.*, p. 185.

31. *Political Problem*, op. cit., p. 23.

32. See: C. W. Hart, "The Hawthorne Experiments," *Canadian Journal of Economics and Political Science*, May 1943.

Daniel Bell, "Adjusting Men to Machines," *Commentary*, January 1947.

Herbert Blumer, "Sociological Theory in Industrial Relations," *American Sociological Review*, June 1947.

W. E. Moore, "Current Issues in Industrial Sociology," *American Sociological Review*, December 1947.

"The Human Factor in Industry," *Political and Economic Planning*, March 5, 1948.

W. E. Moore, "Industrial Sociology, Status and Prospects," *American Sociological Review*, August 1948.

C. W. Mills, "The Contribution of Sociology to Studies of Industrial Relations," *Industrial Relations Research Association Proceedings*, 1948.

C. W. Hart, "Industrial Relations Research and Social Theory," *Canadian Journal of Economics and Political Science*, February 1949.

Harold L. Sheppard, "The Treatment of Unionism in Managerial Sociology," *American Sociological Review*, April 1949.

Reinhard Bendix and Lloyd Fisher, *op. cit.*

George Friedman, "Philosophy Underlying the Hawthorne Investigation," *Social Forces*, December 1949.

E. V. Schneider, "Limitations on Observations in Industrial Sociology," *Social Forces*, March 1950.

John T. Dunlop, "A Framework for the Analysis of Industrial Relations," *Industrial and Labor Relations Review*, April 1950.

Robert C. Sorensen, "Concepts of Conflict in Industrial Sociology," *Social Forces*, March 1951.

W. Koivisto, "Industrial Sociology and the Sociology of Knowledge." (Unpublished manuscript.)

33. For a statement of methods see Burleigh B. Gardner and William Foote Whyte, "Methods for a Study of Human Relations in Industry," *American Sociological Review*, October 1946; also George C. Homans, "The Strategy of Industrial Relations," *American Journal of Sociology*, January 1949.

34. *Pattern for Industrial Peace, op. cit.*, p. 221.

35. *Human Problems, op. cit.*, p. 181.

36. *Idem.*

37. *Ibid.*, p. 182.

38. *Political Problem, op. cit.*, p. 22.

39. *Idem.*

40. *Leadership in a Free Society, op. cit.*, p. 144.

41. *Ibid.*, p. 155. Whitehead thought that, under proper conditions, "the company union . . . has shown great possibilities." (*Ibid.*, p. 154.)

42. "Who Goes Union and Why?" *Personnel Journal*, December 1944.

43. *Industry and Society, op. cit.*, pp. 195-196.

44. *Ibid.*, p. 184.

45. *Pattern for Industrial Peace, op. cit.*, p. 170.

46. *Ibid.*, p. 171.

47. *Idem.*

48. *Ibid.*, p. 179.

49. *Ibid.*, p. 171.

50. *Ibid.*, p. 204.

51. *Ibid.*, p. 228. ("The manager or union leader who can help build a better way of life within industry gains the inner satisfaction of discharging one of the heaviest social responsibilities of modern man." *Ibid.*, p. 213.)

52. This full acceptance of the union as a channel of communication is not original with Whyte. See Gardner, *Human Relations in Industry*, 1945, *op. cit.*

53. These earlier studies, work of other social scientists, deal with (1) a team of workmen engaged in manufacturing an industrial product; (2) a metropolitan street corner gang; (3) a Polynesian tribe; (4) a small New England town; and (5) a company that manufactures electrical equipment. *The Human Group*, op. cit., p. viii, text.

54. *Ibid.*, p. 9.

55. *Ibid.*, p. 16.

56. *Ibid.*, p. 21.

57. *Idem.*

58. *Ibid.*, p. 19.

59. Homans explicitly recognizes the interaction of a social system and its

environment. Ibid., p. 87. Recognition accorded, however, the environment retreats into the shadows and seems to have little explanatory value.

60. *Ibid.,* p. 10.

61. *Ibid.,* p. 18.

62. Homans readily grants that he does not mean that the group is the same kind of organism as the living body, but speaks of a "scale of organicity" upon which the human group occupies a midway point. *Ibid.,* p. 87.

63. *Ibid.,* p. 304.

64. *Ibid.,* pp. 304-305.

65. *Ibid.,* pp. 425-440.

66. *Ibid.,* p. 248.

67. *Ibid.,* p. 243.

68. *Ibid.,* p. 455.

69. *Ibid.,* p. 456.

70. *Idem.*

71. *Idem.*

72. *Ibid.,* p. 457.

73. *Pattern for Industrial Peace, op. cit.,* p. viii.

74. *Pattern for Industrial Peace, op. cit.,* Chapter 11; *The Human Group, op. cit.,* Chapter 2; and *Leadership in a Free Society, op. cit.,* Chapter 1.

75. *The Human Group, op. cit.,* p. 313.

76. *Ibid.,* p. 333.

77. *Ibid.,* p. 459.

78. *Ibid.,* p. 466.

79. *Pattern for Industrial Peace, op. cit.,* Chapter 18.

80. *Industry and Society, op. cit.,* p. 1.

81. Whyte, *Human Relations in the Restaurant Industry, op. cit.*

81. George C. Homans, "The Small Warship," *American Sociological Review,* June 1946.

83. Jerome C. Scott and George C. Homans, "Reflections on the Wildcat strike," *American Sociological Review,* June 1947.

84. *Ibid.,* p. 278.

85. *The Human Group, op. cit.,* p. 465.

86. F. J. Roethlisberger, "Human Relations: Rare, Medium or Well Done?" *Harvard Business Review,* January 1948.

87. Russell Davenport, "The Greatest Opportunity on Earth," *Fortune,* October 1949.

88. *The Human Group, op. cit.,* p. 467.

89. *Idem.*

90. See, for example, William Foote Whyte, "Politics and Ethics," *American Political Science Review,* April 1946.

Plant Sociology: Real Discoveries and New Problems

1. For a detailed sketch of the evolution of industrial sociology see Conrad M. Arensberg, "Behavior and Organization: Industrial Studies," Chapter 14 in John Rohrer and Muzafer Sherif (eds.) *Social Psychology at the Cross Roads,* Harper and Brothers, New York, 1952. For a fuller treatment see Delbert C. Miller and William H. Form, *Industrial Sociology,* Harper and Brothers, New York, 1951. A more recent statement appears in *Money and Motivation,* by William F. Whyte, Harper and Brothers, 1955.

2. Robert K. Merton, *Social Theory and Social Structure,* The Free Press, Glencoe, Ill., 1949.

3. A current account of work in industrial sociology or "human relations research" can be found in a paper as yet unpublished by Chris Argyris of Yale, entitled "The Present State of Research in Human Relations in Industry," dated March 1, 1954.

4. See E. Wight Bakke, *Mutual Survival, The Goals of Unions and Managements*, New York, Harper, 1946, for a documentation of diversity. But even Bakke, confronted with it, laments it. Though he would not have the twain separated by irreconcilable intransigencies, doctrinaire European in fashion, he still seems to overlook history's lesson that constitutional democracy arises out of compromises within agreed-upon limits of disagreement, not upon common goals.

5. *Vide* Conrad M. Arensberg, *op. cit.*

6. Compare Arensberg, *op. cit.*, and George P. Homans, *The Human Group*, Harcourt Brace, New York, 1951, pp. 18-130 (Chapter 5).

7. William Foote Whyte, "Incentive for Productivity, The Case of the Bundy Tubing Company," *Applied Anthropology*, Vol. 1, No. 2, Spring, 1948. Cf. also the events of Chapter 10, in Whyte's *Money and Motivation, op. cit.*

8. See the Argyris paper, already cited, for summaries of the many efforts at many universities working in "Human Relations Research." Researches of Shartle, Bakke, Festinger, Bavelas, Sherif, to name only a few in main line of social psychology development, are in point and are far too numerous to mention here.

8. Cf. Peter M. Blau, "Cooperation and Competition in a Bureaucracy," *The American Journal of Sociology*, Vol. IX, No. 6, May, 1954, pp. 530-535, where the author documents a finding that competition makes for high individual productivity but lower group-wide performances.

10. Roethlisberger, F. J. and Wm. B. Dickson, *Management and the Worker*, Cambridge, Mass., Harvard University Press, 1939.

11. Eliot D. Chapple, "Applied Anthropology in Industry," Chapter No. 45 in *Anthropology Today*, ed. Alfred Kroeber, University of Chicago Press, Chicago, 1953.

12. E. Wight Bakke, *Adaptive Human Behavior*, Yale Labor and Management Center, 1951; also "The Fusion Process," same publisher, 1953. See also *Bonds of Organization*, Harper and Bros., New York, 1950, and Chris Argyris, *Organizational Dynamics and the Fusion Process*, Yale Labor and Management Center, 1953.

13. Chester L. Barnard, *Functions of the Executive*, Harvard University Press, Cambridge, Mass., 1938.

14. Parsons, Talcott, *The Social System*, Harvard University Press, Cambridge, Mass., 1951, and Robert K. Merton, *Social Theory and Social Structure*, The Free Press, Glencoe, Ill., 1949. For Homans, *op. cit.*

15. The word's use in sociology is from Merton, *op. cit.*

15a. Here we must distinguish between fair and unfair criticism. Popular business borrowing of this view, a primitive first fruit of plant sociology, hopefully sees new managerial successes in plans for "two-way communications" and "bottom-up management." But popularization is neither proof nor disproof of a doctrine. Only our most easily frightened economist friends could fear such a humanization of industrial discipline. Nor is social science suddenly Fascist because some fashion-conscious businessmen read "communication" as propaganda and persuasion.

16. Merton, *op. cit.*, p. 151.

17. Goode, Wm. J., and Irving Fowler, "Incentive Factors in a Low Morale Plant," *American Sociological Review*, 14: October, 1949, pp. 618-24. See also Carl Jantke, *Bergmann und Zeche*, J. B. C. Mohr, Tubingen, 1954, for a German study of driving and its effects.

18. D. Cartwright, ed., *Field Theory in Social Sciences*, Harper & Brothers, New York, 1951. See also K. Lewin, Resolving Social Conflicts, Harper & Brothers, New York, 1948.

19. Shartle, Carroll L., "Ohio State Leadership Studies," *Engineering Experiment Station News*, volume XXIV, No. 5, December 1952, pp. 16-21. Also Stogdill, R. M. *Aspects of Leadership and Organization*, Ohio State University Research Foundation, Columbus, 1953.

20. Guetzkow, Harold, ed., *Groups, Leadership* and *Men*, Carnegie Press, Pittsburgh, 1951.

21. Argyris, Chris. *Executive Leaderships: An Appraisal of a Manager in Action*, Harper and Brothers, New York, 1953.

22. Katz, D., and R. L. Kahn, "Some Recent Findings in Human Relations Research" (mimeographed), University of Michigan, Survey Research Center, 1952. For an excellent summary of all the Lewinians' work in industry, see Morris S. Viteles, *Motivation and Morale in Industry*, W. W. Norton and Company, New York: 1953.

23. Coch, L., and J. R. P. French, Jr., "Overcoming Resistance to Change," *Human Relations*, 1948, 1, pp. 512-33.

24. Viteles, *op. cit.* Also cf. E. Jacques, *The Changing Culture of a Factory*, Tavistock Publications, London: 1951, for parallel work in England.

25. Viteles, *op. cit.*, p. 119.

26. Argyris, Chris., *ibid.*, footnote, 3.

27. Argyris, Chris., *ibid.*, quoting Coch and French, cited (23) above.

28. Collins, Orvis, Melville Dalton and Donald Roy, "Restriction of Output and Social Cleavage in Industry," *Applied Anthropology* 7 (Winter 1948), pp. 5-18.

29. Warner, W. Lloyd, and J. O. Low, *The Social System of the Modern Factory. The Strike: A Social Analysis*, Yale University, New Haven, 1947.

30. For a summary of work on classes see Reinhard Bendix and Martin S. Lipset, *Reader in Social Stratification*, Free Press, Glencoe, Ill., 1953.

31. Besides Bendix and Lipset, *op. cit.*, see especially William Lloyd Warner, *American Life, Dream and Reality*, University of Chicago Press, Chicago, 1953.

32. See Lloyd Warner, Robert J. Havighurst and Martin Loeb, *Who Shall Be Educated?* Harper and Brothers, New York, 1944.

33. Robert Merton, "Social Structure and Anomie," reprinted in Robert Merton, *Social Theory and Social Structure, op. cit.*, or for a possibly more general formulation, Talcott Parsons, *The Social System, op. cit.*

34. National Planning Association, "Causes of Industrial Peace: Case Study No. 13, Working Harmony in 18 Companies," Washington, D. C., November 1953, Chapter V.

35. Harbison, Frederick H., and Robert Dubin, *Patterns of Union-Management Relations*, Chicago, Science Research Associates, 1947.

36. Strauss, George, and Leonard R. Sayles, Patterns of Participation in Local Unions," *Industrial and Labor Relations Review*, 6, October 1952, pp. 31-43.

37. See also Chapters 19 and 20 of Whyte, William F. *Money and Motivation, op. cit.*

38. Haskell, E. F., "A Natural Classification of Societies," *Transactions* of the New York Academy of Sciences, March, Series II, Volume 9, No. 5, pp. 186-196.

39. William Foote Whyte, *Street Corner Society*, McGraw-Hill and Company, New York, 1943. Also, *ibid.*, revised edition, 1955.

40. Arensberg, *op. cit.*

41. William Foote Whyte, *Human Relations in the Restaurant Industry,* McGraw-Hill, New York, 1948.

42. F. W. Richardson, Jr., and Charles R. Walker, *Human Relations in an Expanding Company,* Labor and Management Center, Yale University, New Haven, 1948.

43. Arensberg, Conrad M., and Douglas McGregor, "Determination of Morale in an Industrial Company," *Applied Anthropology*, 1 (January-March 1942), pp. 12-34.

44. Horsfall, Alexander B., and Conrad M. Arensberg, "Teamwork and Productivity in a Shoe Factory," *Human Organization*, 8 (Winter 1949), pp. 12-25.

45. Chapple, Eliot D., *op. cit.*

46. Chapple, Eliot D., and Erich Lindemann, "Clinical Implications of Measurements of Interaction Rates in Psychiatric Interviews," *Applied Anthropology*, I, 2 (January-March 1942), pp. 1-12.

47. Chapple, Eliot D., and Gordon Donald, Jr., "A Method for Evaluating Supervisory Personnel," *Harvard Business Review*, Vol. XXIV, Autumn, 1945, Summer, 1946, pp. 197-214.

48. Hart, C. W. M., "Industrial Relations Research and Social Theory," *Canadian Journal of Economic and Political Science*, 15 (February 1949), pp. 53-73.

49. Robert F. Bales, *Interaction Process Analysis*, Cambridge, Massachusetts, Addison Wesley Press, 1950.

50. A. H. Rubinstein, "A Study of Communications in a Manufacturing Company," Department of Industrial Engineering, Columbia University, 1951.

51. Claude Levy-Strauss, "Social Structure," in *Anthropology Today*, eds. Kroeber *et al.*, Chicago University Press, Chicago, 1953.

52. Jean Fourastie, "Predicting Economic Changes in Our Time," *Diogenes*, 5 (Winter 1934), pp. 39-57.

THE NON-ECONOMIC ASSUMPTIONS OF JOHN MAYNARD KEYNES

1. Several definitions may be helpful. Consumption includes expenditures on food, clothing, rent, etc. Saving is that part of income not spent on consumption. Investment entails the acquisition of a machine, a building or an addition to inventories. Speculation is the purchase of titles to wealth, stocks and bonds. As examination of any income distribution—and common sense—prove, one individual may play two or more economic roles. Keynes' discussion runs in terms of groups of pure consumers, pure investors and pure speculators.

2. In Keynesian usage, *actual* saving and investment are always equal. *Planned* saving and investment, as in this example, usually differ and are brought into equality only through changes in national income.

3. There are many explicit qualifications of almost any general statement in Keynes' *General Theory of Employment, Interest and Money*. Although

they do not affect the structure of the theory, they do prove that Keynes was at least as aware of the complexities of the real world as his critics.

4. The relation between national income and consumption is termed interchangeably the consumption function and the propensity to consume. The relation between *additions* to consumption and *additions* to national income is the marginal propensity to consume. The ratio between an increase in income and an increase in investment is called the investment multiplier. The investment multiplier of our example was 2 and the marginal propensity to consume was ½. The higher is the value of the marginal propensity to consume, the larger is the multiplier and the more substantial is the effect of a change in investment on national income.

5. This is an inexact but convenient definition of Keynes' marginal efficiency of capital which is more correctly defined as the highest rate of return over cost obtainable in given economic circumstances.

6. "The" rate of interest in Keynes usually refers to the rate paid on long term government securities, nearly riskless bonds. All other rates exceed this one by amounts which vary according to the differences in risk assumed.

7. Money is also held for other reasons. At any given level of income, the public requires certain sums to bridge the gap between payments of bills and receipt of income, and to guard against unexpected contingencies. But the size of these holdings is a function of the size of income rather than a cause of income shifts.

8. Keynes argues that the existence of any rate of interest at all derives from the natural preference of individuals to hold their liquid assets in the safest of all fashions, in cash. Interest becomes the payment made to them for holding their resources in less safe and less liquid forms.

9. Exigencies of space compel presentation of Keynes' thought in a bare outline which does some injustice to the subtlety of his own account.

10. *Ibid.*, p. 27.

11. *Ibid.*, p. 91.

12. Good correlation is almost certain where variables overlap as much as consumption and income do. Consumption may be as much as 95% of income.

13. The best summary of the methods and the errors of these forecasts is in an article called "Review of Economic Forecasts" by Michael Sapir in *Conference on Research in Income and Wealth*, published by the National Bureau of Economic Research, New York, Volume II (1949), pp. 275-371.

14. All that "spontaneously" means in this connection is a change in consumption caused by events other than changes in income.

15. Keynes, J. M., *The Economic Consequences of the Peace* (1920), p. 237.

16. Wright, D. McC., "The Future of Keynesian Economics," *American Economic Review*, June 1945, p. 320.

17. Business literature is studded with evidence of this statement, although business cycle history demonstrates that the longer individuals expect a given economic situation to continue, the more likely they are to be wrong. Yet, the longer the economic climate is stable, the more confidently will many individuals anticipate continued stability.

18. Keynes, J. M., *The General Theory*, p. 154.

19. See Keynes' essay, "The Villiers Connection" in *Essays in Biography*. In that volume a notable emphasis is placed on blood relationships and on intellectual lineage where other ancestry fails. The point is clearest in the essays on Malthus, Marshall and Edgeworth.

20. This is one Keynesian observation whose lesson labor unions have taken to their hearts. Increasing numbers of wage contracts are tied to changes in the cost of living, in both England and the United States.

21. Keynes, J. M., *Economic Consequences of the Peace*, p. 3.

22. *Ibid.*, pp. 18-20.

23. Keynes, J. M., *Treatise on Money* (1930), Volume II, p. 428.

24. Keynes, J. M., *The General Theory of Employment, Interest and Money*, p. 309.

25. The leading name is Alvin Hansen. See his *Fiscal Policy* and *Business Cycles* and *Full Employment or Stagnation*.

26. *Op. cit.*, p. 380.

27. *Ibid.*, p. 378.

A NOTE ON MICRO- AND MACROECONOMICS

1. As Lekachman has stated: "The pure Keynesian theory is erected within a framework of short-run assumptions."

A NOTE ON "MIDDLE-RANGE" FORMULATION

1. Lekachman is, rightfully, concerned over the fact that survey data on individuals' expenditures and incomes are a collection of observed points on as many different consumption functions as there are individuals. There are two statistical devices to be used in taking this matter into account. By the simultaneous use of many variables, we may attempt to adjust for inter-individual differences in position of expenditure functions. In other words, we "homogenize" individuals by age, family size, recent income change, wealth, home ownership, occupation and other similar variables so that, apart from random variation, we have a collection of observed points on a single function. The other statistical device is to interpret our empirically desired relationships as estimates of average functions, i. e., averages of the individually different functions in case we have not completely "homogenized" individuals. On these points see L. R. Klein, *A Textbook of Econometrics* (Evanston: Row, Peterson and Co., 1952), Chapter V, section 4 (211-26), and references to T. Haavelmo, L. Hurwicz, and H. Rubin, p. 241.

2. F. Modigliani, "Fluctuations in the Savings-Income Ratio: A Problem in Economic Forecasting," *Studies in Income and Wealth*, Vol. 11 (New York: National Bureau of Economic Research, 1949). James S. Duesenberry, *Income Saving and the Theory of Consumer Behavior* (Cambridge, Harvard University Press, 1949).

3. See G. Katona, "Effect of Income Changes on the Rate of Saving," *Review of Economics and Statistics*, Vol. XXXI, May 1949, pp. 95-103.

4. See J. Tobin, "Relative Income, Absolute Income and Saving," *Money, Trade and Economic Growth* (New York: Macmillan Co., 1951), pp. 135-56.
L. R. Klein and H. W. Mooney, "Negro-White Savings Differentials and the Consumption Function Problem," *Econometrica*, Vol. 21, July 1953, pp. 425-56.

REFERENCE GROUP THEORY AND TRADE UNION WAGE POLICY

1. Nevertheless, Perlman's *A Theory of the Labor Movement* (Augustus M. Kelley, New York, 1949), together with Lenin's *What Is To Be Done* to which it is strikingly similar despite their diametrically opposed political preferences, remain the best theoretical interpretations of the labor movement in various contexts that we have. Perlman's theory potentially holds greater value for those political scientists and sociologists who are interested in the political roles and relationships of whole strata within a total social structure than it does for contemporary labor economists who address themselves to the narrower, but no less important, questions surrounding collective bargaining.

2. Arthur M. Ross, *Trade Union Wage Policy* (Berkeley, University of California Press, 1948), pp. 49-50.

3. Ross, A. M., *op. cit.*

4. *Ibid.*, p. 45.

5. *Ibid.*, p. 46.

6. *Ibid.*, p. 47.

7. *Ibid.*, p. 48.

8. Ross, A. M., *op. cit.*, pp. 48-49.

9. *Ibid.*, pp. 49-50.

10. In recent years sociologists and social psychologists have come to recognize that a fuller understanding of many varieties of social behavior requires a knowledge of the processes through which men relate themselves to groups toward whose values they refer their own behavior, and with whom they compare themselves in appraising various aspects of their own situations. Various studies and theoretical works have attempted to analyze the determinants, character, and consequences of reference groups under differing structural conditions. This concept so far has been extremely useful in clarifying the subjective dimensions of stratification systems (see Herbert Hyman, *The Psychology of Status*, Archives of Psychology, No. 269, 1942); processes involved in attitude and opinion formation (see T. M. Newcomb, *Social Psychology* [New York, 1950], pp. 225-232); diverse and apparently unrelated types of behavior of soldiers as reported in Volumes I and II of *The American Soldier* (see Robert K. Merton and Alice Kitt, "Contributions to the Theory of Reference Group Behavior," in R. K. Merton and P. F. Lazarsfeld, eds., *Continuities in Social Research*, Free Press, Glencoe, Ill., 1950). For an application of the reference group concept to the problem of participation in unions, see S. M. Lipset, M. Trow and J. Coleman, *Union Democracy* (Free Press, Glencoe, Ill., 1956).

11. Merton and Kitt, *op cit.*, p. 51 (our emphasis).

12. Merton and Kitt, *op. cit.*, pp. 62-65.

13. Ross, *op. cit.*, pp. 55-56.

14. Ross, *op. cit.*, p. 57.

15. A. M. Ross, *op. cit.*, p. 57. This is certainly a widely held norm in contemporary mass democracy, which is characterized more by such "levelling tendencies" as the demand for uniform treatment according to universalistic criteria than by the minimization of power" associated with the 19th century parliamentary democracy. The norm of "impartiality of treatment" associated with government participation in labor relations is also embodied in statutes—the Walsh-Healy Act, for example, specifies that contractors doing government work shall meet "prevailing rates" as determined by a government agency.

16. *Ibid.*, p. 60.
17. *Ibid.*, p. 61.
18. *Ibid.*, p. 61.
19. See Merton and Kitt, *op. cit.*, p. 57 and footnote 15, on the problem: what are the patterns of response among members of a group category when they are subject to multiple reference groups operating at cross-purposes.
20. S. A. Stouffer, et al., *The American Soldier:* Volume I, Princeton, Princeton University Press, 1949, p. 125.
21. Arthur M. Ross and Donald Irwin, "Strike Experience in Five Countries, 1927–1947: An Interpretation," *Industrial and Labor Relations Review,* Vol. 4, No. 3, April 1951, pp. 323-343.
22. Ross, *op. cit.*, p. 73.
23. Of course, a legitimate differential is not automatically surrendered by a group whom it favors when the basis of its legitimacy has been destroyed. Richard Myers has noted how various unions have attempted to maintain the legitimacy of differentials in their favor in the face of developments which threaten the bases of their legitimacy. For example, he points out that when specific occupations have declined in skill requirements, "union administrators frequently make the attempt to cloak fundamental changes and strive to give the job a traditional appearance. To this end, union workers are urged to maintain their claims to all old operations as well as take over and elevate the standards of any new work where 'shoddy' or 'cut-rate' practices might be introduced. This affirmation of the ethical quality of occupational experience and training makes a strong appeal to the worker who unconsciously accepts his own presence on the job as a guarantee of proper production practices . . ." (Richard R. Myers, "Myth and Status Systems in Industry," *Social Forces,* pp. 333-334.)
Even when the loss of the "objective" (i.e., traditionally accepted) basis for the status or economic superiority of a given craft is not recognized by the members of the craft, nevertheless such a development may upset the structure of legitimacy of wage-rates within an industry if other workers come to recognize this. The retention by various unions of outmoded and unnecessary apprenticeship programs tends to preserve the symbols of high skill even though the rational economic need for them has vanished.
24. *Ibid.*, p. 73.
25. Ross, *op. cit.*, p. 64.
26. *Ibid.*, p. 57.
27. Cf. Lloyd G. Reynolds and Joseph Shister, *Job Horizons* (New York: Harper & Brothers, 1949), pp. 85-89.
28. *Ibid.*, pp. 24-30.
29. An attempt to deal with some of these questions on a theoretical level may be found in "The Political Process in Trade Unions: A Theoretical Statement," by S. M. Lipset in Morroe Berger, et al., *Freedom and Control in Modern Society* (New York: D. Van Nostrand Co., 1954), pp. 82-124.

CONTRIBUTORS

CONRAD M. ARENSBERG, Professor of Anthropology and Executive Officer, Department of Anthropology, Columbia University

LEE BENSON, Research Associate, Bureau of Applied Social Research, Columbia University

HENRY DAVID, Professor of Economics, Graduate School of Business, Columbia University, and Executive Director, National Manpower Council

LLOYD H. FISHER, Late Professor of Political Science and Associate Director, Institute of Industrial Relations, University of California at Berkeley

MARJORIE FISKE, Director of Research and Lecturer, School of Librarianship, University of California at Berkeley

GEORGE KATONA, Director of the Economic Behavior Program of the Survey Research Center, and Professor of Economics and of Psychology, University of Michigan

CLARK KERR, Professor of Industrial Relations and Chancellor of the University of California at Berkeley

L. R. KLEIN, Reader in Econometrics, Oxford University, England

MIRRA KOMAROVSKY, Professor of Sociology and Executive Officer, Department of Sociology, Barnard College, Columbia University

PAUL F. LAZARSFELD, Professor of Sociology and Executive Officer, Department of Sociology, Columbia University

ROBERT LEKACHMAN, Assistant Professor of Economics, Barnard College, Columbia University

SEYMOUR M. LIPSET, Associate Professor of Sociology and Social Institutions, University of California at Berkeley

LEO LOWENTHAL, Professor of Sociology and Social Institutions and Professor of Speech, University of California at Berkeley

RUSSELL E. PLANCK, Associate Professor of History, Seton Hall University

JOSEPH R. STRAYER, Dayton-Stockton Professor of History, Princeton University

GEOFFREY TOOTELL, Department of Sociology, Columbia University

MARTIN TROW, Professor of Sociology, Bennington College

WILLIAM S. VICKREY, Associate Professor of Economics, Department of Economics, Columbia University